T0206006

Lecture Notes in Computer Science   13918

Founding Editors

Gerhard Goos
Juris Hartmanis

The series Lecture Notes in Computer Science (LNCS), including its subseries Lecture Notes in Artificial Intelligence (LNAI) and Lecture Notes in Bioinformatics (LNBI), has established itself as a medium for the publication of new developments in computer science and information technology research, teaching, and education.

LNCS enjoys close cooperation with the computer science R & D community, the series counts many renowned academics among its volume editors and paper authors, and collaborates with prestigious societies. Its mission is to serve this international community by providing an invaluable service, mainly focused on the publication of conference and workshop proceedings and postproceedings. LNCS commenced publication in 1973.

Henning Bordihn · Nicholas Tran · György Vaszil
Editors

Descriptional Complexity of Formal Systems

25th IFIP WG 1.02 International Conference, DCFS 2023
Potsdam, Germany, July 4–6, 2023
Proceedings

 Springer

Editors
Henning Bordihn (ID)
University of Potsdam
Potsdam, Germany

Nicholas Tran (ID)
Santa Clara University
Santa Clara, CA, USA

György Vaszil (ID)
University of Debrecen
Debrecen, Hungary

ISSN 0302-9743 ISSN 1611-3349 (electronic)
Lecture Notes in Computer Science
ISBN 978-3-031-34325-4 ISBN 978-3-031-34326-1 (eBook)
https://doi.org/10.1007/978-3-031-34326-1

This Springer imprint is published by the registered company Springer Nature Switzerland AG
The registered company address is: Gewerbestrasse 11, 6330 Cham, Switzerland

Preface

This volume contains the papers presented at the 25th International Conference on Descriptional Complexity of Formal Systems (DCFS 2023), which was held at the University of Potsdam, Germany, during July 4–6, 2023. It was jointly organized by the Working Group 1.02 on Descriptional Complexity of the International Federation for Information Processing (IFIP) and by the Institute of Computer Science at the University of Potsdam.

The DCFS conference series is an international venue for the dissemination of new results related to all aspects of descriptional complexity including but not limited to the following:

- Automata, grammars, languages, and other formal systems; various modes of operations and complexity measures
- Succinctness of description of objects, state-explosion-like phenomena
- Circuit complexity of Boolean functions and related measures
- Size complexity of formal systems
- Structural complexity of formal systems
- Trade-offs between computational models and modes of operation
- Applications of formal systems (for instance, in software and hardware testing, in dialogue systems, in systems modeling, or in modeling natural languages) and their complexity constraints
- Cooperating formal systems
- Size or structural complexity of formal systems for modeling natural languages
- Complexity aspects related to the combinatorics of words
- Descriptional complexity in resource-bounded or structure-bounded environments
- Structural complexity as related to descriptional complexity
- Frontiers between decidability and undecidability
- Universality and reversibility
- Nature-motivated (bio-inspired) architectures and unconventional models of computing
- Blum static (Kolmogorov/Chaitin) complexity, algorithmic information

DCFS became an IFIP working conference in 2016, continuing the former Workshop on Descriptional Complexity of Formal Systems, which was a merger in 2002 of two other workshops: Formal Descriptions and Software Reliability (FDSR) and Descriptional Complexity of Automata, Grammars and Related Structures (DCAGRS). DCAGRS was previously held in Magdeburg, Germany (1999), London, Ontario, Canada (2000), and Vienna, Austria (2001). FDSR was previously held in Paderborn, Germany (1998), Boca Raton, Florida, USA (1999), and San José, California, USA (2000). Since 2002, DCFS has been successively held in London, Ontario, Canada (2002), Budapest, Hungary (2003), London, Ontario, Canada (2004), Como, Italy (2005), Las Cruces, New Mexico, USA (2006), Nový Smokovec, High Tatras, Slovakia (2007), Charlottetown, Prince Edward Island, Canada (2008), Magdeburg,

Germany (2009), Saskatoon, Canada (2010), Giessen, Germany (2011), Braga, Portugal (2012), London, Ontario, Canada (2013), Turku, Finland (2014), Waterloo, Ontario, Canada (2015), Bucharest, Romania (2016), Milan, Italy (2017), Halifax, Nova Scotia, Canada (2018), and Košice, Slovakia (2019). The next DCFS conferences were planned to be held in Vienna, Austria (2020), and in Seoul, South Korea (2021), but both of these events were canceled as in-person meetings due to the COVID-19 pandemic. The accepted papers appeared only in the conference proceedings. In 2022, the DCFS conference was again held as an on-site event in Debrecen, Hungary.

This year 15 papers were submitted by authors from 10 different countries. As the scientific merit of these submissions was outstanding, the members of the program committee were able to accept 13 submissions after each of the 15 submissions had been single-blind reviewed by three reviewers.

The program also included three invited talks by

- Pascal Caron, University of Rouen, France,
- Friedrich Otto, University of Kassel, Germany,
- Rogério Reis, University of Porto, Portugal.

In addition, Jürgen Dassow (Otto-von-Guericke University of Magdeburg), one of the co-founders of the DCFS conference series, gave a ceremonial address on the occasion of the 25th edition of DCFS.

We thank all invited speakers, contributing authors, Program Committee members, and external referees for their valuable contributions towards the realization of DCFS 2023.

We are also grateful to the editorial staff at Springer for their guidance and help during the process of publishing this volume, and for supporting the event through publication in the LNCS series.

Finally, we would like to thank the members of the organizing committee, whose efforts made it possible to hold this conference, and all participants who contributed to the success of the conference.

We are looking forward to DCFS 2024 to be held at Santa Clara, California, USA.

July 2023   Henning Bordihn
                                                             Nicholas Tran
                                                             György Vaszil

Organization

Steering Committee

Cezar Câmpeanu	University of Prince Edward Island, Canada
Erzsébet Csuhaj-Varjú	Eötvös Loránd University, Hungary
Stavros Konstantinidis	Saint Mary's University, Canada
Martin Kutrib (Chair)	Justus Liebig University, Germany
Giovanni Pighizzini	University of Milan, Italy
Rogério Reis	University of Porto, Portugal
Kai Salomaa	Queen's University, Canada

Program Committee

Henning Bordihn (Co-chair)	University of Potsdam, Germany
Szilárd Zsolt Fazekas	Akita University, Japan
Henning Fernau	University of Trier, Germany
Yo-Sub Han	Yonsei University, South Korea
Michal Hospodár	Slovak Academy of Sciences, Košice, Slovakia
Szabolcs Iván	University of Szeged, Hungary
Galina Jirásková	Slovak Academy of Sciences, Košice, Slovakia
Stavros Konstantinidis	Saint Mary's University, Canada
Orna Kupfermann	Hebrew University, Israel
Sylvain Lombardy	University of Bordeaux, France
Andreas Malcher	Justus Liebig University of Giessen, Germany
Carlo Mereghetti	University of Milan, Italy
Nelma Moreira	University of Porto, Portugal
Dana Pardubska	Comenius University Bratislava, Slovakia
Giovanni Pighizzini	University of Milan, Italy
Kai Salomaa	Queen's University, Canada
Shinnosuke Seki	University of Electro-Communications, Japan
Petr Sosik	Silesian University Opava, Czech Republic
Nicholas Tran (Co-chair)	Santa Clara University, USA
György Vaszil (Co-chair)	University of Debrecen, Hungary

Organizing Committee

Henning Bordihn	University of Potsdam, Germany
Tim Richter	University of Potsdam, Germany
Alexandra Roy	University of Potsdam, Germany

Additional Reviewers

Shamil Asgarli
Jürgen Dassow
Alessandro De Luca
Daniel Gabric
Stefan Hoffmann
Markus Holzer
Christos Kapoutsis
Martin Kutrib
Florin Manea

Lucas Mol
Timothy Ng
Luca Prigioniero
Indhumathi Raman
Narad Rampersad
Bala Ravikumar
Sergey Verlan
Petra Wolf
Chao Yang

Abstracts of Invited Talks

On the Influence of the Various Parameters of the Restarting Automaton on Its Expressive Capacity and Descriptional Complexity

Friedrich Otto

Fachbereich Elektrotechnik/Informatik, Universität Kassel, Kassel, 34109 Germany
f.otto@uni-kassel.de

The *restarting automaton* was introduced by P. *Jančar*, *F. Mráz*, *M. Plátek*, and *J. Vogel* in a talk presented at the FCT'95 in Dresden. It is not just another variant of the Turing machine, but it is a machine model that is motivated by the linguistic technique of *analysis by reduction*. Given a sentence of a natural language, possibly annotated by tags giving morphological, syntactial, and/or semantical information on the various word forms (morphemes) of the sentence, this sentence is repeatedly simplied by local transformations until either an error is detected and the input sentence is rejected, or a correct simple sentence is obtained and the input sentence is accepted. Accordingly, a restarting automaton consists of a finite-state control, a flexible tape (or a linked list) that initially contains the input, and a read/write window of a fixed finite size. Using its window the restarting automaton scans the current sentence stored on its tape, performs one or more local rewrite operations, in this way simplifying the stored sentence, and then it *restarts*. This means that it places its read/write window on the beginning of the tape and resets its finite-state control to the initial state. This sequence of operations, called a *cycle*, is iterated until the automaton either accepts or rejects.

Actually, the restarting automaton is not simply an automaton, but a whole *family of different types of automata*. These types differ with respect to the allowed move and rewrite operations, the size of the read/write window, the number of allowed rewrite operations between restarts, the number of non-input letters in the tape alphabet, and the number of states. Without any restrictions on the allowed rewrite operations, the restarting automaton is equivalent to the Turing machine. In order to restrict the expressive capacity of the restarting automaton, it is therefore generally required that each rewrite operation is *weight-reducing* or even *length-reducing*.

Using different sets of restrictions, the classes of the Chomsky hierarchy have been characterized by various types of restarting automata. In the present talk, these characterizations are presented by considering some of the parameters that are used to specify different types of restarting automata. In addition, the influence of these parameter settings on the descriptional complexity of the restarting automaton is discussed.

Size Matters, But Let's Have It on Average

Rogério Reis

CMUP&DCC, Faculdade de Ciências, Universidade do Porto, R. Campo Alegre s/n,
4169–007 Porto, Portugal
rogerio.reis@fc.up.pt

In the last three decades, descriptional complexity of formal languages, similarly to what happens in computational complexity, is almost always considered for its worst-case. However, in most cases, this worst-case complexity is only achieved for sets of inputs of very small significance. For practical applications, the average-case analysis, where input data is assumed to follow a given probability distribution, can provide much more accurate prediction of the needed computational resources. The study of complexity results on average can be performed through experimentation, for which well behaved random generators for the computational models, and thus rigorous enumerative descriptions of their classes, are needed.

Alternative methods to obtain average results in descriptional complexity can be used in order to avoid the experimentation. Because Kolmogorov incompressible objects have a behaviour that it is, by definition, indistinguishable from the average, its study should give rise to average complexity results in a very elegant and succinct manner.

An elegant alternative is the framework of analytic combinatorics by relating combinatorial objects to algebraic properties of complex analytic generating functions. In particular, the behaviour of these functions around their dominant singularities gives access to the asymptotic form of their (power) series coefficients. In the case of the application to descriptional complexity, because of its natural parametrisation by the size of the alphabet, it is not just one combinatorial class that it is needed to address, but an infinite family of combinatorial classes. This raises problems that do not appear in classical combinatorial classes, such as graphs or trees. Moreover, in many cases, having explicit expressions for the generating functions is unmanageable. Using generating functions implicitly defined by algebraic curves, other methods need to be used to extract the required information for the asymptotic estimates. This allows to find, for the combinatorial classes considered, the behaviour of the generating function without knowing beforehand the explicit value of its singularity. The average results obtained so far, have revealed that asymptoticly, linear complexities in the worst case are halved, on the average case, and square-rooted in the other cases (see [1]). Exceptionally, some results reveal to be much more extreme.

Reference

1. Broda, S., Machiavelo, A., Moreira, N., Reis, R.: Analytic combinatorics and descriptional complexity of regular languages on average. ACM SIGACT News **51**(1), 38–56 (2020)

Contents

Operational State Complexity Revisited: The Contribution of Monsters and Modifiers

Pascal Caron[1(✉)], Jean-Gabriel Luque[2], and Bruno Patrou[1]

[1] LITIS, Université de Rouen, Avenue de l'Université,
76801 Saint-Étienne du Rouvray Cedex, France
{Pascal.Caron,Bruno.Patrou}@univ-rouen.fr
[2] GR2IF, Université de Rouen, Avenue de l'Université,
76801 Saint-Étienne du Rouvray Cedex, France
Jean-Gabriel.Luque@univ-rouen.fr

Abstract. The state complexity of a language L is the number of states of its minimal automaton. The operational (state) complexity of an operation $\otimes$ is the maximal state complexity of the languages $\otimes(L_1, \cdots, L_k)$ where $L_1, \ldots, L_k$ are languages with given state complexities. We highlight two tools that have been developed in recent years and which theorise and summarise a large number of methods used since the 1970 s. A monster is an automaton where any function from states to states is represented by at least one letter. A modifier is a set of functions that allows us to transform a set of automata into an automaton. Thanks to these techniques, we revisit the state complexity of some language transformation operations. These tools allow to propose a unified vision on a large number of known results in a natural way and also to obtain new ones at lower cost. We detail two examples: the star of a boolean operation and the reversal of a boolean operation. By doing so, we directly obtain a new result when the boolean operation is the Xor.

1 Introduction

Operational state complexity is a measure of the power of enlargement of an operation. In the worst case, what is, for instance, the size of the machine recognizing an iteration of words that are in both languages, if we consider two languages recognized by respectively a 3- and a 4-state minimal automaton? The answer (3072) is surprising. In view of this result, it seems important to be able to define the operational complexity upstream in order to reserve the space to store the machine that encodes this operation.

Operational state complexity has been extensively studied in the past years. To our knowledge, the first paper stating results about the state complexity of operations is [26]. In this paper, Maslov gave algorithms for union, Kleene star, square root, catenation and estimate each of these state complexities without

H. Bordihn et al. (Eds.): DCFS 2023, LNCS 13918, pp. 1–20, 2023.
https://doi.org/10.1007/978-3-031-34326-1_1

rigorous proofs. Complexity did not arouse interest for the next 20 years. Birget in [1] brought it back to the forefront for a very long time. An interest that has still not faded and many operations have been studied since, including the Kleene star, reversal, powers, proportional removals, catenation, binary boolean operations [2, 15, 16, 21, 22, 29, 30]. A survey on the state complexity of operations has been published in 2017 [17]. Furthermore, the state complexities of some compositions of well-known operations have been computed, like the star of union, the star of intersection, star-complement-star, multiple compositions of boolean operations and multiple compositions of catenation, among others [8–10, 13, 16, 20, 23–25, 28].

Even though the state complexity of many different operations are known, there are very little general results that can be applied to help us compute the state complexity of a new operation. This is mainly due to the fact that we do not understand well enough how to compute the state complexity of the composition of two operations, even when these operations are simple. Two steps are usually needed when computing the state complexity of a regular operation. The first one is to compute an upper bound using some ingenious tricks. The second is to provide a family of languages, called a witness, whose image by the operation matches this upper bound. Brzozowski [2] pointed out that some particular witnesses could be used for several well-known operations. One of the explanations given by Brzozowski is that they are "complex" in a certain sense: their syntactic monoid is as large as possible.

The paper is organized as follows. Section 2 gives definitions and notations about automata and combinatorics. In Sect. 3, we describe a family containing a large number of well-known operations, the 1-uniform operations, for which we develop tools for state complexity in the next sections. In Sect. 4, we define the algebraic structure of modifiers and give several examples. Section 5 gives examples of combinatorial objects that may encode the states of the output automaton of the modifier. In Sect. 6, we define the monster automaton as the automaton in which every function from state to state is encoded by a letter. We also give several examples of construction. In Sect. 7, we show the impact of modifiers and monsters by easily finding already known results like those of the star (resp. the reversal) of the union and the intersection and by discovering new ones like those of the star (resp. the reversal) of the Xor.

2   Preliminaries

2.1   Conventional Definitions

Let Σ be a finite set of symbols. A <u>word</u> w over Σ is a finite sequence of symbols of Σ. Let us denote by ε the empty word. The catenation of two words $u = a_1 \cdots a_n$ and $v = b_1 \cdots b_m$ denoted by $u \cdot v$ or uv is the word $a_1 \cdots a_n b_1 \cdots b_m$. We define w^n inductively as $w \cdot w^{n-1}$ with $w^0 = \varepsilon$. The set of all finite words over Σ is denoted by Σ^*. A <u>language</u> L over Σ is a subset of Σ^*. We define the <u>complement</u> of $L \subseteq \Sigma^*$ by $\overline{L} = \Sigma^* \setminus L$. For any $n \in \mathbb{N}$, we also define the n-th root of L by

$\sqrt[n]{L} = \{w \in \Sigma^* \mid w^n \in L\}$ and by $\mathrm{Root}(L)$ the union of every n-th root, $n > 0$. The cardinality of a finite set E is denoted by $\#E$, the set of subsets of E is denoted by 2^E and the set of mappings of E into itself is denoted by E^E. We denote by $[\![n]\!]$ the set $\{0, 1, \ldots, n-1\}$. The indicator function is a function that maps elements of a subset X of a set to one, and all other elements to zero. That is, $\mathbf{1}_X(x) = 1$ if $x \in X$, 0 otherwise. For a set E, let $E \cdot 0 = \emptyset$ and $E \cdot 1 = E$.

Let Σ and Γ be two alphabets. A morphism is a function ϕ from Σ^* to Γ^* such that, for all $u, v \in \Sigma^*$, $\phi(uv) = \phi(u)\phi(v)$.

A non-necessarily deterministic finite automaton (NFA) is a 5-tuple $A = (\Sigma, Q, I, F, \delta)$ where Σ is the input alphabet, Q is a finite set of states, $I \subseteq Q$ is the set of initial states, $F \subseteq Q$ is the set of final states and δ is the transition function from $Q \times \Sigma$ to 2^Q which is defined for every $q \in Q$ and every $a \in \Sigma$ and can be extended in a natural way from $Q \times \Sigma^*$ to 2^Q. The automaton A is standard if there is only one initial state and if there is no input transition on this initial state. Formally, $\#I = 1$ and for all $q \in Q$, for all $a \in \Sigma$, $\delta(q, a) \cap I = \emptyset$. A word $w \in \Sigma^*$ is recognized by A if there exists $i \in I$ such that $\delta(i, w) \cap F \neq \emptyset$. The language recognized by A is the set $\mathrm{L}(A)$ of words recognized by A.

We say that A is complete and deterministic (DFA) if $\#I = 1$ and for all $q \in Q$, for all $a \in \Sigma$, $\#\delta(q, a) = 1$. In this case, we consider δ as a function from $Q \times \Sigma$ to Q.

Let $A = (\Sigma, Q, i, F, \delta)$ be a DFA. For any word w, we denote by δ^w the function $q \to \delta(q, w)$. Two states q_1, q_2 of Q are equivalent if for any word w of Σ^*, $\delta(q_1, w) \in F$ if and only if $\delta(q_2, w) \in F$. This equivalence relation is called the Nerode equivalence and is denoted by $q_1 \sim q_2$. If two states are not equivalent, then they are distinguishable. A state q is accessible in A if there exists a word $w \in \Sigma^*$ such that $q = \delta(i, w)$.

Two DFAs are said to be equivalent if they recognize the same language. A DFA is minimal if there does not exist any equivalent DFA with less states and it is well known that for any DFA, there exists a unique, up to a relabeling of the states, minimal equivalent one [19]. Such a minimal DFA is obtained from A by computing $\widehat{A}_{/\sim} = (\Sigma, Q/\sim, [i], F/\sim, \delta_\sim)$ where $\widehat{A}$ is the accessible part of A, and where, for any $q \in Q$, $[q]$ is the $\sim$-class of the state q and satisfies the property $\delta_\sim([q], a) = [\delta(q, a)]$, for any $a \in \Sigma$.

2.2 Operational State Complexity

A k-ary operation over languages (for short an operation) is a map sending every k-tuple of languages sharing the same alphabet Σ to a language over Σ. A k-ary operation is regular if it sends every k-tuple of regular languages to a regular language. To be quite exact, this «operation» is a class of operations, each element of this class depending on the alphabet. We will say that the k-ary operation $\otimes$ over languages (class of operations $\otimes_\sigma$) is alphabet-free if for any pair of alphabets Σ and Γ, for any injective morphism Φ from Σ to Γ and for any k-tuple of regular languages $(L_1, \ldots, L_k)$ over Σ we have $\Phi(\otimes_\Sigma(L_1, \ldots, L_k)) = \otimes_\Gamma(\Phi(L_1), \ldots, \Phi(L_k))$.

As an example, the <u>left quotient</u> operation $L_1^{-1}L_2 = \{v \in \Sigma^* \mid u \in L_1 \vee uv \in L_2\}$ is alphabet-free. On the other hand, the operation which erases every occurrence of the letter 0 in any words of a language is not alphabet-free.

The state complexity of a regular language L denoted by $\mathrm{sc}(L)$ is the number of states of its minimal DFA. This notion extends to regular operations: The state complexity of a k-ary operation $\otimes$ is the k-ary function $\mathrm{sc}_\otimes$ such that, for all $(n_1, \ldots, n_k) \in (\mathbb{N} \setminus 0)^k$,

$$\mathrm{sc}_\otimes(n_1, \ldots, n_k) = \sup\{\mathrm{sc}(\otimes(L_1, \ldots, L_k)) \mid \text{ for all } i \in \{1, \ldots, k\}, \mathrm{sc}(L_i) = n_i\}.$$

A <u>witness</u> for $\otimes$ is a way to assign to each $(n_1, \ldots, n_k)$, assumed sufficiently large, a k-tuple of languages $(L_1, \ldots, L_k)$, over the same alphabet, with $\mathrm{sc}(L_i) = n_i$, for all $i \in \{1, \ldots, k\}$, such that $\mathrm{sc}_\otimes(n_1, \ldots, n_k) = \mathrm{sc}(\otimes(L_1, \ldots, L_k))$.

3   Definitions and Properties of 1-Uniform Operations

In [4] and [14], the authors of the respective papers investigated, independently, the same subclass of alphabet-free regular operations, the class of 1-uniform operations, which are especially handy to manipulate for computing their operational state complexities. The definition of 1-uniform operation is based on that of <u>1-uniform</u> morphism for which the image of a letter is a letter. We recall its definition below.

A morphism ϕ is <u>1-uniform</u> if the image by ϕ of any letter is a letter.

Definition 1. *A k-ary regular operation $\otimes$ is 1-uniform if, for any k-tuple of regular languages $(L_1, \ldots, L_k)$, for any 1-uniform morphism ϕ,*

$$\otimes(\phi^{-1}(L_1), \ldots, \phi^{-1}(L_k)) = \phi^{-1}(\otimes(L_1, \ldots, L_k)).$$

Proposition 1. *Let $\otimes$ be a k-ary 1-uniform operation and Γ be an alphabet. Let $L_1, \ldots, L_k$ be a k-tuple of regular languages over Γ. Then*

- *If $\Sigma \subset \Gamma$ then $\otimes(L_1 \cap \Sigma^*, \cdots, L_k \cap \Sigma^*) = \otimes(L_1, \ldots, L_k) \cap \Sigma^*$.*
- *For any bijection $\varphi : \Sigma \to \Gamma$ extended as an automorphism of monoids, we have $\otimes(\varphi(L_1), \cdots, \varphi(L_k)) = \varphi(\otimes(L_1, \ldots, L_k))$.*

Example 1 (of an alphabet-free operation which is not 1-uniform). Let us consider the binary operation $\otimes$ defined by

$$\otimes(L_1, L_2) = L_1 \cdot L_2^{-1} = \{u \mid uv \in L_1 \text{ for some } v \in L_2\}.$$

This operation is alphabet-free but not 1-uniform because it violates the first condition of Proposition 1. For instance, let $\Gamma = \{a, b, c\}$, $L_1 = \{abc\}$, and $L_2 = \{c\}$. We have

$$\otimes(L_1 \cap \{a, b\}^*, L_2 \cap \{a, b\}^*) = \emptyset \cdot \emptyset^{-1} = \emptyset$$

while

$$\otimes(L_1, L_2) \cap \{a, b\}^* = \{ab\}.$$

One may ask whether there is a connection between alphabet-free operations and 1-uniform ones. From Proposition 1, we deduce the inclusion of the family of 1-uniform operators into the one of alphabet-free ones. The following proposition is the starting point of a hierarchy in rational operations.

Proposition 2. *Any 1-uniform operation is alphabet-free.*

Proof. Let Σ and Γ be two alphabet and Φ be an injective morphism from Σ to Γ extended to a morphism of monoid from Σ^* to Γ^*. Let $\otimes$ be a 1-uniform operation. Let $L^{\Gamma} \subset \Gamma^*$ be a language.

Since Φ is injective, it is obviously left inversible, *i.e.*

$$\Phi^{-1} \circ \Phi = \text{Id} \tag{1}$$

Furthermore, since $\Phi^{-1}(L^{\Gamma}) = \{\phi^{-1}(u) \mid u \in L^{\Gamma} \cap (\Phi(\Sigma))^*\}$, the composition $\Phi \circ \Phi^{-1}$ is just the projection to $2^{(\Phi(\Sigma))^*}$ obtained by erasing the words that do not belong to $(\Phi(\Sigma))^*$. In another word,

$$\Phi \circ \Phi^{-1}(L^{\Gamma}) = \Phi \circ \Phi^{-1}(L^{\Gamma} \cap (\Phi(\Sigma))^*) = L^{\Gamma} \cap (\Phi(\Sigma))^*. \tag{2}$$

From Eq. (1), we have

$$\otimes (L_1^{\Sigma}, \ldots, L_k^{\Sigma}) = \otimes(\Phi^{-1} \circ \Phi(L_1^{\Sigma}), \ldots, \Phi^{-1} \circ \Phi(L_k^{\Sigma})) \tag{3}$$

As $\otimes$ is 1-uniform, from Eq. (3) we deduce

$$\otimes (L_1^{\Sigma}, \ldots, L_k^{\Sigma}) = \Phi^{-1}(\otimes(\Phi(L_1^{\Sigma}), \ldots, \Phi(L_k^{\Sigma}))) \tag{4}$$

Thus

$$\Phi(\otimes(L_1^{\Sigma}, \ldots, L_k^{\Sigma})) = \Phi \circ \Phi^{-1}(\otimes(\Phi(L_1^{\Sigma}), \ldots, \Phi(L_k^{\Sigma})))$$

From Eq. (2) we have

$$\Phi \circ \Phi^{-1}(\otimes(\Phi(L_1^{\Sigma}), \ldots, \Phi(L_k^{\Sigma}))) = \otimes(\Phi(L_1^{\Sigma}), \ldots, \Phi(L_k^{\Sigma})) \cap (\Phi(\Sigma))^* \tag{5}$$

From the first item of Proposition 1 and from Eq. (2), we have

$$\otimes(\Phi(L_1^{\Sigma}), \ldots, \Phi(L_k^{\Sigma})) \cap (\Phi(\Sigma))^* = \otimes(\Phi(L_1^{\Sigma}) \cap (\Phi(\Sigma))^*, \ldots, \Phi(L_k^{\Sigma}) \cap (\Phi(\Sigma))^*)$$
$$= \otimes(\Phi \circ \Phi^{-1} \circ \Phi(L_1^{\Sigma}), \ldots, \Phi \circ \Phi^{-1} \circ \Phi(L_k^{\Sigma}))$$
$$= \otimes(\Phi(L_1^{\Sigma}), \ldots, \Phi(L_k^{\Sigma}))$$

This allows us to conclude.

We check easily that the 1-uniformity is stable by composition.

Proposition 3. *Let $\otimes$ (resp. $\oplus$) be a j-ary (resp. k-ary) 1-uniform operation. Then, for any integer $1 \leq \ell \leq j$, the $(j + k - 1)$-ary operator $\otimes \circ_{\ell} \oplus$ such that*

$$\otimes \circ_{\ell} \oplus(L_1, \ldots, L_{j+k-1}) = \otimes(L_1, \ldots, L_{\ell-1}, \oplus(L_{\ell}, \ldots, L_{\ell+k-1}), L_{\ell+k}, \ldots, L_{j+k-1})$$

is 1-uniform.

Many well-known unary regular operations are 1-uniform. See [14] for a non-exhaustive list of examples like the complement, the Kleene star, the cyclic shift, the mirror, all boolean operations and catenation among others.

4   A Transformation on Automata: The Modifier

We first define a mechanism which unifies automata transformations. This mechanism is called a <u>modifier</u>. A k-modifier is an algorithm taking k automata as input and outputting one automaton. A lot of operations on languages can be described using this mechanism (mirror, complement, Kleene star, ...). As this mechanism works on automata, these operations are necessarily among regular operations. Moreover, these regular operations are exactly 1-<u>uniform</u> operations.

In the same way as we have seen that not all regular operations are 1-uniform, we also show that not all modifiers are <u>coherent</u> (correspond to a regular operation on languages).

4.1   Definition of Modifiers and Examples

A <u>state configuration</u> is a 3-tuple (Q, i, F) such that Q is a finite set, $i \in Q$ and $F \subseteq Q$. A <u>transition configuration</u> is a 4-tuple (Q, i, F, δ) such that (Q, i, F) is a state configuration and $\delta \in Q^Q$. If $A = (\Sigma, Q, i, F, \delta)$ is a DFA, the transition configuration of a letter $a \in \Sigma$ in A is the 4-tuple (Q, i, F, δ^a). The <u>state configuration</u> of $A = (\Sigma, Q, i, F, \delta)$ is the triplet (Q, i, F).

Our purpose is to consider operations on languages that can be encoded on DFA. To this aim, such an operation will be described as a k-ary operator $\mathfrak{m}$, acting on DFAs $A_1, \ldots A_k$ over the same alphabet Σ and producing a new DFA such that

- the alphabet of $\mathfrak{m}(A_1, ..., A_k)$ is Σ,
- the state configuration of $\mathfrak{m}(A_1, ..., A_k)$ depends only on the state configurations of the DFAs $A_1, \ldots, A_k$,
- for any letter $a \in \Sigma$, the transition function of a in $\mathfrak{m}(A_1, \ldots, A_k)$ depends only on the state configurations of the DFAs $A_1, \ldots, A_k$ and on the transition functions of a in each of the DFAs $A_1, ..., A_k$ (not on the letter itself nor on any other letter or transition function).

More formally,

Definition 2. *A modifier $\mathfrak{m}$ is a 4-tuple of mappings $(\mathfrak{Q}, \iota, \mathfrak{f}, \mathfrak{d})$ acting on transition configurations of DFAs $(A_1, \ldots, A_k)$ with $A_j = (\Sigma, Q_j, i_j, F_j, \delta_j)$ to build a DFA $\mathfrak{m}(A_1, \ldots, A_k) = (\Sigma, Q, i, F, \delta)$, where*

$$Q = \mathfrak{Q}((Q_1, i_1, F_1), \ldots, (Q_k, i_k, F_k)), \quad i = \iota((Q_1, i_1, F_1), \ldots, (Q_k, i_k, F_k)),$$
$$F = \mathfrak{f}((Q_1, i_1, F_1), \ldots, (Q_k, i_k, F_k)) \ and$$
$$\forall a \in \Sigma, \quad \delta^a = \mathfrak{d}((i_1, F_1, \delta_1^a), \ldots, (i_k, F_k, \delta_k^a)).$$

Notice that we do not need to put explicitly the dependency of $\mathfrak{d}$ on $(Q_1, \ldots, Q_k)$ because the information is already contained in each δ^a.

Example 2. Let us consider the unary modifier 𝔊tar (see Fig. 1).

$$\mathfrak{Star} = (\mathfrak{Q}, \mathsf{i}, \mathfrak{F}, \mathfrak{d})$$

$$\mathfrak{Q} : (Q, i, F) \longrightarrow 2^Q$$
$$\mathsf{i} : (Q, i, F) \longrightarrow \emptyset$$
$$\mathfrak{F} : (Q, i, F) \longrightarrow \{E \subset Q \mid E \cap F \neq \emptyset\} \cup \{\emptyset\}$$

$$\mathfrak{d} : (i, F, \delta) \longrightarrow
\begin{cases}
\emptyset \longrightarrow
\begin{cases}
\{\delta(i)\} & \text{if} \delta(i) \notin F \\
\{\delta(i), i\} & \text{otherwise}
\end{cases} \\
E \longrightarrow
\begin{cases}
\delta(E) & \text{if } \delta(E) \cap F = \emptyset \\
\delta(E) \cup \{i\} & \text{otherwise}
\end{cases}
\end{cases}$$

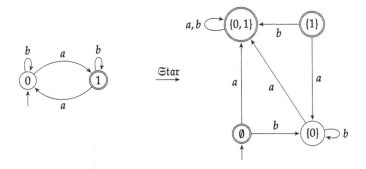

Fig. 1. Application of the 𝔊tar modifier

Example 3. Let us consider the binary modifier ℭonc (see Fig. 2).

$$\mathfrak{Conc} = (\mathfrak{Q}, \mathsf{i}, \mathfrak{F}, \delta)$$

$$\mathfrak{Q} : ((Q_1, i_1, F_1), (Q_2, i_2, F_2)) \longrightarrow Q_1 \times 2^{Q_2}$$
$$\mathsf{i} : ((Q_1, i_1, F_1), (Q_2, i_2, F_2)) \longrightarrow
\begin{cases}
(i_1, \emptyset) & \text{if } i_1 \notin F_1 \\
(i_1, \{i_2\}) & \text{if } i_1 \in F_1
\end{cases}$$
$$\mathfrak{F} : ((Q_1, i_1, F_1), (Q_2, i_2, F_2)) \longrightarrow \{(q_1, E) \mid E \cap F_2 \neq \emptyset\}$$
$$\mathfrak{d} : ((Q_1, i_1, F_1, \delta_1), (Q_2, i_2, F_2, \delta_2)) \longrightarrow$$

$$(q_1, E) \longrightarrow
\begin{cases}
(\delta_1(q_1), \delta_2(E) \cup \{i_2\}) & \text{if } \delta_1(q_1) \in F \\
(\delta_1(q_1), \delta_2(E)) & \text{otherwise}
\end{cases}$$

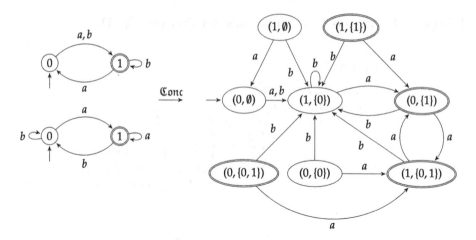

Fig. 2. Application of the $\mathfrak{Conc}$ modifier

4.2 Properties of a Modifier

Definition 3. *A k-ary modifier* $\mathfrak{m}$ *is <u>coherent</u> if, for every pair of k-tuples of DFAs* $(A_1, \ldots, A_k)$ *and* $(B_1, \ldots, B_k)$ *such that* $L(A_j) = L(B_j)$ *for all* $j \in \{1, \ldots, k\}$, *we have* $L(\mathfrak{m}(A_1, \ldots, A_k)) = L(\mathfrak{m}(B_1, \ldots, B_k))$.

If $\mathfrak{m}$ is a coherent modifier then we denote by $\otimes_\mathfrak{m}$ the operation such that for any k-tuple of regular languages $(L_1, \cdots, L_k)$ we have $\otimes_\mathfrak{m}(L_1, \ldots, L_k) = L(\mathfrak{m}(A_1, \ldots, A_k))$ for any k-tuple of DFAs $(A_1, \ldots, A_k)$ such that each A_i recognizes L_i.

The correspondence between coherent modifiers and 1-uniform operations is stated in the following Theorem and proved in [4].

Theorem 1. *A k-ary operation* $\otimes$ *is 1-uniform if and only if there exists a coherent k-ary modifier* $\mathfrak{m}$ *such that* $\otimes = \otimes_\mathfrak{m}$.

For some usual operations on languages (Comp, Union, Inter, Xor, Conc, Star and SRoot), we give one of their modifiers in Table 1. Thus these operations are 1-uniform.

We give in Example 4 an illustration of a modifier, $\mathfrak{S}\mathfrak{to}\mathfrak{S}\mathfrak{tar}$, which is not coherent. This modifier has however a great algorithmic importance. Indeed, it is used for the step by step (or Glushkov) construction of an automaton from a regular expression. What allows it to work in software like AUTOMATE[12] or AG [3] is the certainty of taking as input automata that are standard.

Example 4. $\mathfrak{S}\mathfrak{to}\mathfrak{S}\mathfrak{tar} = (\mathfrak{Q}, \mathfrak{i}, \mathfrak{F}, \mathfrak{d})$

$$\mathfrak{Q} : (Q, i, F) \longrightarrow 2^Q$$
$$\mathfrak{i} : (Q, i, F) \longrightarrow \{i\}$$
$$\mathfrak{F} : (Q, i, F) \longrightarrow \{E \subset Q \mid E \cap F \neq \emptyset\} \cup \{\{i\}\}$$
$$\mathfrak{d} : (Q, i, F, \delta) \longrightarrow E \longrightarrow \begin{cases} \delta(E) & \text{if } E \cap F = \emptyset \\ \delta(E) \cup \{\delta(i)\} & \text{otherwise} \end{cases}$$

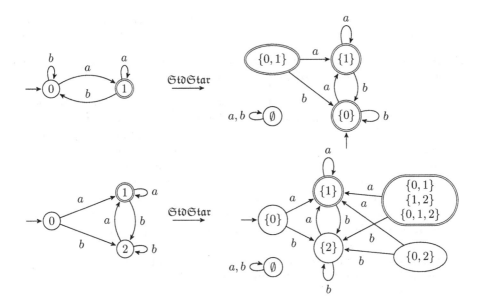

In this last figure, we have represented the three states $\{0,1\}, \{1,2\}$ and $\{0,1,2\}$ in one to make the drawing clearer.

Table 1. Description of some classical modifiers

	$\mathfrak{Q}$	$\mathfrak{i}$	$\mathfrak{f}$	$\mathfrak{d}$
Comp	Q_1	i_1	$Q_1 \setminus F_1$	$\delta_1(q_1)$
Union	$Q_1 \times Q_2$	(i_1, i_2)	$F_1 \times Q_2 \cup Q_1 \times F_2$	$(\delta_1(q_1), \delta_2(q_2))$
Inter	$Q_1 \times Q_2$	(i_1, i_2)	$F_1 \times F_2$	$(\delta_1(q_1), \delta_2(q_2))$
Xor	$Q_1 \times Q_2$	(i_1, i_2)	$F_1 \times (Q_2 \setminus F_2)$ $\cup (Q_1 \setminus F_1) \times F_2$	$(\delta_1(q_1), \delta_2(q_2))$
Conc	$Q_1 \times 2^{Q_2}$	$(i_1, \emptyset)$	$\{(q_1, E) \mid E \cap F_2 \neq \emptyset\}$	$\begin{cases} (\delta_1(q_1), \delta_2(E) \cup \{i_2\}) \\ \quad \text{if } \delta_1(q_1) \in F \\ (\delta_1(q_1), \delta_2(E)) \\ \quad \text{otherwise} \end{cases}$
Star	2^{Q_1}	$\emptyset$	$\{E \mid E \cap F_1 \neq \emptyset\} \cup \{\emptyset\}$	$\emptyset \rightarrow \begin{cases} \{\delta(i_1)\} \\ \quad \text{if } \delta(i) \notin F \\ \{\delta(i_1), i_1\} \\ \quad \text{otherwise} \end{cases}$ $E \rightarrow \begin{cases} \delta(E) \\ \quad \text{if } \delta(E) \cap F = \emptyset \\ \delta(E) \cup \{i_1\} \\ \quad \text{otherwise} \end{cases}$
SRoot	$Q_1^{Q_1}$	Id	$\{g \mid g^2(i_1) \in F_1\}$	$g \rightarrow (\delta_1^a \circ g)$

We easily check that, for modifiers, the property of coherence is stable by composition.

Proposition 4. *Let* m_1 *and* m_2 *be two coherent modifiers. The modifier* $m_1 \circ_\ell m_2$ *is coherent and describes a regular operation* $\otimes_{m_1} \circ_\ell \otimes_{m_2}$ *for a suitable value* ℓ.

Many complexity studies have been conducted on the composition of operations [13, 18, 25]. Using tricks, the authors informally define combinatorial objects that represent their states. This is the case in [16] and in [9] for multiple catenation where a state of a multiple catenation is denoted by a sequence of subsets of states of these catenation. These objects generally correspond exactly to the states as defined in the modifiers. It is often handy to describe the states of the resulting automaton this way. Let us give some examples of operations from Table 1. For the modifiers 𝔘nion, 𝔍nter and 𝔛or, a state is an element of the cartesian product of the states of the input. For the 𝕮onc modifier, a state is a pair composed of a state of the first input and a subset of states of the second input. For the 𝕾tar modifier, a state is a subset of states of the input. For the 𝕾ℜoot modifier, each state is a function from the set of states to the set of states of the input.

5   Valid States and Combinatorial Objects

In the case of modifiers, states are represented by combinatorial objects. These objects can be lists of subsets as in Example 5, tableaux as in Example 6 or lists of functions as in Example 7. The valid states of a modifier are exactly the set of possible states resulting from applying this modifier to any k-tuple of automata.

Example 5. Let's take as an example the concatenation of k languages. Each state is represented by a list $(e_1, E_2, \ldots, E_k)$ of subsets of states, but not all these states are valid.
$$\mathfrak{Conc}_k = (\mathfrak{Q}, \mathfrak{i}, \mathfrak{F}, \mathfrak{d})$$

$$\mathfrak{Q} : ((Q_1, i_1, F_1), \ldots, (Q_k, i_k, F_k)) \to Q_1 \times 2^{Q_2} \times \ldots \times 2^{Q_k}$$
$$\mathfrak{i} : ((Q_1, i_1, F_1), \ldots, (Q_k, i_k, F_k)) \to (i_1, \emptyset, \ldots, \emptyset)$$
$$\mathfrak{F} : ((Q_1, i_1, F_1), \ldots, (Q_k, i_k, F_k)) \to \{(q_1, E_2, \ldots, E_k) \mid E_k \cap F_k \neq \emptyset\}$$
$$\mathfrak{d} : ((Q_1, i_1, F_1, \delta_1), \ldots, (Q_k, i_k, F_k, \delta_k)) \to$$
$$(q_1, E_2, \ldots, E_k) \longrightarrow (\delta_1(q_1), \delta_2(E_2) \cup \{i_2\} \cdot \mathbf{1}_{F_1}(\delta_1(q_1)),$$
$$\ldots, \delta_k(E_k) \cup \{i_k\} \cdot \mathbf{1}_{F_{k-1}}(\delta_{k-1}(E_{k-1})))$$

To be valid, the states defined by the modifier $\mathfrak{Conc}_k$ must have specific properties:

- $\forall 0 < j < k, (E_j = \emptyset \Rightarrow E_{j+1} = \emptyset)$ (to access a DFA of the list, we must go through its predecessors)
- $\forall 0 < j < k, (S_j \cap F_j \neq \emptyset \Rightarrow i_{j+1} \in E_{j+1})$.

Moreover, we can see in this example that not all valid states are necessarily accessible. Indeed, in this example, we can see that if one of the final sets $F_{0 \leq j < k}$ is empty then all the states $(e_1, E_2, \ldots, E_k)$ of which a set $E_{l > j}$ is not empty will not be accessible but these states can be valid.

Example 6. Proposition 4 together with Theorem 1 show that the star of any boolean operation is 1-uniform. We thus define the modifier

$$\mathfrak{StarUnion} = \mathfrak{Star} \circ \mathfrak{Union} = (\mathfrak{Q}, \mathfrak{i}, \mathfrak{F}, \mathfrak{d}).$$

$\mathfrak{Q} : ((Q_1, i_1, F_1), (Q_2, i_2, F_2)) \to 2^{Q_1 \times Q_2}$
$\mathfrak{i} : ((Q_1, i_1, F_1), (Q_2, i_2, F_2)) \to \emptyset$
$\mathfrak{F} : ((Q_1, i_1, F_1), (Q_2, i_2, F_2)) \to$
$\qquad \{E \in 2^{Q_1 \times Q_2} \mid E \cap (F_1 \times Q_2 \cup Q_1 \times F_2) \neq \emptyset\} \cup \{\emptyset\}$
$\mathfrak{d} : ((Q_1, i_1, F_1, \delta_1), (Q_2, i_2, F_2, \delta_2)) \to$

$$
\begin{cases}
\emptyset & \longrightarrow \begin{cases} \{(\delta_1(i_1), \delta_2(i_2))\} \\ \quad \text{if } (\delta_1(i_1), \delta_2(i_2)) \notin F \\ \{(\delta_1(i_1), \delta_2(i_2)), (i_1, i_2)\} \\ \quad \text{otherwise} \end{cases} \\[2em]
\{(e_1, e_2) \mid e_1 \in Q_1, e_2 \in Q_2\} \longrightarrow \begin{cases} \{(\delta_1(e_1), \delta_2(e_2))\} \\ \quad \text{if } (\delta_1(e_1), \delta_2(e_2)) \notin F \\ \{(\delta_1(e_1), \delta_2(e_2)), (i_1, i_2)\} \\ \quad \text{otherwise} \end{cases}
\end{cases}
$$

In this modifier, a state is a subset of couples and is represented by a tableau. In this tableau, lines (resp. columns) are representing states of the first (resp. second) automaton. It is easy to see that the two modifiers $\mathfrak{StarInter}$ ($\mathfrak{Star} \circ \mathfrak{Inter}$) and $\mathfrak{StarXor}$ ($\mathfrak{Star} \circ \mathfrak{Xor}$) can be defined the same way just changing the computation of the final states $\{E \in 2^{Q_1 \times Q_2} \mid E \cap (F_1 \times Q_2 \cap Q_1 \times F_2) \neq \emptyset\} \cup \{\emptyset\}$, and $\{E \in 2^{Q_1 \times Q_2} \mid E \cap (F_1 \times Q_2 \oplus Q_1 \times F_2) \neq \emptyset\} \cup \{\emptyset\}$.

To be valid, the states defined by the modifier $\mathfrak{StarUnion}$ (resp. $\mathfrak{StarInter}$, $\mathfrak{StarXor}$) must have a cross in the circle red zone (the initial zone (state)) if there is a cross in the grey zone (the final zone).

Example 7. Our last example will be devoted to composition of Boolean operations and root operations (Boolean-root operations). The language we deal with is the intersection of the square root of a language L_1 and the cube root of a second language L_2. The modifier of this operation is defined by the following modifier:

$$\mathfrak{InterRoot} = (\mathfrak{Q}, \mathfrak{i}, \mathfrak{F}, \mathfrak{d}).$$

$\mathfrak{Q} : ((Q_1, i_1, F_1), (Q_2, i_2, F_2)) \rightarrow Q_1^{Q_1} \times Q_2^{Q_2}$
$\mathfrak{i} : ((Q_1, i_1, F_1), (Q_2, i_2, F_2)) \rightarrow (\mathrm{Id}, \mathrm{Id})$
$\mathfrak{F} : ((Q_1, i_1, F_1), (Q_2, i_2, F_2)) \rightarrow$
$\qquad \left\{ (f, g) \in Q_1^{Q_1} \times Q_2^{Q_2} \mid f^2(i_1) \in F_1 \wedge g^3(i_2) \in F_2 \right\}$
$\mathfrak{d} : ((Q_1, i_1, F_1, \delta_1), (Q_2, i_2, F_2, \delta_2)) \rightarrow (f, g) \longrightarrow (\delta_1 \circ f, \delta_2 \circ g)$

Generalizing this example, each state is an array of functions. The transition function by a letter is also an array of functions. We go from one state to the other by composing only the functions which are at the same index of the array. These family of modifiers is called <u>friendly modifiers</u>. The family of Boolean root operations they encode has been studied in detail in [6]. It has been shown that the state complexity of such a k-ary operator taking input, languages of complexity $(n_1, \ldots, n_k)$ is $n_1^{n_1} \times \ldots \times n_k^{n_k}$ for $k > 1$. Moreover, it has been shown that there is always a witness with at most $3k$ letters.

6   A Set of Automata Containing All State to State Functions: The Monster

In [2], Brzozowski gives a series of properties that would make a language L_n of state complexity n sufficiently complex to be a good candidate for constructing witnesses for numerous classical regular operations. One of these properties is that the size of the syntactic semigroup is n^n, which means that each transformation of the minimal DFA of L_n can be associated to a transformation by some non-empty word. This upper bound is reached when the set of transition functions of the DFA is exactly the set of transformations from state to state.

The idea of using combinatorial objects to denote letters has already been used by Sakoda and Sipser [27] to obtain results for two-way automata, or by Birget [1] to obtain deterministic state complexity.

We thus consider the set of transformations of $[\![n]\!]$ as an alphabet where each letter is simply named by the transition function it defines. This leads to the following definition:

Definition 4. *A 1-monster is an automaton* $\mathrm{Mon}_n^F = (\Sigma, [\![n]\!], 0, F, \delta)$ *defined by*

- *the alphabet* $\Sigma = [\![n]\!]^{[\![n]\!]}$,
- *the set of states* $[\![n]\!]$,
- *the initial state* 0,
- *the set of final states* F,
- *the transition function* δ *defined for any* $a \in \Sigma$ *by* $\delta(q, a) = \delta^a(q)$.

The language recognized by a 1-monster DFA is called a <u>1-monster language</u>.

Example 8. The 1-monster $\mathrm{Mon}_2^{\{1\}}$ is

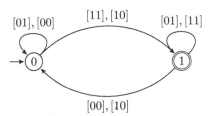

where, for all $i, j \in \{0, 1\}$, the label $[ij]$ denotes the transformation sending 0 to i and 1 to j, which is also a letter in the DFA above.

Let us notice that some families of 1-monster languages are witnesses for the Star and Reverse operations ([7]). The following claim is easy to prove and captures a universality-like property of 1-monster languages:

Proposition 5. *Let L be any regular language recognized by a DFA $A = (\Sigma, [\![n]\!], 0, F, \delta)$. The language L is the preimage of $\mathrm{L}(\mathrm{Mon}_n^F)$ by the 1-uniform morphism ϕ such that, for all $a \in \Sigma$, $\phi(a) = \delta^a$, i.e.*

$$L = \phi^{-1}(\mathrm{L}(\mathrm{Mon}_n^F)).$$

This is an important and handy property that we should keep in mind. We call it the restriction-renaming property.

We wonder whether the notions above could be extended to provide witnesses for k-ary operators. In the unary case, the alphabet of a monster is the set of all possible transformations we can apply on the states. In the same way, a k-monster DFA is a k-tuple of DFAs, and its construction must involve the set of k-tuples of transformations as an alphabet. Indeed, the alphabet of a k-ary monster has to encode all the transformations acting on each set of states independently one from the others (see Fig. 3). This leads to the following definition :

Definition 5. *A k-monster is a k-tuple of automata $\mathrm{Mon}_{n_1,\ldots,n_k}^{F_1,\ldots,F_k} = (\mathbb{M}_1, \ldots, \mathbb{M}_k)$ where, for any $j \in \{1, \ldots, k\}$, $\mathbb{M}_j = (\Sigma, [\![n_j]\!], 0, F_j, \delta_j)$ is defined by*

- *the common alphabet $\Sigma = [\![n_1]\!]^{[\![n_1]\!]} \times \ldots \times [\![n_k]\!]^{[\![n_k]\!]}$,*
- *the set of states $[\![n_j]\!]$,*
- *the initial state 0,*
- *the set of final states F_j,*
- *the transition function δ_j defined for any $(a_1, \ldots, a_k) \in \Sigma$ by $\delta_j(q, (a_1, \ldots, a_k)) = \delta^{a_j}(q)$.*

A k-tuple of languages $(L_1, \ldots, L_k)$ is called a monster k-language if there exists a k-monster $(\mathbb{M}_1, \ldots, \mathbb{M}_k)$ such that $(L_1, \ldots, L_k) = (\mathrm{L}(\mathbb{M}_1), \ldots, \mathrm{L}(\mathbb{M}_k))$.

Fig. 3. An example of transition function in a 2-monster.

Proposition 6. *When F_j is different from $\emptyset$ and $[\![n_j]\!]$, $\mathbb{M}_j$ is minimal.*

Definition 5 allows us to extend the restriction-renaming property in a way that is still easy to check.

Proposition 7. *Let $(L_1, \ldots, L_k)$ be a k-tuple of regular languages recognized by the DFAs $(A_1, \ldots A_K)$ where $A_{1 \leq j \leq k} = (\Sigma, [\![n_j]\!], 0, F_j, \delta_j)$. Let $\mathrm{Mon}^{F_1, \ldots, F_k}_{n_1, \ldots, n_k} = (\mathbb{M}_1, \ldots, \mathbb{M}_k)$. For all $j \in \{1, \ldots, k\}$, the language L_j is the preimage of $\mathrm{L}(\mathbb{M}_j)$ by the 1-uniform morphism ϕ such that, for all $a \in \Sigma$, $\phi(a) = (\delta_1^a, \ldots, \delta_k^a)$, i.e.*

$$(L_1, \ldots, L_k) = (\phi^{-1}(\mathrm{L}(\mathbb{M}_1)), \ldots, \phi^{-1}(\mathrm{L}(\mathbb{M}_k))).$$

Monsters are relevant for the study of state complexity of 1-uniform operations as shown in the theorem below.

Theorem 2. *Any k-ary 1-uniform operation admits a family of monster k-languages as a witness.*

Proof. Suppose now that $\otimes$ is a k-ary 1-uniform operation. Then, if $(L_1, \ldots, L_k)$ is a k-tuple of regular languages over Σ, $(A_1, \ldots, A_k)$ the k-tuple of DFAs such that each $A_j = (\Sigma, Q_j, i_j, F_j, \delta_j)$ is the minimal DFA of L_i, and ϕ the 1-uniform morphism such that, for all $a \in \Sigma$, $\phi(a) = (\delta_1^a, \ldots, \delta_k^a)$, and if

$$\mathrm{Mon}^{F_1, \ldots, F_k}_{n_1, \ldots, n_k} = (\mathbb{M}_1, \ldots, \mathbb{M}_k),$$

then

$$\otimes(L) = \otimes(\phi^{-1}(\mathrm{L}(\mathbb{M}_1)), \ldots, \phi^{-1}(\mathrm{L}(\mathbb{M}_k))) = \phi^{-1}(\otimes(\mathrm{L}(\mathbb{M}_1), \ldots, \mathrm{L}(\mathbb{M}_k))).$$

It follows that

$$\mathrm{sc}(\otimes(L)) = \mathrm{sc}(\phi^{-1}(\otimes(\mathrm{L}(\mathbb{M}_1), \ldots, \mathrm{L}(\mathbb{M}_k)))) \leq \mathrm{sc}(\otimes(\mathrm{L}(\mathbb{M}_1), \ldots, \mathrm{L}(\mathbb{M}_k)))$$

by Property 5. In addition, each $\mathrm{L}(\mathbb{M}_j)$ has the same state complexity as L_j.

7   Computing State Complexity with the Help of Monsters and Modifiers

The classical method to compute the state complexity of an operation is first to provide an algorithm for this operation. In the aim to obtain an upper bound, we count the states created by the algorithm. In order to have a tight bound, all these states have to be both accessible and distinguishable. Finally, to complete the proof, we provide a witness (a set of languages given by their minimal automata) that reaches this bound. In this paper, we are mainly interested in the state complexity of combined operations. We will see what modifiers and monsters can do for the following two combined operations: the star of a boolean operation and the reversal of a boolean operation.

7.1   The Star of a Boolean Operation

The algorithm proposed in [28] to obtain a minimal DFA A recognizing $(L_1 \cup L_2)^*$ acts in the same way as our modifier $\mathfrak{StarUnion}$ defined in Example 6 but the defined states are different. Indeed, the states defined for A are these: Let $A_1 = (\Sigma, Q_1, i_1, F_1, \delta_1)$ and $A_2 = (\Sigma, Q_2, i_2, F_2, \delta_2)$ be two minimal DFA such that $L(A_1) = L_1$ and $L(A_2) = L_2$. The states of A are

$$\{q_0\} \cup \mathcal{P} \cup \mathcal{R} \tag{6}$$

where

$$\mathcal{P} = \{P_1 \cup P_2 \mid P_1 \in 2^{Q_1 \setminus F_1} \setminus \{\emptyset\}, P_2 \in 2^{Q_2 \setminus F_2} \setminus \{\emptyset\}\} \tag{7}$$

and

$$\mathcal{R} = \{R \subset Q_1 \cup Q_2 \mid i_1, i_2 \in R, \ R \cap (F_1 \cup F_2) \neq \emptyset\} \tag{8}$$

These states are a subpart of the states of the modifier $\mathfrak{StarUnion}$ which are $2^{Q_1 \times Q_2}$. The state q_0 is our state $\emptyset$. The states of $\mathcal{P}$ are the non-final states and the states of $\mathcal{R}$ are the final states. these states are exactly those which are accessible and pairwise distinguishable. On the other hand, the transition function is the same in both modifiers. What is possibly problematic is the sentence:

"*It is easy to verify that $L(A) = (L(A_1) \cup L(A_2))^*$*".

Things seems to be swept under the rug a bit. The coherent modifiers (see Table 1) and their composition provide a formal positive answer (see Proposition 4) to the question of language recognition by application of the algorithm.

For the case of the star of intersection, the same authors only give an upper bound for the state complexity of this operation and do not guarantee that it is reached. It is Jiraskova and Okhotin [23] who show, thanks to Brzozowski automata, that this upper bound is tight. In these two papers, the algorithms used (the modifiers) are the same as the one we defined in [6]. One measures here immediately the interest of the monster which gives us a witness for the operation star of intersection. Another advantage of modifiers is uniformity. States defined by any modifier $\mathfrak{StarBool}$ of the star of any Boolean operation are the same. These states are represented by the same combinatorial object: a tableau. However, for the star of each of these Boolean operations, the state complexity is not the same. For each of these boolean operations, we have highlighted an equivalence relation on tableaux which represents the states such that all tableaux (states) of a same class are equivalent. For the star of intersection operation, two distinct tableaux are in two distinct equivalence classes. For the star of union, if there exist four integers $k_1 \neq k_2$, $\ell_1 \neq \ell_2$ and a tableau containing crosses including two crosses in (k_1, ℓ_1) and in (k_2, ℓ_2) then it is equivalent to the tableau containing the same crosses plus those in (k_1, ℓ_2) and in (k_2, ℓ_1) (see Fig. 4).

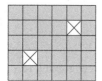 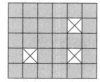

Fig. 4. Three indistinguishable tableaux computed by the $\mathfrak{Star}\mathfrak{Union}$ modifier.

This uniformity in modifiers also allows us, thanks to the results of [8], to catch the state complexity of the star of xor operation. This time, the equivalence relation defined on the tableaux is as follows: if there exist four integers $k_1 \neq k_2$, $\ell_1 \neq \ell_2$ and a tableau containing crosses including three crosses in (k_1, ℓ_1) and in (k_1, ℓ_2) and (k_2, ℓ_1) then it is equivalent to the tableau containing the same crosses plus the one in (k_2, ℓ_2) (see Fig. 5).

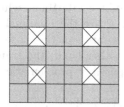 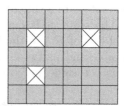

Fig. 5. Two indistinguishable tableaux computed by the $\mathfrak{Star}\mathfrak{Xor}$ modifier.

7.2   The Reversal of a Boolean Operation

The algorithms proposed in [25] to compute the reversal of a Boolean operation are based on two observations. The first of them comes from the juxtaposition-union algorithm. Indeed, if L_1 (resp. L_2) is recognized by the DFA $A_1 = (\Sigma, Q_1, i_1, F_1, \delta_1)$ (resp. $A_2 = (\Sigma, Q_2, i_2, F_2, \delta_2)$) then $L_1 \cup L_2$ is recognized by the NFA $A = A_1 \uplus A_2 = (\Sigma, Q_1 \uplus Q_2, \{i_1, i_2\}, F_1 \uplus F_2, \delta_1 \uplus \delta_2)$ and $\overleftarrow{L_1 \cup L_2}$ is recognized by the NFA $\overleftarrow{A} = (\Sigma, Q_1 \uplus Q_2, F_1 \uplus F_2, \{i_1, i_2\}, \overleftarrow{\delta_1} \uplus \overleftarrow{\delta_2})$ with $\overleftarrow{\delta_i}(p, a) = \{q \mid p = \delta_i(q, a)\}$, $i \in \{1, 2\}$. We also note that $\overleftarrow{A}$ is an NFA for the language $\overleftarrow{L_1} \cup \overleftarrow{L_2}$, which allows us to deduce that operations reversal and union commute for languages but also that operations reversal and juxtaposition-union commute for automata. The authors thus obtain a DFA for $\overleftarrow{L_1 \cup L_2}$ by computing $\widehat{\mathrm{Det}}(\overleftarrow{A})$.

The second observation concerns a property of languages. By applying DeMorgan's law, we find that $L_1 \cap L_2 = \overline{\overline{L_1} \cup \overline{L_2}}$. First, On a DFA A, we obtain its complementary language $\overline{A}$ by reversing the final and non-final states. The computation of a DFA recognizing $\overleftarrow{L_1 \cap L_2}$ from A_1 and A_2 recognizing respectively L_1 and L_2 is thus done in the following way:

$$\widehat{\mathrm{Det}}(\overleftarrow{\overline{A_1} \uplus \overline{A_2}}) \tag{9}$$

States defined by this algorithm are exactly those:

"a $pair$ $[R, S]$ of $sets$ $where$ $\emptyset \neq R \subseteq Q_1$ and $\emptyset \neq S \subseteq Q_2$ and a $state$ t $which$ is a $sink$

$state$." $\tag{10}$

The method proposed by the authors does not allow to conclude for the reversal of the Xor. Here we give a family of $\mathfrak{ReversalBool}_\circ$ modifiers that can compute the reversal of any boolean operation. This one is based on the fact that any boolean operation commutes with the reversal operation.

The main idea is as follows: Let $A_1 = (\Sigma, Q_1, i_1, F_1, \delta_1)$ and $A_2 = (\Sigma, Q_2, i_2, F_2, \delta_2)$ be two automata recognizing respectively L_1 and L_2. The modifier $\mathfrak{ReversalBool}_\circ$ computes

$$\widehat{\mathrm{Det}}(\overleftarrow{A_1} \circ \overleftarrow{A_2})$$

where $\circ$ denotes the computation of any of the boolean operations $\cup, \cap$ or $\oplus$ and is realized by a Cartesian product of the two automata which means that each state of $\mathfrak{ReversalBool}_\circ(A_1, A_2)$ is a set of couples. It is the set of final states which will define the kind of boolean operation. These final states are the set of couples (p, q) where $p \in F_1 \circ q \in F_2$. The modifier for the reversal of any boolean operation is therefore this one:
$\mathfrak{ReversalBool}_\circ = (\mathfrak{Q}, \mathfrak{i}, \mathfrak{F}, \mathfrak{d})$

$\mathfrak{Q} : ((Q_1, i_1, F_1), (Q_2, i_2, F_2)) \to 2^{Q_1 \times Q_2}$

$\mathfrak{i} : ((Q_1, i_1, F_1), (Q_2, i_2, F_2)) \to F_1 \times F_2$

$\mathfrak{F} : ((Q_1, i_1, F_1), (Q_2, i_2, F_2)) \to \{E \in 2^{Q_1 \times Q_2} \mid E \cap (\{i_1\} \times Q_2 \circ Q_1 \times \{i_2\}) \neq \emptyset\}$

$\mathfrak{d} : ((Q_1, i_1, F_1, \delta_1), (Q_2, i_2, F_2, \delta_2)) \to$
$\qquad\qquad\qquad E \longrightarrow \{(p, q) \in Q_1 \times Q_2 \mid (\delta_1(p), \delta_2(q)) \in E\}$

The difference between the modifier we provide and the algorithm given in [25] is only due to the definition of states. It is enough to consider only the accessible states of our modifiers, to have a bijection with the states of the algorithm. These correspond to the empty array ($\emptyset$) which is the image of the state t and saturated tableaux (R, S) having crosses in (r, s) $r \in R$, $s \in S$ which are images of the states $[R, S]$.

We know thanks to (10) that all states of (9), corresponding to our valid tableaux, are accessible. We deduce that the upper bound for the three operations of reversal of union, reversal of catenation and reversal of Xor which corresponds to the number of valid states for the equivalence relation of the union in the tableaux is $(2^m - 1)(2^n - 1) + 1$. In the case of union-reversal and intersection-reversal, as states are also pairwise non-equivalent, this bound is tight. We conjecture that this bound is also tight for the reversal of Xor operation.

8   Conclusion

A quick reading might lead one to think that modifiers and monsters are *ad-hoc* structures defined in order to study operational state complexities of 1-uniform operations. In this last section, we will try to argue, that these objects deserve to be studied for themselves and that their deep knowledge will allow the development of applications in Language theory.

First, let us illustrate the first part of the statement: these objects are perfectly suited to the study of the state complexity of 1-uniform operations. When a modifier acts on a k-tuple of automata, the 1-uniform property is translated by the fact that the image of a k-tuple of transitions does not depend on the others. As a consequence, since each monster contains all the possible k-tuples of transitions, it is a natural candidate to be a witness. As a consequence, we can describe, as follows, a strategy to compute the state complexity of an operation using monsters and modifiers:

1. Describe the transformation with the help of a modifier whose states are represented by combinatorial objects;
2. Apply the modifier to well-chosen k-monsters. We will have to discuss which states are final;
3. Minimize the resulting automaton and estimating its size.

Let us point out that in the first step, we describe in a combinatorial way the action of the modifier. The pair (modifier, monster) can be seen as an algebraic tool allowing to migrate a problem of language theory to a pure problem of combinatorics, and so use appropriate tools, like generating functions and formal power series, to solve them.

Some notions need to be deepened. For example, the notion of alphabetic simplicity, which can be defined as the size of the smallest alphabet for which the state complexity bound is reached. For the moment, we do not have a general theory but a case by case analysis using the combinatorial properties revealed by our method [4–7,9–11]. Notice that in our earliest papers, the modifiers are not explicitly used. It is precisely the observation that the use of combinatorics is quite natural in that context that revealed to us the existence of these objects that we described, studied and explicitly used in the next papers.

There are several directions that would be interesting to consider. First, as we did with the friendly operators [6], we could examine sub-families of operators with particular properties that can be translated on modifiers. Then, in a second step, it seems interesting to look for algebraic structures allowing to encode super-families of operators like for example alphabet-free operators.

References

1. Birget, J.-C.: Intersection and union of regular languages and state complexity. Inf. Process. Lett. **43**(4), 185–190 (1992)
2. Brzozowski, J.A.: In search of most complex regular languages. Int. J. Found. Comput. Sci. **24**(6), 691–708 (2013)
3. Caron, P.: AG: A set of maple packages for manipulating automata and semigroups. Softw. Pract. Exper. **27**(8), 863–884 (1997)
4. Caron, P., Hamel-De le court, E., Luque, J.B.: Algebraic and combinatorial tools for state complexity: Application to the star-xor problem. In: Leroux, J., Raskin, J.-F., (eds.) Proceedings Tenth International Symposium on Games, Automata, Logics, and Formal Verification, GandALF 2019, Bordeaux, France, 2–3rd September 2019, volume 305. EPTCS, pp. 154–168 (2019)
5. Caron, P., Hamel-de-le-court, E., Luque, J.-G.: A study of a simple class of modifiers: product modifiers. In: Jonoska, N., Savchuk, D. (eds.) DLT 2020. LNCS, vol. 12086, pp. 110–121. Springer, Cham (2020). https://doi.org/10.1007/978-3-030-48516-0_9
6. Caron, P., Hamel-De le Court, E., Luque, J.B.: Combination of roots and boolean operations: An application to state complexity. Inf. Comput. **289**(Part), 104961 (2022)
7. Caron, P., Hamel-De le court, E., Luque, J.-G., Patrou, B.: New tools for state complexity. Discret. Math. Theor. Comput. Sci. **22**(1) (2020)
8. Caron, P., Luque, J.-G., Mignot, L., Patrou, B.: State complexity of catenation combined with a boolean operation: A unified approach. Int. J. Found. Comput. Sci. **27**(6), 675–704 (2016)
9. Caron, P., Luque, J.-G., Patrou, B.: State complexity of multiple catenations. Fundam. Inform. **160**(3), 255–279 (2018)
10. Caron, P., Luque, J.-G., Patrou, B.: State complexity of combined operations involving catenation and binary boolean operations: beyond the brzozowski conjectures. Theor. Comput. Sci. **800**, 15–30 (2019)
11. Caron, P., Luque, J.-G., Patrou, B.: A combinatorial approach for the state complexity of the shuffle product. J. Autom. Lang. Comb. **25**(4), 291–320 (2020)
12. Champarnaud, J.-M., Hansel, G.: Automate, a computing package for automata and finite semigroups. J. Symb. Comput. **12**(2), 197–220 (1991)
13. Cui, B., Gao, Y., Kari, L., Sheng, Yu.: State complexity of two combined operations: Catenation-union and catenation-intersection. Int. J. Found. Comput. Sci. **22**(8), 1797–1812 (2011)

14. Davies, S.: A general approach to state complexity of operations: formalization and limitations. In: Hoshi, M., Seki, S. (eds.) DLT 2018. LNCS, vol. 11088, pp. 256–268. Springer, Cham (2018). https://doi.org/10.1007/978-3-319-98654-8_21

15. Domaratzki, M.: State complexity of proportional removals. J. Autom. Lang. Comb. **7**(4), 455–468 (2002)

16. Ésik, Z., Gao, Y., Liu, G., Sheng, Yu.: Estimation of state complexity of combined operations. Theor. Comput. Sci. **410**(35), 3272–3280 (2009)

17. Gao, Y., Moreira, N., Reis, R., Sheng, Yu.: A survey on operational state complexity. J. Autom. Lang. Comb. **21**(4), 251–310 (2017)

18. Gao, Y., Salomaa, K., Sheng, Yu.: The state complexity of two combined operations: Star of catenation and star of reversal. Fundam. Inform. **83**(1–2), 75–89 (2008)

19. Hopcroft, J.E., Ullman, J.D.: Introduction to Automata Theory. Addison-Wesley, Languages and Computation (1979)

20. Jirásek, J., Jirásková, G.: The exact complexity of star-complement-star. In: Câmpeanu, C. (ed.) CIAA 2018. LNCS, vol. 10977, pp. 223–235. Springer, Cham (2018). https://doi.org/10.1007/978-3-319-94812-6_19

21. Jirásek, J., Jirásková, G., Szabari, A.: State complexity of concatenation and complementation. Int. J. Found. Comput. Sci. **16**(3), 511–529 (2005)

22. Jirásková, G.: State complexity of some operations on binary regular languages. Theor. Comput. Sci. **330**(2), 287–298 (2005)

23. Jirásková, G., Okhotin, A.: On the state complexity of star of union and star of intersection. Fundam. Inform. **109**(2), 161–178 (2011)

24. Jirásková, G., Shallit, J.: The state complexity of star-complement-star. In: Yen, H.-C., Ibarra, O.H. (eds.) DLT 2012. LNCS, vol. 7410, pp. 380–391. Springer, Heidelberg (2012). https://doi.org/10.1007/978-3-642-31653-1_34

25. Liu, G., Martín-Vide, C., Salomaa, A., Sheng, Yu.: State complexity of basic language operations combined with reversal. Inf. Comput. **206**(9–10), 1178–1186 (2008)

26. Maslov, A.N.: Estimates of the number of states of finite automata. Soviet Math. Dokl. **11**, 1373–1375 (1970)

27. Sakoda, W.J., Sipser, M.: Nondeterminism and the size of two way finite automata. In Lipton, R.J., Burkhard, W.A., Savitch, W.J., Friedman, E.P., Aho, A.V., (eds.) Proceedings of the 10th Annual ACM Symposium on Theory of Computing, 1–3 May 1978, San Diego, California, USA, pp. 275–286. ACM (1978)

28. Salomaa, A., Salomaa, K., Sheng, Yu.: State complexity of combined operations. Theor. Comput. Sci. **383**(2–3), 140–152 (2007)

29. Salomaa, A., Wood, D., Sheng, Yu.: On the state complexity of reversals of regular languages. Theor. Comput. Sci. **320**(2–3), 315–329 (2004)

30. Sheng, Yu., Zhuang, Q., Salomaa, K.: The state complexities of some basic operations on regular languages. Theor. Comput. Sci. **125**(2), 315–328 (1994)

Hypercubes and Isometric Words Based on Swap and Mismatch Distance

Marcella Anselmo[1], Giuseppa Castiglione[2], Manuela Flores[1,2],

Dora Giammarresi[3(✉)], Maria Madonia[4], and Sabrina Mantaci[2]

[1] Dipartimento di Informatica, Università di Salerno, Fisciano, Italy
manselmo@unisa.it, mflores@unisa.it
[2] Dipartimento di Matematica e Informatica, Università di Palermo, Palermo, Italy
giuseppa.castiglione@unipa.it, sabrina.mantaci@unipa.it
[3] Dipartimento di Matematica, Università Roma "Tor Vergata", Rome, Italy
giammarr@mat.uniroma2.it
[4] Dipartimento di Matematica e Informatica, Università di Catania, Catania, Italy
madonia@dmi.unict.it

Abstract. The hypercube of dimension n is the graph whose vertices are the 2^n binary words of length n, and there is an edge between two of them if they have Hamming distance 1. We consider an edit distance based on swaps and mismatches, to which we refer as *tilde-distance*, and define the *tilde-hypercube* with edges linking words at tilde-distance 1. Then, we introduce and study some isometric subgraphs of the tilde-hypercube obtained by using special words called *tilde-isometric words*. The subgraphs keep only the vertices that avoid a given tilde-isometric word as a factor. An infinite family of tilde-isometric words is described; they are isometric with respect to the tilde-distance, but not to the Hamming distance. In the case of word 11, the subgraph is called *tilde-Fibonacci cube*, as a generalization of the classical Fibonacci cube. The tilde-hypercube and the tilde-Fibonacci cube can be recursively defined; the same holds for the number of their edges. This allows an asymptotic estimation of the number of edges in the tilde-Fibonacci cube, in comparison to the total number in the tilde-hypercube.

Keywords: Swap and mismatch distance · Isometric words · Hypercube

1 Introduction

The n-dimensional *hypercube*, Q_n, encloses all the binary strings of length n and hence it is a model that deserves a starring role in graph theory. It is defined as a graph whose vertices are in correspondence with the 2^n words of length n and there is an edge

Partially supported by INdAM-GNCS Project 2022 and 2023, FARB Project ORSA229894 of University of Salerno, TEAMS Project and PNRR MUR Project PE0000013-FAIR University of Catania, PNRR MUR Project ITSERR CUP B53C22001770006 and FFR fund University of Palermo, MUR Excellence Department Project MatMod@TOV, CUP E83C23000330006, awarded to the Department of Mathematics, University of Rome Tor Vergata.

© IFIP International Federation for Information Processing 2023
Published by Springer Nature Switzerland AG 2023
H. Bordihn et al. (Eds.): DCFS 2023, LNCS 13918, pp. 21–35, 2023.
https://doi.org/10.1007/978-3-031-34326-1_2

between two vertices if the corresponding words differ in one position, that is if their *Hamming distance* is 1. Hence, the distance between two vertices in the graph is equal to the Hamming distance of the corresponding words. During the years, the notion of hypercube has been extensively investigated (see [11] for a survey). Hypercubes are used for designing interconnection networks and they found applications also in theoretical chemistry (see [15] for a survey). However, hypercubes have a critical limitation due to the fact that they have an exponential number of vertices. For this, various modifications have been proposed by considering subgraphs that are *isometric*, that is the distance of any pair of vertices in such subgraphs is the same as the distance in the complete hypercube. With this aim, in 1993, Hsu introduced the *Fibonacci cubes* [12]. They are isometric subgraphs of Q_n obtained by selecting only the vertices whose corresponding words do not contain 11 as factor. They have many remarkable properties also related to Fibonacci numbers.

Generalized Fibonacci cubes $Q_n(f)$ were introduced in 2012 as the subgraphs of Q_n keeping only vertices associated to binary words that do not contain f as a factor, i.e. f-free binary words [13]. Note that, in order to get an isometric subgraph of Q_n, the avoided word should satisfy some special conditions; if this is the case, then the word is said isometric. Indeed, a binary word f is *isometric* (or Ham-isometric) when, for any $n \geq 1$, $Q_n(f)$ can be isometrically embedded into Q_n, and *non-isometric*, otherwise [16]. The structure of binary Ham-isometric words has been characterized in [14, 16, 22, 25, 26] and the research on the topic is still very active [7, 23, 24].

Recently, binary Ham-isometric words have been considered in the two-dimensional setting, and Ham-non-isometric pictures (also called *bad pictures*) have been investigated [6]. Moreover, the notion of isometric word has been extended to the case of alphabets of size k, with $k > 2$, by considering k-ary n-cubes, Q_n^k, and k-ary n-cubes avoiding a word f, $Q_n^k(f)$. In this setting, the distance between two vertices is no longer their Hamming distance, but their Lee distance. Taking into account this distance, Lee-isometric k-ary words have been introduced, studied and characterized [3–5]. Using the characterizations of Ham- and Lee-isometric words, in [4, 8], some linear-time algorithms are provided in order to check whether a word is isometric and to give some interesting information on non-isometric words. Worthily, Ham- and Lee-isometric words can be defined and studied by ignoring hypercubes and adopting a point of view closer to combinatorics on words. Actually, a word f is Ham- (Lee-, resp.) isometric, if for any pair of f-free words u and v of the same length, u can be transformed in v by a sequence of f-free words, starting with u and ending with v, such that the sequence has length equal to the Hamming (Lee, resp.) distance between u and v and every two consecutive words in the sequence have Hamming (Lee, resp.) distance equal to 1.

In some applications coming from computational biology, it seems natural to consider the *swap* operation, exchanging two adjacent different symbols in a word; therefore an edit distance based on swap and mismatch errors seems worth to be considered [1, 10]. Actually, this distance was defined in 70's by Wagner and Fischer [20, 21] who proved that it can be efficiently computed.

In [2] this distance is referred to as *tilde-distance*, since the $\sim$ symbol somehow evokes the swap operation. Tilde-isometric words have been defined using the tilde-distance, in place of Hamming or Lee distance, and studied from a combinatorial point of view.

In this paper, the tilde-distance serves as the base to define the *tilde-hypercube*, $\tilde{Q}_n$; it has again all the n-binary strings as vertices, but the edges correspond to tilde-distance equal to 1. This implies that $\tilde{Q}_n$ has more edges than Q_n; in particular, since a swap corresponds to two mismatches, some vertices having distance 2 in Q_n, become adjacent in $\tilde{Q}_n$.

Over the years, many variations of the hypercube have been introduced in order to improve some of its features. For example, folded hypercubes (cf. [9]) and enhanced hypercubes (cf. [19]) have been defined by adding some edges to the hypercube and present many advantages for some topological features. Here we introduce the tilde-hyperube that has some extras edges to the hypercube but it is defined by changing the concept of distance and allow the definition of isometric subgraphs.

In this paper we give a recursive construction of tilde-hypercubes and enumerate the number of their edges. Then, we consider subgraphs of the tilde-hypercubes $\tilde{Q}_n(f)$ by selecting the vertices corresponding f-free words, for a given word f. It is easy to show that f is *tilde-isometric* if and only if $\tilde{Q}_n(f)$ is an isometric subgraph of $\tilde{Q}_n$. We present an infinite family of tilde-isometric words that are not Hamming isometric. The last part of the paper is devoted to select special words f. For what concern the word $f = 11$, that is both Hamming- and tilde-isometric, the subgraph $\tilde{Q}_n(11)$ is referred to as the *tilde-Fibonacci cube*. We present a recursive construction for it and we compare it with the classic Fibonacci cube. We show that the number of edges in the tilde-Fibonacci cube is about 1/7 less than the number of edges in the whole tilde-hypercube. We also examine this ratio, with some experimental results, for $Q_n(1010)$, where 1010 is a tilde-non-isometric but Ham-isometric word and for $\tilde{Q}_n(11100)$, where 11100 is Ham-non-isometric and tilde-isometric word, for $n = 4, \ldots, 16$.

2 Preliminaries

In this paper we only focus on the binary alphabet $\Sigma = \{0, 1\}$. A word (or string) w over Σ of length $|w| = n$, is $w = a_1 a_2 \cdots a_n$, where $a_1, a_2, \ldots, a_n$ are symbols in Σ. The set of all words over Σ is denoted Σ^*. Finally, ϵ denotes the *empty word* and $\Sigma^+ = \Sigma^* - \{\epsilon\}$. For any word $w = a_1 a_2 \cdots a_n$, the *reverse* of w is the word $w^{rev} = a_n a_{n-1} \cdots a_1$. If $x \in \Sigma$, $\bar{x}$ denotes the opposite of x, i.e. $\bar{x} = 1$ if $x = 0$ and viceversa. Then we define *complement* of w the word $\overline{w} = \bar{a}_1 \bar{a}_2 \cdots \bar{a}_n$.

Let $w[i]$ denote the symbol of w in position i, i.e. $w[i] = a_i$. Then, $w[i..j] = a_i \ldots a_j$, for $1 \leq i \leq j \leq n$, denotes a *factor* u of w. We say that $I = [i..j]$ is the *interval* where the factor u occurs in w. The *prefix* (resp. *suffix*) of w of length l, with $1 \leq l \leq n - 1$ is $\text{pre}_l(w) = w[1..l]$ (resp. $\text{suf}_l(w) = w[n - l + 1..n]$). When $\text{pre}_l(w) = \text{suf}_l(w) = u$ then u is here referred to as an *overlap* of w of length l; in other frameworks, it is also called border, or bifix. A word w is said *f-free* if w does not contain f as a factor.

An *edit operation* is a function $O : \Sigma^* \to \Sigma^*$ that transforms a word into another one. Let OP be a *set of edit operations*. The *edit distance* of words $u, v \in \Sigma^*$, with respect to the set OP, is the minimum number of edit operations in OP needed to transform u into v.

In this paper, we consider the edit distance that uses only *swap* and *replacement* operations to fix *swap* and *mismatch* errors. Note that these operations preserve the length of the word.

Definition 1. *Let* $w = a_1 a_2 \ldots a_n$ *be a word over* Σ.
The replacement operation *(or* replacement, *for short) on* w *at position* i, *with* $i = 1, \ldots, n$, *is defined by*

$$R_i(a_1 a_2 \ldots a_{i-1} \boldsymbol{a_i} a_{i+1} \ldots a_n) = a_1 a_2 \ldots a_{i-1} \boldsymbol{\bar{a}_i} a_{i+1} \ldots a_n.$$

The swap operation *(or* swap, *for short) on* w *at position* i, *with* $i = 1, \ldots, n-1$ *and* $a_i \neq a_{i+1}$, *is defined by*

$$S_i(a_1 a_2 \ldots a_{i-1} \boldsymbol{a_i} \boldsymbol{a_{i+1}} a_{i+2} \ldots a_n) = a_1 a_2 \ldots a_{i-1} \boldsymbol{a_{i+1}} \boldsymbol{a_i} a_{i+2} \ldots a_n.$$

Note that one swap corresponds to the replacement of two consecutive symbols.

The *Hamming distance* $\operatorname{dist}_H(u, v)$ of $u, v \in \Sigma^*$ is defined as the minimum number of replacements needed to get v from u. A word f is *Ham-isometric* if for any pair of f-free words u and v, there exists a sequence of replacements of length $\operatorname{dist}_H(u, v)$ that transforms u into v where all the intermediate words are also f-free. A word w has a 2-*error overlap* if there exists l such that $\operatorname{pre}_l(w)$ and $\operatorname{suf}_l(w)$ have Hamming distance 2 (cf. [22]). Then, the following characterization of Ham-non-isometric words is proved.

Proposition 2 ([22]). *A word* f *is Ham-non-isometric if and only if* f *has a 2-error overlap.*

Let G be a graph, $V(G)$ be the set of its nodes and $E(G)$ be the set of its edges. The distance of $u, v \in V(G)$, $\operatorname{dist}_G(u, v)$, is the length of the shortest path connecting u and v in G. The *diameter* of G, denoted by $d(G)$, is the maximum distance of two vertices in G. A subgraph S of a (connected) graph G is an *isometric subgraph* if for any $u, v \in V(S)$, $\operatorname{dist}_S(u, v) = \operatorname{dist}_G(u, v)$.

Let us recall the notion of hypercube and Fibonacci cube, related to the Hamming distance. The n-*hypercube*, or binary n-cube, Q_n, is a graph with 2^n vertices, each associated to a binary word of length n. The vertices are often identified with the associated word. Two vertices u and v in Q_n are adjacent when their associated words differ in exactly 1 position, i.e. when $\operatorname{dist}_H(u, v) = 1$. Therefore, $\operatorname{dist}_{Q_n}(u, v) = \operatorname{dist}_H(u, v)$.

Denote by f_n the n-th Fibonacci number, defined by $f_1 = 1, f_2 = 1$ and $f_i = f_{i-1} + f_{i-2}$, for $i \geq 3$. The *Fibonacci cube* F_n of order n is the subgraph of Q_n whose vertices are binary words of length n avoiding the factor 11. It is well known that F_n is an isometric subgraph of Q_n (cf. [15]). Isometric subgraphs of hypercubes are also called *partial cubes*.

One of the main properties of Q_n and F_n is their *recursive structure* that have been extensively studied (cf. [12, 15, 17]).

The following results are well-known, but are hereby stated for future reference.

Proposition 3. *Let* Q_n *be the hypercube of order* n *and* F_n *be the Fibonacci cube. Then*

- $|V(Q_n)| = 2^n$ and $|E(Q_n)| = n2^{n-1}$
- $|V(F_n)| = f_{n+2}$
- $|E(F_1)| = 1$, $|E(F_2)| = 2$ and $|E(F_n)| = |E(F_{n-1})| + |E(F_{n-2})| + f_n, \forall n > 2$

$$|E(F_n)| = \frac{2(n+1)f_n + nf_{n+1}}{5}$$

The number of edges of a hypercube with $N = 2^n$ vertices is $(N \log N)/2$.

The sequence $|E(F_n)|$ is Sequence A001629 in [18]. Hence, the number of edges of a Fibonacci cube with N vertices, $N = f_{n+2}$, is $O(N \log N)$, asymptotically equal to the number of edges of a hypercube with the same number of vertices.

3   Tilde-Isometric Words

In this section, we consider the edit distance based on swap and replacement operations used to fix swap and mismatch errors between two words. In [2] it is called tilde-distance and denoted by $dist_\sim$. We give the definition of tilde-isometric words and then present a family of tilde-isometric words.

Definition 4. *Let* $u, v \in \Sigma^*$ *be words of equal length. The* tilde-distance $dist_\sim(u, v)$ *between* u *and* v *is the minimum number of replacements and swaps needed to transform* u *into* v.

Definition 5. *Let* $u, v \in \Sigma^*$ *be words of equal length.*
A tilde-transformation τ *of length* h *from* u *to* v *is a sequence of words* $(w_0, w_1, \ldots, w_h)$ *such that* $w_0 = u$, $w_h = v$, *and for any* $k = 0, 1, \ldots, h-1$, $dist_\sim(w_k, w_{k+1}) = 1$.
Further, τ *is* f-*free if for any* $i = 0, 1, \ldots, h$, *word* w_i *is* f-*free.*
A tilde-transformation from u *to* v *is* minimal *if its length is equal to* $dist_\sim(u, v)$.

A tilde-transformation $(w_0, w_1, \ldots, w_h)$ from u to v is associated to a sequence of h operations $(O_{i_1}, O_{i_2}, \ldots O_{i_h})$ such that, for any $k = 1, \ldots, h$, $O_{i_k} \in \{R_{i_k}, S_{i_k}\}$ and $w_k = O_{i_k}(w_{k-1})$; it can be represented as follows:

$$u = w_0 \xrightarrow{O_{i_1}} w_1 \xrightarrow{O_{i_2}} \cdots \xrightarrow{O_{i_h}} w_h = v.$$

With a little abuse of notation, in the sequel we will refer to a tilde-transformation both as a sequence of words and as a sequence of operations. Furthermore, when the tilde-transformation is minimal, the positions $i_1, i_2, \ldots, i_h$ are all distinct.

Note that the definition of minimal tilde-transformation given in [2] is more restrictive than the one presented here, since in that case the operations are required not to operate twice on the same position.

In the following we give some examples that show some special features of tilde-transformations, which never occur when Hamming-transformations are considered. This highlights on one hand the richness of new situations that can occur by adding the swap operation, but also forecasts new and harder techniques for handling such more challenging scenario. First of all we point out that when only replacements are used, the different minimal transformations from u to v use the same set of operations, possibly applied in a different order. This is not the case for the tilde-transformations.

Example 6. Let $u = 1011, v = 0110$. Below, τ_1 and τ_2 are two tilde-transformations from u to v with different lengths and using different operations. Note that τ_1 is minimal since its length is equal to dist$_\sim (u, v) = 2$.

$$\tau_1 : 1011 \xrightarrow{S_1} 0111 \xrightarrow{R_4} 0110 \qquad \tau_2 : 1011 \xrightarrow{R_1} 0011 \xrightarrow{R_2} 0111 \xrightarrow{R_4} 0110$$

Let $u' = 100, v' = 001$. In this case σ_1 and σ_2 are two minimal tilde-transformations from u' to v' on different sets of operations. In particular observe that σ_1 flips twice the bit in the second position.

$$\sigma_1 : 100 \xrightarrow{S_1} 010 \xrightarrow{S_2} 001 \qquad \sigma_2 : 100 \xrightarrow{R_1} 000 \xrightarrow{R_3} 001$$

This is not the only situation where two minimal tilde-transformations on different sets of operations can occur. Consider for instance $u'' = 010$ and $v'' = 101$ and the minimal tilde-transformations ρ_1 and ρ_2 from u'' to v'', where in both cases each symbol is changed just once:

$$\rho_1 : 010 \xrightarrow{S_1} 100 \xrightarrow{R_3} 101 \qquad \rho_2 : 010 \xrightarrow{S_2} 001 \xrightarrow{R_1} 101$$

The variety of situations described above gives the expectation of a higher degree of difficulty of the tilde-transformations (compared to the Hamming transformations) when handling some property like, for instance, isometricity.

Remark 7. Let $u, v \in \Sigma^m$ and τ be a minimal tilde-transformation from u to v. If τ contains two swaps, S_i and S_{i+1}, at consecutive positions i and $i + 1$ of u, then such swaps can be substituted by two replacements, namely R_i and R_{i+2}, still obtaining a minimal tilde-transformation from u to v. An example of this case is shown in Example 6 for u' and v'.

Let us now define isometric words based on the tilde distance.

Definition 8. *Let $f \in \Sigma^*$ be a word of length n with $n \geq 1$. The word f is tilde-isometric if for any pair of f-free words u and v of equal length $m \geq n$, there exists a minimal tilde-transformation from u to v that is f-free. It is tilde-non-isometric if it is not tilde-isometric.*

In order to prove that a word is tilde-non-isometric it is sufficient to exhibit a pair (u, v) of words contradicting Definition 8. More challenging is to prove that a word is tilde-isometric.

Example 9. The word $f = 1010$ is tilde-non-isometric. In fact, let $u = 11000$ and $v = 10110$; u and v are f-free; moreover the only possible minimal tilde-transformations from u to v are $11000 \xrightarrow{S_2} 10100 \xrightarrow{R_4} 10110$ and $11000 \xrightarrow{R_4} 11010 \xrightarrow{S_2} 10110$, and in both cases 1010 appears as factor after the first step. On the other side, observe that f is Ham-isometric by Proposition 2.

Let us highlight the following straightforward property of tilde-isometric binary words that is very helpful to simplify proofs and computations.

Remark 10. A word f is tilde-isometric iff $\overline{f}$ is tilde-isometric iff f^{rev} is tilde-isometric.

In view of Remark 10, we will focus on words starting with 1. The following proposition explicitly explores the tilde-isometricity for all words of length 2, 3 and 4.

Proposition 11. *The following statements hold.*

1. *All words of length 2 are tilde-isometric*
2. *All words of length 3, except for 101 and 010, are tilde-isometric*
3. *The words 1111, 1110, 1000, 0000, 0001, 0111 are tilde-isometric. All the other words of length 4 are tilde-non-isometric.*

Proof. Consider the different cases:

1. If $|f| = 2$, two cases arise, up to reverse and complement: $f = 10$ and $f = 11$. They are both tilde-isometric words because of next Proposition 13.
2. If $|f| = 3$, three cases arise, up to complement and reverse.
   - $f = 111$ and $f = 100$, are tilde-isometric because of Proposition 13.
   - $f = 101$, is tilde-non-isometric. In fact, $u = 1111$ and $v = 1001$ contradict isometricity of f, since they are f-free, and all the minimal transformations of u into v need to change u into a word that has 101 as a factor.
3. If $|f| = 4$, the following cases arise, up to complement and reverse.
   - $f = 1111$ and $f = 1110$ are tilde-isometric because of Proposition 13.
   - $f = 1100$. Then $u = 110100$ and $v = 101010$ contradict isometricity of f.
   - $f = 1001$. Then $u = 11011$ and $v = 10001$ contradict isometricity of f.
   - $f = 1010$ is tilde-non-isometric (see Example 9).
   - $f = 1011$. Then $u = 11111$ and $v = 10011$ contradict isometricity of f.   □

Let us show an infinite family of words that are tilde-isometric, but not Hamisometric, by Proposition 2. First, prove next technical lemma.

Lemma 12. *Let $f \in \Sigma^n$ be a tilde-non-isometric word, let (u, v), with $u, v \in \Sigma^m$, be a pair of words contradicting Definition 8, with minimal $d = \mathrm{dist}_\sim(u, v)$ among all such pairs of words with length m. Let $\{O_{i_1}, O_{i_2}, \ldots, O_{i_d}\}$ be the set of operations of a minimal tilde-transformation from u to v that does not contain two swaps at two consecutive positions.*
Then, for $j = 1, 2, \ldots, d$, f occurs in $O_{i_j}(u)$ at the interval that we denote by I_j. Moreover, there exist $s, t \in \{i_1, i_2, \ldots i_d\}$, such that I_s and I_t both contain at least one position modified by O_t and at least one position modified by O_s.

Proof. Let $\{O_{i_1}, O_{i_2}, \ldots, O_{i_d}\}$ be the set of operations as in the hypothesis. Further suppose that for any $j = 1, 2, \ldots, d$, $O_{i_j} \in \{R_{i_j}, S_{i_j}\}$ and $1 \leq i_1 < i_2 < \cdots < i_d \leq m$.

Since the transformation does not contain two consecutive swaps, each O_{i_j} can be applied to u. Let us show that for $j = 1, 2, \ldots, d$, $O_{i_j}(u)$ has an occurrence of f. In fact, if $O_{i_j}(u)$ were f-free then the pair $(O_{i_j}(u), v)$ would still contradict Definition 8, but with $\mathrm{dist}_\sim(O_{i_j}(u), v) < d$, against the minimality of d. Let I_j be the interval where f occurs in $O_{i_j}(u)$. This interval contains at least one position modified by O_{i_j}, because u is f-free; let $o(j)$ denote the smallest position in I_j modified by O_{i_j}. Moreover, this occurrence of f must disappear in a tilde-transformation from u to v, because v is f-free. Hence, I_j contains a position modified by another operation in $\{O_{i_1}, O_{i_2}, \ldots, O_{i_d}\}$; let $p(j)$ denote the smallest such position. Overall, there exist $s, t \in \{i_1, i_2, \ldots i_d\}$, such that I_s contains at least one position modified by O_t and I_t contains at least one position modified by O_s. To prove this, consider for any $j = 1, \ldots, d$, interval I_j and the two positions $o(j)$ and $p(j)$ in I_j. Note that $p(1) > o(1)$, whereas $p(d) < o(d)$. Let i_k be the smallest position in $\{i_1, i_2, \ldots i_d\}$, such that $p(k) < o(k)$; then $p(k-1) > o(k-1)$. Since I_k contains $o(k)$ and $p(k)$, with $p(k) < o(k)$, then I_k also contains $o(k-1)$ because $p(k) \leq o(k-1) < o(k)$. Finally, I_k and I_{k-1} both contain $o(k-1)$ and $o(k)$ and can play the role of I_s and I_t.   □

Proposition 13. *Let* $f_{h,k} = 1^h 0^k$, *with* $h, k \geq 0$. *Then,* $f_{h,k}$ *is tilde-isometric for any* $h, k \geq 0$, *except for* $h = k = 2$, *i.e.,* $f_{2,2} = 1100$ *is tilde-non-isometric.*

Proof. Suppose that $f = f_{h,k} = 1^h 0^k$, $f \neq 1100$, is tilde-non-isometric and let (u, v), with $u, v \in \Sigma^m$, be a pair of words contradicting Definition 8, with minimal $\text{dist}_\sim(u, v)$ among all such pairs of words with length m. Then, no minimal tilde-transformation from u to v is f-free. In view of Remark 7, consider a minimal tilde-transformation from u to v without swaps at two consecutive positions.

Let I_s and I_t be the corresponding intervals as in Lemma 12 and let $I = [p..q]$ be their intersection. Without loss of generality on s and t, interval I is the interval in which a suffix of f occurs in $O_s(u)$ and the interval in which a prefix of f in $O_t(u)$ occurs, of the same length l, with $l = q - p + 1$. In other words, $\text{dist}_\sim(suf_l(f), pref_l(f)) = 2$. Note that this implies $f \neq 1^h, 0^k$.

Interval $I = [p..q]$ can contain either four, or three, or two among the positions modified by O_s and O_t, of which at least one is modified by O_s and at least one by O_t. One can show that a contradiction follows in all cases. We give details only in some cases that involve swap operations; the other ones can be treated in a similar way.

Consider the case that I contains four positions modified by O_s and O_t. Therefore, O_s and O_t are non-consecutive swaps, i.e. $O_s = S_s$ and $O_t = S_t$, with $s, t \in [p..q]$. Since $(S_s(u))[p..q] = suf_l(f)$, one has $u[p..q] \in 1^*010^*$. But, then, there exists no other swap operation in $u[p..q]$ that can give a prefix of f, as it should be for S_t.

Consider now the case that I contains two positions modified by O_s and O_t. Three cases are possible following that O_s and O_t are both replacement operations, or both swap operations, or one is a swap and the other a replacement. Note that if O_s or O_t is a swap then it must be either S_{p-1} or S_q.

Let us consider the case that O_s and O_t are both swap operations and that $O_s = S_{p-1}$ and $O_t = S_q$. Then, the two positions in $u[p..q]$ which are modified by O_s and O_t must be p and q. First, suppose $q = p + 1$. If $u[p..q] = 10$ then $u[p-1..q+1] = 0101$. The application of S_{p-1} on u implies that f ends with 100, whereas the application of S_q implies that f begins with 110. Hence, $f = 1100$, against the hypothesis. The application of S_{p-1} on u in the cases that $u[p..q] = 00, 01, 11$, respectively, would result in a suffix $010, 011, 101$ of f, and this is a contradiction. Suppose now $q > p + 1$. If $u[p] = 1$ then $u[p..q] \in 1000^*$, since $(S_{p-1}(u))[p..q] = suf_l(f)$. Subsequently, S_q cannot give a prefix of f. An analogous reasoning shows that $u[p] = 0$ cannot hold either.   □

The notion of tilde-isometricity is not comparable with the one of Ham-isometricity. Furthermore, the following result holds.

Proposition 14. *The word* 11100 *is the shortest tilde-isometric word that is not Ham-isometric. The word* 1010 *is the shortest Ham-isometric word that is not tilde-isometric.*

Proof. The word 11100 is tilde-isometric (Proposition 13) but Ham-non-isometric (Proposition 2). On the other hand 1010 is tilde-non-isometric (Proposition 11), and it is Ham-isometric (Proposition 2). The minimality of the length of these words comes from Proposition 11. □

4   The Tilde-Hypercube

Classical binary hypercubes connect vertices following their Hamming distance, while the distance of vertices in a k-ary n-cube represents their Lee-distance. This suggests to investigate hypercubes based on other distances. In this paper we introduce the *tilde-hypercube*, whose vertices are the binary words and edges connect vertices with tilde-distance equal to 1. Then, its recursive structure is explored.

Definition 15. *The n-tilde-hypercube $\tilde{Q}_n$, or tilde-hypercube of order n, is a graph with 2^n vertices, each associated to a binary word of length n. Two vertices in $\tilde{Q}_n$, are adjacent whenever the tilde-distance of their associated words is 1.*

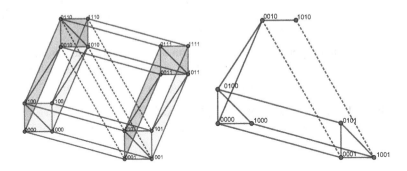

Fig. 1. The tilde-hypercube of order 4 (a) the tilde-Fibonacci cube of order 4 (b)

Figure 1(a) shows the tilde-hypercube of order 4.

Remark 16. Q_n is a proper subgraph of $\tilde{Q}_n$. In fact for $u, v \in \Sigma^*$, $\text{dist}_H(u, v) = 1$ implies $\text{dist}_\sim(u, v) = 1$. Further, for any $n \geq 2$, there exist words u_n, v_n of length n such that $\text{dist}_\sim(u_n, v_n) = 1$ and $\text{dist}_H(u_n, v_n) \neq 1$. For instance, for any $0 \leq k, h \leq n - 2$, $h + k = n - 2$, consider words $u_n = 0^h010^k$ and $v_n = 0^h100^k$; then $\text{dist}_\sim(u_n, v_v) = 1$ and $\text{dist}_H(u_n, v_n) = 2$, therefore (u_n, v_n) is an edge in $\tilde{Q}_n$ but not in Q_n.

As mentioned before, many variations of the hypercube have been introduced such as, for instance, the folded hypercube [9] and the enhanced hypercube [19]. The n-tilde-hypercube here defined has no inclusion relation with any of the above mentioned hypercubes.

The following lemma is the main tool to exhibit a recursive definition of the tilde-hypercube, in analogy with the classical hypercube.

Lemma 17. *For any* $u, v \in \Sigma^{n-1}$, $\mathrm{dist}_\sim(u0, v0) = \mathrm{dist}_\sim(u, v) = \mathrm{dist}_\sim(u1, v1)$ *and* $\mathrm{dist}_\sim(u0, u1) = 1$. *Moreover, for any* $u' \in \Sigma^{n-2}$, $\mathrm{dist}_\sim(u'01, u'10) = 1$.

Proposition 18. *The* n-*tilde-hypercube* $\tilde{Q}_n$ *can be recursively defined, with* $n \geq 1$.

Proof. If $n = 1$, $\tilde{Q}_1$ has just two vertices 0 and 1 connected by an edge.

Suppose all the tilde-hypercubes of dimension smaller than n have been defined. The hypercube $\tilde{Q}_n$ is recursively constructed as follows. Start with a copy of $\tilde{Q}_{n-1}$, say $\tilde{\mathbf{Q}}_{n-1}^0$, where every vertex u is replaced by $u0$ and a second copy, say $\tilde{\mathbf{Q}}_{n-1}^1$, where every vertex u is replaced by $u1$. By Lemma 17, if u and v are connected in $\tilde{Q}_{n-1}$, then $u0$ and $v0$ ($u1$ and $v1$, respectively) are connected in $\tilde{Q}_n$, this means that $\tilde{\mathbf{Q}}_{n-1}^0$ and $\tilde{\mathbf{Q}}_{n-1}^1$ are subgraphs of $\tilde{Q}_n$. Moreover for any $u \in \Sigma^{n-1}$, an edge in $\tilde{Q}_n$ links vertices $u0$ in $\tilde{\mathbf{Q}}_{n-1}^0$ and $u1$ in $\tilde{\mathbf{Q}}_{n-1}^1$. Finally, for any $u' \in \Sigma^{n-2}$ an edge of $\tilde{Q}_n$ links $u'10$ in $\tilde{\mathbf{Q}}_{n-1}^0$ and $u'01$ in $\tilde{\mathbf{Q}}_{n-1}^1$. In Fig. 1(a), these latter edges added in the fourth step of recursion, are depicted with dotted edges. For any other pair of words $u, v \in \{0, 1\}^n$, $\mathrm{dist}_\sim(u, v) > 1$, then (u, v) is not an edge of $\tilde{Q}_n$. □

Corollary 19. *Let* $\tilde{Q}_n$ *be the tilde-hypercube of order* n. *Then,* $|E(\tilde{Q}_1)| = 1$ *and, for any* $n \geq 2$

$$|E(\tilde{Q}_n)| = 2|E(\tilde{Q}_{n-1})| + 2^{n-1} + 2^{n-2}$$

Proof. By the recursive construction in Proposition 18, $\tilde{Q}_n$ has twice the number of edges of $\tilde{Q}_{n-1}$ (since it contains $\tilde{\mathbf{Q}}_{n-1}^0$ and $\tilde{\mathbf{Q}}_{n-1}^1$), plus one edge for each vertex of $\tilde{Q}_{n-1}$, i.e. 2^{n-1}, plus one edge for each vertex of $\tilde{Q}_{n-1}$ ending on 1, i.e. 2^{n-2}. □

By solving the above recurrence, we find the exact formula $|E(\tilde{Q}_n)| = (3n - 1) \cdot 2^{n-2}$ (Sequence A053220 in [18]). Let $\tilde{E}Q(N)$ be the number of edges of the tilde-hypercube with N vertices, $N = 2^n$. Then,

$$\tilde{E}Q(N) = N(3 \log N - 1)/4 \qquad (1)$$

5   The Tilde-Hypercube Avoiding a Word

The so-called generalized Fibonacci cube has been defined in [13] as the subgraph of the hypercube where the vertices having a given word as factor are removed. In analogy, we introduce the definitions of the tilde-hypercube avoiding a word and the tilde-Fibonacci cube.

Definition 20. *The* n-*tilde-hypercube avoiding a word* f, *or the tilde-hypercube of order* n *avoiding a word* f, *denoted* $\tilde{Q}_n(f)$, *is the subgraph of* $\tilde{Q}_n$ *obtained by removing those vertices which contain* f *as a factor.*

Next proposition states the relationship between tilde-isometric words and subgraphs of the tilde-hypercube avoiding a word. The proof can be easily derived from the definitions.

Proposition 21. *A word $f \in \Sigma^*$ is tilde-isometric if and only if for all $n \geq |f|$, $\tilde{Q}_n(f)$ is an isometric subgraph of $\tilde{Q}_n$.*

Example 22. All binary words of length 2 are both tilde-isometric (Proposition 11) and Ham-isometric. Further, for each $n \geq 1$, $\tilde{Q}_n(10)$ and $Q_n(10)$ coincide. In fact, $V(\tilde{Q}_n(10)) = \{0^h 1^k | h, k \geq 0, \quad h + k = n\}$ and $E(\tilde{Q}_n(10)) = \{(0^i 1^j, 0^{i-1} 1^{j+1}) | 1 \leq i, j \leq n\}$. The case of word 11 deserves to be treated in a separated section. The other words of length 2 are tilde-isometric by complement (see Remark 10).

5.1 The Tilde-Fibonacci Cube

The tilde-hypercube avoiding word 11 is called the tilde-Fibonacci cube, in analogy to the Fibonacci cube introduced by Hsu [12]. Here, we show a recursive construction of the tilde-Fibonacci cube; it allows to enumerate the number of its edges and then to compare it with the number of edges of the tilde-hypercube with the same number of vertices.

Definition 23. *The n-tilde-Fibonacci cube, or tilde-Fibonacci cube of order n, denoted $\tilde{F}_n$, is $\tilde{F}_n = \tilde{Q}_n(11)$, $n \geq 1$.*

By Proposition 3, $|V(\tilde{F}_n)| = |V(F_n)| = f_{n+2}$. Among these vertices, f_{n+1} end with a 0 and f_n end with a 1. Figure 1(b) shows the tilde-Fibonacci cube of order 4.

Remark 24. Let $u \in V(F_{n-1})$, $x \in \Sigma$. If u ends with 1, then $ux \in V(\tilde{F}_n)$ iff $x = 0$. If u ends with 0 then $ux \in V(\tilde{F}_n)$, for any $x \in \{0, 1\}$.

Proposition 25. *The n-tilde-Fibonacci cube $\tilde{F}_n$ can be recursively defined, with $n \geq 1$.*

Proof. If $n = 1$, $\tilde{F}_1$ has two vertices 0 and 1 connected by an edge. If $n = 2$, $\tilde{F}_2$ has three vertices 00, 01 and 10 and $E(\tilde{F}_2) = \{(00, 10), (00, 01), (01, 10)\}$.

Let $n \geq 3$ and suppose $\tilde{F}_i$ are defined for all $i < n$. Then, $\tilde{F}_n$ can be constructed from a copy of $\tilde{F}_{n-1}$ (say $\mathbf{\tilde{F}}^0_{n-1}$) where each vertex u is replaced by $u0$, and a copy of $\tilde{F}_{n-2}$ (say $\mathbf{\tilde{F}}^{01}_{n-2}$), where each vertex v is replaced by $v01$ in $\mathbf{\tilde{F}}^{01}_{n-2}$. If there is an edge linking u and u' in $\tilde{F}_{n-1}$, then there is en edge linking $u0$ and $u'0$ in $\tilde{F}_n$, i.e. $\mathbf{\tilde{F}}^0_{n-1}$ is a subgraph of $\tilde{F}_n$. For similar reasons $\mathbf{\tilde{F}}^{01}_{n-2}$ is a subgraph of $\tilde{F}_n$. Further, for any $v0 \in V(\tilde{F}_{n-1})$, there is an edge linking $v00$ in $\mathbf{\tilde{F}}^0_{n-1}$ and $v01$ in $\mathbf{\tilde{F}}^{01}_{n-2}$ and for any $u1 \in V(\tilde{F}_{n-1})$ there is an edge linking $u10$ in $\mathbf{\tilde{F}}^0_{n-1}$ and $u01$ in $\mathbf{\tilde{F}}^{01}_{n-2}$ (see the dotted edges in Fig. 1(b)). By Remark 24 and Lemma 17 no further edges exist in $\tilde{F}_n$. $\square$

Corollary 26. *Let $\tilde{F}_n$ be the n-tilde-Fibonacci cube. Then, $|E(\tilde{F}_1)| = 1, |E(\tilde{F}_2)| = 3$ and, for any $n \geq 2$*

$$|E(\tilde{F}_n)| = |E(\tilde{F}_{n-1})| + |E(\tilde{F}_{n-2})| + f_{n+1}.$$

Proof. From the proof of Proposition 25, $\tilde{F}_1$ has 1 edge and $\tilde{F}_2$ has 3 edges. Moreover, $|E(\tilde{F}_n)|$ is the sum of $|E(\tilde{F}_{n-1})|$ with $|E(\tilde{F}_{n-2})|$, plus one edge for each vertex in $\tilde{F}_{n-1}^0$, i.e. f_{n+1}, by Proposition. 3.   □

By solving the recurrence in Corollary 26, we find the following exact formula:

$$|E(\tilde{F}_n)| = \frac{(n+1)f_{n+3} + (n-2)f_{n+1}}{5}$$

(Sequence A023610 in [18] for $|E(\tilde{F}_{n+1})|$).

Since the number of vertices of $\tilde{F}_n$ is f_{n+2}, from the previous formula it follows that the tilde-Fibonacci cube has $O(N \log N)$ edges, where N is the number of vertices, as for the tilde-hypercube (see Eq. (1)).

To compare the number of edges of the Fibonacci cube and the hypercube, in [12] the authors prove that the ratio between the number of edges $EF(N)$ and $EQ(N)$ in the Fibonacci cube and the hypercube with N vertices, respectively, is asymptotically bounded by $0.79 < EF(N)/EQ(N) < 0.80$. In analogy with this result, by using the same method as in [12], we have the following corollary.

Corollary 27. *Let $\tilde{E}F(N)$ and $\tilde{E}Q(N)$ be the number of edges of the tilde-Fibonacci cube and of the tilde-hypercube with N vertices, respectively. Then, their ratio is asymptotically bounded by*

$$0.85 < \frac{\tilde{E}F(N)}{\tilde{E}Q(N)} < 0.86$$

Proof. By Eq. (1) and Proposition 3, $\tilde{E}Q(f_{n+2}) = f_{n+2}(3 \log f_{n+2} - 1)/4$ and by Corollary 26, $\tilde{E}F(f_{n+2}) = ((n+1)f_{n+3} + (n-2)f_{n+1})/5$. By considering $\tilde{E}F(f_{n+2})/\tilde{E}Q(f_{n+2})$ asymptotically, the thesis follows.   □

This proves that the number of edges of the tilde-Fibonacci cube is about $1/7$ less than the number of edges of the tilde-hypercube, with fixed number of vertices. The ratio is just slightly higher than in the Hamming case. This fact is not surprising because the swap operation adds new edges, but, on the other hand, it shortens the average distances between vertices because a swap corresponds to two replacement operations. More formally, we have the following remark.

Remark 28. In [12] it is proven that the diameter of F_n is $d(F_n) = n$ and that the maximal distance involves the words $(10)^{n/2}$ and $(01)^{n/2}$ for even n, and $(01)^{\lfloor n/2 \rfloor}0$ and $(10)^{\lfloor n/2 \rfloor}1$ for odd n. If the tilde-distance is considered, then $d(\tilde{F}_n) = \lceil n/2 \rceil$. Indeed, the same words have maximal tilde-distance in $\tilde{F}_n$ and the minimal 11-free tilde-transformation from one to the other consists of $n/2$ swaps for even n and $\lfloor n/2 \rfloor$ swaps and one replacement for odd n.

5.2 Some Experimental Results

In the previous subsection, Corollary 27 gives the upper and lower bound of the ratio between the number of edges of the n-tilde-Fibonacci cube and the number of edges of the n-tilde-hypercube having the same number of vertices; in this way it is possible to compare the bounds in the tilde case with the bounds in the Hamming case. It is likely that in the future the same kind of asymptotic bounds can be proved for the hypercubes and tilde-hypercubes avoiding words that are both Hamming and tilde-isometric.

In this section we collect some experimental values regarding the hypercube avoiding 1010 and the tilde-hypercube avoiding 11100. The choice of investigating such words is motivated by the fact that they are the shortest words to prove the difference between the set of Ham-isometric words and the set of tilde-isometric-words (cf. Proposition 14). In fact, according to Proposition 14, the word 1010 is tilde-non-isometric but it is Ham-isometric, hence, $Q_n(1010)$ is an isometric subgraph of Q_n, whereas $\tilde{Q}_n(1010)$ is not an isometric subgraph of $\tilde{Q}_n$. On the contrary, according to Proposition 14, the word 111000 is tilde-isometric and Ham-non-isometric, therefore, $\tilde{Q}_n(11100)$ is an isometric subgraph of $\tilde{Q}_n$, whereas $Q_n(11100)$ is not an isometric subgraph of Q_n (cf. Proposition 21). By now, in both cases we are not able to enumerate the edges and vertices, hence we give in Table 1 the values for n up to 16, computed by construction. In order to compare data in the same way as in [12], it is necessary to normalize the number of edges to the same number of vertices. From Proposition 3, the number of edges of the hypercube with N vertices is equal to $(N \log N)/2$. Then, with $N = |V(Q_n(1010))|$, for each n we have

$$R_H\,(1010) = \frac{|E(Q_n(1010))|}{(|V(Q_n(1010))| \log |V(Q_n(1010))|)/2}$$

From Eq. 1, the number of edges of the tilde-hypercube with N vertices is equal to $N(3 \log N - 1)/4$. Then, with $N = |V(\tilde{Q}_n(11100))|$, for each n we have

$$R_\sim\,(11100) = \frac{|E(\tilde{Q}_n(11100))|}{|V(\tilde{Q}_n(11100))|(3 \log |V(\tilde{Q}_n(11100))| - 1)/4.}$$

We can see that the ratios for $n = 4, \ldots, 16$, for these two words are close and encourage a future research on generalized tilde-Fibonacci cubes.

Table 1. Vertices and edges cardinality and ratio of some cubes of order $n = 4, \ldots, 16$

n	4	5	6	7	8	9	10	11	12	13	14	15	16
$|V(Q_n)|=|V(\tilde{Q}_n)|$	16	32	64	128	256	512	1024	2048	4096	8192	16384	32768	65536
$|E(Q_n)|$	32	80	192	448	1024	2304	5120	11264	24576	53248	114688	245760	524288
$|E(\tilde{Q}_n)|$	44	112	272	640	1472	3328	7424	16384	35840	77824	167936	360448	770048
$|V(Q_n(1010))|$	15	28	53	100	188	354	667	1256	2365	4454	8388	15796	29747
$|E(Q_n(1010))|$	28	62	138	299	632	1323	2746	5645	11520	23377	47192	94830	189808
$R_H\,(1010)$	0,96	0,92	0,91	0,90	0,89	0,88	0,88	0,87	0,869	0,866	0,863	0,861	0,859
$|V(\tilde{Q}_n(11100))|$	16	31	60	116	224	432	833	1606	3096	5968	11504	22175	42744
$|E(\tilde{Q}_n(11100))|$	44	106	245	550	1208	2609	5569	11773	24691	51440	106566	219696	451005
$R_\sim\,(11100)$	1	0,99	0,98	0,97	0,96	0,96	0,95	0,95	0,944	0,941	0,939	0,937	0,935

6 Conclusion and Future Work

In this paper we have introduced the tilde-hypercube and the tilde-Fibonacci cube as a generalization of the corresponding classical notions, with the tilde-distance in place of the Hamming one. We have shown that, as in the classical case, the tilde-hypercube and the tilde-Fibonacci cube can be recursively defined. This made it possible to provide recursive and closed formulas for their number of edges with respect to the order. We used such results to quantify how many edges the tilde-Fibonacci cube has compared to the tilde-hypercube with the same number of vertices, and it turned out that this value is very close to the classical case. However, the investigation definitely deserves some deepening, since the hypercubes and the tilde-hypercubes are defined on different distances, which are supposed to be used for different applications.

We guess that both Fibonacci cubes and tilde-Fibonacci cubes are the best isometric cubes avoiding a word in terms of reduction of the number of edges, but at the moment the investigation is too germinal. We plan to continue the research in this direction and, above all, to study in deep structural and topological properties of tilde-Fibonacci cubes.

References

1. Amir, A., Eisenberg, E., Porat, E.: Swap and mismatch edit distance. Algorithmica **45**(1), 109–120 (2006)
2. Anselmo, M., Castiglione, G., Flores, M., Giammarresi, D., Madonia, M., Mantaci, S.: Isometric words based on swap and mismatch distance. CORR abs/2303.03086 (2023)
3. Anselmo, M., Flores, M., Madonia, M.: Quaternary n-cubes and isometric words. In: Lecroq, T., Puzynina, S. (eds.) WORDS 2021. LNCS, vol. 12847, pp. 27–39. Springer, Cham (2021). https://doi.org/10.1007/978-3-030-85088-3_3
4. Anselmo, M., Flores, M., Madonia, M.: Fun slot machines and transformations of words avoiding factors. In: 11th International Conference on Fun with Algorithms. LIPIcs, vol. 226, pp. 4:1–4:15 (2022)
5. Anselmo, M., Flores, M., Madonia, M.: On k-ary n-cubes and isometric words. Theor. Comput. Sci. **938**, 50–64 (2022)
6. Anselmo, M., Giammarresi, D., Madonia, M., Selmi, C.: Bad pictures: some structural properties related to overlaps. In: Jirásková, G., Pighizzini, G. (eds.) DCFS 2020. LNCS, vol. 12442, pp. 13–25. Springer, Cham (2020). https://doi.org/10.1007/978-3-030-62536-8_2
7. Azarija, J., Klavžar, S., Lee, J., Pantone, J., Rho, Y.: On isomorphism classes of generalized Fibonacci cubes. Europ. J. Comb. **51**, 372–379 (2016)
8. Béal, M., Crochemore, M.: Checking whether a word is Hamming-isometric in linear time. Theor. Comput. Sci. **933**, 55–59 (2022)
9. El-Amawy, A., Latifi, S.: Properties and performance of folded hypercubes. IEEE Trans. Parallel Distrib. Syst. **2**(1), 31–42 (1991)
10. Faro, S., Pavone, A.: An efficient skip-search approach to swap matching. Comput. J. **61**(9), 1351–1360 (2018)
11. Harary, F., Hayes, J., Wu, H.: A survey of the theory of hypercube graphs. Comput. Math. Appl. **15**(4), 277–289 (1988)
12. Hsu, W.J.: Fibonacci cubes-a new interconnection topology. IEEE Trans. Parallel Distrib. Syst. **4**(1), 3–12 (1993)
13. Ilić, A., Klavžar, S., Rho, Y.: Generalized Fibonacci cubes. Discrete Math. **312**(1), 2–11 (2012)

14. Ilić, A., Klavžar, S., Rho, Y.: The index of a binary word. Theor. Comput. Sci. **452**, 100–106 (2012)

15. Klavžar, S.: Structure of Fibonacci cubes: a survey. J. Comb. Optim. **25**(4), 505–522 (2013)

16. Klavžar, S., Shpectorov, S.V.: Asymptotic number of isometric generalized Fibonacci cubes. Eur. J. Comb. **33**(2), 220–226 (2012)

17. Munarini, E., Salvi, N.Z.: Structural and enumerative properties of the Fibonacci cubes. Discret. Math. **255**(1–3), 317–324 (2002)

18. Sloane, N.: On-line encyclopedia of integer sequences. http://oeis.org/

19. Tzeng, N., Wei, S.: Enhanced hypercubes. IEEE Trans. Comput. **40**(3), 284–294 (1991)

20. Wagner, R.A., Fischer, M.J.: The string-to-string correction problem. J. ACM **21**(1), 168–173 (1974)

21. Wagner, R.A.: On the complexity of the extended string-to-string correction problem. In: Rounds, W.C., Martin, N., Carlyle, J.W., Harrison, M.A. (eds.) Proceedings of the 7th Annual ACM Symposium on Theory of Computing, 5–7 May 1975, Albuquerque, New Mexico, USA, pp. 218–223 (1975)

22. Wei, J.: The structures of bad words. Eur. J. Comb. **59**, 204–214 (2017)

23. Wei, J.: Proof of a conjecture on 2-isometric words. Theor. Comput. Sci. **855**, 68–73 (2021)

24. Wei, J., Yang, Y., Wang, G.: Circular embeddability of isometric words. Discret. Math. **343**(10), 112024 (2020)

25. Wei, J., Yang, Y., Zhu, X.: A characterization of non-isometric binary words. Eur. J. Comb. **78**, 121–133 (2019)

26. Wei, J., Zhang, H.: Proofs of two conjectures on generalized Fibonacci cubes. Eur. J. Comb. **51**, 419–432 (2016)

Defying Gravity and Gadget Numerosity: The Complexity of the Hanano Puzzle

Michael C. Chavrimootoo[✉][iD]

Department of Computer Science,
University of Rochester, Rochester, NY 14627, USA
michael.chavrimootoo@rochester.edu

Abstract. Using the notion of visibility representations, our paper establishes a new property of instances of the Nondeterministic Constraint Logic (NCL) problem (a PSPACE-complete problem that is very convenient to prove the PSPACE-hardness of reversible games with pushing blocks). Direct use of this property introduces an explosion in the number of gadgets needed to show PSPACE-hardness, but we show how to bring that number from 32 down to only three in general, and down to two in a specific case! We propose it as a step towards a broader and more general framework for studying games with irreversible gravity, and use this connection to guide an indirect polynomial-time many-one reduction from the NCL problem to the Hanano Puzzle—which is NP-hard—to prove it is in fact PSPACE-complete.

Keywords: Computational complexity · Irreversible games · Hardness of games · Minimizing gadgets

1 Introduction

The application of complexity theory to the study of games has allowed us to understand the hardness of many popular games. Many games that are limited to a single player are NP-complete (with respect to many-one polynomial-time reductions, which is what we will always refer to when using the terms "-hard" and "-complete"), while two-player games are typically PSPACE-complete [8]. However, the moment the board layout becomes dynamic or the number of moves becomes unbounded, the complexity of a one-player game can jump to being PSPACE-complete [8]. Surprisingly, the presence of irreversible gravity, which limits the number of moves possible, can yield complex games [8].

The Hanano Puzzle is a one-player game with a dynamic board, unbounded moves, and gravity developed by video game creator Qrostar [10]. Liu and Yang recently proved that the language version of the Hanano Puzzle is NP-hard [9]. In their paper, they ask if the problem is NP-complete and leave the question open. We pinpoint the problem's complexity by proving Hanano Puzzle's language version to be PSPACE-complete. We do so by providing an indirect

Work supported in part by NSF Grant CCF-2006496.

H. Bordihn et al. (Eds.): DCFS 2023, LNCS 13918, pp. 36–50, 2023.
https://doi.org/10.1007/978-3-031-34326-1_3

reduction from the Nondeterministic Constraint Logic (NCL) problem (a known PSPACE-complete problem [8]). One of the major challenges of the reduction is overcoming the effects of gravity. We define a method that leverages graph-theoretic techniques to circumvent unwanted effects of gravity, thereby making reductions from NCL easier. To our knowledge, this method (of abstracting away the "harmful" effects of gravity) is new in this area, which makes our study interesting in this sense. We are also able to significantly reduce the number of gadgets that we need to build by constructing "base gadgets" from which other gadgets can be built. This design is entirely independent of the Hanano Puzzle, and so we believe it might have applications to other similar games.

2   Preliminaries

A simple planar graph is one that is loop-free, has no multi-edges (i.e., for each pair of vertices, there is at most one edge between the pair of vertices), and is planar (i.e., can be drawn on a piece of paper so that its edges only intersect at their common endpoints). Given a graph $G = (V, E)$, a *visibility representation* Γ for G maps every vertex $v \in V$ to a vertical vertex segment $\Gamma(v)$ and every edge $(u, v) \in E$ to a horizontal edge segment $\Gamma(u, v)$ such that each horizontal edge segment $\Gamma(u, v)$ has its respective endpoints lying on the vertical vertex segments $\Gamma(u)$ and $\Gamma(v)$, and no other segment intersections or overlaps occur [12] (See Fig. 3 for an example)[1].

2.1   The Hanano Puzzle

This section expands on definitions by Liu and Yang [9]. The Hanano Puzzle comprises different levels. A level of the game is an $n \times m$ grid (with $n, m > 0$) that contains only the following components: immovable gray blocks, movable gray blocks, (movable) colored blocks, colored flowers, and empty spaces. Each colored block/flower can be red, blue, or yellow. Each flower is immovable and is affixed to some block. If that block is movable, then whenever it moves, the affixed flower moves with the block (see Fig. 1d). Gray blocks can be of arbitrary shape and size, while all other components are 1×1 objects. In our gadgets, we try to the best of our ability to minimize the number of sides of each movable gray block. A block can slide (see Fig. 1a) left or right, one step at a time. For a slide to occur, the space that the block will occupy after the slide must either be empty or be occupied by part of the block that is sliding. Two adjacent blocks of width one can also be swapped in one step (see Fig. 1b) the positions of the two blocks can be swapped without moving any other component of the grid.

Figure 1 shows screenshots of the game that show sample game moves. Note that the checkered cells are what we call "immovable gray blocks." Movable gray blocks are not depicted in these figures. Because this is a game with gravity, after

---

[1]   This definition deviates slightly from the standard one in that the standard definition, vertices are mapped to horizontal segments, and edges are mapped to vertical segments. For our purposes, both definitions are equivalent.

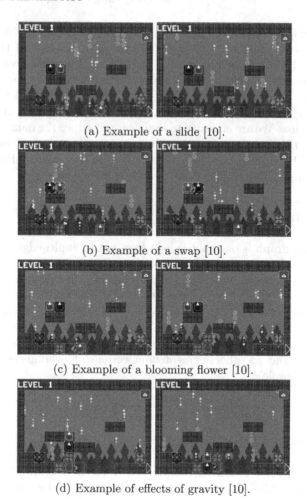

(a) Example of a slide [10].

(b) Example of a swap [10].

(c) Example of a blooming flower [10].

(d) Example of effects of gravity [10].

Fig. 1. Screenshots of the Hanano Puzzle (reproduced with permission from Qrostar [11]).

the player makes a move, every movable block that is not directly supported will fall (see Fig. 1d). This can be viewed as happening in a single step. Each colored block contains an arrow, pointing either up, down, left, or right. If a colored block touches (by sharing a side; touching corners have no effect) a flower of the same color, a flower will bloom from the side of the colored block indicated by the arrow (see Fig. 1c), and the new flower will stay affixed/attached to that block. We will sometimes say that the block has bloomed when this happens. If the blooming side is in contact with a block, the blooming flower attempts to "force" its way out by pushing against the surface in contact with the blooming side. This may result in that block in contact with the blooming side to be shifted, or in the blooming block to be shifted. If no shift is possible, then the flower does not bloom. A block can only bloom once and that action cannot be undone. Additionally, if the new flower is in contact with a different block of the same color, chain bloomings can occur within the same step. To solve (complete) a level, one must make every colored block bloom. Formally, we determine the complexity of HANANO = {H | H is a solvable level of the Hanano Puzzle}.

2.2   Nondeterministic Constraint Logic (NCL)

The notions introduced in this section are from Hearn and Demaine [8]. An NCL graph is a directed graph consisting of edges of weights one or two (respectively called red and blue edges) that connect vertices while subject to the constraint that the sum of weights of edges into each vertex is at least two (aka the minimum inflow requirement/constraint). The only operation allowed on an NCL graph is flipping the direction of an edge such that the new graph is still an NCL graph. Given an NCL graph G and an edge e in the graph, deciding if there is a sequence of edge flips that eventually flip e is PSPACE-complete. It turns out that the problem remains PSPACE-complete even if the NCL graph is a planar AND/OR NCL graph, i.e., it is simple planar, each vertex is connected to exactly three edges, and each vertex is either an AND vertex (i.e., one incident edge is blue and the other two are red) or an OR vertex (i.e., all incident edges are blue). In this paper, we will tacitly assume that our NCL graphs are planar AND/OR NCL graphs. For readability and accessibility purposes, in addition to being colored, the blue edges in this paper will be solid and the red edges will be dashed. Typically, to show that NCL reduces to a problem A, it suffices to construct an AND gadget and an OR gadget. However, because of the effects of gravity, we will see in Sect. 3 that the gadgets need to "interact" properly.

Fig. 2. An NCL graph.

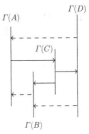

Fig. 3. A visibility representation of Fig. 2.

3   PSPACE-Completeness

The HANANO is clearly in PSPACE, since the configure of the game at any point in time can be stored in polynomial space.

3.1 Defying Gravity with Structure

Part of the difficulty in devising a correct reduction is the fact that in NCL, every action is fully reversible while in HANANO, due to gravity and blooms, some moves are irreversible, so we cannot give direct gadgets. Liu and Yang [9] did not encounter this issue as their reduction from CIRCUIT-SAT leveraged the fact that in a boolean circuit, bits only need to move in one direction once. The technique behind their construction is very similar to that used by Friedman [6] to show the NP-hardness of a simple game (Cubic) with gravity. We thus need to be careful in our construction to make sure we do not prematurely make irreversible moves. Additionally, we shall build into our gadgets the constraints of the NCL game to help simulate NCL using HANANO.

Given an NCL graph, each node in the graph will be simulated using gadgets. To help identify the colored blocks and flowers of the gadgets in proofs, we label those items with special text. E.g., the label "B2", indicates the second blue block in the gadget, whereas the label "BF1" indicates the first blue flower. Blue blocks will represent both red and blue edges. It's important to note that *all our blocks bloom upwards.* Next to each flower will be a boldfaced white line to indicate where the flower is attached. Additionally, our gadgets will contain some grid lines to help the reader better gauge the distances. The presence of a block in a gadget will indicate that the edge represented by the block is directed into the node represented by the gadget. Blocks will only be allowed to move between gadgets by following the constraints imposed by NCL. This means that those constraints must be encoded within the gadgets, using the rules of the Hanano Puzzle. This is the first challenge. The second challenge is to overcome the nonreversibility induced by gravity. To help ensure that most block moves are reversible, the effects of gravity must be circumvented. Luckily, this is possible due to the planarity of NCL graphs. We shall start by addressing the second challenge. The first challenge will be resolved by designing the gadgets. One such way is by having blooms "force" a certain setting of the game when the inflow constraints are violated.

Theorem 1 ([12,13]). *A graph admits a visibility representation if and only if it is planar. Furthermore, a visibility representation for a planar graph can be constructed in linear time.*[2]

Since our NCL graphs are planar, we can compute the visibility representation of an NCL graph in linear time. This has the advantage that if we're trying to reduce to a game of sliding blocks, and we wish to represent the direction of the edges by using blocks that are sliding from one gadget (where each vertex is represented using a gadget) to another, then by having all the edges be horizontal, we remove the danger of having gravity make an "edge flip" irreversible. Implicit in this, is that our gadgets will need to be "size-adaptable," i.e., as

---

[2] In an earlier version of this paper, we independently proved a weaker version of this theorem. Our result established the "if" direction (the "only if" direction is trivial), but our polynomial-time algorithm did not run in linear time.

we will see based on the length of the segment to which a vertex is mapped, a gadget's height may need to change. Our constructions will have the property that they can be internally padded so as to make gadgets artificially long without affecting their correctness. Thus those "edge flips" in the game of interest (here, the Hanano Puzzle) are fully reversible, to the extent that is required to be compatible with NCL's reversibility.

3.2   Gadgets and Schemas

Each vertex in the NCL graph will be represented using a gadget and those gadgets will be connected using tunnels that will represent the edges. For each of these tunnels, there will be a blue block and that block will be placed in the gadget representing the vertex to which the edge is incident. Thus, flipping edges will be represented by moving blocks from one gadget to another. For gadgets to interact properly, we must ensure that a block can only travel through its designated tunnel and that the minimum inflow requirement is always met, i.e., for each gadget, there is always either one blue block representing a blue edge or two blue blocks each representing a red edge in the gadget, at any point in time. Since each vertex in the NCL graph is connected to exactly three edges, each gadget will have three entry points that can each lie either on the left or the right of the gadget. Consider the following notation to represent a gadget: $x_1 x_2 x_3 | y_1 y_2 y_3$, where for each $i \in \{1, 2, 3\}$, $\{x_i, y_i\} \in \{\{R, \cdot\}, \{B, \cdot\}\}$, and the list $[x_1, x_2, x_3, y_1, y_2, y_3]$ contains either exactly three Bs, or exactly one B and two Rs. (The last condition simply captures the idea that each vertex is either an AND vertex or an OR vertex.) For example, $R \cdot \cdot | \cdot B R$ means that the top entry point on the left side of the gadget is for a red edge's blue block, the middle on the right side is for a blue edge's blue block, and the bottom on the right side is for a red edge's blue block. The remaining entry points are considered blocked off, i.e., not entry points. It's easy to see that due to this structure enforced, the number of gadgets needed to show the reduction goes up from two to *32* (8 OR gadgets + 24 AND gadgets).[3] However, we will show how, by giving only three gadgets, we can derive all the remaining gadgets (i.e., show their existence). The approach will in fact not rely on properties of the Hanano Puzzle, and thus will be reusable for other purposes. However, if one restricts their attention to HANANO, then we will argue that one of the gadgets need not be constructed. Let us first look at how to construct the OR gadgets.

Lemma 1. *The gadget in Fig. 4a satisfies the same constraints as an NCL OR vertex.*

---

[3] One could try to argue that given one OR gadget and one AND gadget, it suffices to "just place the tunnels on the correct side" to obtain the remaining 30 gadgets, but that approach does not take into account the structure of the gadget. This suggested approach certainly works for our OR gadgets (see Fig. 4a), but not for our AND gadgets (see Fig. 4b). However, we do show how to derive all the OR/AND gadgets in a way that is independent of the structure of the underlying gadgets.

Proof. First notice that each movable gray block has very limited movement. G2 can only move up by one "unit," and G1 can either move up or move down by

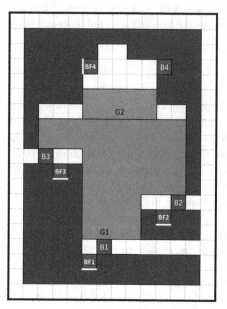

(a) $B \cdots | \cdot BB$ gadget.

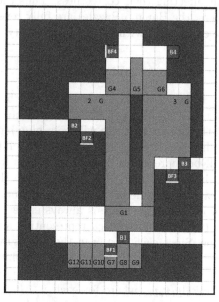
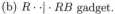

(b) $R \cdots | \cdot RB$ gadget.

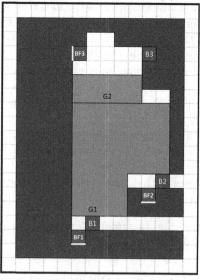

(c) Red bend gadget.

Fig. 4. Our three gadgets: an OR gadget ($B \cdots | \cdot BB$), an AND gadget ($R \cdots | \cdot RB$), and a red bend gadget. (Color figure online)

one unit. Thus for any blue block Bx, the only flower that it can reach in that gadget is BFx. Now, the only way for B4 to bloom is if B4 is in contact with BF4, and it must be on BF4's right side (the only other exposed side of BF4 is the bottom side, but if B4 is directly under BF4 it will not have enough room to bloom). Thus B4 can bloom iff G2 moves up by one unit. This can happen exactly if G1 moves up by one unit, which can happen iff one of B1, B2, or B3 blooms. Finally, notice that if B1, B2, and B3 all leave the gadget, then G1 and G2 both drop by one unit with no possibility of returning to their original configuration, thus making it impossible to bloom B4. We conclude by noting that we could have merged G1 and G2 into a single block, but opted not to as we sought to minimize the number of sides on each movable gray block.   □

We will show how to construct certain gadgets from other gadgets, by essentially chaining certain gadgets together. For our convenience we define a "constrained blue edge terminator" gadget, that will allow us to force an edge from pointing out of a gadget, without connecting the edge to other nodes. This allows us to simplify the design of our gadgets. We state the following proposition in a general form, i.e., its proof will not depend on the Hanano Puzzle's properties.

Proposition 1. *The constrained blue edge terminator gadget can be constructed using any gadget that satisfies the same constraints as an NCL OR vertex.*

Proof. We want the constrained blue edge terminator to be a gadget that, when attached to a tunnel that represents a blue edge, will force the block that represents the edge's orientation to be inside itself (i.e., inside the constrained blue edge terminator) so as to not violate the inflow constraints.

Fix a gadget that satisfies the same constraints as an NCL OR vertex. There must exist a configuration of the gadget that corresponds to the NCL OR with one (blue) edge pointing into the vertex and the remaining edges (i.e., two blue edges) pointing out of the vertex. Now, block off the tunnels that correspond to the two edges pointing of the vertex. This configuration of the gadget correctly constraints the represented blue edge's orientation.   □

A natural question to ask is whether $B \cdot \cdot | \cdot BB$ is special, or whether this result can be achieved using any of the other OR gadgets, and we answer in the positive that indeed, any of the eight OR gadgets suffices. We first note that it suffices to consider the gadgets for $B \cdot \cdot | \cdot BB$, $\cdot B \cdot | B \cdot B$, $\cdot \cdot B | BB \cdot$, and $\cdot \cdot \cdot | BBB$, as the remaining ones can be obtained via vertical symmetry. In an abuse of notation, we will sometimes use the shorthand for a gadget to refer to the gadget that is obtained from it via vertical symmetry in our schemas. Edges that are connected to the constrained blue edge terminator have a direction assigned and point to a $\oslash$ to indicate the termination. The remaining edges have no direction, indicating that they can be assigned in any way that satisfies the minimum inflow constraints.

Lemma 2. *For each gadget G in the following list, the remaining gadgets in that same list can be constructed from G: 1. $B \cdot \cdot | \cdot BB$, 2. $\cdot B \cdot | B \cdot B$, 3. $\cdot \cdot B | BB \cdot$, and 4. $\cdot \cdot \cdot | BBB$.*

Proof. We prove this lemma by showing how to construct 2 from 1, how to construct 3 from 2, how to construct 4 from 3, and finally how to construct 1 from 4. In each case, we will have a gadget that satisfies the same constraints as an NCL OR vertex, so we tacitly appeal to Proposition 1 to, for "free," have a constrained blue edge terminator. We construct in Fig. 5 schematic diagrams to aid in our proof.

From 1 to 2. Figure 5a depicts the construction. The edges of the $\cdot B \cdot |B \cdot B$ gadget are 2, 4, and 5. If those edges all point out (i.e., 2 points left and the other two point right), then the minimum inflow constraint is violated as 3 cannot be flipped and 1 can only point into one the two gadgets. Thus one of 2, 4, or 5 must always be pointed inwards, and this gadgets satisfies the same constraints and as NCL OR vertex.

From 2 to 3. Figure 5b depicts the construction. The edges of the $\cdot B \cdot |B \cdot B$ gadget are 2, 4, and 5. If those edges all point out (i.e., 2 points left and the other two point right), then the minimum inflow constraint is violated as 3 cannot be flipped and 1 can only point into one the two gadgets. Thus one of 2, 4, or 5 must always be pointed inwards, and this gadgets satisfies the same constraints and as NCL OR vertex.

From 3 to 4. Figure 5c depicts the construction. The edges of the $\cdot B \cdot |B \cdot B$ gadget are 2, 4, and 5. If those edges all point out (i.e., they all point right), then the minimum inflow constraint is violated as 3 cannot be flipped and 1 can only point into one the two gadgets. Thus one of 2, 4, or 5 must always be pointed inwards, and this gadgets satisfies the same constraints and as NCL OR vertex.

From 4 to 1. Figure 5d depicts the construction. The edges of the $\cdot B \cdot |B \cdot B$ gadget are 2, 4, and 5. If those edges all point out (i.e., 2 points left and the other two point right), then the minimum inflow constraint is violated as 3 cannot be flipped and 1 can only point into one the two gadgets. Thus one of 2, 4, or 5 must always be pointed inwards, and this gadgets satisfies the same constraints and as NCL OR vertex.   □

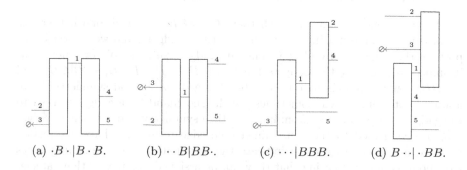

(a) $\cdot B \cdot |B \cdot B$.   (b) $\cdot \cdot B|BB\cdot$.   (c) $\cdots |BBB$.   (d) $B \cdot \cdot | \cdot BB$.

Fig. 5. Schemas showing the "equivalence" of the OR gadgets.

The AND gadgets are trickier, but we can construct all of them using two gadgets: a gadget that satisfies the same constraints as an NCL AND vertex, and a "red bend" gadget. The red bend gadget will allow us to, in some sense, reorient the direction of a tunnel that corresponds to a red edge (hence the "red" in the name even though all our blocks are blue; in the context of HANANO, the red bend gadget also works on "blue edges" but that does not necessarily hold in general). Lemma 4 gives an analogous result to Lemma 2.

Lemma 3. *The gadget in Fig. 4b satisfies the same constraints as an* NCL AND *vertex, with B1 representing the blue edge, and with B3 and B4 representing the red edges.*

Proof. Let us first describe the gadget before arguing its correctness.

G4 and G6 can only move up by 1 "unit," and G2 and G3 can each either move up or move down by one unit. Thus each colored block, can only reach one flower. If both B2 and B3 exit the gadget, then B1 must remain to support G1 (which in turn supports G2 and G3), as otherwise, G2 and G3 will drop by 1 unit and G4 and G6 will never be able to move up. Similarly, if B1 is to exit, all the gray blocks must remain supported. This is only possible if G1 is stowed to the left and B2 and B3 remain in the gadget to, respectively, support G3 and G2. Additionally, the area underneath B1 is made up of multiple movable gray blocks for a simple reason. B1 must be able to move horizontally without blooming (either to exit the gadget or two carry G1 to "stow" it). By this setting, we can move the location of BF1 (by swapping G7 with an adjacent movable block of width one; BF1 is affixed to G7 and the two will move as if they were one 2×1 block) to make sure it is always on the left of B1.

Now, the only way for B4 to bloom is if B4 is in contact with BF4, and it must be on BF4's right side (the only other exposed side of BF4 is the bottom side, but if B4 is directly under BF4 it will not have enough room to bloom). Thus B4 can bloom if and only if G4 and G6 move up by one unit. This can happen exactly if both G2 and G3 move up by one unit. There are two ways this can happen: Either both B2 and B3 bloom, or B1 blooms (thus pushing G1 up by one unit). Thus B4 blooms if and only if either B2 and B3 bloom in the gadget, or B1 blooms in the gadgets. □

We now define an important property of the red bend gadget that is used in the proof of Lemma 4. Intuitively, the results means that the inflow constraint on red bend gadgets is one (or two under the "blue bend" interpretation).

Proposition 2. *The red bend gadget in Fig. 4c is solvable if and only if either B1 or B2 blooms while supporting G1.*

Proof. The design of the gadget is simply a restricted/modified version of that in Fig. 4a, so we omit the description of the gadget.

$\implies$: Suppose the gadget is solvable. Then B3 must come in contact with BF3. This is only possible if both G1 and G2 move up by one unit. For this to happen, either B1 or B2 must bloom while supporting G1.

$\impliedby$: Suppose that either B1 or B2 blooms while supporting G1. In both cases, G1 moves up by one unit, thus also pushing G2 up by one unit, hence allowing B3 to come in contact with BF3 to bloom. □

Earlier, we mentioned that when our attention is focus on HANANO, we only need two gadgets. This is indeed possible because all the blocks that we use are of the same color, and so we can define the red bend gadget to be a restricted version of the OR gadget. Consider the gadget in Fig. 4a. If we place a constrained blue edge terminator at the tunnel for B3, then the resulting gadget is essentially the red bend gadget.

Lemma 4. *For each gadget G in the following list, the remaining gadgets in that same list can be constructed from G, the red bend gadget, and any OR gadget:*
1. $R \cdots | \cdot RB$, 2. $\cdot R \cdot | R \cdot B$, 3. $\cdots | RRB$, 4. $\cdots B | RR\cdot$, 5. $\cdots | BRR$, 6. $\cdots R | BR\cdot$, 7. $B \cdots | \cdot RR$, 8. $\cdot R \cdot | B \cdot R$, 9. $\cdots | RBR$, 10. $R \cdots | \cdot BR$, 11. $\cdot B \cdot | R \cdot R$, and 12. $\cdots R | RB\cdot$.

Proof. We represent our red bend gadgets using a vertex with exactly two red edges on the same side of the gadget. The structure of this proof resembles that of Lemma 2.

From 1 to 2. Figure 6a depicts the construction. If edge 5 points right, then edge 1 points right and edge 4 points left. Thus edge two must point left, leaving edge 3 to point right. If edge 5 points left, then edge 4 is free to point in either direction. In that case, we can fix edge 1 to point left and edge 2 to point right, thus leaving edge 3 to point in any direction. Therefore, this gadget satisfies the same constraints as an NCL AND vertex.

From 2 to 3. Figure 6b depicts the construction. If 4 points right, then 2 must point right and 3 must point left. Thus 1 must point left. If 4 points left, we can fix 2 to point left, leaving 1 and 3 free to point in either direction. Therefore, this gadget satisfies the same constraints as an NCL AND vertex.

From 3 to 4. Figure 6c depicts the construction. If 4 points left, then 3 must point right, forcing both 1 and 2 to point left. If 4 points right, we can fix 3 to point left, thus leaving 1 and 2 free to point in either direction. Therefore, this gadget satisfies the same constraints as an NCL AND vertex.

From 4 to 5. Figure 6d depicts the construction. If 4 points right, then 3 must point left, forcing both 1 and 2 to point left. If 4 points left, we can fix 3 to point right, thus leaving 1 and 2 free to point in either direction. Therefore, this gadget satisfies the same constraints as an NCL AND vertex.

From 4 to 6. Figure 6e depicts the construction. If 1 points right, then 2 and 3 must point left, and so 4 must point left. If 1 points left, then we can fix 3 to point right, leaving 2 and 4 free to point in either direction. Therefore, this gadget satisfies the same constraints as an NCL AND vertex.

From 6 to 7. Figure 6f depicts the construction. If 1 points right, then 2 must point left and 3 must point right, and so 4 must point right. If 1 points left, then we can fix 2 to point right, leaving 3 and 4 free to point in either direction. Therefore, this gadget satisfies the same constraints as an NCL AND vertex.

From 7 to 8. Figure 6g depicts the construction. If 1 points right, then 2 and 3 must point right too, and so 4 must point left. If 1 points left, then we can fix 3 to point left, leaving 2 and 4 free to point in either direction. Therefore, this gadget satisfies the same constraints as an NCL AND vertex.

From 8 to 9. Figure 6h depicts the construction. If 1 points right, then 2 must point right and 3 must point left, and so 4 must point left. If 1 points left, then we can fix 2 to point left, leaving 3 and 4 free to point in either direction. Therefore, this gadget satisfies the same constraints as an NCL AND vertex.

From 9 to 10. Figure 6i depicts the construction. If 1 points right, then 2 and 3 must point left, and so 4 must point right. If 1 points left, then we can fix 3 to point right, leaving 2 and 4 free to point in either direction. Therefore, this gadget satisfies the same constraints as an NCL AND vertex.

From 10 to 11. Figure 6j depicts the construction. If 1 points right, then 2 must point left and 3 must point right, and so 4 must point right. If 1 points left, then we can fix 2 to point right, leaving 3 and 4 free to point in either direction. Therefore, this gadget satisfies the same constraints as an NCL AND vertex.

From 11 to 12. Figure 6k depicts the construction. If 1 points right, then 2 and 3 must point right, and so 4 must point left. If 1 points left, then we can fix 3 to point left, leaving 2 and 4 free to point in either direction. Therefore, this gadget satisfies the same constraints as an NCL AND vertex.

From 12 to 1. Figure 6l depicts the construction. If 1 points right, then 2 must point right and 3 must point left, and so 4 must point left, and 5 must point right. If 1 points left, then we can fix 2 to point left and fix 4 to point right, leaving 3 and 5 free to point in either direction. Therefore, this gadget satisfies the same constraints as an NCL AND vertex. $\square$

3.3   Main Result

Theorem 2. HANANO *is* PSPACE-*complete even if (1) all flowers and colored blocks have the same color, and (2) colored blocks can only bloom upwards.*

Proof. Since HANANO $\in$ PSPACE, it suffices to show that NCL $\leq_m^p$ HANANO. Consider the clearly-polynomial-time-computable function that we describe in the next paragraph. We assume without loss of generality that the input is an NCL graph and a valid target edge, as we can easily detect in polynomial time if is not and map to a fixed element that is not in HANANO.

Construct in polynomial time a visibility representation for the input NCL graph and construct a game grid based on the visibility representation, replacing each vertex of the graph by a suitable gadget, and replacing edges with the appropriate tunnels. The game grid will be polynomially larger than the visibility representation since the gadgets have constant-bounded size. We must ensure that the game is only solvable when the target edge $e = (u, v)$ is flipped. If the flower than blooms b is attached to an immovable gray block, replace that flower with an immovable gray block. Otherwise, the flower that blooms b must be attached to the top of a 1×1 movable gray block. Replace that gray block with a 2×1 movable gray block. There is now no flower in the gadget for v that can bloom b, so to bloom, b must move the gadget for u. If the game is solvable, then b must bloom, and so there will exist a sequence of block movements corresponding to edge flips, so the edge e can be flipped in G. If there is a sequence of edge

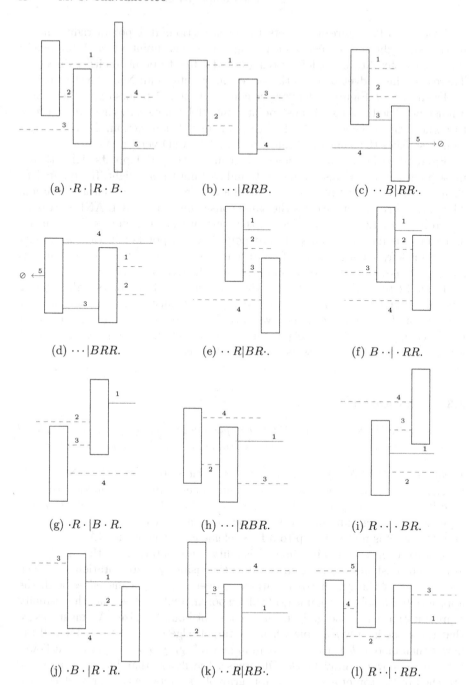

Fig. 6. Schemas showing the "equivalence" of the AND gadgets.

flips that eventually flips edge e in G, there is sequence of block movements that respect the inflow constraints and eventually see b move from the gadget representing v to the gadget representing u. Thus the colored block b (and all the other ones in the game) can bloom and the game is solvable. Finally note that all the colored blocks in our gadgets have their arrows pointing up, and that we only use blue blocks/flowers.   □

4   Related Work

The literature on the complexity of games is rich and covers a variety of games. We refer readers to Appendix A of Hearn and Demaine's book [8], which contains an extensive survey of games whose complexity were known at their time of writing. The introduction of NCL [7] helped simplify the process of showing that many games with sliding blocks are PSPACE-complete by limiting the number of gadgets to simulate to two. The work on motion planning through doors [1] provides a framework to show the PSPACE-hardness of certain problems by simulating *one* gadget. However, that paper's contribution does not solve the major problem faced by classifying the Hanano Puzzle: circumventing certain effects of gravity. There are games with gravity that were studied prior to the introduction of NCL. For example, Friedman [6] proved Cubic to be NP-hard. Clickomania is another game with gravity that was studied before the introduction of NCL. This game is a one-player game with a bounded number of moves and it is in fact NP-complete [3]. Solving a level of Super Mario Brothers (SMB), which is another game with gravity, has also been proven to be PSPACE-complete [5]. However, the framework used in that proof does not rely on NCL, since SMB is not a game that involves pulling blocks. Another famous game with gravity is Tetris. While the "offline" version is NP-complete [4], in the general case, it is NP-hard [2]. On the other hand, Jelly-no-Puzzle, also by Qrostar, is known to be NP-hard is the general case [14]. Our paper uses NCL to study a game with sliding blocks and irreversible gravity, and extends this line of work by providing a framework to study such games using only three gadgets in general, and by having only two gadgets when focusing on HANANO.

5   Conclusion and Open Directions

After establishing the NP-hardness of HANANO, Liu and Yang stated as an open problem the task of determining whether HANANO $\in$ NP. It follows from our PSPACE-completeness result that HANANO $\notin$ NP unless NP = PSPACE.

Another contribution of this paper is the use of the visibility representations. Our Proposition 1 and our Lemmas 2 and 4 helped significantly reduce the number of gadgets needed. Since these proofs are independent of HANANO, we believe that they can be reused to analyze additional games.

By leveraging schemas and symmetry, we only needed to provide three gadgets (instead of 32 gadgets). If we focus our attention to HANANO, then we can derive the red bend gadget from $B \cdot \cdot | \cdot BB$. And so, an interesting direction would be to investigate whether the reduction could be carried out using only two gadgets (or even one) in the general case. (One might posit that by placing a constrained blue edge terminator on the blue edge for $\cdots|BRR$, we get what looks like a red bend gadget, but that omits the inflow constraint of two. Thus both red edges would need to face into the gadget, which is too strong of a requirement.) Finally, we mention that our movable gray blocks have up to six sides in two gadgets and up to eight sides in the third gadget. We followed the closest paper in the literature, which states that those movable gray blocks can have "any size or shape" [9]. However, it would be interesting if our result could be strengthened to only have movable gray blocks with exactly four sides.

Acknowledgments. We thank Benjamin Carleton, Lane A. Hemaspaandra, David E. Narváez, Conor Taliancich, and Henry B. Welles, and the anonymous reviewers for their helpful comments and suggestions.

References

1. Ani, J., Bosboom, J., Demaine, E., Diomidov, Y., Hendrickson, D., Lynch, J.: Walking through doors is hard, even without staircases: Proving PSPACE-hardness via planar assemblies of door gadgets. In: Proceedings of the 10th International Conference on Fun with Algorithms, vol. 157, pp. 3:1–3:23 (2020)
2. Asif, S., et al.: Tetris is NP-hard even with $O(1)$ rows or columns. J. Inf. Process. **28**, 942–958 (2020)
3. Biedl, T., Demaine, E., Demaine, M., Fleischer, R., Jacobson, L., Munro, J.I.: The complexity of Clickomania. In: Nowakowski, R.J. (ed.) More Games of No Chance, pp. 389–404. Cambridge University Press, Cambridge (2002)
4. Breukelaar, R., Demaine, E., Hohenberger, S., Hoogeboom, H., Kosters, W., Liben-Nowell, D.: Tetris is hard, even to approximate. Int. J. Comput. Geometry Appl. **14**(1–2), 41–68 (2004)
5. Demaine, E., Viglietta, G., Williams, A.: Super Mario Bros. is harder/easier than we thought. In: Proceedings of the 9th International Conference on Fun with Algorithms, pp. 13:1–13:14 (2016)
6. Friedman, E.: Cubic is NP-complete. Presented at the 34th Annual Florida MAA Section Meeting (2001)
7. Hearn, R., Demaine, E.: PSPACE-completeness of sliding-block puzzles and other problems through the nondeterministic constraint logic model of computation. Theoret. Comput. Sci. **343**(1–2), 72–96 (2005)
8. Hearn, R., Demaine, E.: Games, Puzzles, and Computation. CRC Press (2009)
9. Liu, Z., Yang, C.: Hanano puzzle is NP-hard. Inf. Process. Lett. **145**, 6–10 (2019)
10. Qrostar: Hanano Puzzle (2011). https://qrostar.skr.jp/en/hanano/
11. Qrostar: (2022). Personal communication
12. Tamassia, R.: Handbook of Graph Drawing and Visualization. Chapman and Hall/CRC (2016)
13. Tamassia, R., Tollis, I.G.: A unified approach to visibility representations of planar graphs. Discrete Comput. Geom. **1**(4), 321–341 (1986). https://doi.org/10.1007/BF02187705
14. Yang, C.: On the complexity of Jelly-no-Puzzle. In: Japanese Conference on Discrete and Computational Geometry, Graphs, and Games, pp. 165–174 (2018)

Existential and Universal Width
of Alternating Finite Automata

Yo-Sub Han[1], Sungmin Kim[1], Sang-Ki Ko[2], and Kai Salomaa[3(⊠)]

[1] Department of Computer Science, Yonsei University, 50, Yonsei-Ro, Seodaemun-Gu, Seoul 120-749, Republic of Korea
{emmous,rena_rio}@yonsei.ac.kr
[2] Department of Computer Science and Engineering, Kangwon National University, 1 Kangwondaehak-gil, Chuncheon-si, Gangwon-do 24341, Republic of Korea
sangkiko@kangwon.ac.kr
[3] School of Computing, Queen's University, Kingston, ON K7L 3N6, Canada
salomaa@queensu.ca

Abstract. The existential width of an alternating finite automaton (AFA) A on a string w is, roughly speaking, the number of nondeterministic choices that A uses in an accepting computation on w that uses least nondeterminism. The universal width of A on string w is the least number of parallel branches an accepting computation of A on w uses. The existential or universal width of A is said to be finite if it is bounded for all accepted strings. We show that finiteness of existential and universal width of an AFA is decidable. Also we give hardness results and give an algorithm to decide whether the existential or universal width of an AFA is bounded by a given integer.

Keywords: alternating finite automaton · universal and existential choices · measure of nondeterminism · space complexity · decidability

1 Introduction

The amount of nondeterminism in computations of finite automata can be quantified in various ways [4,7]. Tree width, a.k.a. path size or leaf size, counts the number of all computations [6,12,17,24], the degree of ambiguity [11,22,26,29] counts the number of accepting computations, and the guessing and branching measures [5] quantify the amount of nondeterminism on a best accepting computation.

An alternating finite automaton (AFA) extends a nondeterministic finite automaton (NFA) by allowing both existential choices and universal branching in the computation. Alternating finite automata were introduced in the early 1980's [1]. They recognize only the regular languages but can be double exponentially more succinct than deterministic finite automata. Universal and existential width quantify separately the universal branching (i.e., the number of parallel computations) and the number of existential (i.e., nondeterministic) choices in an alternating computation [15,16].

© IFIP International Federation for Information Processing 2023
Published by Springer Nature Switzerland AG 2023
H. Bordihn et al. (Eds.): DCFS 2023, LNCS 13918, pp. 51–64, 2023.
https://doi.org/10.1007/978-3-031-34326-1_4

The goal here is to measure in an alternating computation separately existential and universal choices, so while a general definition of AFA [2,9,19] defines transitions in terms of general Boolean functions, we divide the states into existential states (corresponding to disjunction) and universal states (corresponding to conjunction). This model was originally used for alternating Turing machines [1], and for finite automata it is used e.g. in [3,10]. In the classification of Boolean and alternating automata from [13] our model is the most restricted alternating one-way finite automaton model.

A pruned computation tree of an AFA [14,15] is obtained from the "full" computation tree by following all branches of a universal computation step and one nondeterministically chosen branch in an existential computation step. An AFA accepts a string w if it has a pruned computation tree on w with all leaves labeled by accepting states and, in this sense, a pruned computation tree corresponds to one computation of an AFA. A pruned computation tree of an NFA consists of a single path.

Universal width counts the number of branches in a pruned computation tree and existential width counts the number of existential choices not followed by a pruned computation tree. Existential and universal width can be defined as either worst-case or best-case measures. For complexity measures that are based on one nondeterministically chosen computation the best-case variant is, arguably, the more relevant measure. For example, the best-case branching and guessing are "measures of the extent to which a regular language, viewed as a computational task for finite automata, can benefit from nondeterminism [5]", while worst-case branching has more marginal interest [25].

The maximal universal (respectively, maximal existential) width of an AFA A on a string w is the largest number of parallel computations (respectively, the largest number of existential choices encountered) in a pruned computation tree of A on w. Earlier work has considered growth rates and decision problems of the maximal width measures [16].

This paper considers the corresponding best-case measures. The universal (respectively, existential) width of an AFA A on a string w accepted by A is the smallest number of leaves (respectively, the smallest number of existential choices encountered) in an accepting pruned tree of A on w. Note that the accepting pruned tree that has optimal universal width may not be optimal for existential width, and vice versa. Since existential width is defined in terms of the "best" computation, the measure is similar to the guessing or branching measures for NFAs considered by Goldstine et al. [5] or the "number of nondeterministic moves" measure considered by Leung [21]. For an NFA where all nondeterministic transitions have exactly two choices, existential width coincides with the guessing measure and with the number of nondeterministic moves measure of the NFA.

We consider decision problems for the existential and universal width of an AFA. Using a decidable property of distance automata [8,23], we show that finiteness of these measures is decidable. For general AFAs the algorithm uses exponential space. From existing results [5,21,23] it follows that deciding

Table 1. Complexity landscape of decision problems for existential and universal width. UFA refers to an AFA with only universal states. Table entries that are divided in two parts indicate complexity upper bound and lower bound.

problem			NFA	AFA	UFA
Existential width	∞		PSPACE-complete [5,21,23]	EXPSPACE (Thm 10)	N/A
				PSPACE-hard	
	$\leq k$		PSPACE-complete (Corollary 17)	EXPSPACE (Proposition 15)	
				PSPACE-hard	
Universal width	∞		N/A	EXPSPACE (Thm 4)	PSPACE-complete (Corollary 7)
				PSPACE-hard	
	$\leq k$			EXPSPACE (Prop. 12)	PSPACE-complete (Corollary 14)
				PSPACE-hard	

finiteness of existential width of an NFA is PSPACE-complete. We show that for an AFA with only universal states, deciding finiteness of universal width is also PSPACE-complete. Additionally we consider the complexity of the decision problems whether the existential or universal width of an AFA is bounded by a given positive integer. Table 1 summarizes the known complexity results for existential and universal width.

2   Preliminaries

We assume that the reader is familiar with basics of formal languages and finite automata. For more information see e.g. the texts [27,28] or the survey [9].

In the following Σ is always a finite alphabet, the set of strings over Σ is Σ^* and ε is the empty string and $|w|$ is the length of string w. The set of prefixes of a set of strings S is prefix(S). By slight abuse of notation, the cardinality of a finite set S is also denoted $|S|$. The set of positive integers is $\mathbb{N}$. When considering decision problems with integer inputs, we assume that the integers are given in unary notation.[1]

An *alternating finite automaton* (AFA) is a 5-tuple, $A = (Q, \Sigma, \delta, q_0, F)$ where $Q = Q_e \cup Q_u$ is the finite set of states, Q_e is the set of *existential states*, Q_u is the set of *universal states* ($Q_e \cap Q_u = \emptyset$), Σ is the input alphabet, $\delta : Q \times \Sigma \to 2^Q$ is the transition function, $q_0 \in Q$ is the initial state, and $F \subseteq Q$ is the set of final states.

The AFA A is a nondeterministic finite automaton (NFA) if all states are existential (that is, $Q_u = \emptyset$). Similarly, A is a universal finite automaton (UFA) if all states are universal (and $Q_e = \emptyset$). The AFA A is a deterministic finite automaton (DFA) if the transition function is one-valued $\delta : Q \times \Sigma \to Q$.

By a *transition* of A we mean a triple (q_1, b, q_2), $q_2 \in \delta(q_1, b)$, $q_1, q_2 \in Q$, $b \in \Sigma$. A transition (q_1, b, q_2) is *properly existential* if $q_1 \in Q_e$ and $|\delta(q_1, b)| \geq 2$. Similarly (q_1, b, q_2) is a *properly universal* transition if $q_1 \in Q_u$ and $|\delta(q_1, b)| \geq 2$.

---

[1] With binary representation of integers some results, for example, the upper bound of Proposition 15, would change.

When it is convenient we view the transition relation δ of A as a subset of $Q \times \Sigma \times Q$, and use the two ways of representing the set of transitions of A interchangeably.

2.1   Computation Trees and Their Prunings

The membership of a string w in the language of an AFA A is usually defined inductively on the length of w [1–3]. Since we want to measure the number of existential choices and the amount of universal branching we represent computations of A explicitly in terms of pruned computation trees, and also define the set of strings accepted by A using this terminology. Below general computation trees are first defined in the same way as for NFAs [12,24], and the pruning operation defines a particular computation of an AFA.

For $q \in Q$ and $w \in \Sigma^*$, the *q-computation tree of A on w*, is a finite ordered tree $T_{A,q,w}$ defined inductively on the length of w where the nodes are labeled by elements of $Q \times (\Sigma \cup \{\varepsilon\}) \cup \{\bot\}$. First $T_{A,q,\varepsilon}$ is a singleton tree where the only node is labeled by (q, ε). For the inductive step consider $w = bu$, $b \in \Sigma$, $u \in \Sigma^*$. If $\delta(q, b) = \{q_1, \ldots, q_m\}$, $m \geq 1$, $T_{A,q,bu}$ is the tree where the root labeled by (q, b) has m immediate subtrees $T_{A,q_i,u}$, $i = 1, \ldots, m$.[2] If $\delta(q, b) = \emptyset$, $T_{A,q,bu}$ has root labeled by (q, b) and it has one child labeled by $\bot$ representing a failed computation.[3]

In a computation tree $T_{A,q,w}$ a path from the root to a leaf has length at most $|w|$. An element (p, ε) labels a leaf at the end of a branch that has consumed the entire string w. A leaf labeled by (p, ε) is also said to be labeled by the state p, for short.

Next we define the *pruning operation* on computation trees that replaces some children of existential states with a cut-symbol ψ. The definition is done inductively on the length of the string. For $q \in Q$, the unique pruning of $T_{A,q,\varepsilon}$ is the singleton tree with only node labeled by (q, ε). For a string bv, where $b \in \Sigma$ and $v \in \Sigma^*$, a pruning of the q-computation tree of A on bv, $q \in Q$, where $\delta(q, b) = \{p_1, \ldots, p_k\}$, $k \geq 1$, is obtained recursively from the tree $T_{A,q,bv}$ as follows:

(i) If $q \in Q_e$, then we replace $k - 1$ of the immediate subtrees of the root by a node labeled by ψ (representing a pruning of that branch), and the remaining subtree $T_{A,p_i,v}$ by a pruning of the computation tree $T_{A,p_i,v}$.
(ii) If q is a universal state, then we replace each immediate subtree $T_{A,p_i,v}$ of the root by a pruning of $T_{A,p_i,v}$, $1 \leq i \leq k$.

---

[2] The order of children of a node is not important and we can assume that elements of $\delta(q, b)$ are ordered by an arbitrary linear order.

[3] Alternatively, it would be possible to indicate a failed computation by a leaf labeled by (q, b). The failure symbol is used for clarity.

Finally, if $\delta(q, b) = \emptyset$, the pruning operation does not change the computation tree $T_{A,q,bv}$ (which consists of the root and a child node labeled by the failure symbol $\perp$).

The set of all prunings of a computation tree T is denoted $\succcurlyeq(T)$. The leaves of a pruned tree are either *state-leaves* labeled by (p, ε), $p \in Q$, *cut-leaves* labeled by ψ, or *fail-leaves* labeled by $\perp$.

A pruned computation tree T^p in $\succcurlyeq(T_{A,q_0,w})$ represents one particular computation of the AFA A on w, and usually the tree $T_{A,q_0,w}$ has multiple prunings, that is, $\succcurlyeq(T_{A,q_0,w})$ has cardinality greater than one. A pruned tree is *accepting* if all leaves are labeled by accepting states or the cut-symbol ψ and the set of accepting pruned trees of A on string w is $\succcurlyeq^{acc}(T_{A,q_0,w})$. The language accepted by the AFA A is $L(A) = \{w \in \Sigma^* \mid \succcurlyeq^{acc}(T_{A,q_0,w}) \neq \emptyset\}$.

Intuitively, the cut-leaves labeled by ψ represent existential choices in the computation that are not followed. Any pruned computation tree of an NFA consists of a single path to a state leaf or to the fail symbol $\perp$, where the nodes representing properly existential transitions have additional children labeled by the cut-symbol ψ.

We will need the following notion of levels of a pruned tree.

Definition 1. *Consider a pruned computation tree T^p of A on input w. The ith level of T^p, $i = 0, 1, \ldots$ consists of states that are reached after reading the prefix of w of length i. In a failed computation, the ith level may also contain a failure symbol $\perp$.*

We say that level i of T^p increases the universal width of T^p if the computation represented by T^p applies a properly universal transition to some state occurring on level i.

We say that level i of T^p increases the existential width of T^p if either

(i) T^p *applies a properly existential transition to a state occurring on level i, or,*

(ii) T^p *applies a properly universal transition to a state occuring on level i and the computations represented by the subtrees of T^p corresponding to at least two of the children both contain a properly existential transition.*

The second way of increasing the existential width of a pruned tree in Definition 1 is illustrated by Example 2 in the next subsection.

2.2   Universal and Existential Width

As mentioned above a pruned computation tree represents a particular computation of an AFA and we use these terms interchangeably. Universal width measures the number of (parallel) branches of a computation of an AFA and existential width measures the number of existential choices in a computation, strictly speaking, the number of existential choices that are not followed.

In the following $A = (Q, \Sigma, \delta, q_0, F)$ is always an AFA.

The *universal width* of a pruned computation tree T^p of A, $\mathrm{uw}(T^p)$, is the number of state-leaves and fail-leaves of T^p.[4] The *existential width* of T^p, $\mathrm{ew}(T^p)$, is the number of cut-leaves in T^p. The universal (respectively, existential) width of A on a string w is the width of the accepting pruned tree with least width:

$$\mathrm{uw}(A, w) = \min\{\mathrm{uw}(T^p) \mid T^p \in \mathord{\prec}^{\mathrm{acc}}(T_{A,q_0,w})\},$$

$$\mathrm{ew}(A, w) = \min\{\mathrm{ew}(T^p) \mid T^p \in \mathord{\prec}^{\mathrm{acc}}(T_{A,q_0,w})\},$$

Generally, a tree in $\mathord{\prec}^{\mathrm{acc}}(T_{A,q_0,w})$ that minimizes universal width of A on w would not minimize the existential width of A on w.

If A is an NFA then $\mathrm{uw}(A, w)$ is one for any string accepted by A, and if A is an UFA then $\mathrm{ew}(A, w)$ is always zero. If A is a DFA, $\mathrm{uw}(A, w) = 1$ and $\mathrm{ew}(A, w) = 0$ for any string accepted by A. Note that if A is an NFA where all properly existential transitions have exactly two choices, then $\mathrm{ew}(A, w)$ equals the *guessing* [5] or the *number of nondeterministic moves* [21] of A on w.

The universal width (respectively, existential width) of the AFA A is defined by taking the supremum over all accepted strings. If $L(A) \neq \emptyset$,

$$\mathrm{uw}(A) = \sup\{\mathrm{uw}(A, w) \mid w \in L(A)\}, \quad \mathrm{ew}(A) = \sup\{\mathrm{ew}(A, w) \mid w \in L(A)\}.$$

If $L(A) = \emptyset$, we set $\mathrm{uw}(A) = \mathrm{ew}(A) = 0$. If the values $\mathrm{uw}(A, w)$ (respectively, $\mathrm{ew}(A, w)$) are unbounded for strings accepted by A then $\mathrm{uw}(A)$ (respectively, $\mathrm{ew}(A)$) is infinite. The AFA A_1 depicted in Example 2 has infinite universal width and infinite existential width.

Example 2. Consider the AFA A_1 with universal states u_1, u_2 and existential state e depicted in Fig. 1. Here only the last computation step is existential but, for all $k \in \mathbb{N}$, $\mathrm{ew}(A_1, a^k ba) = 2^k$.

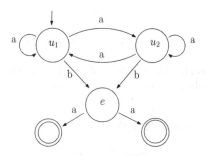

Fig. 1. AFA A_1

---

[4] Fail-leaves are included for the worst-case variant of the measure considered in [16]. For the best-case variant considered here it does not make a difference whether we count also fail-leaves.

2.3   Distance Automata

Our decision algorithm for finiteness of existential or universal width uses existing results on limitedness of distance automata. We introduce also the notion of a (computation) path of a nondeterministic automaton. Let $A = (Q, \Sigma, \delta, q_0, F)$ be an NFA. For $p_0, p_k \in Q$, a *path* of A from state p_0 to p_k with underlying string $a_1 a_2 \cdots a_k$, $a_i \in \Sigma$, $i = 1, \ldots, k$, is $(p_0, a_1, p_1, a_2, \ldots, p_{k-1}, a_k, p_k)$ where $p_j \in \delta(p_{j-1}, a_j)$, $j = 1, \ldots, k$.

Intuitively, a distance automaton [8,23] is an NFA where the transitions are assigned weight 0 or 1. More formally, a *distance automaton* is a pair $\mathcal{D} = (D, d)$, where $D = (Q, \Sigma, \delta, q_0, Q_F)$ is the underlying NFA of $\mathcal{D}$ and $d : Q \times \Sigma \times Q \to \{0, 1, \infty\}$ is the distance function that satisfies the following:

$$\text{for any } q_1, q_2 \in Q, \ b \in \Sigma, \ d(q_1, b, q_2) = \infty \text{ iff } q_2 \notin \delta(q_1, b).$$

The distance of a path $(q_1, a_1, q_2, \ldots, q_m, a_m, q_{m+1})$, $a_i \in \Sigma$, $q_j \in Q$, $1 \le i \le m$, $1 \le j \le m + 1$, is $\sum_{i=1}^{m} d(q_i, a_i, q_{i+1})$. Then d is extended as a function on $Q \times \Sigma^* \times Q$ by setting, for $q_1, q_2 \in Q$, $w \in \Sigma^*$, $d(q_1, w, q_2)$ to be the smallest distance of a path from q_1 to q_2 with underlying string w. The distance of a string w accepted by $\mathcal{D}$ is $d(w) = \min_{q \in Q_F} d(q_0, w, q)$ and the distance of the automaton $\mathcal{D}$ is defined to be $\sup_{w \in L(D)} d(w)$. The distance automaton is said to be *limited* if the distance of $\mathcal{D}$ is finite.

The limitedness problem was shown to be decidable by Hashiguchi [8] and later Leung and Podolskiy [20,23] gave the following complexity bound.

Proposition 3 ([20,23]). *Deciding limitedness of a distance automaton is PSPACE-complete.*

3   Deciding Finiteness of Universal and Existential Width

To decide the finiteness of the universal width of an AFA A we convert A to an NFA that keeps track of all states occuring on one level of a pruned computation tree and define a distance function for the NFA where a transition has weight one if and only if the universal width of the pruned tree increases on the corresponding level of the simulated computation.

Theorem 4. *For a given AFA A it is decidable in EXPSPACE whether or not uw(A) is finite.*

For an AFA A with only universal states, the NFA used in the proof of Theorem 4 to simulate A is, in fact, deterministic. In this case we can decide finiteness of uw(A) directly without relying on distance automata and this yields a better complexity bound than Theorem 4.

Lemma 5. *For an UFA A we can decide whether uw(A) is finite in PSPACE.*

Deciding finiteness of universal width is PSPACE-hard and this holds already for UFAs. The proof uses a reduction from the intersection emptiness problem for k DFAs, $k \ge 1$ [18].

Lemma 6. *Given an UFA A it is PSPACE-hard to decide whether* $\mathrm{uw}(A)$ *is finite.*

For general AFA's the lower bound of Lemma 6 does not match the upper bound of Theorem 4, however, by combining it with Lemma 5 we have:

Corollary 7. *For a given UFA A it is PSPACE-complete to decide whether* $\mathrm{uw}(A)$ *is finite.*

Next we consider the question of deciding finiteness of existential width of a general AFA. As for deciding finiteness of universal width in Theorem 4, we first convert the given AFA A to an equivalent NFA that keeps track of all states occurring on a given level of a pruned computation tree of A. However, now the construction is more involved because existential width can be increased both directly by properly existential transitions and indirectly by universal branching that, at a later stage, in at least two successors leads to existential choices. The situation was illustrated by Example 2.

The correctness of the algorithm deciding finiteness of existential width is based on the following observation. Recall that the notion of a level increasing the existential width of a pruned tree is defined in Definition 1.

Lemma 8. *The existential width of an AFA A is infinite if and only if for all* $m \in \mathbb{N}$ *there exists* $w_m \in L(A)$ *such that any accepting pruned tree of w has at least m levels that increase the existential width of the tree.*

Note that the number of levels that increase the existential width of a pruned tree does not in any way directly give the value of the existential width of the tree. Lemma 8 simply gives a characterization of when the existential width of an AFA is infinite.

Analogously as in the proof of Theorem 4, we construct an NFA that simulates a pruned computation tree of an AFA A one level at a time, and then give weights to transitions in a way that exactly the non-zero weighted transitions increase the existential width of the simulated pruned tree of A. As discussed above, the existential width can be increased both directly and indirectly (via universal transitions) and for this reason the NFA is not obtained by a straightforward subset construction as in the proof of Theorem 4.

Consider an AFA $A = (Q, \Sigma, \delta, q_0, F)$, $Q = Q_e \cup Q_u$. Let $Q^{(i)} = \{q^{(i)} \mid q \in Q\}$, $i = 1, 2$, be two marked copies of the set Q. We define an NFA B equivalent to A, $B = (\Sigma, P, \gamma, \{q_0\}, F_B)$, where P is the powerset of $Q \cup Q^{(1)} \cup Q^{(2)} \cup \{p_{\mathrm{sink}}\}$, the set of final states of B is

$$F_B = \{X \in P \mid X \subseteq F \cup \{q^{(2)} \mid q \in F\}\},$$

and the transition relation γ is defined as follows for $b \in \Sigma$ and $X = \{x_1, \ldots, x_m\} \in P$. The set $\gamma(X, b)$ consists of all sets $\bigcup_{i=1}^{m} \phi(x_i, b)$ where each $\phi(x_i, b)$ is a subset of $Q \cup Q^{(1)} \cup Q^{(2)} \cup \{p_{\mathrm{sink}}\}$, selected nondeterministically as follows:

(i) if $x_i \in Q_e$, then $\phi(x_i, b)$ is a singleton set consisting of one element of $\delta(x_i, b) \neq \emptyset$. If $\delta(x_i, b) = \emptyset$, $\phi(x_i, b) = \{p_{\text{sink}}\}$. [Intuitive idea: in a state of Q_e, B simulates a nondeterministic choice of A. If $\delta(x_i, b) = \emptyset$, the computation of B fails.]

(ii) if $x_i \in Q_u$ and $\delta(x_i, b) = \{p_1, \ldots, p_k\}$, $k \geq 1$, then $\phi(x_i, b)$ can be any of the sets

$$\{p_1^{(r_1)}, \ldots, p_k^{(r_k)}\}, \quad r_j \in \{1, 2\}, \ j = 1, \ldots, k.$$

If $\delta(x_i, b) = \emptyset$, $\phi(x_i, b) = \{p_{\text{sink}}\}$. [Intuitive idea: B simulates all universal choices of A and nondeterministically assigns a superscript (1) or (2) for the state.]

(iii) if $x_i = q^{(1)}$, $q \in Q_e$ and $\delta(q, b) = \{p_1, \ldots, p_k\}$, where $k \geq 2$, then $\phi(x_i, b)$ is a singleton set $\{p_i\}$, $1 \leq i \leq k$. [Intuitive idea: in a state of $Q_e^{(1)}$, B simulates a properly existential step of A and erases the superscript (1).]

(iv) if $x_i = q^{(1)}$, $q \in Q_e$ and $\delta(q, b) = \{p_1\}$, then $\phi(x_i, b) = \{p_1^{(1)}\}$. If $\delta(q, b) = \emptyset$, $\phi(x_i, b) = \{p_{\text{sink}}\}$. [Intuitive idea: B simulates a deterministic step of A and keeps the superscript (1). There is only one choice for $\phi(x_i, b)$.]

(v) if $x_i = q^{(1)}$, $q \in Q_u$ and $\delta(q, b) = \{p_1, \ldots, p_k\}$, $k \geq 1$, then $\phi(x_i, b)$ can be any of the sets

$$\{p_1^{(r_1)}, \ldots, p_k^{(r_k)}\}, \quad r_j \in \{1, 2\}, \ j = 1, \ldots, k, \text{ and, } (\exists j) : r_j = 1.$$

If $\delta(q, b) = \emptyset$, $\phi(x_i, b) = \{p_{\text{sink}}\}$. [Intuitive idea: B simulates all universal choices of A and nondeterministically chooses a superscript (1) or (2) for each state. Since original state has superscript (1), at least one of the successor states must have superscript (1).]

(vi) if $x_i = q^{(2)}$, $q \in Q_e$, and $\delta(q, b) = \{p_1, \ldots, p_k\}$, where $k \geq 2$ or $k = 0$, then $\phi(x_i, b) = \{p_{\text{sink}}\}$. [Intuitive idea: if B encounters a properly existential transition in a state with superscript (2), this leads to failure.]

(vii) if $x_i = q^{(2)}$, $q \in Q_e$ and $\delta(q, b) = \{p_1\}$, then $\phi(x_i, b) = \{p_1^{(2)}\}$. [Intuitive idea: B simulates a deterministic step of A and keeps the superscript (2).]

(viii) if $x_i = q^{(2)}$, $q \in Q_u$ and $\delta(q, b) = \{p_1, \ldots, p_k\}$, $k \geq 1$, then $\phi(x_i, b)$ consists of the set $\{p_1^{(2)}, \ldots, p_k^{(2)}\}$. If $\delta(q, b) = \emptyset$, $\phi(x_i, b) = \{p_{\text{sink}}\}$. [Intuitive idea: B simulates all universal choices of A and in all branches retains the superscript (2). Also in this case there is only one choice for $\phi(x_i, b)$.]

(ix) if $x_i = p_{\text{sink}}$, then $\phi(x_i, b) = \{p_{\text{sink}}\}$.

Roughly speaking, the NFA B operates as follows. States of B consist of sets of states of A that occur on one level of a pruned computation tree, with possible superscripts added to the states that contain information about the subsequent computation on the remaining suffix. If B is in a state X and we ignore the superscripts of the states of A in X, for each state of X, a computation step of B simulates one existential choice of A and all universal choices of A. When simulating a universal step of A in a state of Q_u or $Q_u^{(1)}$, B nondeterministically assigns superscripts (1) and (2) to the resulting states. If the state occurring in an accepting computation of B contains an element of $Q^{(1)}$ when processing the remaining suffix the simulated computation of A must pass through at least one properly existential computation step. The superscript (1) does not appear in final states of B and the superscript (1) can be removed only when simulating a properly existential step of A by rule (iii). On the other hand, a part of the computation of B starting from a state of $Q^{(2)}$ cannot erase the superscript (2) and, according to definitions (vi), (vii), (viii), this computation cannot simulate any properly existential transitions of A. A subcomputation of B originating from a state of $Q^{(2)}$ is completely "deterministic" in the sense that it is uniquely determined by the remaining input. Note that a state of B can together with elements of $Q^{(2)}$ contain other elements and other parts of the computation of B can make properly existential choices.

We note the following concerning the correspondence between a pruned tree T^p of A on input w and a computation C_{T^p} of B that simulates T^p. At a given level of T^p the nodes are labeled by elements of Q and in the simulating computation the corresponding state of B is a subset of $Q \cup Q^{(1)} \cup Q^{(2)}$. That is, the set of labels of nodes of T^p is a multiset, whereas the state of C_{T^p} is a set. The crucial point of the construction is that for two nodes of T^p on a given level labeled by the same state q or $q^{(1)}$ where $q \in Q_u$ it is not possible that a simulating computation of B according to rules (ii) or (v) would need to make a different nondeterministic selection of superscripts (1) and (2) for the successor states. For a given suffix of the input only one selection of the superscripts is possible and any other selection cannot lead to a final state of B. This means that B can always make the selections in (ii) and (v) correctly, to simulate any accepting computation of A on the remaining input. This observation is stated as the following lemma:

Lemma 9. *Consider an accepting computation of B starting from state $X \in P$ on input bw, $b \in \Sigma$, $w \in \Sigma^*$. In the transition of B, according to cases (ii) and (v) the assignment of superscripts (1) and (2) to the elements of $\gamma(X, b)$ is unambiguous in the sense that for q or $q^{(1)}$ in X where $q \in Q_u$, $\delta(q, b) = \{p_1, \ldots, p_k\}$, the sequence $p_1^{(r_1)}, \ldots, p_k^{(r_k)}$, $1 \leq r_i \leq 2$, $i = 1, \ldots, k$, added to $\gamma(X, b)$ is uniquely determined.*

Now we assign weights to transitions of B as follows to obtain a distance automaton B_{dist}. Consider a transition of B on input symbol $b \in \Sigma$: $t = (\{x_1, \ldots, x_m\}, b, \{p_1, \ldots, p_k\})$, $p_i \in Q \cup Q^{(1)} \cup Q^{(2)} \cup \{p_{\text{sink}}\}$. The transition t is assigned weight 1 in the following cases where the numbering of the cases corresponds to the numbering used in the definition of the transition relation γ of B:

(i) one of the states x_i is in Q_e and $\delta(x_i, b)$ has at least two elements.
(ii) one of the states x_i is in Q_u and, when selecting $\phi(x_i, b)$, the transition t assigns superscript (1) to at least two of the elements of $\delta(x_i, b)$.
(iii) one of the states x_i is $q^{(1)}$, $q \in Q_e$ and $\delta(q, b)$ has at least two elements.
(v) one of the states x_i is $q^{(1)}$, $q \in Q_u$ and, when selecting $\phi(x_i, b)$, the transition t assigns superscript (1) to at least two elements of $\delta(q, b)$.

In all other cases, the weight of the transition t is 0.

Each transition t of B simulates the computation of A on one level of a pruned computation tree. The above selection of weights means that a transition t is assigned weight one if and only if in the simulated computation of A the corresponding level increases the existential width of the pruned tree as defined in Definition 1. Applying Proposition 3 to the distance automaton B_{dist}, and relying on Lemmas 8 and 9, yields the following:

Theorem 10. *For a given AFA A it is decidable in EXPSPACE whether or not $\mathrm{ew}(A)$ is finite.*

In the special case when A is an NFA, the construction in the proof of Theorem 10 yields an NFA where states are singleton subsets of the state set of A. This means that the algorithm of Theorem 10 works in polynomial space. Goldstine et al. [5] have shown that finiteness of the branching measure of an NFA is decidable using the Hashiguchi algorithm [8] for distance automata. Since the branching of an NFA is finite if and only if its existential width is finite, together with the PSPACE complexity upper bound from [23] this also implies that deciding finiteness of existential width of an NFA is in PSPACE. Furthermore, Leung [21] has shown that deciding the limitedness problem for the number of nondeterministic moves of an NFA is PSPACE-hard. Since, for an NFA A, the number of nondeterministic moves in an optimal computation is limited if and only if $\mathrm{ew}(A)$ is finite, combining these observations we have:

Corollary 11. *Deciding the finiteness of the existential width of a given NFA is PSPACE-complete.*

For general AFAs we do not have a hardness result that would match the exponential space upper bound of Theorem 10.

4   Deciding Whether Width of an AFA is at Most k

It is known that for a given AFA A and given $k \in \mathbb{N}$ it is decidable whether or not $\mathrm{uw}(A) \leq k$ [14]. Below we give a more detailed construction that yields a complexity upper bound.

Proposition 12. *For a given AFA A and $k \in \mathbb{N}$ we can decide in EXPSPACE whether $\mathrm{uw}(A) \leq k$.*

An UFA A has a unique pruned tree on a given input and we can check whether $\mathrm{uw}(A)$ is greater than k by finding a string w such that $\mathrm{uw}(A, w) > k$, and the inequality can be verified by simulating A on the nondeterministically guessed string w one symbol at a time.

Proposition 13. *For a given UFA A and $k \in \mathbb{N}$ we can decide in PSPACE whether $\mathrm{uw}(A) \leq k$.*

PSPACE-hardness of checking $uw(A) \leq k$ applies already for UFAs. This is proved, similarly as Lemma 6, using a reduction from the intersection emptiness of DFAs and the proof is omitted. Combining this observation with Proposition 13 we have:

Corollary 14. *For a given UFA A and $k \in \mathbb{N}$ it is PSPACE-complete to decide whether $uw(A) \leq k$.*

Finally we consider the question of deciding whether, for a given AFA A, $ew(A) \leq k$. In principle, we would want to do an NFA simulation analogous to Proposition 12. Note that in order to keep track of the number of cut-symbols encountered, the computation would need to keep track of multiplicities of states. Here a complication is that because universal width is unbounded a finite state simulation cannot store an arbitrary multiset of states. However, it turns out that the construction can place an upper bound on the multiplicities of states of A that need to be stored in the multiset.

Proposition 15. *For a given AFA A and $k \in \mathbb{N}$, we can decide in EXPSPACE whether or not $ew(A) \leq k$.*

For an NFA A, the construction of the proof of Proposition 15 yields an NFA B identical to A and, consequently, the value of existential width can be decided in polynomial space. Using a construction modified from [21] we get a matching hardness result.

Lemma 16. *For a given NFA A and $k \in \mathbb{N}$, it is PSPACE-hard to decide whether or not $ew(A) \leq k$.*

Combining the previous observation that for NFAs the algorithm of Proposition 15 works in PSPACE and Lemma 16 we have:

Corollary 17. *For a given NFA A and $k \in \mathbb{N}$, deciding whether or not $ew(A) \leq k$ is PSPACE-complete.*

5   Conclusion

We have shown that deciding finiteness of the existential and universal width of an AFA is decidable and given complexity upper and lower bounds for the questions. For general AFAs finiteness of existential or universal width can be decided in EXPSPACE. From earlier results it follows that deciding finiteness of existential width of NFAs is PSPACE-complete and deciding finiteness of universal width of an UFA was also shown to be PSPACE-complete. Additionally, we have considered the complexity of deciding whether existential or universal width of an AFA has a given integer value.

Future work could consider descriptional complexity comparisons of AFAs with different existential or universal width. For example, it is known that an NFA with finite path size can be determinized with a polynomial size blow-up [24]. Furthermore, the existential and universal width measures could be extended as a function of input length. The literature contains fundamental work on the succinctness comparison of NFAs with, respectively, bounded, polynomial or exponential growth rate of the degree of ambiguity [11,22,26,29].

Acknowledgements. We thank the anonymous referees for a careful reading of the paper and useful suggestions. Han, Kim and Ko were supported by the NRF grant (RS-2023-00208094). Salomaa was supported by Natural Sciences and Engineering Research Council of Canada (NSERC).

References

1. Chandra, A.K., Kozen, D.C., Stockmeyer, L.J.: Alternation. J. ACM **28**(1), 114–133 (1981)
2. Fellah, A., Jürgensen, H., Yu, S.: Constructions for alternating finite automata. Int. J. Comput. Math. **35**, 117–132 (1990)
3. Geffert, V.: An alternating hierarchy for finite automata. Theor. Comput. Sci. **445**, 1–24 (2012)
4. Goldstine, J., Kappes, M., Kintala, C.M.R., Leung, H., Malcher, A., Wotschke, D.: Descriptional complexity of machines with limited resources. J. Univ. Comput. Sci. **8**(2), 193–234 (2002)
5. Goldstine, J., Kintala, C.M.R., Wotschke, D.: On measuring nondeterminism in regular languages. Inf. Comput. **86**(2), 179–194 (1990)
6. Han, Y.S., Ko, S.K., Salomaa, K.: Deciding path size of nondeterministic (and input-driven) pushdown automata. Theor. Comput. Sci. **939**, 170–181 (2023)
7. Han, Y.S., Salomaa, A., Salomaa, K.: Ambiguity, nondeterminism and state complexity of finite automata. Acta Cybernetica **23**, 141–157 (2017)
8. Hashiguchi, K.: Limitedness theorem on finite automata with distance functions. J. Comput. Syst. Sci. **24**, 223–244 (1982)
9. Holzer, M., Kutrib, M.: Descriptional and computational complexity of finite automata: a survey. Inf. Comput. **209**(3), 456–470 (2011)
10. Hromkovič, J.: On the power of alternation in automata theory. J. Comput. Syst. Sci. **31**, 28–39 (1985)
11. Hromkovič, J., Schnitger, G.: Ambiguity and communication. Theory Comput. Syst. **48**, 517–534 (2011)
12. Hromkovič, J., Seibert, S., Karhumäki, J., Klauck, H., Schnitger, G.: Communication complexity method for measuring nondeterminism in finite automata. Inf. Comput. **172**, 202–217 (2002)
13. Kapoutsis, C., Zakzok, M.: Alternation in two-way finite automata. Theor. Comput. Sci. **870**, 75–102 (2021)
14. Keeler, C., Salomaa, K.: Alternating finite automata with limited universal branching. In: Leporati, A., Martín-Vide, C., Shapira, D., Zandron, C. (eds.) LATA 2020. LNCS, vol. 12038, pp. 196–207. Springer, Cham (2020). https://doi.org/10.1007/978-3-030-40608-0_13
15. Keeler, C., Salomaa, K.: Combining limited parallelism and nondeterminism in alternating finite automata. In: Jirásková, G., Pighizzini, G. (eds.) DCFS 2020. LNCS, vol. 12442, pp. 91–103. Springer, Cham (2020). https://doi.org/10.1007/978-3-030-62536-8_8

16. Keeler, C., Salomaa, K.: Width measures of alternating finite automata. In: International Conference Descriptional Complexity of Formal Systems, DCFS. Lecture Notes in Computer Science, vol. 13037, pp. 88–99. Springer, Heidelberg (2021). https://doi.org/10.1007/978-3-030-93489-7_8

17. Keeler, C., Salomaa, K.: Structural properties of NFAs and growth rates of nondeterminism measures. Inf. Comput. **284**, 104690 (2022)

18. Kozen, D.: Lower bounds for natural proof systems. In: Proceedings of 18th Annual Symposium on Foundations of Computer Science, pp. 254–266 (1977)

19. Leiss, E.: Succinct representation of regular languages by Boolean automata. Theor. Comput. Sci. **13**, 323–330 (1981)

20. Leung, H.: Limitedness theorem on finite automata with distance functions: an algebraic proof. Theor. Comput. Sci. **81**, 137–145 (1991)

21. Leung, H.: On finite automata with limited nondeterminism. Acta Informatica **35**, 595–624 (1998)

22. Leung, H.: Separating exponentially ambiguous finite automata from polynomially ambiguous finite automata. SIAM J. Comput. **27**, 1073–1082 (1998)

23. Leung, H., Podolskiy, V.: The limitedness problem on distance automata: Hashiguchi's method revisited. Theor. Comput. Sci. **310**, 147–158 (2004)

24. Palioudakis, A., Salomaa, K., Akl, S.G.: State complexity of finite tree width NFAs. J. Automata Lang. Comb. **17**(2–4), 245–264 (2012)

25. Palioudakis, A., Salomaa, K., Akl, S.G.: Worst case branching and other measures of nondeterminism. Int. J. Found. Comput. Sci. **28**(3), 195–210 (2017)

26. Ravikumar, B., Ibarra, O.H.: Relating the type of ambiguity of finite automata to the succinctness of their representation. SIAM J. Comput. **18**(6), 1263–1282 (1989)

27. Shallit, J.: A Second Course in Formal Languages and Automata Theory. Cambridge University Press, Cambridge (2008)

28. Sipser, M.: Introduction to the Theory of Computation, 3rd edn. Cengage (2013)

29. Weber, A., Seidl, H.: On the degree of ambiguity of finite automata. Theor. Comput. Sci. **88**(2), 325–349 (1991)

On Jaffe's Pumping Lemma, Revisited

Markus Holzer[(✉)] and Christian Rauch

Institut für Informatik, Universität Giessen, Arndtstr. 2, 35392 Giessen, Germany
{holzer,christian.rauch}@informatik.uni-giessen.de

Abstract. We consider Jaffe's pumping lemma [J. JAFFE. A necessary and sufficient pumping lemma for regular languages. *SIGACT News*, Summer, 1978] from a descriptional complexity perspective. Jaffe's pumping lemma is a necessary and sufficient condition for a language for being regular. In this way we improve a result of [A. YEHUDAI. A note on the pumping lemma for regular languages. *Inform. Proc. Lett.*, 9(3):135–136, 1979] by showing that there is a regular language over the alphabet Σ of size at least two with deterministic state complexity between p, the minimal pumping constant for Jaffe's pumping lemma, and $\sum_{i=0}^{p-1} |\Sigma|^i$. This is in line with recent research on minimal pumping constants for various pumping lemma conducted in [J. DASSOW and I. JECKER. Operational complexity and pumping lemmas. *Acta Inform.*, 59:337–355, 2022]. Moreover, we also compare the minimal pumping constant of Jaffe's pumping lemma with those of other well-known pumping lemmata from the literature.

Keywords: finite automata · Jaffe's pumping lemma · regular languages · finite-state devices · descriptional complexity

1 Introduction

Pumping lemmata or iteration theorems are basic tools in automata theory and formal languages to prove non-regularity or non-context-freedom. For an annotated bibliography on pumping lemmata we refer to [8]. In most cases pumping lemmata provide a necessary condition for a language L to be regular or context-free. To our knowledge the first pumping lemma that also provided a sufficient condition was Jaffe's pumping lemma [6] for regular languages from 1978. Roughly speaking, there the pumping property maintains the Myhill-Nerode equivalence classes (also for the non-accepted words of the language)—see Lemma 4 on page 4. Because Jaffe's pumping lemma gives a necessary and sufficient condition for a language L to be regular, it is natural to ask how the pumping constant given in the lemma relates to the state complexity of L. In fact, a first answer to this question was already given in 1979 by Yehudai [10]. He showed, by obtaining a relation between the minimal pumping constant of Jaffe's pumping lemma and the deterministic state complexity of a language, that Jaffe's construction in the proof of the lemma is optimal. To this end he

ⓒ IFIP International Federation for Information Processing 2023
Published by Springer Nature Switzerland AG 2023
H. Bordihn et al. (Eds.): DCFS 2023, LNCS 13918, pp. 65–78, 2023.
https://doi.org/10.1007/978-3-031-34326-1_5

constructed a language L over a binary alphabet such that the minimal pumping constant that satisfies Jaffe's pumping lemma is p and the deterministic state complexity of L is $2^p - 1 = \sum_{i=0}^{p-1} 2^i$. Apart from this, there has been a recent study [2] on the operational complexity of minimal pumping constants for certain other variants of the pumping lemmata, e.g., [1,5,7,9]. The sole outcome linking minimal pumping constants and deterministic state complexity on regular languages from a descriptional complexity standpoint is investigated in more detail in this paper.

At first glance, we revisit Jaffe's pumping lemma and prove some simple facts about the minimal constant satisfying the lemma. It turns out that this measure nicely fits to some other minimal constants induced by some well-known pumping lemmata [1,5,7,9] and the deterministic state complexity. Then we recall Yehudai's construction [10] and generalize it to languages over an arbitrary alphabet of size at least two. As a further step we show how to alter this construction by making certain states unreachable in order to show a relation between Jaffe's minimal pumping constant p of a regular language L over the alphabet Σ and its deterministic state complexity n, namely

$$p \leq n \leq \sum_{i=0}^{p-1} |\Sigma|^i = \frac{|\Sigma|^p - 1}{|\Sigma| - 1}.$$

This in turn induces a lower bound of $\log_{|\Sigma|}(n)$ on p; recall that p is trivially bounded by n from above. Finally, we take a closer look on how to regulate the values of multiple minimal pumping constants concurrently of the aforementioned pumping lemmata for a single regular language. As shown in [2] this is possible for certain combinations of pumping lemmata. How does Jaffe's pumping lemma behave w.r.t. this question? We give a partial answer by showing that for a large number of combinations this is also possible if one takes Jaffe's pumping lemma into account. Nevertheless, some combinations are left open, which serve for further investigations on the subject. In particular, combinations for large values seem to be complicated to obtain, because simultaneously fulfilling the requirements for different pumping lemmata seems to be complicated somehow. For instance, Jaffe's pumping lemma requires that during pumping one remains in the same Myhill-Nerode equivalence class of the considered language, while another pumping lemma may restrict the pumping position only for accepted words.

2   Preliminaries

We recall some definitions on finite automata as contained in [3]. Let Σ be an alphabet. Then, as usual Σ^* refers to the set of all words over the alphabet Σ, including the empty word λ, and $\Sigma^{\leq k}$ denotes the set of all words of length at most k.

A *deterministic finite automaton* (DFA) is a quintuple $A = (Q, \Sigma, \cdot, q_0, F)$, where Q is the finite set of *states*, Σ is the finite set of *input symbols*, $q_0 \in Q$

is the *initial state*, $F \subseteq Q$ is the set of *accepting states*, and the *transition function* · maps $Q \times \Sigma$ to Q. The *language accepted* by the DFA A is defined as $L(A) = \{ w \in \Sigma^* \mid q_0 \cdot w \in F \}$, where the transition function is recursively extended to a mapping $Q \times \Sigma^* \to Q$ in the usual way. Finally, a finite automaton is *unary* if the input alphabet Σ is a singleton set, that is, $\Sigma = \{a\}$, for some input symbol a.

We define the *deterministic state complexity of a regular language* L as

$$\mathsf{sc}(L) = \min\{ |Q| \mid A \text{ is a DFA with state set } Q \text{ accepting } L, \text{ i.e., } L = L(A) \}.$$

An automaton is *minimal* if it admits no smaller equivalent automaton w.r.t. the number of states. For DFAs minimality can be easily verified. It suffices to show that all states are reachable from the initial state and all states are pairwise inequivalent. An alternative characterization of minimal DFAs comes from the *Myhill-Nerode* equivalence relation $\equiv_L$ which is defined as follows—let $L \subseteq \Sigma^*$— then for $u, v \in \Sigma^*$ let $u \equiv_L v$ if and only if $uw \in L \iff vw \in L$, for all $w \in \Sigma^*$. The equivalence class of u is referred to as $[u]_L$ or simply $[u]$ if the language is clear from the context and is the set of all words that are equivalent to u w.r.t. the relation $\equiv_L$, i.e., $[u]_L = \{ v \mid u \equiv_L v \}$. It is well known that the number of states of a minimal DFA accepting the language L (which is unique up to isomorphisms) equals the number of equivalence classes of $\equiv_L$.

Finally, let us recall some results from [2] on minimal pumping constants for two pumping lemmata from the literature. The first pumping lemma allows pumping anywhere in the considered word, while the other pumping lemma restricts the pumping to a length-bounded prefix of the considered word. The following pumping or iteration lemma can be found in [7, page 70, Theorem 11.1]

Lemma 1. *Let L be a regular language over Σ. Then there is a constant p (depending on L) such that the following holds: If $w \in L$ and $|w| \geq p$, then there are words $x \in \Sigma^*$, $y \in \Sigma^+$, and $z \in \Sigma^*$ such that $w = xyz$ and $xy^t z \in L$ for $t \geq 0$. Let $\mathsf{mpc}(L)$ denote the smallest number p satisfying the aforementioned statement.*

We say that the word y in the previous lemma can be *pumped* in w. The next lemma is shown in [9, page 119, Lemma 8], [1, page 252, Folgerung 5.4.10], and [5, page 56, Lemma 3.1]:

Lemma 2. *Let L be a regular language over Σ. Then there is a constant p (depending on L) such that the following holds: If $w \in L$ and $|w| \geq p$, then there are words $x \in \Sigma^*$, $y \in \Sigma^+$, and $z \in \Sigma^*$ such that $w = xyz$, $|xy| \leq p$, and $xy^t z \in L$ for $t \geq 0$. Let $\mathsf{mpl}(L)$ denote the smallest number p satisfying the aforementioned statement.*

Obviously, Lemma 2 implies Lemma 1. Besides some simple facts such as (1) $\mathsf{mpc}(L) = 0$ if and only if $\mathsf{mpl}(L) = 0$ if and only if $L = \emptyset$, (2) for every non-empty finite language L we have $\mathsf{mpc}(L) \geq 1 + \min\{ |w| \mid w \in L \}$, (3) $\mathsf{mpc}(L) = 1$

implies $\lambda \in L$, and (4) if $\mathtt{mpl}(L) = 1$, then L is suffix closed,[1] also (5) the inequalities $\mathtt{mpc}(L) \leq \mathtt{mpl}(L) \leq \mathtt{sc}(L)$ were shown in [2]. The upper bound on the minimal pumping constants by the deterministic state complexity is obvious. These inequalities were specified more precisely in the following theorem which can also be found in [2] and requires a growing size alphabet—recently this was improved to binary languages in [4]:

Theorem 3. *Let p_1, p_2, and p_3 be natural numbers with $1 \leq p_1 \leq p_2 \leq p_3$. Then, there exists a regular language L (over a binary alphabet) such that $\mathtt{mpc}(L) = p_1$, $\mathtt{mpl}(L) = p_2$, and $\mathtt{sc}(L) = p_3$.*

3   Jaffe's Pumping Lemma, Revisited

In general (regular) pumping lemmata give necessary conditions for languages to be regular. Nevertheless, one can find also pumping lemmata that are sufficient and necessary for being regular. One of the first lemmata of this kind can be found in [6]. It reads as follows:

Lemma 4. *Let L be a language over an alphabet Σ. Then the language L is regular if and only if there is a constant p (depending on L) such that the following holds: If $w \in \Sigma^*$ and $|w| = p$, then there are words $x \in \Sigma^*$, $y \in \Sigma^+$, and $z \in \Sigma^*$ such that $w = xyz$ and*

$$wv = xyzv \in L \iff xy^t zv \in L$$

for all $t \geq 0$ and each $v \in \Sigma^*$. Let $\mathtt{mpe}(L)$ denote the smallest number p satisfying the aforementioned statement.

An alternative version of Lemma 4 appeared in [11, page 86, Lemma 4.3], where the requirement $|w| = p$ is replaced by the condition $|w| \geq p$. This slight change in condition will *not* effect the minimal pumping constant as argued next. For a regular language L we refer to the minimal number p satisfying Lemma 4 with the modified condition $|w| \geq p$ as $\widetilde{\mathtt{mpe}}(L)$. Obviously, $\mathtt{mpe}(L) \leq \widetilde{\mathtt{mpe}}(L)$ by definition. On the other hand, $\widetilde{\mathtt{mpe}}(L) \leq \mathtt{mpe}(L)$, because for every word $\tilde{w}$ that is longer than $\mathtt{mpe}(L)$ there are words $w \in \Sigma^*$ and $v \in \Sigma^*$ with $|w| = \mathtt{mpe}(L)$ and $\tilde{w} = wv$. But word w can be pumped, i.e., there are words $x \in \Sigma^*$, $y \in \Sigma^+$, and $z \in \Sigma^*$ such that $w = xyz$ and

$$\tilde{w} = wv = xyzv \in L \iff xy^t zv \in L$$

for $t \geq 0$ and $v \in \Sigma^*$. Hence $\tilde{w}$ can be pumped, too. This implies that $\widetilde{\mathtt{mpe}}(L) \leq \mathtt{mpe}(L)$, which proves equality. That is $\mathtt{mpe}(L) = \widetilde{\mathtt{mpe}}(L)$. Moreover, it is easy to see that a further condition on the length of the pumped word or prefix such as, e.g., $|y| \leq |xy| \leq p$ will not change $\mathtt{mpe}(L)$ or $\widetilde{\mathtt{mpe}}(L)$ either. Thus, the above given definition of $\mathtt{mpe}(L)$ is robust against the previously discussed changes.

---

[1] A language $L \subseteq \Sigma^*$ is *suffix closed* if $L = \{\, x \mid yx \in L,$ for some $y \in \Sigma^* \,\}$, i.e., the word x is a member of L whenever yx is in L, for some $y \in \Sigma^*$.

First we prove some basic facts in similar vein as done in [2] for the other minimal pumping constants. Therefore the proof of Lemma 4 will be very useful so we present its main concepts. The proof idea for the one direction is that for a given DFA with state set Q we can always use $k = |Q|$ since every word of length $|Q|$ forms a computation over the states of the automaton where at least one state is visited twice. For the other direction we construct an automaton that viewed as a graph is a full $|\Sigma|$-ary tree of height k, for a given k, if we ignore the transitions that emanate from the leaves of this tree. Let us call such an automaton an automaton with a tree-like graph structure. The nodes of the tree are named q_w, if the word w maps the root to it, e.g., the root is labeled by q_λ. Now each node q_w is accepting if the word w is in the language L. For adding the transitions for states that are at the leaves of the tree we observe that each word that maps the root to such a state has length $k-1$ and therefore each word that maps the root to a state at the leaf and afterwards to another state has length k. Since each word of length k can be pumped, the transitions of states at the leaves have to end in a node of the tree.

By using this method we directly obtain the following theorem.

Theorem 5. *Let L be a regular language over the alphabet Σ. Then we have $mpe(L) = 1$ if and only if L is universal or empty, i.e., $L = \Sigma^*$ or $L = \emptyset$.*

We obtain $\mathtt{mpc}(L) \leq \mathtt{mpe}(L) \leq \mathtt{sc}(L)$ by definition. Whether we can come up with a stronger result also taking the value of $\mathtt{mpl}(L)$ into account is answered next.

Theorem 6. *Let L be any regular language. Then $mpl(L) \leq mpe(L)$.*

Thus, we have

$$\mathtt{mpc}(L) \leq \mathtt{mpl}(L) \leq \mathtt{mpe}(L) \leq \mathtt{sc}(L).$$

Then the question arises whether we can come up with a similar statement as shown in Theorem 3 for all four minimal pumping lemma constants. It turns out that the situation is more involved in this case. First we concentrate on the relation between $\mathtt{mpe}(L)$ and $\mathtt{sc}(L)$. Obviously, there is a language L over an arbitrary alphabet (even unary) such that $\mathtt{mpe}(L) = \mathtt{sc}(L)$, e.g., for every integer $k \geq 1$ the language $(a^k)^*$ suffices $\mathtt{mpe}((a^k)^*) = \mathtt{sc}((a^k)^*) = k$. On the other hand, in [10] it was shown that for every integer $m \geq 1$ there is a language L over a binary alphabet such that $\mathtt{mpe}(L) = m$ and $\mathtt{sc}(L) = \sum_{i=0}^{m-1} 2^i$. Basically, Yehudai's construction relies on Jaffe's original proof [6] that constructs a full binary tree of height m for one of the implications of the if-and-only-if pumping lemma statement. To keep the presentation self-contained we (almost literally) recall the proof of [10] and generalize it to alphabets of size at least two. It is worth mentioning that the generalization to alphabets of size larger than two is not entirely obvious since the introduction of new symbols must also increase the deterministic state complexity of the language in question, while not changing Jaffe's minimal pumping constants.

Theorem 7. *Let $p \geq 1$ be a natural number. Then there exists a language L over the alphabet Σ of size at least two such that $mpe(L) = p$ and $sc(L) = \sum_{i=0}^{p-1} |\Sigma|^i$.*

Proof. For $p = 1$, the statement is obvious, because $\sum_{i=0}^{p-1} |\Sigma|^i = 1$ regardless of the size of Σ. Therefore we can assume for the rest of the proof that $p \geq 2$.

Let Σ be an alphabet of size at least two and a_1 be any fixed letter from Σ. We define a DFA $A = (Q, \Sigma, \cdot, q_\lambda, F)$ with state set $Q = \{ q_w \mid w \in \Sigma^{\leq p-1} \}$, set of final states $F = \{ q_w \mid w \in \Sigma^{p-2} a_1 \}$, and for each $q_w \in Q$, letters $a, b \in \Sigma$, and $c \in \Sigma \setminus \{a_1\}$ the transitions function is set to

1. a tree-like structure by $q_w \cdot a = q_{wa}$, if $|w| < p - 1$, and
2. if $|w| = p - 1$, then we distinguish the cases
   (a) word $w = ba_1^{p-2}$, then $q_w \cdot a = q_\lambda$, if $a = b$, and $q_w \cdot a = q_w$, otherwise,
   (b) word $w = w''bca_1^m$, for $m = p - |w''| - 3 > 0$, then $q_w \cdot a = q_{w''b}$, if $a = b$, and $q_w \cdot a = q_w$, otherwise, and finally
   (c) word $w = w'c$, then $q_w \cdot a = q_{w'}$, if $a = c$, and $q_w \cdot a = q_w$, otherwise,

which map a state/word onto one of its prefixes, which ensures that we have the inequality $mpe(L(A)) \leq p$. This completes the description of the DFA A of height p. Note that if A is minimal, then we have $mpe(L(A)) = p$. It remains to show that A is minimal.

For proving two states q_u and q_v of A to be inequivalent, i.e., $q_u \not\equiv q_v$, we define the following helpful measure for accepting states of A. For each $q_w \in F$, we define $r(q_w) = 0$, if $w \in \Sigma a_1^{p-2}$, otherwise there is a unique word w' such that $w = w'ca_1^+$, for $c \in \Sigma \setminus \{a_1\}$, so we set $r(q_w) = |w'|$. Then the following two claims, proven by induction on the function r, imply A's minimality.

Claim 1. If q_u and q_v are different accepting states then $q_u \not\equiv q_v$.

The second claim reads as follows:

Claim 2. If q_u and q_v are different non-accepting states then $q_u \not\equiv q_v$.

By the above two claims we obtain that in all cases $u \neq v$ implies $q_u \not\equiv q_v$. Hence, A is minimal and by construction has $\sum_{i=0}^{p-1} |\Sigma|^i$ states.   □

With the help of the previous theorem we are able to prove the reachability of all possible combinations of $mpe(L)$ and $sc(L)$ satisfying

$$mpe(L) \leq sc(L) \leq \sum_{i=0}^{mpe(L)-1} |\Sigma|^i,$$

where Σ is of size at least two, by making states in the tree-like automaton constructed in the proof of Theorem 7 unreachable. Before we describe how to alter this automaton let us mention the following useful lemma on the minimal pumping constant w.r.t. Lemma 4, which we state without proof.

Theorem 8. *Let $A = (Q, \Sigma, \cdot_A, q_0, F)$ be a minimal DFA, state $q \in Q$, and letter $a \in \Sigma$. Define the finite automaton $B = (Q, \Sigma, \cdot_B, q_0, F)$ with the transition function $\cdot_B$ that is equal to the transition function of $\cdot_A$, except for the state q and the letter a, where $q \cdot_B a = q$. Then, $mpe(L(B)) \leq mpe(L(A))$.*

Now we are able to prove the main theorem.

Theorem 9. *Let Σ be an alphabet of size at least two and p_1, p_2 be natural numbers with $p_1 \leq p_2 \leq \sum_{i=0}^{p_1-1} |\Sigma|^i$. Then there is a regular language L over Σ such that $\mathsf{mpe}(L) = p_1$ and $\mathsf{sc}(L) = p_2$.*

Proof. We will adapt the construction of the automaton A shown in the proof of Theorem 7 for the value p_1 by making certain complete sub-trees of A unreachable from the initial state. Therefore, the proof is divided into three parts: (i) first we demonstrate the recursive procedure for adapting the construction from the previous proof such that we obtain an automaton with the requested number of states, (ii) afterwards we show that this automaton is minimal, and (iii) finally we prove that for the constructed automaton that accepts the language L the value of $\mathsf{mpe}(L)$ is p_1 as required.

Let $A = (Q, \Sigma, \cdot, q_\lambda, F)$ be the automaton constructed in the proof of Theorem 7 with parameter p_1. We assume w.l.o.g. that $\Sigma = \{a_1, a_2, \ldots, a_k\}$ and that a_1 is the fixed letter that is used in the construction of A. The recursive procedure TREE-CUT moves through the automaton and alters some transitions of the form $q_w \cdot a = q_{wa}$, if $|w| < p_1 - 1$, in order to make sub-trees unreachable; all other transitions, in particular those with states of the form q_w with $|w| = p_1 - 1$, will remain as they are. Next we describe how the tree cutting procedure operates on A.

Procedure TREE-CUT has three parameters: state q_w, height h, and number of states x. It is called under the assertion $1 \leq h \leq x$ and returns a sub-automaton below q_w, that viewed as a graph without self-loops is a tree of height h and size x with certain properties, which are explained later. Initially it is called with the values q_λ, p_1, and p_2 or for short (q_λ, p_1, p_2); obviously the assertion is fulfilled by the assumption of the theorem. Then besides termination were $h = 1$ and $x = 1$ must hold, and nothing is changed on the automaton structure anymore, we distinguish two cases—here T_k^h is the size of a complete k-ary tree of height h, where the height of a tree is the maximal number of nodes on any root-leaf path:

1. Cut-tree-stem case: If

$$1 + \ell \cdot T_k^{h-1} < x \leq 1 + \ell \cdot T_k^{h-1} + (h-1), \tag{1}$$

for $0 \leq \ell \leq k-1$, where $T_k^h = \sum_{i=0}^{h-1} k^i$, then we proceed as follows depending on ℓ, where we distinguish two sub-cases:
(a) If $\ell = 0$, then by Eq. 1 and the assertion $h \leq x$, we deduce $x = h$. Thus we change the following transitions on the state q_w to self-loops by re-defining

$$q_w \cdot a_i = q_w, \quad \text{for } 2 \leq i \leq k,$$

which makes the sub-trees with the roots q_{wa_i}, for $2 \leq i \leq k$, of the original automaton A unreachable. Then a recursive call of TREE-CUT with parameters $(q_{wa_1}, h-1, h-1)$ is made. Here the assertion is obviously fulfilled.

(b) Otherwise, let $\ell \geq 1$. Then the following transitions are changed to self-loops

$$q_w \cdot a_i = q_w, \quad \text{for } \ell + 2 \leq i \leq k,$$

which makes the sub-trees with the roots q_{wa_i}, for $\ell + 2 \leq i \leq k$, of the original automaton A unreachable, and as mentioned above all other transitions for q_w remain as they are in A. Then recursive calls of TREE-CUT with parameters $(q_{wa_\ell}, h-1, t)$ and $(q_{wa_{\ell+1}}, h-1, h-1)$ in sequence are made, where $t = x - (\ell - 1) \cdot T_k^{h-1} - h$. The assertion on the second call of TREE-CUT is obviously fulfilled. Whether this is also the case for the first one will be shown after the description of the procedure is completed—see below.

2. Cut-tree case: If

$$1 + \ell \cdot T_k^{h-1} + (h - 1) < x \leq 1 + (\ell + 1) \cdot T_k^{h-1} \tag{2}$$

for $0 \leq \ell \leq k - 1$, then the situation is sightly simpler than Case (newinlinkPar43item:casespsone1), because we do not have to distinguish between different sub-cases for ℓ. The transitions

$$q_w \cdot a_i = q_w, \quad \text{for } \ell + 2 \leq i \leq k,$$

are re-defined, which makes the sub-trees with the roots q_{wa_i}, for $\ell+2 \leq i \leq k$, of the original automaton A unreachable. Then a single call of TREE-CUT with the parameters $(q_{wa_{\ell+1}}, h - 1, t)$ for $t = x - \ell \cdot T_k^{h-1} - 1$ is done. Again, whether the assertion for the call is fulfilled will be shown below.

This completes the description of the procedure TREE-CUT—see Fig. 1 for a drawing on the recursive calls of the procedure. It remains to show the left open assertions for the recursive calls above. First note that $T_k^h \geq 2h$, if $k \geq 2$ and $h \geq 3$ or $k \geq 3$ and $h \geq 2$. Consider the call of TREE-CUT with parameters $(q_{wa_\ell}, h-1, t)$ with $t = x - (\ell-1) \cdot T_k^{h-1} - h$, from the first case (second sub-case), where Eq. 1 holds. Here we deduce

$$t = x - (\ell - 1) \cdot T_k^{h-1} - h > 1 + \ell \cdot T_k^{h-1} - (\ell - 1) \cdot T_k^{h-1} - h$$
$$= 1 + T_k^{h-1} - h$$
$$\geq 1 + 2(h - 1) - h = 1 + 2h - 2 - h = h - 1,$$

for appropriate values of k and h guaranteeing $T_k^h \geq 2h$, which shows the correctness of the assertion. For the missing cases $h = 1$ and $h = k = 2$ it follows that Inequality (2) holds.

Finally, the call of TREE-CUT with the parameters $(q_{wa_{\ell+1}}, h - 1, t)$ with $t = x - \ell \cdot T_k^{h-1} - h$ from the second case has to be looked at. Recall that Eq. 2 holds. We find the estimate

$$t = x - \ell \cdot T_k^{h-1} - 1 > 1 + \ell \cdot T_k^{h-1} + (h - 1) - \ell \cdot T_k^{h-1} - 1 = h - 1.$$

Hence, also in this case the assertion holds true. By construction, the altered automaton A' with transition function $\cdot_{A'}$ satisfies the following properties:

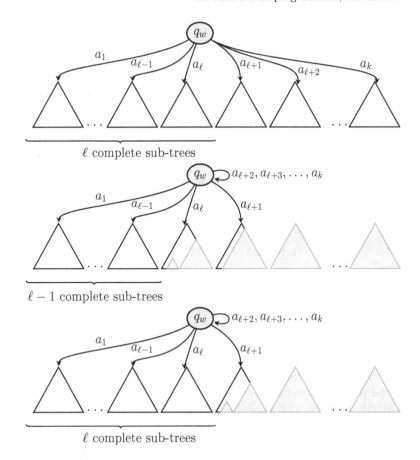

Fig. 1. Schematic drawing for the application of the TREE-CUT procedure. On the top the sub-tree of q_w is shown before the call of the procedure. The drawing in the middle and at the bottom show the situation after the procedure is called in the cut-tree-stem and cut-tree case, respectively. Observe, that there remain $\ell - 1$ and ℓ complete reachable sub-trees for those two cases, respectively. The sub-tree of q_{wa_ℓ} (top right) and $q_{wa_{\ell+1}}$ (lower right), respectively, is a sub-tree which may consist of at least $h - 1$ and at most T_k^{h-1} reachable states. For the cut-tree-stem case the sub-tree of $q_{wa_{\ell+1}}$ contains exactly $h - 1$ reachable states.

1. the automaton has exactly p_2 reachable states,
2. every reachable state q_w of A' is reached by w from the initial state, that is, $q_\lambda \cdot_{A'} w = q_w$, and w induces a simple path, which is a path with no repetitions of states,
3. for every reachable state q_w, for $|w| < p_1 - 1$, the a_1-transition is part of A' and moves to state $q_{wa_1} = q_w \cdot_{A'} a_1$—as a consequence the word $a_1^{p_1-1-|w|}$ moves q_w towards $q_{w'}$ with $w' = wa_1^{p_1-1-|w|}$, i.e., a state of maximal height, satisfying $|w'| = p_1 - 1$.

A schematic drawing of the recursive calls of TREE-CUT with the parameters q_λ, $h = 5$, and $t = 25$ on the automaton A with binary input alphabet is shown in Fig. 2.

From these properties together with the construction given in the proof of Theorem 7 we can deduce the following useful fact that is satisfied by A' and the original automaton A. It implies that neither A nor A' accepts $\emptyset$ or Σ^* if the height is at least two. The next claim is interesting on its own.

Claim 3. Let Σ be the input alphabet and $\cdot$ be the transition function of A' with distinguished fixed letter a_1 from Σ. Further, let A' be of height at least two, and q be any state of A'. Then, if q is non-accepting (accepting, respectively), then there is a word $w \in a_1^*$ ($w \in \Sigma^*$, respectively), such that the state $q \cdot w$ is accepting (non-accepting, respectively). The statement remains valid for the automaton A from Theorem 7. □

In order to prove the statement of Theorem 9 it suffices to prove the following two claims:

Claim 4. The DFA A' is minimal when considering only the reachable states.

The second claim reads as follows:

Claim 5. The language L' accepted by A' satisfies $\mathtt{mpe}(L') = p_1$.

This proves the stated theorem. □

In the preceding theorem, we have demonstrated the concurrent regulation of the minimal pumping constant w.r.t. Lemma 4 and the deterministic state complexity. Simultaneously managing multiple minimal pumping constants together with $\mathtt{mpe}(L)$, for a regular language, and the deterministic state complexity in similar vein as in Theorem 3 of [2] is more challenging and an ambitious undertaking. The concurrent regulation of the aforementioned pumping constants for languages defined over a growing alphabet is comparatively less challenging. For instance, if one considers $\mathtt{mpc}(L)$, $\mathtt{mpe}(L)$, and $\mathtt{sc}(L)$, then it is easy to see that the unary language $L = a^{p_1-1}(a^{p_2 i})^*$ satisfies $\mathtt{mpc}(L) = p_1$ and $\mathtt{mpe}(L) = p_2$, and $\mathtt{sc}(L) = p_2$. Thus, in order to increase the state complexity a suitable union of languages of the form c_i^+, for new symbols c_i, can be used—this is the same trick used in [2]. Hence, for all possible values $1 \le p_1 \le p_2 \le p_3$ there is a regular language L such that $\mathtt{mpc}(L) = p_1$, $\mathtt{mpe}(L) = p_2$, and $\mathtt{sc}(L) = p_3$. Analogous results can be obtained for combinations of other pumping lemma constants. Subsequently, we address the inquiry of simultaneously regulating the four constants $\mathtt{mpc}(L)$, $\mathtt{mpl}(L)$, $\mathtt{mpe}(L)$, and $\mathtt{sc}(L)$ for languages defined over an alphabet of constant size. Here we give a partial answer to this problem:

Theorem 10. *Let p_1, p_2, p_3, and p_4 be four natural numbers with $1 \le p_1 \le p_2 \le p_3 \le p_4$ satisfying $p_2 \ge 3$ and*[2]

$$p_2 + p_3 + \langle p_3 > 3 \rangle \le p_4 \le p_2 + \sum_{i=0}^{p_3-3} |\Sigma|^i + 2 + \langle p_3 > 3 \rangle.$$

---

[2] Let P be a Boolean predicate. Then $\langle P \rangle := 1$, if P is *true*; otherwise $\langle P \rangle := 0$.

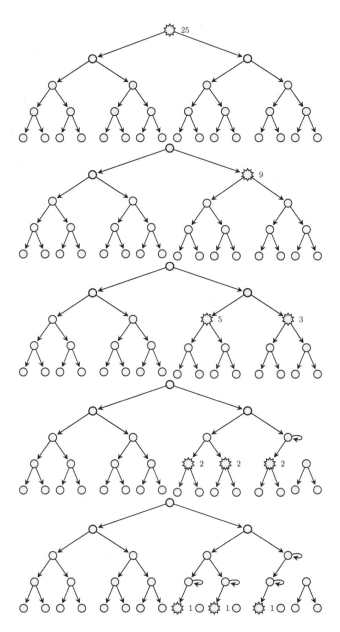

Fig. 2. A schematic drawing of the recursive calls of TREE-CUT with the parameters q_λ, $h = 5$, and $t = 25$ on the automaton A (only the tree-like graph structure is shown). Here the zigzag-bordered nodes are the ones the TREE-CUT procedure is called with. The number besides those nodes is the third value of the respective call of the procedure.

Then there exists a regular language over an alphabet Σ of size at least three such that $mpc(L) = p_1$, $mpl(L) = p_2$, $mpe(L) = p_3$, and $sc(L) = p_4$.

Proof. We only prove the statement for a three letter alphabet $\Sigma = \{a_1, a_2, a_3\}$. The below given construction easily generalizes to alphabets of larger size. We use the automaton A' of height $p_3 - 2$ with distinguished fixed letter a_1 from Theorem 9 as a basic build block in our construction. Assume that Q is the state set, $\cdot$ is the transition function, and q_λ is the initial state, and F is the set of final states of A'. Roughly speaking the to-be-constructed automaton B consists of an a_1-cycle of length p_2, an accepting and a rejecting sink state, as well as A' and an intermediate state for connecting the components. Formally, let $B = (Q_B, \Sigma, \cdot_B, q_\lambda, F_B)$, where

$$Q_B = \{q_{a_3 a_2 w} \mid q_w \in Q\} \cup \{q_{a_1^i} \mid 0 \le i \le p_2 - 1\} \cup \{q_{a_2}, q_{a_3}, q_{a_3 a_1}, q_{a_3 a_3}\}$$

and

$$F_B = \{q_{a_3 a_2 w} \mid q_w \in F\} \cup \{q_{a_1^{p_1 - 1}}\} \cup \{q_{a_2}, q_{a_3}, q_{a_3 a_3}\}.$$

Observe, that all states of the form $q_{a_3 a_2 w}$ are induced by the automaton A'. The transition function is set to:

1. on the initial state let $q_\lambda \cdot_B a_i = q_{a_i}$, for $1 \le i \le |\Sigma|$,
2. the a_1-cycle of length p_2 is given by $q_{a_1^i} \cdot_B a_1 = q_{a_1^{i+1}}$, if $0 \le i < p_2 - 2$; otherwise $q_{a_1^{p_2 - 1}} \cdot_B a_1 = q_\lambda$,
3. next $q_{a_3} \cdot_B a_i = q_{a_3 a_i}$, for $1 \le i \le |\Sigma|$, and
4. finally copying the A'-structure by $q_{a_3 a_2 w} \cdot_B a_i = q_{a_3 a_2 v}$, if $q_w \cdot a_i = q_v$ in A', for $a_i \in \Sigma$—this is not only replicating the tree-like graph structure of A', but also the backward transitions on the states of maximal height into the tree-like graph structure.

All non-specified transitions are self-loops. This completes the description of B—a schematic drawing is given in Fig. 3. In abuse of notation we say that a state pair (q, p) is inequivalent if the states q and p are inequivalent.

Claim 6. Let Q be the state set of A'. Then except for the pair $(q_{a_2}, q_{a_3 a_3})$ all other pairs of different states of B are inequivalent, if $|Q| > 1$; otherwise only the state pairs from $\{q_{a_2}, q_{a_3 a_2}, q_{a_3 a_3}\}$ are equivalent. Thus, the minimal automaton accepting the language $L(B)$ has $|Q| + p_2 + 3$ states, if $|Q| > 1$, and $|Q| + p_2 + 2$ states otherwise.

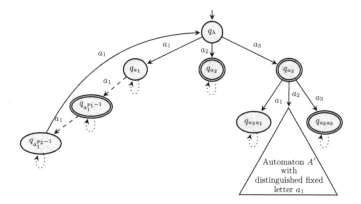

Fig. 3. Schematic drawing of the automaton B where the sub-automaton A' with its distinguished fixed letter a_1 of height $p_3 - 2$ is not drawn explicitly. Dotted loop transitions indicate self-loops on the states with the appropriate (non-shown) letters.

Next it remains to show that the pumping constants are met.

Claim 7. The language $L(B)$ satisfies the requirements on the minimal pumping constants under consideration.

Both claims prove the stated result.   □

With more effort put into the construction of the automaton in the proof of Theorem 10 one can improve the upper bound for the deterministic state complexity, by increasing the alphabet size. The schematic drawing shown in Fig. 4 gives an overview of the modifications of the original automaton construction in the proof of Theorem 10—cf. Fig. 3.

Here sub-automata of different heights (at most $p_3 - 2$) are used, but it is required that at least one of these sub-automata is of height $p_3 - 2$, in order to induce that the minimal pumping constant of Jaffe's pumping lemma is p_3. The detailed construction and the tedious analysis are left to the interested reader. It is worth mentioning that the different sub-automata are all inequivalent due to the difference in the fixed distinguished letters. In summary one obtains the following theorem—the lower bound remains the same as in Theorem 10:

Theorem 11. *Let p_1, p_2, p_3, and p_4 be four natural numbers with $1 \leq p_1 \leq p_2 \leq p_3 \leq p_4$ satisfying $p_2 \geq 3$ and*

$$p_2 + p_3 + \langle p_3 > 3 \rangle \leq p_4 \leq p_2 + \sum_{i=0}^{p_3-2} |\Sigma|^i - 2 \left(\sum_{i=0}^{p_3-3} |\Sigma|^i \right) + |\Sigma| - 1.$$

Then there is a regular language over an alphabet Σ of size at least three such that $\mathtt{mpc}(L) = p_1$, $\mathtt{mpl}(L) = p_2$, $\mathtt{mpe}(L) = p_3$, and $\mathtt{sc}(L) = p_4$.   □

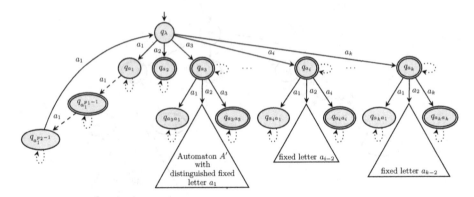

Fig. 4. Schematic drawing of modifications of the automaton constructed in the proof of Theorem 10. All sub-automata A' are with different distinguished fixed letters to make their states inequivalent to each other. These sub-automata are of height at most $p_3 - 2$ and there is one sub-automaton with height exactly $p_3 - 2$.

References

1. Brauer, W.: Automatentheorie: Eine Einführung in die Theorie endlicher Automaten. Leitfäden und Monographien der Informatik, Teubner Stuttgart (1984). (in German)
2. Dassow, J., Jecker, I.: Operational complexity and pumping lemmas. Acta Inform. **59**, 337–355 (2022)
3. Harrison, M.A.: Introduction to Formal Language Theory. Addison-Wesley (1978)
4. Holzer, M., Rauch, C.: More on the descriptional complexity of pumping (März 2023), (in preparation)
5. Hopcroft, J.E., Ullman, J.D.: Introduction to Automata Theory. Addison-Wesley, Languages and Computation (1979)
6. Jaffe, J.: A necessary and sufficient pumping lemma for regular languages. SIGACT News **10**(2), 48–49 (1978)
7. Kozen, D.C.: Automata and Computability. Undergraduate Texts in Computer Science. Springer (1997). https://doi.org/10.1007/978-1-4612-1844-9
8. Nijholt, A.: YABBER–yet another bibliography: Pumping lemma's. An annotated bibliography of pumping. Bull. EATCS **17**, 34–53 (1982)
9. Rabin, M.O., Scott, D.: Finite automata and their decision problems. IBM J. Res. Dev. **3**, 114–125 (1959). https://doi.org/10.1147/rd.32.0114
10. Yehudai, A.: A note on the pumping lemma for regular languages. Inform. Process. Lett. **9**(3), 135–136 (1979)
11. Yu, S.: Chapter 2: Regular languages. In: Rozenberg, G., Salomaa, A. (eds.) Handbook of Formal Languages, vol. 1, pp. 41–110. Springer (1997)

Operational Complexity: NFA-to-DFA Trade-Off

Michal Hospodár[1] , Jozef Jirásek[2] , Galina Jirásková[1(✉)] ,
and Juraj Šebej[2]

[1] Mathematical Institute, Slovak Academy of Sciences,
Grešákova 6, 040 01 Košice, Slovakia
{hospodar,jiraskov}@saske.sk
[2] Department of Computer Science, P. J. Šafárik University,
Jesenná 5, 040 01 Košice, Slovakia
{jozef.jirasek,juraj.sebej}@upjs.sk

Abstract. We examine operational complexity assuming that the arguments are given as nondeterministic finite automata and the resulting language is represented by a deterministic finite automaton. We show that the known upper bounds for Boolean operations and concatenation are met by ternary languages, and we prove that they are asymptotically tight in the binary case. For the cut and square operations, we get tight upper bounds $2^{m-1}(2^n+1)$ and $\frac{3}{4}2^{2n}$, respectively. Our witnesses are described over a four-letter alphabet for cut, and a ten-letter alphabet for square. We also show that the tight upper bound on the syntactic complexity of a language given by an n-state NFA is 2^{n^2}. For the square root operation, we provide a lower bound 2^{n^2-n} and an upper bound 2^{n^2}.

1 Introduction

The state complexity of a regular operation is the number of states that are sufficient and necessary in the worst case for a deterministic finite automaton (DFA) to accept the language resulting from the operation, considered as a function of sizes of DFAs representing the arguments of the operation. If arguments and the resulting languages are represented by nondeterministic finite automata (NFAs), then we speak about the nondeterministic state complexity of regular operations.

M. Hospodár—This publication was supported by the Operational Programme Integrated Infrastructure (OPII) for the project 313011BWH2: "InoCHF - Research and development in the field of innovative technologies in the management of patients with CHF", co-financed by the European Regional Development Fund.

M. Hospodár and G. Jirásková—Supported by the Slovak Grant Agency for Science (VEGA) under contract 2/0096/23 "Automata and Formal Languages: Descriptional and Computational Complexity".

J. Jirásek and J. Šebej—Supported by the Slovak Grant Agency for Science (VEGA) under contract 1/0177/21 "Descriptional and Computational Complexity of Automata and Algorithms".

H. Bordihn et al. (Eds.): DCFS 2023, LNCS 13918, pp. 79–93, 2023.
https://doi.org/10.1007/978-3-031-34326-1_6

The first results on the state complexity of regular operations were published by Maslov [16] and Yu, Zhuang, and Salomaa [22], while the nondeterministic state complexity of operations was introduced by Holzer and Kutrib [8].

Some other models of finite automata were considered in the literature. Operational complexity on two-way finite automata was investigated by Jirásková and Okhotin [14]. Jirásek Jr. et al. [11,12] used the representation of regular languages by self-verifying and unambiguous automata. In all of these papers, the arguments and the resulting languages were represented by the same model of automata.

In this paper we examine operational complexity assuming that the arguments of an operation are represented by NFAs, but the resulting language is required to be represented by a DFA. Our motivation comes from two problems studied in the literature: the complexity of combined operations [19], and the operational complexity on self-verifying [11] and unambiguous [12] finite automata.

If a given combined operation does not contain complementation, then we can perform all included operations on NFAs. This gives an NFA representation of arguments for the outermost operation. Then, the NFA-to-DFA trade-off for this operation can be used to get an upper bound on the complexity of the given combined operation. Self-verifying and unambiguous finite automata are special kinds of NFAs, while every DFA is self-verifying as well as unambiguous. Thus, the NFA-to-DFA trade-off for a regular operation provides an upper bound on the complexity of this operation on self-verifying or unambiguous automata.

The first results on NFA-to-DFA trade-offs for regular operations were presented by Jirásková and Krajňáková [13]. They obtained tight upper bounds for union, intersection, difference, symmetric difference, concatenation, reversal, star, shuffle, left quotient, and right quotient. To describe witnesses, they used a quaternary alphabet for Boolean operations and concatenation, and a binary alphabet otherwise.

Here we continue this research, and improve the results for Boolean operations and concatenation by describing witnesses over a ternary alphabet. We also prove that the corresponding upper bounds are asymptotically tight in the binary case. Then we examine NFA-to-DFA trade-offs for less common regular operations, namely, cut, square, and square root. While for cut and square we provide tight upper bounds with witnesses defined over a fixed alphabet, for square root we only have a lower and upper bound, although we conjecture that the tight upper bound is given by the expression $\sum_{k=0}^{n} \binom{n}{k}\left(1+(2^k-1)2^{n-k}\right)^{n-1}$. Finally, we get the tight upper bound on the syntactic complexity of languages represented by NFAs.

2   Preliminaries

We assume that the reader is familiar with the basic notions in formal languages and automata theory. For details and all unexplained notions, we refer to [9,20,21].

Let Σ be a finite non-empty alphabet of symbols. Then Σ^* denotes the set of all strings over Σ including the empty string ε, and $\Sigma^+ = \Sigma^* \setminus \{\varepsilon\}$. For a finite set S, the symbol $|S|$ denotes the size of S, and the symbol 2^S denotes the power set of S. For two integers i and j, we denote the set $\{i, i+1, \ldots, j\}$ by $[i, j]$.

A *nondeterministic finite automaton* (NFA) is a quintuple $A = (Q, \Sigma, \cdot, s, F)$ where Q is a finite non-empty set of states, Σ is a finite non-empty input alphabet, $\cdot : Q \times \Sigma \to 2^Q$ is the transition function, $s \in Q$ is the initial state, and $F \subseteq Q$ is the set of final states. The transition function can be extended to the domain $2^Q \times \Sigma^*$ in the natural way. The language accepted by A is the set of strings $L(A) = \{w \in \Sigma^* \mid s \cdot w \cap F \neq \emptyset\}$. For states p, q and a symbol a we write (p, a, q) whenever $q \in p \cdot a$.

A nondeterministic automaton is a *deterministic finite automaton* (DFA) if $|q \cdot a| = 1$ for each state q and each input symbol a. We usually write $p \cdot a = q$ instead of $p \cdot a = \{q\}$ and we use $p \xrightarrow{a} q$ to denote that $p \cdot a = q$. A non-final state q_d of a DFA is called *dead* if $q_d \cdot a = q_d$ for each symbol a. A DFA is *minimal* if all its states are reachable from the initial state, and no two distinct states are equivalent. The *state complexity* of a regular language L, $\mathrm{sc}(L)$, is the number of states in a minimal DFA accepting L.

Sometimes, a model of nondeterministic finite automata with multiple initial states (MNFA) is considered. Every MNFA $A = (Q, \Sigma, \cdot, I, F)$ can be converted to an equivalent DFA $\mathcal{D}(A) = (2^Q, \Sigma, \cdot, I, \{S \in 2^Q \mid S \cap F \neq \emptyset\})$; here $\cdot$ is the transition function of A extended to the domain $2^Q \times \Sigma$. The DFA $\mathcal{D}(A)$ is called the *subset automaton* of the MNFA A. The subset automaton may not be minimal since some of its states can be unreachable or equivalent to other states.

The *reverse* of an MNFA $A = (Q, \Sigma, \cdot, I, F)$ is the MNFA $A^R = (Q, \Sigma, \cdot^R, F, I)$ where $q \cdot^R a = \{p \mid q \in p \cdot a\}$. We say that a subset S of Q is *reachable* in A if there exists a string w such that $S = I \cdot w$. A subset S is *co-reachable* in A if it is reachable in A^R. The co-reachability of all singleton sets guarantees that the corresponding subset automaton does not have equivalent states [13, Lemma 1].

Throughout the paper we always assume that $m, n \geq 2$.

3   Boolean Operations and Cut

It is shown in [13, Theorem 8] that tight upper bounds on NFA-to-DFA trade-offs for union, symmetric difference, intersection, and difference are 2^{m+n}, 2^{m+n}, $2^{m+n} - 2^m - 2^n + 2$, and $2^{m+n} - 2^m + 1$, respectively, with witnesses described over a quaternary alphabet. Our next result shows that the corresponding upper bounds can be met by ternary languages.

Theorem 1. *Let K and L be languages accepted by NFAs A and B from Fig. 1. Then*

(a) $\mathrm{sc}(K \cup L) = \mathrm{sc}(K \oplus L) = 2^{m+n}$,
(b) $\mathrm{sc}(K \cap L) = 2^{m+n} - 2^m - 2^n + 2$,
(c) $\mathrm{sc}(K \setminus L) = 2^{m+n} - 2^n + 1$.

Proof. Notice that transitions on b are the same in both automata. The roles of the transitions on a and c are mutually exchanged. In the subset automaton $\mathcal{D}(A)$, each singleton set is reached from $\{1\}$ by a string in a^*, and the

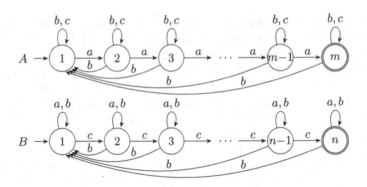

Fig. 1. Ternary witnesses for Boolean operations.

empty set is reached from $\{m\}$ by a. Next, for each set S with $1 \notin S$, the set $\{1\} \cup S$ is reached from S by b, and the set S is reached from a set containing 1 by a string in a^*. This proves the reachability of all subsets of $[1, m]$ in $\mathcal{D}(A)$ via strings in $\{a, b\}^*$ by induction. Hence for every $S \subseteq [1, m]$ there is a string $u_S \in \{a, b\}^*$ such that $1 \cdot_A u_S = S$. Symmetrically, for every $T \subseteq [1, n]$, there is a string $v_T \in \{b, c\}^*$ such that $1 \cdot_B v_T = T$.

Let $\circ \in \{\cup, \oplus, \cap, \setminus\}$. Construct the product automaton $M_\circ$ from DFAs $\mathcal{D}(A)$ and $\mathcal{D}(B)$. The initial state of $M_\circ$ is $(\{1\}, \{1\})$. Let $S \subseteq [1, m]$ and $T \subseteq [1, n]$. Then each state (S, T) with $1 \in S$ is reachable in $M_\circ$ from the initial state by the string $u_S v_T$ and each state (S, T) with $1 \notin S$ is reached from a state (S', T) with $1 \in S'$ by a string in a^*. Hence each state of $M_\circ$ is reachable.

To prove distinguishability first consider union. Then (S, T) is final in $M_\cup$ if $m \in S$ or $n \in T$. Let (S, T) and (S', T') be two distinct states of $M_\cup$. Then $S \neq S'$ or $T \neq T'$. In the first case, without loss of generality, let $s \in S \setminus S'$. Then $(S, T) \xrightarrow{a^{m-s}c^n} (\{m\} \cup S_1, \emptyset)$ for some S_1 and $(S', T') \xrightarrow{a^{m-s}c^n} (S_1', \emptyset)$ for some S_1' with $m \notin S_1'$. It follows that $a^{m-s}c^n$ is accepted by $M_\cup$ from (S, T) and rejected from (S', T'). The case of $T \neq T'$ is symmetric. The proof of distinguishability for symmetric difference is exactly the same as for union.

Now consider intersection. A state (S, T) is final in $M_\cap$ iff $m \in S$ and $n \in T$. All states $(\emptyset, T)$ with $T \subseteq [1, n]$ and $(S, \emptyset)$ with $S \subseteq [1, m]$ are dead in $M_\cap$. If $s \in S$ and $t \in T$, then the string $a^{m-s}c^{n-t}$ is accepted by $M_\cap$ from (S, T), so (S, T) is not dead. Let S, T, S', T' be non-empty such that $(S, T) \neq (S', T')$. Then $S \neq S'$ or $T \neq T'$. In the first case, let $s \in S \setminus S'$ and $t \in T$. Consider the string $a^{m-s}c^{n-t}$. Notice that

$$(S, T) \xrightarrow{a^{m-s}c^{n-t}} (\{m\} \cup S_1, \{n\} \cup T_1) \text{ for some } S_1, T_1,$$

$$(S', T') \xrightarrow{a^{m-s}c^{n-t}} (S_1', T_1') \text{ for some } S_1', T_1' \text{ with } m \notin S_1'.$$

Thus $a^{m-s}c^{n-t}$ is accepted by $M_\cap$ from (S, T) and rejected from (S', T'). The case of $T \neq T'$ is symmetric.

Finally, consider the difference $K \setminus L$. A state (S,T) is final in $M_\setminus$ if and only if $m \in S$ and $n \notin T$. All states $(\emptyset, T)$ with $T \subseteq [1, n]$ are dead in $M_\setminus$. Let $S \neq \emptyset$. If $s \in S$, then the string $a^{m-s}c^n$ is accepted from (S,T), so (S,T) is not dead. Let $S \neq \emptyset$, $S' \neq \emptyset$, $(S,T) \neq (S',T')$. If $s \in S \setminus S'$, then

$$(S,T) \xrightarrow{a^{m-s}c^n} (\{m\} \cup S_1, \emptyset) \text{ for some } S_1,$$

$$(S',T') \xrightarrow{a^{m-s}c^n} (S'_1, \emptyset) \text{ for some } S'_1 \text{ with } m \notin S'_1.$$

Thus the string $a^{m-s}c^n$ is accepted by $M_\setminus$ from (S,T) and rejected from (S',T'). If $S = S'$, $s \in S$, and $t \in T \setminus T'$, then take the string $a^{m-s}c^{n-t}$:

$$(S,T) \xrightarrow{a^{m-s}c^{n-t}} (\{m\} \cup S_1, \{n\} \cup T_1) \text{ for some } S_1, T_1;$$

$$(S',T') \xrightarrow{a^{m-s}c^{n-t}} (\{m\} \cup S_1, T'_1) \text{ where } n \notin T'_1.$$

Thus $a^{m-s}c^{n-t}$ is rejected by $M_\setminus$ from (S,T) and accepted from (S',T').   □

The next theorem shows that the upper bounds for Boolean operations are asymptotically tight already in the binary case.

Theorem 2. *Let K and L be languages accepted by NFAs A and B from Fig. 2. Then*

(a) $\mathrm{sc}(K \cup L) = \mathrm{sc}(K \oplus L) = 2^{m+n-1} + m + n,$
(b) $\mathrm{sc}(K \cap L) = 2^{m+n-1} + m + n - 2^m - 2^n + 2,$
(c) $\mathrm{sc}(K \setminus L) = 2^{m+n-1} + m + n - 2^m + 1.$

Proof. Construct the product automaton $M_\cup$ for $K \cup L$ using the subset automata $\mathcal{D}(A)$ and $\mathcal{D}(B)$. The initial state of $M_\cup$ is $(\{1\}, \{1\})$. Let $S \subseteq [1,m]$ and $T \subseteq [1,n]$. If $s \leq \min S$, then we denote $S \ominus s = \{i - s + 1 \mid i \in S\}$. The set $T \ominus t$ is defined analogously. Notice that by reading a from any (S,T) we reach state $(S \cdot a, T \cup \{1\})$ and by reading b we reach state $(S \cup \{1\}, T \cdot b)$. It follows that exactly one of S or T contains state 1, except for the initial state $(\{1\}, \{1\})$. So, the set of possible reachable states $\mathcal{R}$ consists of pairs (S,T) of four types:

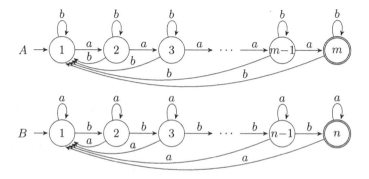

Fig. 2. Binary NFAs A and B with $\mathrm{sc}(L(A) \cup L(B)) = 2^{m+n-1} + m + n$.

(1) $(S, \emptyset)$, $(\emptyset, T)$;
(2) $(\{1\}, \{j\})$, $(\{i\}, \{1\})$, where $i \in Q_A$ and $j \in Q_B$;
(3) (S, T), where $1 \in S$, $1 \notin T$, and $T \neq \emptyset$,
(4) (S, T), where $1 \in T$, $1 \notin S$, and $S \neq \emptyset$,

and it contains $(2^m + 2^n - 1) + (m + n - 1) + (2^{m+n-1} - 2^m - 2^n + 2) = 2^{m+n-1} + m + n$ pairs. Let us show that all pairs in $\mathcal{R}$ are reachable.

As shown in the proof of Theorem 1, for each $S \subseteq [1, m]$ and each $T \subseteq [1, n]$, there exists a string $u_S \in \{a, b\}^*$ such that $\{1\} \cdot u_S = S$ and a string $u_T \in \{a, b\}^*$ such that $\{1\} \cdot u_T = T$ in $\mathcal{D}(A)$ and $\mathcal{D}(B)$, respectively. We consider four cases:

(1) $S = \emptyset$ or $T = \emptyset$. Then $(\{1\}, \{1\}) \xrightarrow{a^m} (\{\emptyset\}, \{1\}) \xrightarrow{u_T} (\emptyset, T)$, and the proof for $T = \emptyset$ is symmetric.
(2) Let $S = \{1\}$ and $T = \{j\}$, or $S = \{i\}$ and $T = \{1\}$. Then

$$(\{1\}, \{1\}) \xrightarrow{b^{j-1}} (\{1\}, \{j\}), \text{ and } (\{1\}, \{1\}) \xrightarrow{a^{i-1}} (\{i\}, \{1\}).$$

(3) $(1 \in S$ and $T = \{j\}$ where $j \neq 1)$ or $(1 \in T$ and $S = \{i\}$ where $i \neq 1)$. We prove this case by induction on the size of S. The basis, $|S| = 1$, is shown in (2). Let $|S| \geq 2$. Set $S' = (S \setminus \{1\})$ and $s = \min S'$, so $1 \in S' \ominus s$ and $|S' \ominus s| = |S| - 1$. Then $(S' \ominus s, \{n\})$ is reachable by induction, it is sent to $(S', \{1, n\})$ by a^{s-1}, and then to $(S, \{j\})$ by b^{j-1}. Symmetrically, by swapping a and b, we prove the other case.
(4) $(1 \in S, 1 \notin T, T \neq \emptyset)$ or $(1 \in T, 1 \notin S, S \neq \emptyset)$. We prove the first sub-case by induction on $|T|$. The basis, $|T| = 1$, is proved in case (3). Assume that the claim holds if $|T'| = k$. Let $|T| = k + 1$. Set $S' = S \setminus \{1\}$ and $s = \min S' \geq 2$. Next, set $t = \min T \geq 2$ and $T' = (T \setminus \{t\})$. Then the pair $(S' \ominus s, T' \ominus t)$ is reachable by induction since $1 \in (S' \ominus s)$, $1 \notin T' \ominus t$, and $|T' \ominus t| = k \geq 1$. We have $(S' \ominus s, T' \ominus t) \xrightarrow{a^{s-1}} (S', (T' \ominus t) \cup \{1\}) \xrightarrow{b^{t-1}} (S, T)$. second sub-case is proved in a symmetric way.

The proof for distinguishability is the same as in the proof of Theorem 1 but we replace the letter c with b. This gives the desired state complexities. $\square$

The *cut* of languages K and L is the language

$$K \,!\, L = \{uv \mid u \in K, v \in L, \text{ and } uv' \notin K \text{ for every non-empty prefix } v' \text{ of } v\}.$$

If regular languages K and L are accepted by DFAs $A = (Q_A, \Sigma, \circ, s_A, F_A)$ and $B = (Q_B, \Sigma, \bullet, s_B, F_B)$, then the language $K \,!\, L$ is accepted by the cut automaton $A \,!\, B = (Q_A \cup (Q_A \times Q_B), \Sigma, \cdot, s, F)$ where $s = s_A$ if $s_A \notin F_A$ and $s = (s_A, s_B)$ otherwise, $F = Q_A \times F_B$, and for $p \in Q_A$, $q \in Q_B$, and $a \in \Sigma$, the transitions are as follows:

$$p \cdot a = \begin{cases} p \circ a, & \text{if } p \circ a \notin F_A; \\ (p \circ a, s_B), & \text{if } p \circ a \in F_A, \end{cases} \quad (p, q) \cdot a = \begin{cases} (p \circ a, q \bullet a), & \text{if } p \circ a \notin F_A; \\ (p \circ a, s_B), & \text{if } p \circ a \in F_A, \end{cases}$$

cf. [1, 6, 7, 10].

If $p \in F_A$, then the state (p, s_B) is called a *resetting state*, and it follows from the construction of the cut automaton that if $p \in F_A$ then neither p nor (p, q) with $q \neq s_B$ are reachable in $A!B$. If automaton B has a dead state q_d, then each state (p, q_d) is equivalent to the corresponding state p [10, Lemma 1(b)]. Our aim is to get tight upper bound for the NFA-to-DFA trade-off for the cut operation.

Theorem 3. *Let $K, L \subseteq \Sigma^*$ be languages accepted by an m- and n-state NFA. Then $\mathrm{sc}(K!L) \leq 2^{m-1}(2^n + 1)$, and this upper bound is tight if $|\Sigma| \geq 4$.*

Proof. Let K and L be accepted by some NFAs A and B, respectively. If A or B has no final states, then $K!L = \emptyset$. Otherwise, the subset automaton $\mathcal{D}(A)$ has at least 2^{m-1} final states, so the cut automaton $\mathcal{D}(A)!\mathcal{D}(B)$ has at least 2^{m-1} resetting states. Moreover, the subset automaton $\mathcal{D}(B)$ has 2^n states including the dead state $\emptyset$. It follows that in the cut automaton, each state $(p, \emptyset)$ is equivalent to the state p. This gives the desired upper bound $2^{m-1} + 2^{m-1}2^n = 2^{m-1}(2^n + 1)$.

For tightness, let $\Sigma = \{a, b, c, d\}$. Let K be the language accepted by the m-state NFA A in which transitions on a and b are shown in Fig. 3 (left) and the symbols c and d perform the identity. Symmetrically, let L be the language accepted by the n-state NFA B in which transitions on c and d are shown in Fig. 3 (right) and the symbols a and b perform the identity.

Since each state $(p, \emptyset)$ is equivalent to p, we may assume that the initial state of the cut automaton $\mathcal{D}(A)!\mathcal{D}(B)$ is $(\{1\}, \emptyset)$. Consider the following family of $2^{m-1}(2^n + 1)$ states in the cut automaton $\mathcal{D}(A)!\mathcal{D}(B)$

$$\mathcal{R} = \{(S, \{1\}) \mid S \subseteq [1, m] \text{ and } m \in S\} \cup$$
$$\{(S, T) \mid S \subseteq [1, m], m \notin S, \text{ and } T \subseteq [1, n]\},$$

and let us show that all states in $\mathcal{R}$ are reachable and pairwise distinguishable.

Notice that in $\mathcal{D}(A)$, each subset S can be shifted cyclically by one either by a (if $1 \notin S$ or $\{1, m\} \subseteq S$) or by ab (otherwise). Moreover, symbol b eliminates state 1 from each set containing the state 1. It follows that each subset of $[1, m]$ is reachable from $[1, m]$. Hence for each $S \subseteq [1, m]$ there exists a string u_S in $\{a, b\}^*$ which sends $[1, m]$ to S in $\mathcal{D}(A)$, and symmetrically, for each $T \subseteq [1, n]$ there exists a string v_T in $\{c, d\}^*$ which sends $[1, n]$ to T in $\mathcal{D}(B)$. Then in the cut automaton, we have $(\{1\}, \emptyset) \xrightarrow{a^m} ([1, m], \{1\}) \xrightarrow{u_S} (S, \{1\})$. Moreover, if $m \notin S$, then $(S, \{1\}) \xrightarrow{c^n} (S, [1, n]) \xrightarrow{v_T} (S, T)$. This shows reachability.

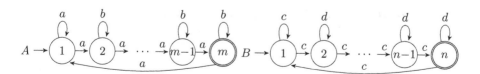

Fig. 3. The transitions on a and b in the NFA A (left) and on c and d in B (right).

To prove distinguishability, let (S,T) and (S',T') be two distinct pairs in $\mathcal{R}$. First let $S \neq S'$, and let $s \in S \setminus S'$. Set $w_s = (ab)^{m-s}a(ab)^{s-1}$. Then the string $w_s = (ab)^{m-s}a(ab)^{s-1}$ sends S to $\{s\}$ while going through the final state m, and it sends S' to the empty set. Therefore for $T'' \in \{T', \{1\}\}$, which is sent to the empty set by $(cd)^n$, we have

$$(S,T) \xrightarrow{w_s} (\{s\},\{1\}) \xrightarrow{a^{m-s}} (\{m\},\{1\}) \xrightarrow{(cd)^n} (\{m\},\{1\}) \xrightarrow{ab} (\emptyset,\{1\}) \xrightarrow{c^{n-1}} (\emptyset,\{n\})$$

$$(S',T') \xrightarrow{w_s} (\emptyset,T'') \xrightarrow{a^{m-s}} (\emptyset,T'') \xrightarrow{(cd)^n} (\emptyset,\emptyset) \xrightarrow{abc^{n-1}} (\emptyset,\emptyset);$$

notice that the resetting state $(\{m\},\{1\})$ goes to itself on c and d. So the string $w_s a^{m-s}(cd)^n abc^{n-1}$ distinguishes (S,T) and (S',T'). Now let $S = S'$ and $T \neq T'$ (so $m \notin S$) and let $t \in T \setminus T'$. Then c^{n-t} distinguishes the two pairs. $\qquad\square$

4   Concatenation and Square

In this section we consider the concatenation and square operations. The state complexity of these two operations is $m2^n - 2^{n-1}$ and $n2^n - 2^{n-1}$, respectively [16, 18] with binary witnesses. The tight upper bound $\frac{3}{4}2^{m+n}$ on the NFA-to-DFA trade-off for concatenation is provided in [13, Theorem 6], and witnesses are described over a quaternary alphabet. We first show that this upper bound can be met by ternary languages. Then we discuss the binary case. In the second part of this section, we get the tight upper bound $\frac{3}{4}2^{2n}$ on the NFA-to-DFA trade-off for square. To describe witnesses, we use a ten-letter alphabet.

Theorem 4. *Let K and L be languages accepted by NFAs A and B from Fig. 4. Then $sc(KL) = \frac{3}{4}2^{m+n}$.*

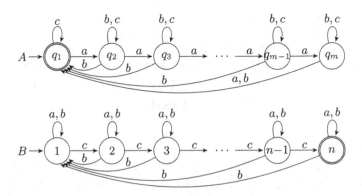

Fig. 4. Ternary witnesses for concatenation meeting the upper bound $\frac{3}{4}2^{m+n}$.

Proof. Construct an MNFA N for KL from A and B by adding the transitions $(q_1, c, 1)$, $(q_m, a, 1)$, and $(q_i, b, 1)$ for $i = 2, 3, \ldots, m$. The initial states of N are q_1 and 1. The set of final states is $\{n\}$.

Notice that in N^R each singleton set $\{j\}$ is reachable from the initial set $\{n\}$ via a string in c^*, and each $\{q_i\}$ is reachable from $\{1\}$ via a string in ca^*. It follows that for each state p of N, there is a string w_p which is accepted from and only from p. Hence all states of the subset automaton $\mathcal{D}(N)$ are pairwise distinguishable.

We now show that the subset automaton $\mathcal{D}(N)$ has $\frac{3}{4}2^{m+n}$ reachable states. Each state of $\mathcal{D}(N)$ consists of a subset S' of $\{q_1, q_2, \ldots, q_m\}$ and a subset T of $[1, n]$; we denote such state by (S, T) where $S = \{i \mid q_i \in S'\} \subseteq [1, m]$. Moreover having $1 \in S$ implies $1 \in T$, so in total we have $\frac{3}{4}2^{m+n}$ reachable states. Let us show the reachability of each such state (S, T).

In the same way as in the proof of Theorem 1, we show that for each $S \subseteq [1, m]$ there is a string $u_S \in \{a, b\}^*$ such that $1 \cdot_A u_S = S$, except for the empty set which is reached from 1 by b. Next, for each $T \subseteq [1, n]$ there is a string $v_T \in \{b, c\}^*$ such that $1 \cdot_B v_T = T$. To prove reachability, consider several cases:

Case 1: $S = \emptyset$. The initial state $(\{1\}, \{1\})$ is sent to $(\emptyset, T)$ by bv_T.

Case 2: $S \neq \emptyset$ and $1 \in T$.

Case 2.a: $S = \{1\}$. By induction on $|T|$ we show that $(\{1\}, T)$ with $1 \in T$ is reachable. The base case, $T = \{1\}$, holds true since $(\{1\}, \{1\})$ is the initial state of $\mathcal{D}(N)$. Assume that the claim holds true for each set of size k and let $|T| = k + 1$. Let $T = \{1, i_1, \ldots, i_k\}$ where we have $1 < i_1 < \cdots < i_k \leq n$. Set $T' = \{1, i_2 - i_1 + 1, \ldots, i_k - i_1 + 1\}$. Then $|T'| = k$, so the pair $(\{1\}, T')$ is reachable by induction, and it is sent to $(\{1\}, T)$ by $a^{m-1}c^{i_1-1}a$.

Case 2.b: $1 \in S$, where $|S| \geq 2$. The pair $(\{1\}, T)$ is reachable by (2.a), and it is sent to (S, T) by u_S since $1 \in T$.

Case 2.c: $1 \notin S$. Let $S = \{i_1, i_2, \ldots, i_k\}$ where we have $2 \leq i_1 < \cdots < i_k \leq m$. Set $S' = \{1, i_2 - i_1 + 1, \ldots, i_k - i_1 + 1\}$. Then (S', T) is reachable by (2.a) or (2.b), and it is sent to (S, T) by $a^{i_1 - 1}$.

Case 3: $S \neq \emptyset$ and $1 \notin T$. This means that $1 \notin S$. The pair $(S, \emptyset)$ is reached from $(\{1\}, \{1\})$ by $u_S c^n$. If $T = \{i_1, i_2 \ldots, i_k\}$ where $2 \leq i_1 < i_2 < \cdots < i_k \leq n$, then we set $T' = \{1, i_2 - i_1 + 1, \ldots, i_k - i_1 + 1\}$. The pair (S, T') is reachable by (2) since $1 \in T'$, and it is sent to (S, T) by $c^{i_1 - 1}$ since $1 \notin S$.   □

Proposition 5. *Consider languages* $K = (a+b)^*a(a+b)^{m-2}$ *and* $L = (a+b)^{n-1}$. *Then* $\mathrm{sc}(KL) \geq \frac{1}{4}2^{m+n}$.

Proof. The languages K and L are accepted by binary NFAs of m and n states, respectively. We have $KL = (a+b)^*a(a+b)^{m+n-3}$, and it is well known that every DFA for this language has at least 2^{m+n-2} states.   □

Theorem 6. *Let* L *be a language over an alphabet* Σ *accepted by an n-state NFA. Then* $\mathrm{sc}(L^2) \leq \frac{3}{4}2^{2n}$, *and this upper bound is tight if* $|\Sigma| \geq 10$.

Proof. The desired upper bound follows from the upper bound $\frac{3}{4}2^{m+n}$ for NFA-to-DFA trade-off for concatenation [13, Theorem 6]. For tightness, consider the ten-letter alphabet $\Sigma = \{a, b, c, d, e, f, m, g, o, s\}$. Let $A = ([1, n], \Sigma, \cdot, 1, \{n\})$ be the n-state NFA in which the transitions are as follows:

$i \cdot a = \{i + 1\}$ if $i \leq n - 1$,
$n \cdot b = \{n\}$,
$1 \cdot c = \{1\}, 2 \cdot c = \{2, n\}, n \cdot c = \{2\}$,
$1 \cdot d = \{1, n\}, 2 \cdot d = \{2\}, n \cdot d = \{n\}$,
$2 \cdot e = \{2, 3\}, i \cdot e = \{i\}$ if $i \neq 2$,
$1 \cdot f = \{1, 3\}, i \cdot f = \{i\}$ if $i \neq 1$,
$1 \cdot m = \{1\}, 2 \cdot m = \{2\}, i \cdot m = \{i + 1\}$ if $3 \leq i \leq n - 2, n \cdot m = \{n\}$,
$2 \cdot g = \{1, 2\}, i \cdot g = \{i\}$ if $i \neq 2$,
$2 \cdot o = \emptyset, i \cdot o = \{i\}$ if $i \neq 2$,
$1 \cdot s = \{2\}, 2 \cdot s = \{1\}, i \cdot s = \{i\}$ if $i \notin \{1, 2\}$,

and all the remaining transitions go to the empty set. Figure 5 illustrates the transitions in A.

Construct the NFA A^2 for the language $L(A)^2$ from two copies of A in which the state set is $Q \cup \{\bar{q} \mid q \in Q\}$, the initial state is 1, and the unique final state is $\bar{n}$, by adding the transitions $(n - 1, a, \bar{1})$, $(2, c, \bar{1})$, $(1, d, \bar{1})$, and $(n, \sigma, \bar{1})$ for each σ in $\{b, d, e, f, m, g, o, s\}$. In the NFA A^2, each singleton set is co-reachable via a string in $a^* \cup a^* b a^*$. It follows that all subsets in the subset automaton $\mathcal{D}(A^2)$ are pairwise distinguishable, as shown in the proof of Theorem 4. Hence we only need to show that the subset automaton has $\frac{3}{4}2^{2n}$ reachable states.

To simplify the notation, we write the states of this subset automaton as pairs (S, T) where $S, T \subseteq [1, n]$ and (S, T) represents the subset $S \cup \{\bar{q} \mid q \in T\}$ in the subset automaton. In this notation, we need not to use different names for

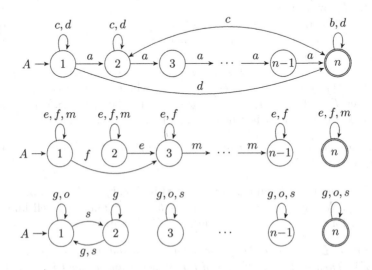

Fig. 5. The transitions in the NFA A.

Table 1. Reachability of different types of pairs of sets.

$S_1 \backslash T_1$	$\emptyset$	$\{1\}$	$\{2\}$	$\{1,2\}$	$S_1 \backslash T_1$	$\{1\}$	$\{1,2\}$
$\emptyset$	oso	o	os	osg	$\{n\}$	o	os
$\{1\}$	so	sgo	s	sg	$\{1,n\}$	so	s
$\{2\}$	sos	ε	$sgos$	sgs	$\{2,n\}$	ε	ss
$\{1,2\}$	$sosg$	g	gs	gsg	$\{1,2,n\}$	g	gs

states in the first and second copy. It follows from the construction of A^2 that in $\mathcal{D}(A^2)$, the transition function works for each symbol σ as follows:

$$(S,T) \circ \sigma = \begin{cases} (S \cdot \sigma, T \cdot \sigma), & \text{if } S \cdot \sigma \cap F = \emptyset; \\ (S \cdot \sigma, \{1\} \cup (T \cdot \sigma)), & \text{if } S \cdot \sigma \cap F \neq \emptyset. \end{cases}$$

Our first aim is to reach four specific pairs using symbols a, c, d:

$$\rightarrow (\{1\}, \emptyset) \xrightarrow{a^{n-1}c} (\{2\}, \{1\}) \xrightarrow{d} (\{2\}, \{1,n\}),$$

$$(\{2\}, \{1\}) \xrightarrow{c} (\{2,n\}, \{1\}) \xrightarrow{d} (\{2,n\}, \{1,n\}).$$

From $(\{2\}, \{1\})$ we can reach each pair $(\{2\} \cup S, \{1\} \cup T)$ with $S, T \subseteq [3, n-1]$ since we always can add state 3 either from state 2 or 1 by symbols e and f, respectively, and we can shift states $3, 4, \ldots, n-2$ to states $4, 5, \ldots, n-1$ by symbol m. Then we can reach each pair $(S_1 \cup S, T_1 \cup T)$ with $S_1, T_1 \subseteq \{1,2\}$ using symbols g (generate 1 from 2), o (omit 2), and s (swap 1 and 2) as shown in Table 1 (left).

From $(\{2\}, \{1,n\})$, we can reach each pair $(S, T \cup \{n\})$ with $S, T \subseteq [1, n-1]$ in the same way since $n \cdot \sigma = \{n\}$ if $\sigma \in \{e, f, m, g, o, s\}$.

From $(\{2,n\}, \{1\})$, we can reach each pair $(\{2,n\} \cup S, \{1\} \cup T)$ with $S, T \subseteq [3, n-1]$ using e, f, m, and then we reach $(S_1 \cup S, T_1 \cup T)$ as in Table 1 (right); recall that $n \in S$ implies $1 \in T$ for each pair (S, T).

Finally, from $(\{2,n\}, \{1,n\})$, we can reach each pair $(\{2,n\} \cup S, \{1,n\} \cup T)$ with $S, T \subseteq [3, n-1]$ using e, f, m, and then we continue in the same way as in the previous case to reach $(S_1 \cup S, T_1 \cup T \cup \{n\})$.

The four cases give reachability of $2^{n-1}2^{n-1} + 2^{n-1}2^{n-1} + 2^{n-1}2^{n-2} + 2^{n-1}2^{n-2}$ states. This gives the desired lower bound $\frac{3}{4}2^{2n}$. □

5   Syntactic Complexity and Square Root

For any language L over Σ, an equivalence relation $\approx_L$ on Σ^* is the *syntactic congruence* [3,17] if, for all x, y in Σ^*,

$$x \approx_L y \text{ if and only if } uxv \in L \Leftrightarrow uyv \in L \text{ for all } u, v \in \Sigma^*.$$

The semigroup $\Sigma^+/\approx_L$ of equivalence classes of the relation $\approx_L$ is the *syntactic semigroup* of L. The *syntactic complexity* of L is the cardinality of its syntactic semigroup.

In a DFA, each string w in Σ^* induces a transformation on the state set given by $q \mapsto q \cdot w$. It is known that the syntactic complexity of L is equal to the number of transformations induced by all non-empty strings in the minimal DFA accepting L. It follows that if L is accepted by an n-state DFA, then the syntactic complexity of L is at most n^n. This upper bound is met by a ternary DFA whose symbols perform the cyclic permutation, transposition, and contraction [16](5) since these three transformations are the generators of the transition semigroup.

In an NFA with state set $[1, n]$, each symbol sends a state in $[1, n]$ to a subset of $[1, n]$. Hence each symbol can be described by an n-tuple of subsets of $[1, n]$. Thus the largest alphabet containing all possible symbols is of size 2^{n^2}. The following theorem provides a tight upper bound on the syntactic complexity of a language represented by an NFA.

Theorem 7. *Let L be a language over Σ accepted by an n-state NFA. Then the syntactic complexity of L is at most 2^{n^2}. This upper bound is tight if $|\Sigma| = 2^{n^2}$.*

Proof. Let $A = (Q, \Sigma, \cdot, s, F)$ be an n-state NFA accepting L. Then in A, each string x performs a mapping from Q to 2^Q given by $q \mapsto q \cdot x$. If two strings x and y perform the same mapping, then $S \cdot x = S \cdot y$ for each subset S of Q. Now, if $u, v \in \Sigma^*$, then $s \cdot uxv = (s \cdot u) \cdot x \cdot v = (s \cdot u) \cdot y \cdot v = s \cdot uyv$, hence both uxv and uyv are either accepted or rejected, and therefore $x \approx_L y$. Since the number of mappings from Q to 2^Q is 2^{n^2}, the upper bound on the syntactic complexity of L follows.

For tightness, consider NFA $([1, n], \Sigma, \cdot, 1, \{n\})$ where $\Sigma = \{a_{S_1, S_2, \ldots, S_n} \mid S_i \subseteq [1, n] \text{ for each } i\}$ and $i \cdot a_{S_1, S_2, \ldots, S_n} = S_i$ for each state i and each symbol in Σ. Denote by a the symbol $a_{\{2\}, \{3\}, \ldots, \{n\}, \{1\}}$ that maps i to $\{i + 1\}$ if $i \neq n$ and it maps n to $\{1\}$. Let b and c be two distinct symbols in Σ. Then there is a state i such that $i \cdot b \neq i \cdot c$ and, without loss of generality, let $q \in (i \cdot b) \setminus (i \cdot c)$. Set $u = a^{i-1}$ and $v = a^{n-q}$. Then the string ubv is accepted by A through an accepting computation $1 \xrightarrow{u} i \xrightarrow{b} q \xrightarrow{v} n$ and ucv is rejected since $q \notin i \cdot c$ and v is accepted only from q. It follows that b and c are in distinct equivalence classes of $\approx_L$, which gives the desired lower bound.   □

The *square root* of a language L is the language
$$\sqrt{L} = \{w \mid ww \in L\}.$$

If L is accepted by a DFA $A = ([1, n], \Sigma, \cdot, 1, F)$, then $\sqrt{L}$ is accepted by the DFA $([1, n]^n, \Sigma, \circ, (1, 2, \ldots, n), F')$ where $(i_1, i_2, \ldots, i_n) \circ a = (i_1 \cdot a, i_2 \cdot a, \ldots, i_n \cdot a)$ and $F' = \{(i_1, i_2, \ldots, i_n) \mid i_{i_1} \in F\}$ [16](7). This provides an upper bound n^n on the state complexity of square root, and it is known that the tight upper bound is $n^n - \binom{n}{2}$ [5, Theorem 3]. Now, we consider the NFA-to-DFA trade-off.

Theorem 8. *Let L be a language over an alphabet Σ accepted by an n-state NFA. Then $\mathrm{sc}(\sqrt{L}) \leq 2^{n^2}$. A lower bound $2^{n^2 - n}$ can be met if $|\Sigma| = 2^{n^2}$.*

Proof. Let L be accepted by an NFA $A = ([1, n], \Sigma, \cdot, 1, F)$. We show that $\sqrt{L}$ is accepted by the DFA $A' = ((2^{[1,n]})^n, \Sigma, \circ, (\{1\}, \{2\}, \ldots, \{n\}), F')$ where

$$(S_1, S_2, \ldots, S_n) \circ a = (S_1 \cdot a, S_2 \cdot a, \ldots, S_n \cdot a) \text{ for each } S_i \subseteq [1, n] \text{ and } a \in \Sigma,$$
$$F' = \{(S_1, S_2, \ldots, S_n) \mid (\bigcup_{i \in S_1} S_i) \cap F \neq \emptyset\},$$

that is, an n-tuple of subsets of $[1, n]$ is final in A' if it has a final state in a set whose index is given by a state in the set S_1; notice that each n-tuple with $S_1 = \emptyset$ is not final. A string w is accepted by A' if and only if $\bigcup_{i \in \{1\} \cdot w} (\{i\} \cdot w) \cap F \neq \emptyset$ which holds if and only if ww is accepted by A. Hence A' accepts $\sqrt{L}$, which gives the desired upper bound 2^{n^2}.

To get lower bound $2^{n^2 - n}$, consider the NFA $A = ([1, n], \Sigma, \cdot, 1, [1, n])$ where $\Sigma = \{a_{S_1, S_2, \ldots, S_n} \mid S_i \subseteq [1, n] \text{ for each } i\}$ is an alphabet which contains all possible symbols, and we have $i \cdot a_{S_1, S_2, \ldots, S_n} = S_i$ for each i and each symbol. Let A' be the DFA for $\sqrt{L(A)}$ described above. Then each state $(S_1, S_2, \ldots, S_n)$ in A' is reached from the initial state $(\{1\}, \{2\}, \ldots, \{n\})$ by symbol $a_{S_1, S_2, \ldots, S_n}$.

Let us show that all states with $S_1 = [1, n]$ are pairwise distinguishable. Let $([1, n], S_2, S_3, \ldots, S_n)$ and $([1, n], T_2, T_3, \ldots, T_n)$ be two distinct states. Then, without loss of generality, we have $s \in S_k \setminus T_k$ for some $k \geq 2$ and $s \in [1, n]$. Then the symbol $a_{E_1, E_2, \ldots, E_n}$ with $E_i = \emptyset$ if $i \neq s$ and $E_s = \{k\}$ sends the first n-tuple to an n-tuple $(\{k\}, S'_2, S'_3, \ldots, S'_k = \{k\}, S'_{k+1}, \ldots, S'_n)$ and it sends the second n-tuple to an n-tuple $(\{k\}, T'_2, T'_3, \ldots, T'_k = \emptyset, T'_{k+1}, \ldots, T'_n)$. Hence this symbol is accepted from the first n-tuple and rejected from the second one. This gives $(2^n)^{n-1} = 2^{n^2 - n}$ reachable and pairwise distinguishable states. □

We can prove that in the lower bound example from the previous proof, in which we have $F = [1, n]$, the number of reachable and pairwise distinguishable states is $\sum_{k=0}^n \binom{n}{k} (1 + (2^k - 1)2^{n-k})^{n-1}$, which seems to be at least $2^{n^2 - 1}$, so the upper bound 2^{n^2} would be asymptotically tight.

Conjecture 9. Let L be a language over Σ accepted by an NFA with n states. Then $\mathrm{sc}(\sqrt{L}) \leq \sum_{k=0}^n \binom{n}{k} (1 + (2^k - 1)2^{n-k})^{n-1}$. This bound is tight if $|\Sigma| = 2^{n^2}$.

6   Conclusions

We investigated the NFA-to-DFA trade-off for some operations on regular languages, continuing the research from [13]. Our results are summarized in Table 2 which also recalls the results from [13], and compares NFA-to-DFA trade-offs to the known results on the state complexity, that is, DFA-to-DFA trade-off, of the corresponding operations. The table also shows the size of alphabets that we used to describe our witnesses.

For Boolean operations and concatenation, we improved known results by decreasing the size of the alphabet used to describe witnesses from 4 to 3. We also showed that the upper bounds for these operations are asymptotically tight in the binary case. Finally, we obtained a tight upper bound 2^{n^2} on syntactic complexity of a language represented by an n-state NFA.

Since every unary n-state NFA can be simulated by a DFA of $2^{\Theta(\sqrt{n \ln n})}$ states, no our upper bound can be met in the unary case. We believe that the NFA-to-DFA trade-off for star in the unary case is $(n-1)^2 + 2$, while the trade-offs for the other operations in the unary case remain open. A smaller alphabet for square root would be of interest as well.

Table 2. The NFA-to-DFA trade-offs and state complexities of regular operations.

operation	NFA-to-DFA	$|\Sigma|$	Source	DFA-to-DFA	
union	2^{m+n}	3	Thm. 1	mn	[16]
symmetric difference	2^{m+n}	3	Thm. 1	mn	[2]
intersection	$2^{m+n} - 2^m - 2^n + 2$	3	Thm. 1	mn	[22]
difference	$2^{m+n} - 2^n + 2$	3	Thm. 1	mn	[2]
cut	$2^{m-1}(2^n + 1)$	4	Thm. 3	$mn - n + m$	[6]
concatenation	$\frac{3}{4}2^{m+n}$	3	Thm. 4	$m2^n - 2^{n-1}$	[16]
square	$\frac{3}{4}2^{2n}$	10	Thm. 6	$n2^n - 2^{n-1}$	[18]
square root	$2^{n^2-n} \le \cdot \le 2^{n^2}$	2^{n^2}	Thm. 8	$n^n - \binom{n}{2}$	[5]
complementation	2^n	2	[13, Thm. 3]	n	folklore
reversal	2^n	2	[13, Thm. 4]	2^n	[15]
star	2^n	2	[13, Thm. 5]	$\frac{3}{4}2^n$	[16]
shuffle	2^{mn}	4	[13, Thm. 9]	$\Theta(2^{mn})$	[4]
left quotient	2^m	2	[13, Thm. 10]	$2^m - 1$	[22]
right quotient	2^m	2	[13, Thm. 10]	m	folklore

Acknowledgment. We would like to thank Ivana Krajňáková for her wide and long-term contribution to some parts of this research.

References

1. Berglund, M., Björklund, H., Drewes, F., van der Merwe, B., Watson, B.W.: Cuts in regular expressions. In: Béal, M., Carton, O. (eds.) DLT 2013. LNCS, vol. 7907, pp. 70–81. Springer (2013). https://doi.org/10.1007/978-3-642-38771-5_8
2. Brzozowski, J.A.: Quotient complexity of regular languages. J. Autom. Lang. Comb. 15(1/2), 71–89 (2010). https://doi.org/10.25596/jalc-2010-071
3. Brzozowski, J.A., Szykuła, M., Ye, Y.: Syntactic complexity of regular ideals. Theory Comput. Syst. **62**(5), 1175–1202 (2017). https://doi.org/10.1007/s00224-017-9803-8
4. Câmpeanu, C., Salomaa, K., Yu, S.: Tight lower bound for the state complexity of shuffle of regular languages. J. Autom. Lang. Comb. **7**(3), 303–310 (2002). https://doi.org/10.25596/jalc-2002-303
5. Caron, P., Hamel-De le Court, E., Luque, J.G., Patrou, B.: New tools for state complexity. Discret. Math. Theor. Comput. Sci. **22**(1) (2020). https://doi.org/10.23638/DMTCS-22-1-9

6. Drewes, F., Holzer, M., Jakobi, S., van der Merwe, B.: Tight bounds for cut-operations on deterministic finite automata. Fundam. Inform. **155**(1–2), 89–110 (2017). https://doi.org/10.3233/FI-2017-1577
7. Holzer, M., Hospodár, M.: The range of state complexities of languages resulting from the cut operation. In: Martín-Vide, C., Okhotin, A., Shapira, D. (eds.) LATA 2019. LNCS, vol. 11417, pp. 190–202. Springer (2019). https://doi.org/10.1007/978-3-030-13435-8_14
8. Holzer, M., Kutrib, M.: Nondeterministic descriptional complexity of regular languages. Int. J. Found. Comput. Sci. **14**(6), 1087–1102 (2003). https://doi.org/10.1142/S0129054103002199
9. Hopcroft, J.E., Ullman, J.D.: Introduction to Automata Theory. Addison-Wesley, Languages and Computation (1979)
10. Hospodár, M., Olejár, V.: The cut operation in subclasses of convex languages (extended abstract). In: Caron, P., Mignot, L. (eds.) CIAA 2022. LNCS, vol. 13266, pp. 152–164. Springer (2022). https://doi.org/10.1007/978-3-031-07469-1_12
11. Jirásek, J.Š., Jirásková, G., Szabari, A.: Operations on self-verifying finite automata. In: Beklemishev, L.D., Musatov, D.V. (eds.) CSR 2015. LNCS, vol. 9139, pp. 231–261. Springer (2015). https://doi.org/10.1007/978-3-319-20297-6_16
12. Jirásek, J., Jr., Jirásková, G., Šebej, J.: Operations on unambiguous finite automata. Int. J. Found. Comput. Sci. **29**(5), 861–876 (2018). https://doi.org/10.1142/S012905411842008X
13. Jirásková, G., Krajňáková, I.: NFA-to-DFA trade-off for regular operations. In: Hospodár, M., Jirásková, G., Konstantinidis, S. (eds.) DCFS 2019. LNCS, vol. 11612, pp. 184–196. Springer (2019). https://doi.org/10.1007/978-3-030-23247-4_14
14. Jirásková, G., Okhotin, A.: On the state complexity of operations on two-way finite automata. Inf. Comput. **253**, 36–63 (2017). https://doi.org/10.1016/j.ic.2016.12.007
15. Jirásková, G., Šebej, J.: Reversal of binary regular languages. Theoret. Comput. Sci. **449**, 85–92 (2012). https://doi.org/10.1016/j.tcs.2012.05.008
16. Maslov, A.N.: Estimates of the number of states of finite automata. Soviet Math. Doklady **11**, 1373–1375 (1970)
17. Myhill, J.: Finite automata and representation of events. Wright Air Development Center Technical Report, pp. 57–624 (1957)
18. Rampersad, N.: The state complexity of L^2 and L^k. Inf. Process. Lett. **98**(6), 231–234 (2006). https://doi.org/10.1016/j.ipl.2005.06.011
19. Salomaa, A., Salomaa, K., Yu, S.: State complexity of combined operations. Theor. Comput. Sci. **383**(2–3), 140–152 (2007). https://doi.org/10.1016/j.tcs.2007.04.015
20. Sipser, M.: Introduction to the theory of computation. Cengage Learning (2012)
21. Yu, S.: Regular languages. In: Rozenberg, G., Salomaa, A. (eds.) Handbook of Formal Languages, vol. 1: Word, Language, Grammar, pp. 41–110. Springer (1997). https://doi.org/10.1007/978-3-642-59136-5_2
22. Yu, S., Zhuang, Q., Salomaa, K.: The state complexities of some basic operations on regular languages. Theor. Comput. Sci. **125**(2), 315–328 (1994). https://doi.org/10.1016/0304-3975(92)00011-F

The Word Problem for Finitary Automaton Groups

Maximilian Kotowsky[1] and Jan Philipp Wächter[2]([⊠])

[1] Insitut für Formale Methoden der Informatik (FMI), Universität Stuttgart,
Universitätsstraße 38, 70569 Stuttgart, Germany
`kotowsmn@studi.informatik.uni-stuttgart.de`
[2] Dipartimento di Matematica, Politecnico di Milano, Piazza Leonardo da Vinci, 32,
20133 Milano, Italy
`j.ph.waechter@gmail.com`

Abstract. A finitary automaton group is a group generated by an invertible, deterministic finite-state letter-to-letter transducer whose only cycles are self-loops at an identity state. We show that, for this presentation of finite groups, the uniform word problem is coNP-complete. Here, the input consists of a finitary automaton together with a finite state sequence and the question is whether the sequence acts trivially on all input words. Additionally, we also show that the respective compressed word problem, where the state sequence is given as a straight-line program, is PSPACE-complete. In both cases, we give a direct reduction from the satisfiablity problem for (quantified) boolean formulae.

Keywords: Automaton Group · Word Problem · Finitary · Activity

1 Introduction

There are many connections between groups and automata (see e. g. [20]). In this article, we are mostly concerned with automaton groups, where the term automaton usually refers to an invertible, deterministic finite-state letter-to-letter transducer. In such an automaton, every state q induces a function mapping an input word u to the output word obtained by starting in q and following the path labeled by u in the input. Since the automaton is invertible, every such function is a bijection and the closure under composition of these functions (and their inverses) forms a group. This is the group generated by the automaton and any group arising in this way is an automaton group. Not every group is an automaton group but the class of automaton groups contains some very interesting examples (see e. g. [4]). Probably the most famous one is Grigochuk's group, which – among other interesting properties – was the historically first group of intermediate growth (i. e. the numbers of elements that can be written as a word of length at most n over the generators grows slower than any exponential function but faster than any polynomial; see [13] for an introduction to this topic).

J. Ph. Wächter: The second author is funded by the Deutsche Forschungsgemeinschaft (DFG, German Research Foundation) - 492814705.

© IFIP International Federation for Information Processing 2023
Published by Springer Nature Switzerland AG 2023
H. Bordihn et al. (Eds.): DCFS 2023, LNCS 13918, pp. 94–108, 2023.
https://doi.org/10.1007/978-3-031-34326-1_7

These interesting examples also led to an investigation of the algorithmic properties of automaton groups, where the presentation using automata is an alternative to the classical one using (typically finitely many) generators and relations. It turns out that this presentation is still quite powerful as many decision problems remain undecidable. For example, it is known that there is an automaton group with an undecidable conjugacy problem [22] (given two group elements, check whether they are conjugate) and one with an undecidable order problem [3, 12] (given a group element, check whether it has finite order). Decidability of the finiteness problem for automaton groups (given an automaton, check whether its generated group is finite) is still an open problem but the corresponding problem for semigroups has been shown to be undecidable [11].

The word problem (given a group element, check whether it is the neutral element), however, seems to have a special role for automaton groups. It is well known to be decidable and a guess and check approach also yields that the problem can be solved in non-deterministic linear space, even in the uniform case (where the generating automaton is also part of the input) [10, 21]. Regarding lower bounds, Armin Weiß and the second author proved that there is an automaton group with a PSPACE-complete word problem [23].

In this work, we will apply similar ideas to investigate the complexity of the word problem for the lowest level of the activity hierarchy for automaton groups introduced by Sidki [19]. This hierarchy classifies automaton groups based on the structure of the cycles in the generating automaton. At the lowest level, which belongs to the class of finitary automata and finitary automaton groups, the only cycles are the self-loops at an identity state (i. e. a state where the output word is always the same as the input word). It turns out that this class coincides with the class of (all) finite groups.

On the next level, the class of bounded automata and bounded automaton groups, every path in the automaton may contain at most one cycle (not counting self-loops at an identity state). This class still seems "finite enough" for many problems to be decidable. For example, the finiteness problem [7] and the order problem [8] are decidable and there are positive results on the conjugacy problem [8]; the word problem of a bounded automaton group can be solved in deterministic logarithmic space [2, 17] and its complement is an ET0L language [6].

We will be interested in the finitary level. As we have discussed, studying the word problem of these groups is the same as studying the word problem of arbitrary finite groups. It is well known that a group is finite if and only if its word problem (i. e. the formal language of words over the generators representing the neutral element) is regular. While this does not settle the precise complexity for the individual groups entirely, we will approach this setting from a different perspective. We will consider the uniform word problem, where the group is part of the input in a suitable presentation. Typical such presentations include, for example, the classical one with generators and relations, Caley graphs and tables or presenting the elements as matrices or permutations (where the representation as permutations may be considered a special case of the representation as matrices). For Cayley tables, the problem can be solved in deterministic logarithmic space (by iterated lookups in the table) and the same is true for matrix representations [15]. Since the word problem of every non-solvable finite group is NC^1-complete [1], we immediately get a lower bound for any group representation. For permutations, there are also lower bound results regarding deterministic logarithmic space [9].

Our presentation of choice is that of using an automaton (in the way described above). Here, we will show that the uniform word problem is coNP-complete by giving a direct reduction from the satisfiability problem for boolean formulae. Then, we will show that the uniform compressed word problem, where the input state sequence is not given directly but only compressed in the form of a context-free grammar (or, more precisely, a straight-line program), is PSPACE-complete and, thus, exponentially harder (under common complexity theoretic assumptions). This reflects a similar (provable) exponential gap in the general case [23]. We prove this latter result by giving a direct reduction from the satisfiability problem for quantified boolean formulae. This approach of simulating logical formulae in automata is similar to the techniques used in [23] and we hope that the general idea can be extended to further settings, for example, to obtain lower bound results for further levels of the activity hierarchy. The underlying idea is to use certain commutators for simulating logical conjunctions. This is often attributed to Barrington, who used this approach to show the above-mentioned result on the NC^1-completeness of the word problem of non-solvable finite groups [1] (see [2] for more results in that direction). However, there are also similar ideas predating Barrington (see [23] for references).

2   Preliminaries

Logic. For this paper, we will require some basic knowledge about propositional and first-order logic. We use $\bot$ to denote a *false* truth value and $\top$ to denote the truth value *true*. We let $\mathbb{B} = \{\bot, \top\}$ and may evaluate the truth value $\mathcal{A}(\varphi)$ of a formula φ over the *variables* $\mathbb{X}$ under an *assignment* $\mathcal{A} : \mathbb{X} \to \mathbb{B}$ in the usual way. If this evaluates to $\top$, we say that $\mathcal{A}$ *satisfies* φ and φ is *satisfiable* if it is satisfied by some assignment. A *literal* is either a variable x or the negation $\neg x$ of a variable. In the first case, the literal is *positive* and, in the second case, it is *negative*. A *clause* is a disjunction $\bigvee_{i=1}^{n} L_i$ of literals L_i. A conjunction $\bigwedge_{k=1}^{K} C_k$ of clauses C_k is a formula in *conjunctive normal form* (*CNF* for short). If all the clauses contain exactly 3 distinct literals, we say that the formula is in *3-conjunctive normal form* (*3-CNF* for short).

Words and Group Operations. An alphabet is a non-empty, finite set Σ. A finite sequence $w = a_1 \ldots a_\ell$ of elements $a_1, \ldots, a_\ell \in \Sigma$ is a *word* and its *length* is $|w| = \ell$. The unique word of length 0 is denoted by ε and the set of all words over Σ is Σ^*, which forms a monoid whose operation is the concatenation of words (and whose neutral element is ε).

We will often work with words in the context of generating a group. In this case, we assume that, for an alphabet Q, we have a disjoint copy $Q^{-1} = \{q^{-1} \mid$

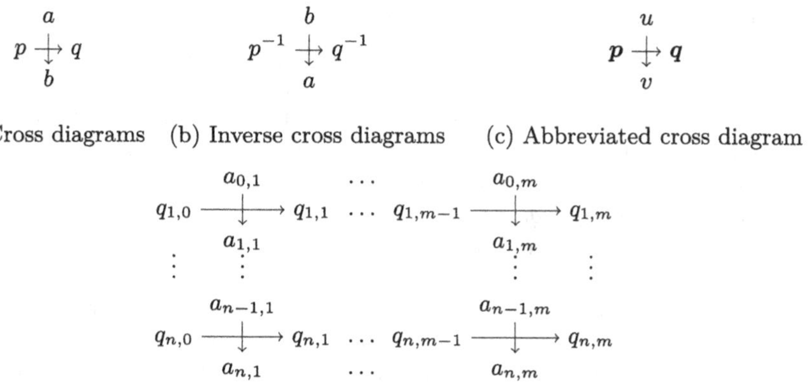

$$a$$
$$p \xrightarrow{} q$$
$$b$$

$$b$$
$$p^{-1} \xrightarrow{} q^{-1}$$
$$a$$

$$u$$
$$p \xrightarrow{} q$$
$$v$$

(a) Cross diagrams (b) Inverse cross diagrams (c) Abbreviated cross diagram

$$
\begin{array}{ccccc}
& a_{0,1} & \cdots & a_{0,m} & \\
q_{1,0} \xrightarrow{} q_{1,1} & \cdots & q_{1,m-1} \xrightarrow{} q_{1,m} & \\
& a_{1,1} & & a_{1,m} & \\
\vdots & \vdots & & \vdots & \vdots \\
& a_{n-1,1} & & a_{n-1,m} & \\
q_{n,0} \xrightarrow{} q_{n,1} & \cdots & q_{n,m-1} \xrightarrow{} q_{n,m} & \\
& a_{n,1} & \cdots & a_{n,m} &
\end{array}
$$

(d) Multiple crosses combined in one diagram

Fig. 1. Single, inverted, combined and abbreviated cross diagrams

$q \in Q\}$ of formal inverse letters. For the set of words over such positive and negative letters, we write $Q^{\pm *} = (Q \cup Q^{-1})^*$ and we may extend the notation q^{-1} to words by letting $(q_1 \ldots q_\ell)^{-1} = q_\ell^{-1} \ldots q_1^{-1}$ where we additionally use the convention $(q^{-1})^{-1} = q$. We say a group G is *generated* by Q if there is a monoid homomorphism $\pi : Q^{\pm *} \to G$ with $\pi(q^{-1}) = \pi(q)^{-1}$. In this context, we write $\boldsymbol{p} = \boldsymbol{q}$ *in* G for $\pi(\boldsymbol{p}) = \pi(\boldsymbol{q})$ (where $\boldsymbol{p}, \boldsymbol{q} \in Q^{\pm *}$) and also $\boldsymbol{p} = g$ *in* G if $\pi(\boldsymbol{p}) = g$. So, for example, we write $\boldsymbol{p} = \mathbb{1}$ in G if $\pi(\boldsymbol{p})$ is the neutral element of the group G, which we usually denote by $\mathbb{1}$.

In addition to taking the inverse, we lift further group operations to words. In analogy to the *conjugation* $g^k = k^{-1}gk$ of some group element $g \in G$ by another one $k \in G$, we also write $\boldsymbol{q}^{\boldsymbol{p}}$ for the word $\boldsymbol{q}^{\boldsymbol{p}} = \boldsymbol{p}^{-1}\boldsymbol{q}\boldsymbol{p}$ (where $\boldsymbol{p}, \boldsymbol{q} \in Q^{\pm *}$). Note that this notation is compatible with the conjugation as we have $\pi(\boldsymbol{q}^{\boldsymbol{p}}) = \pi(\boldsymbol{q})^{\pi(\boldsymbol{p})}$. We also do the same for the *commutator* $[h, g] = h^{-1}g^{-1}hg$ of two group elements $g, h \in G$ and write $[\boldsymbol{q}, \boldsymbol{p}]$ for the word $[\boldsymbol{q}, \boldsymbol{p}] = \boldsymbol{q}^{-1}\boldsymbol{p}^{-1}\boldsymbol{q}\boldsymbol{p}$. Again, this is compatible with the projection $\pi: \pi([\boldsymbol{q}, \boldsymbol{p}]) = [\pi(\boldsymbol{q}), \pi(\boldsymbol{p})]$.

Automata and Automaton Groups. In the context of this paper, an automaton is a finite state letter-to-letter transducer. Formally, an *automaton* $\mathcal{T}$ is a triple (Q, Σ, δ) where Q is a finite, non-empty set of *states*, Σ is the (input and output) *alphabet* of $\mathcal{T}$ and $\delta \subseteq Q \times \Sigma \times \Sigma \times Q$ is the *transition* relation. In this context, we usually write $p \xrightarrow{a/b} q$ for the tuple $(p, a, b, q) \in Q \times \Sigma \times \Sigma \times Q$. This is a transition *starting* in p, *ending* in q with *input* a and *output* b.

An automaton $\mathcal{T} = (Q, \Sigma, \delta)$ is *deterministic* and *complete* if we have $d_{p,a} = |\{p \xrightarrow{a/b} q \mid b \in \Sigma, q \in Q\}| = 1$ for all $p \in Q$ and $a \in \Sigma$. It is additionally *invertible* if we also have $d'_{p,b} = |\{p \xrightarrow{a/b} q \mid a \in \Sigma, q \in Q\}| = 1$ for all $p \in Q$ and $b \in \Sigma$. A deterministic, complete and invertible automaton is a $\mathscr{G}$-*automaton*.

Another way of indicating that we have a transition $p \xrightarrow{a/b} q \in \delta$ is to use the cross diagram in Fig. 1a. Multiple cross diagrams may be combined into a larger one. For example, the cross diagram in Fig. 1d indicates $q_{i,j-1} \xrightarrow{a_{i-1,j}/a_{i,j}} q_{i,j} \in \delta$

for all $1 \leq i \leq n$ and $1 \leq j \leq m$. Typically, we will omit unnecessary intermediate states if we do not need to name them. Additionally, we also allow abbreviations in the form of words (instead of only single letters) in the input and output and state sequences (i. e. words over Q) on the left and right. Note, however, that here the right-most state of the sequence is considered to be the first state,[1] which results in the abbreviated cross diagram in Fig. 1c for $\boldsymbol{p} = q_{n,0} \cdots q_{1,0}$, $u = a_{0,1} \cdots a_{0,m}$, $v = a_{n,1} \cdots a_{n,m}$ and $\boldsymbol{q} = q_{n,m} \cdots q_{1,m}$.

For a deterministic and complete automaton $\mathcal{T} = (Q, \Sigma, \delta)$, there exists exactly one cross diagram of the form in Fig. 1c for every $\boldsymbol{p} \in Q^*$ and $u \in \Sigma^*$. If $\mathcal{T}$ is additionally invertible (i. e. it is a $\mathcal{G}$-automaton), we define that we have the cross diagram in Fig. 1b for $p, q \in Q$ and $a, b \in \Sigma$ whenever we have the one from Fig. 1a. Note that we have flipped the cross diagram along its horizontal axis and inverted the states. In this case, the cross diagram in Fig. 1c uniquely exists for all $\boldsymbol{p} \in Q^{\pm*}$ and all $u \in \Sigma^*$ (despite the additional states from Q^{-1}).

This allows us to define a left action of $Q^{\pm*}$ on Σ^* where the action of $\boldsymbol{q} \in Q^{\pm*}$ on a word $u \in \Sigma^*$ is given by $\boldsymbol{q} \circ u = v$ where v is uniquely obtained from the cross diagram in Fig. 1c (the empty state sequence acts as the identity on all words by convention). The reader may verify that we indeed have $\boldsymbol{q}^{-1}\boldsymbol{q} \circ u = u = \boldsymbol{q}\boldsymbol{q}^{-1} \circ u$ with our definition of inverting cross diagrams.

For two state sequences $\boldsymbol{p}, \boldsymbol{q} \in Q^{\pm*}$ of a $\mathcal{G}$-automaton $\mathcal{T} = (Q, \Sigma, \delta)$, let

$$\boldsymbol{p} =_{\mathcal{T}} \boldsymbol{q} \iff \forall u \in \Sigma^* : \boldsymbol{p} \circ u = \boldsymbol{q} \circ u.$$

It turns out that this relation is a congruence, which allows us to consider the monoid $Q^{\pm*}/=_{\mathcal{T}}$ formed by its classes. In fact, this monoid has a group structure (where the class of $\boldsymbol{q}^{-1}$ is the inverse of the class of $\boldsymbol{q}$) and this is the *group generated* by $\mathcal{T}$. Any group generated by some $\mathcal{G}$-automaton is called an *automaton group*.

We use the common graphical depiction of automata, which results in a $\Sigma \times \Sigma$-labeled finite directed graph. If this graph does not have any cycles except for the a/a labeled self-loops at an identity state,[2] we say that the automaton is *finitary*. The *depth* of a finitary $\mathcal{G}$-automaton is the minimal number d such that, after reading at least d many letters, we are always in the identity state (regardless of where we started). A group generated by a finitary $\mathcal{G}$-automaton is a *finitary* automaton group. Since, with a finitary $\mathcal{G}$-automaton, a state sequence may only act non-trivially on the first d letters (where d is the depth of the generating automaton), a finitary automaton group is necessarily finite. On the other hand, any finite group G is generated by the finitary automaton (G, G, δ) with $\delta = \{g \xrightarrow{h/gh} \mathbb{1} \mid g, h \in G\}$. Thus, studying finitary automaton groups is the same as studying finite groups but we are interested in a certain way of presenting these groups.

Complexity. We need some notions from complexity theory for this paper. For these, we refer the reader to standard textbooks on the topic (such as [18]). We

---

[1] This makes sense as we will later on define a *left* action of the states on the words.

[2] Note that any complete finite automaton must contain a cycle and, therefore, every finitary $\mathcal{G}$-automaton has an identity state.

will encounter the complexity classes NP, CONP, PSPACE as well as many-one LOGSPACE-reductions, which we use for our hardness results.

Balanced Iterated Commutators. In addition to the normal commutator of two elements, we also need certain iterated commutators.

Definition 1 (compare to [23, Definition 3]). *For words* $\alpha, \beta, q_1, \ldots, q_D \in Q^{\pm*}$ *where* $D = 2^d$ *is a power of two, we define* $B_{\beta,\alpha}[q_D, \ldots, q_1]$ *by induction on* d *and let*

$$B_{\beta,\alpha}[q_1] = q_1 \quad and$$

$$B_{\beta,\alpha}[q_D, \ldots, q_1] = \left[B_{\beta,\alpha}[q_D, \ldots, q_{\frac{D}{2}+1}]^\beta, \; B_{\beta,\alpha}[q_{\frac{D}{2}}, \ldots, q_1]^\alpha \right].$$

This also immediately yields an operation $B_{\beta,\alpha}[g_D, \ldots, g_1]$ for group elements $g_1, \ldots, g_D$ using the natural evaluation in the group.

The reason for introducing balanced iterated commutators is that we may use them to simulate a D-ary logical conjunction in groups. The idea here is that the neutral element $\mathbb{1}$ belongs to $\bot$ and all other elements are considered to belong to $\top$. One direction of the simulation then works in any group as we state in the following fact.[3]

Fact 1 (see [23, Fact 4]). *Let a group* G *be generated by the alphabet* Q *and let* $\alpha, \beta, q_1, \ldots, q_D \in Q^{\pm*}$ *for some* $D = 2^d$. *If there is some* $1 \leq i \leq D$ *with* $q_i = \mathbb{1}$ *in* G, *we have* $B_{\beta,\alpha}[q_D, \ldots, q_1] = \mathbb{1}$ *in* G.

We use balanced iterated commutators (instead of the usual ones of the form $[g_D, [g_{D-1}, \ldots, g_1]]$) because their depth remains logarithmic in the number of entries allowing us to compute them in logarithmic space.

Fact 2 (see [23, Lemma 7]). *The balanced commutator* $B_{\beta,\alpha}[q_D, \ldots, q_1]$ *can be computed from* $q_1, \ldots, q_D \in Q^{\pm*}$ *and* $\alpha, \beta \in Q^{\pm*}$ *in logarithmic space.*

Normally, we cannot simply add balanced iterated commutators to cross diagrams and expect the resulting diagram to still hold. However, this is possible if all the entries (and the conjugating elements α and β) act trivially on the input word (which can be seen by a simple induction).

Fact 3 (see [23, Fact 8]). *Let* $\mathcal{T} = (Q, \Sigma, \delta)$ *be a* $\mathscr{G}$-*automaton,* $u \in \Sigma^*$, $\alpha, \beta, q_1, \ldots, q_D \in Q^{\pm*}$ *with* $D = 2^d$ *then the cross diagrams*

$$\begin{array}{ccc} u & u & u \\ q_i \stackrel{}{+}\!\!\!\rightarrow q_i', & \alpha \stackrel{}{+}\!\!\!\rightarrow \alpha', & \beta \stackrel{}{+}\!\!\!\rightarrow \beta' \\ u & u & u \end{array}$$

for all $1 \leq i \leq D$ *imply the cross diagram*

---

[3] The fact can be proved using a simple induction on the structure of the balanced iterated commutators, see [23, Fact 4].

$$B_{\beta,\alpha}[\boldsymbol{q}_D, \dots, \boldsymbol{q}_1] \xrightarrow[u]{\ u\ } B_{\beta',\alpha'}[\boldsymbol{q}'_D, \dots, \boldsymbol{q}'_1] \ .$$

The Group A_5. We have already seen in Fact 1 that the balanced iterated commutator collapses to $\mathbb{1}$ (which corresponds to $\bot$) if one of its entries is equal to $\mathbb{1}$ (i.e. corresponds to $\bot$). This is one of the two directions to use the commutators as logical conjunctions. The other direction, however, does not hold for all elements of all groups. That is why we next look at the group A_5 of even permutations on the five-element set $\{a_1, \dots, a_5\}$. Here, we have a non-identity element which is its own commutator (up to suitable conjugation).[4] This can be used as a conjunction.

Fact 4 (compare to [23, Example 5]). *For the elements $\sigma = (13254)$, $\alpha = (23)(45)$ and $\beta = (245)$ of A_5, we have $\sigma \neq \mathbb{1}$ and $\sigma = [\sigma^\beta, \sigma^\alpha]$.*

Fact 5 (compare to [23, Example 5]). *For $\sigma, \alpha, \beta \in A_5$ from Fact 4, we have $B_{\beta,\alpha}[\sigma, \dots, \sigma] = \sigma$ for any number 2^d of entries.*

Example 1. How can we use Fact 1 and Fact 5 to simulate a D-ary logical conjunction for $D = 2^d$ using A_5? We have already stated that we use $\mathbb{1}$ as the truth value $\bot$ and we will use σ (from Fact 4) as the truth value $\top$. Now, for calculating (or computing) the logical conjunction of $g_1, \dots, g_D \in \{\mathbb{1}, \sigma\} \subseteq A_5$ (where each group element represents $\bot$ or $\top$, accordingly), we use the balanced iterated commutator $B_{\beta,\alpha}[g_D, \dots, g_1]$ (with α and β also referring to the elements from Fact 4). If one of the entries is $\mathbb{1}$ (i.e. represents $\bot$), the entire commutator collapses to $\mathbb{1}$ (again representing $\bot$) by Fact 1. If all of the entries are equal to σ (i.e. they all represent $\top$), the commutator itself will also evaluate to σ by Fact 5 (and, thus, represent $\top$). Thus, it indeed behaves like a logical conjunction.

3   The Word Problem

Theorem 1. *The uniform word problem for finitary automaton groups*

    Input: *a finitary $\mathscr{G}$-automaton $\mathcal{T} = (Q, \Sigma, \delta)$ and*
                  a state sequence $\boldsymbol{q} \in Q^{\pm*}$
    Question: *is $\boldsymbol{q} = \mathbb{1}$ in $\mathscr{G}(\mathcal{T})$?*

is CONP-*complete (under many-one* LOGSPACE-*reductions), even for $|\Sigma| = 5$.*

Proof. That the complement of the problem is in NP follows from a "guess and check" approach: we guess a witness on which $\boldsymbol{q}$ acts non-trivially. The length of the witness is bounded by the depth (and, thus, the size) of $\mathcal{T}$ and the checking can be done state by state.

---

[4] Such an element exists since there are two five-cycles in A_5 whose commutator is again a five-cycle and since five-cycles are always conjugate (see [1, Lemma 1 and 3]).

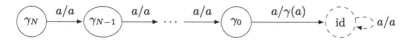

Fig. 2. Schematic depiction of the automaton part for the states $\{\alpha_n, \beta_n \mid 0 \le n \le N\}$. This part exists for $\gamma \in \{\alpha, \beta\}$ (where α and β refer to the elements defined in Fact 4) and the dashed state refers to the already defined identity state. All transitions exist for all $a \in \Sigma$.

For the other direction, we reduce the NP-hard[5] satisfiability problem for boolean formulae in 3-CNF to the complement of the stated problem by using a many-one LOGSPACE-reduction. In other words, we need to map (in logarithmic space) a boolean formula φ in 3-CNF over a set of variables $\mathbb{X} = \{x_1, \dots, x_N\}$ to a finitary $\mathscr{G}$-automaton $\mathcal{T}$ and a state sequence $\mathbf{q}$ such that $\mathbf{q}$ does **not** act as the identity if and only if φ is satisfiable.

As φ is in 3-CNF, we may write $\varphi = \bigwedge_{k=1}^{K} C_k$ where every $C_k = (\neg)x_{n_1} \vee (\neg)x_{n_2} \vee (\neg)x_{n_3}$ with $1 \le n_1 < n_2 < n_3 \le N$ (without loss of generality, no clause may contain a positive and a negative literal of the same variable).

As the alphabet of the automaton $\mathcal{T}$, we use $\Sigma = \{a_1, \dots, a_5\}$. From this set, we take two arbitrary letters and identify them with $\bot$ and $\top$, respectively. This allows us to encode an assignment $\mathcal{A} : \mathbb{X} \to \mathbb{B}$ as the word $\langle \mathcal{A} \rangle = \mathcal{A}(x_N) \dots \mathcal{A}(x_1)$ of length N.[6] Note that a word $w \in \Sigma^*$ of length N encodes an assignment (i. e. $w = \langle \mathcal{A} \rangle$ for some assignment $\mathcal{A}$) if and only if $w \in \{\bot, \top\}^*$.

The general idea is now that we check for every clause C_k whether the first N letters of the input form an encoding of an assignment satisfying C_k. If this is not the case (i. e. if a letter different to $\bot$ and $\top$ appears or if the encoded assignment does not satisfy C_k), we will go into an identity state, which can be thought of as a "fail" state. Otherwise, we end in a state corresponding to σ from Fact 4. Finally, we will use the balanced commutator from Definition 1 to make a conjunction of all these checks.

We will give a precise definition of the automaton $\mathcal{T} = (Q, \Sigma, \delta)$ by describing various parts. The reader may verify that each of these parts may be computed in logarithmic space and that none of them introduces any cycles (except for the self-loops at the identity state). First, we need the mentioned identity state $\mathrm{id} \in Q$ (with the transitions $\{\mathrm{id} \xrightarrow{a/a} \mathrm{id} \mid a \in \Sigma\} \subseteq \delta$).

In order to eventually realize the balanced iterated commutator as a logical conjunction, we also need some technical states for the elements α and β from Fact 4. These states ignore the first N letters and then act as α or β on the $(N+1)$-th letter. For this, we use the states $\{\alpha_n, \beta_n \mid 0 \le n \le N\} \subseteq Q$ with the transitions

$$\{\alpha_n \xrightarrow{a/a} \alpha_{n-1}, \beta_n \xrightarrow{a/a} \beta_{n-1} \mid 0 < n \le N, a \in \Sigma\}$$
$$\cup \{\alpha_0 \xrightarrow{a/\alpha(a)} \mathrm{id}, \beta_0 \xrightarrow{a/\beta(a)} \mathrm{id} \mid a \in \Sigma\} \subseteq \delta.$$

---

[5] This is a well-known classical NP-complete problem, see e. g. [18, Problem 9.5.5].

[6] Note that the right-most letter here corresponds to the first variable x_1. We could have done this the other way round as well but it turns out that this numbering has some technical advantages.

This results in the automaton part graphically depicted in Fig. 2 (for $\gamma \in \{\alpha, \beta\}$). Note that, for $\gamma \in \{\alpha, \beta\}$ and all $1 \leq n \leq N$, we have the cross diagram

$$
\gamma_n \xrightarrow[w]{w} \gamma_0 \xrightarrow[\gamma(a)]{a} \text{id} \tag{1}
$$

for all $w \in \Sigma^*$ of length n and $a \in \Sigma$. In particular, we have the invariant that γ_N acts trivially on the first N letters of all words.

Then, we need states that check whether the first N letters are either $\perp$ or $\top$ and, if this is the case, act like σ (from Fact 4) on the $(N+1)$-th letter. Otherwise, they will go to the identity state as a "fail" state. For this, we use the states $\{\sigma_n \mid 0 \leq n \leq N\} \subseteq Q$ together with the transitions

$$
\left\{ \sigma_n \xrightarrow{\perp/\perp} \sigma_{n-1}, \sigma_n \xrightarrow{\top/\top} \sigma_{n-1}, \sigma_n \xrightarrow{b/b} \text{id} \mid 0 < n \leq N, b \in \Sigma \setminus \{\perp, \top\} \right\}
$$
$$
\cup \left\{ \sigma_0 \xrightarrow{a/\sigma(a)} \text{id} \mid a \in \Sigma \right\} \subseteq \delta.
$$

See Fig. 3 for a graphical representation. By construction, we obtain for all $0 \leq n \leq N$ the cross diagram

$$
\sigma_n \xrightarrow[w]{w} \begin{cases} \sigma_0 & \text{if } w \in \{\perp, \top\}^* \\ \text{id} & \text{otherwise} \end{cases} \tag{2}
$$

for all $w \in \Sigma^*$ of length n. Recall that, for a word $w \in \Sigma^*$ of length N, we have $w = \langle \mathcal{A} \rangle$ for some assignment $\mathcal{A}$ if and only if $w \in \{\perp, \top\}^*$ (i.e. if we are in the upper case in the above diagram). We have, in particular, that σ_N does not change the first N letters.

Most interesting are those parts of the automaton which are used to verify whether a clause is satisfied. For each $1 \leq k \leq K$, consider the clause $C_k = L_1 \vee L_2 \vee L_3$ with $L_i = (\neg) x_{n_i}$ for $1 \leq n_1 < n_2 < n_3 \leq N$. We say that x_n appears *positively* in C_k if $L_i = x_n$ and it appears *negatively* if $L_i = \neg x_n$ (for some i); otherwise it does *not* appear in C_k.

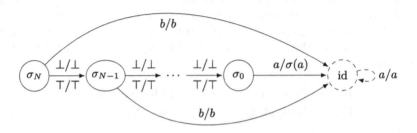

Fig. 3. The automaton part for the states $\{\sigma_n \mid 0 \leq n \leq N\}$ where σ refers to the element defined in Fact 4, the dashed state refers to the already defined identity state and the transitions exist for all $a \in \Sigma$ and $b \in \Sigma \setminus \{\perp, \top\}$.

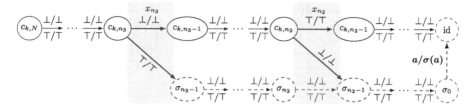

Fig. 4. Part of the automaton for the states $\{c_{k,n} \mid 0 < n \leq N\}$. We assume x_{n_3} to appear positively in C_k while x_{n_2} is assumed to appear negatively. The part for x_{n_1} is not drawn for space reasons. Dashed states and transitions are already defined above. The transition on the right exists for all $a \in \Sigma$ and missing transitions are of the form b/b and go to id (for $b \in \Sigma \setminus \{\perp, \top\}$).

Now, in order to verify that the clause C_k is satisfied, we use the states $\{c_{k,n} \mid 0 < n \leq N\} \subseteq Q$ with the transitions

$$\{c_{k,n} \xrightarrow{\perp/\perp} c_{k,n-1}, c_{k,n} \xrightarrow{\top/\top} c_{k,n-1} \mid 0 < n \leq N, x_n \text{ does not appear in } C_k\}$$
$$\cup \{c_{k,n} \xrightarrow{\perp/\perp} c_{k,n-1}, c_{k,n} \xrightarrow{\top/\top} \sigma_{n-1} \mid 0 < n \leq N, x_n \text{ appears positively in } C_k\}$$
$$\cup \{c_{k,n} \xrightarrow{\perp/\perp} \sigma_{n-1}, c_{k,n} \xrightarrow{\top/\top} c_{k,n-1} \mid 0 < n \leq N, x_n \text{ appears negatively in } C_k\}$$
$$\cup \{c_{k,n} \xrightarrow{b/b} \text{id} \mid 0 < n \leq N, b \in \Sigma \setminus \{\perp, \top\}\} \subseteq \delta$$

where we identify $c_{k,0}$ with the identity state id. This results in the automaton part schematically depicted in Fig. 4.

The reader may verify that we obtain the cross diagram

$$c_{k,N} \underset{w}{\overset{w}{+}} \begin{cases} \sigma_0 & \text{if } w = \langle \mathcal{A} \rangle \text{ such that } \mathcal{A} \text{ satisfies } C_k \\ \text{id} & \text{otherwise} \end{cases} \tag{3}$$

for all $w \in \Sigma^*$ of length N and all $1 \leq k \leq K$ by construction of the automaton. Note here that the "otherwise" case occurs if w contains a letter different to $\perp$ and $\top$ (i.e. it does not encode an assignment) and if w encodes an assignment which does not satisfy C_k.

This concludes the definition of $\mathcal{T}$ and it remains to define q. For this, we assume without loss of generality that K is a power of two (we may simply repeat clauses otherwise). To define q, we use the balanced commutator from Definition 1. In order to simplify our notation, we simply write $B_n[q_\ell, \ldots, q_1]$ for any $0 \leq n \leq N$ instead of $B_{\beta_n, \alpha_n}[q_\ell, \ldots, q_1]$ (for any $q_1, \ldots, q_\ell \in Q^{\pm *}$). Using this convention, we let

$$q = B_N[c_{K,N}, \ldots, c_{1,N}].$$

Please note that q may be computed in logarithmic space by Fact 2.

This concludes the definition of the reduction function and it remains to show $q \neq_\mathcal{T}$ id if and only if φ is satisfiable. From the cross diagrams (3), we obtain the black part of the cross diagram

$$
q = \left\{\begin{array}{ccc} \overrightarrow{c_{1,N}} & \xrightarrow{w} & \overrightarrow{q_1} \\[2pt] & w & \\ \vdots & \vdots & \vdots \\ & w & \\ c_{K,N} & \xrightarrow{w} & q_K \\ \underbracket{B_N}\!\! & w & \!\!\underbracket{B_0} \end{array}\right\} =_{\mathcal{T}} \begin{cases} \sigma_0 & \text{if } w = \langle \mathcal{A} \rangle \text{ s.\,t. } \mathcal{A} \text{ satisfies } \varphi = \bigwedge_{k=1}^{K} C_k \\ \text{id} & \text{otherwise} \end{cases} \tag{4}
$$

for all $w \in \Sigma^*$ of length N where we have $q_k = \sigma_0$ if $w = \langle \mathcal{A} \rangle$ for some assignment $\mathcal{A}$ that satisfies C_k and $q_k = \text{id}$ otherwise (i.e. if w does not encode a suitable assignment or if the assignment does not satisfy C_k). By Fact 3, we may add the balanced commutators to the cross diagram (gray additions above). Now, if w encodes an assignment satisfying all clauses, we obtain $B_0[\sigma_0, \ldots, \sigma_0] =_{\mathcal{T}} \sigma_0$ (by Fact 5) on the right, which acts non-trivially on some letter. Otherwise (and this is the case for all w if φ is not satisfiable), one entry will be id and the whole commutator collapses to id (by Fact 1).

Remark 1. The automaton constructed by the reduction for Theorem 1 has $(3 + K) \cdot (N + 1) + 1$ many states where N is the numbers of variables and K is the number of clauses. The depth of the automaton is $N + 1$.

4   The Compressed Word Problem

Straight-line Programs. A *straight-line program* (or *SPL*) is a context-free grammar which generates exactly one word. We refer the reader to a standard textbook (such as [14]) for definitions and details. By convention, non-terminal symbols are usually capitalized while terminal symbols are lowercase.

The Compressed Word Problem. Using SLPs allows for the input state sequence to be given in a compressed form. This results in the *compressed word problem* (for details on this problem and why it is important, we refer the reader to [5, 16]).

Theorem 2. *The uniform compressed word problem for finitary automaton groups*

> **Input:** *a finitary $\mathscr{G}$-automaton $\mathcal{T} = (Q, \Sigma, \delta)$ and*
> *a straight-line program generating a state sequence $q \in Q^{\pm*}$*
> **Question:** *is $q = \mathbb{1}$ in $\mathscr{G}(\mathcal{T})$?*

is PSPACE-complete (under many-one LOGSPACE-reductions), even for $|\Sigma| = 5$.

Proof (sketch). That the problem is in PSPACE can again be seen by using a "guess and check" approach (as the length of a witness depends only on $\mathcal{T}$). Note that we cannot simply uncompress the SLP for the "check" part, though. We have to apply the states one by one directly from the SLP where we start with the rule for the start symbol. Terminal symbols can be applied directly but, for non-terminal symbols, we have to recursively descend into their corresponding rules. An important point here is that no non-terminal symbol may appear twice on a branch of the syntax tree of a/the generated word as this would imply that the grammar already generated infinitely many words. Thus, for the recursion, we only need to store up to one position in every rule, which we may do in PSPACE.

For the PSPACE-hardness, we use a special form of the PSPACE-complete (see e. g. [18, Theorem 19.1]) satisfiability problem for quantified boolean formulae where the input formula is of the form $\varphi = \neg\forall x_N \neg\forall x_{N-1} \ldots \neg\forall x_1 : \varphi_0$ with φ_0 in 3-CNF and variables from $\{x_1, \ldots, x_N\}$. That this special form remains PSPACE-complete can be seen using standard techniques.

Then, we build on the reduction from Theorem 1 applied to φ_0. Roughly speaking, this yields a finitary $\mathscr{G}$-automaton $\mathcal{T} = (Q_0, \Sigma, \delta_0)$ with $\Sigma = \{a_1, \ldots, a_5\}$ and a state sequence $\boldsymbol{q_0} \in Q_0^{\pm*}$ such that $\boldsymbol{q_0}$ acts only non-trivially on those words that encode assignments satisfying φ_0.

The idea is now that we use states for toggling the individual truth values encoded in the input word. For this, we enrich $\mathcal{T}_0$ with the states $\{t_n \mid 0 \le n < N\}$ and the transitions

$$\left\{ t_n \xrightarrow{\perp/\perp} t_{n-1}, t_n \xrightarrow{\top/\top} t_{n-1}, t_n \xrightarrow{b/b} \mathrm{id} \mid 0 < n < N, b \in \Sigma \setminus \{\perp, \top\} \right\}$$
$$\cup \left\{ t_0 \xrightarrow{\perp/\top} \mathrm{id}, t_0 \xrightarrow{\top/\perp} \mathrm{id}, t_0 \xrightarrow{b/b} \mathrm{id} \mid b \in \Sigma \setminus \{\perp, \top\} \right\} \subseteq \delta$$

(where $\perp, \top \in \Sigma$ were chosen in Theorem 1). See Fig. 5 for a graphical depiction. The state t_n skips n letters and then toggles between $\perp$ and $\top$. With suitable balanced iterated commutators, we can use this to simulate the $\forall x_n$ quantifiers. To simulate the logical negation, we use the trick that, for $g \in \{1, \sigma\} \subseteq A_5$, we have $g^{-1}\sigma = \sigma \iff g = 1$ (and $g^{-1}\sigma = 1$ otherwise). This yields the inductive definition of

$$q'_n = B_N[q_{n-1}^{t_{N-n}}, \boldsymbol{q}_{n-1}] \text{ and } \boldsymbol{q}_n = (q'_n)^{-1} \sigma_N$$

(using the notation B_n for B_{β_n, α_n} introduced in the proof of Theorem 1) where $q'_0 = \boldsymbol{q}_0$ is already given by the first reduction. This inductive structure immediately yields a LOGSPACE-computable SLP for $\boldsymbol{q} = \boldsymbol{q}_N$ and it remains to show that $\boldsymbol{q}_N$ indeed acts non-trivially if and only if φ holds. We will do this using induction on n.

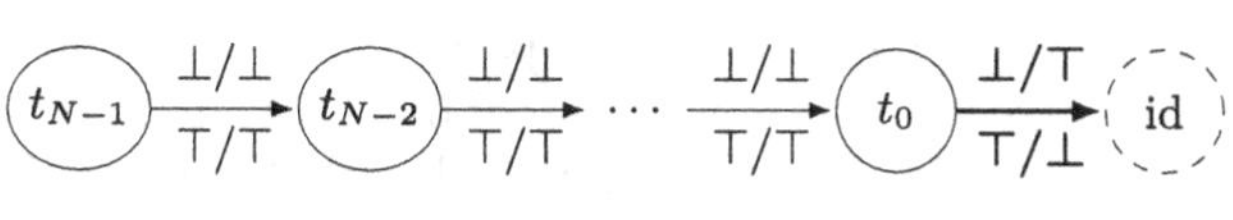

Fig. 5. The additional automaton part with the states $\{t_n \mid 0 \le n < N\}$. Missing transitions are b/b transitions to the identity state (for $b \in \Sigma \setminus \{\perp, \top\}$).

By construction, we obtain the cross diagram

$$w \quad a$$
$$t_n \xrightarrow{} t' \xrightarrow{} \mathrm{id} \tag{5}$$
$$w \quad \tilde{a}$$

for all $w \in \Sigma^*$ of length $0 < n < N$ and letters $a \in \Sigma$, where we have $t' = t_0$ and $\tilde{a} = \neg a$ (i.e. $\tilde{a} = \top$ if $a = \bot$ and $\tilde{a} = \bot$ if $a = \top$) if $wa \in \{\bot, \top\}^*$ and $t' = \mathrm{id}$ and $\tilde{a} = a$ otherwise.

In order to state our actual induction invariant, let $\varphi_0' = \varphi_0$, $\varphi_n' = \forall x_n : \varphi_{n-1}$ and $\varphi_n = \neg\varphi_n'$ for $0 < n \le N$. This means $\varphi_n = \neg\forall x_n \ldots \neg\forall x_1 : \varphi_0$ and φ_n' is the same without the out-most negation. We extend the notation $\langle \mathcal{A} \rangle$ from the proof of Theorem 1 to assignments $\mathcal{A} : \{x_{n+1}, \ldots, x_N\} \to \mathbb{B}$ (for $0 \le n \le N$) by letting $\langle \mathcal{A} \rangle = \mathcal{A}(x_N) \ldots \mathcal{A}(x_{n+1}) \in \{\bot, \top\}^* \subseteq \Sigma^*$. Note that $\langle \mathcal{A} \rangle$ has length $N - n$ and that the empty word is the encoding of an empty assignment.

Now, the invariant is that, for all $0 \le n \le N$, all words $u \in \Sigma^*$ of length $N - n$ and all words $v \in \Sigma^*$ of length n, we have the black part of

$$q_n = \begin{cases} \sigma_N \xrightarrow{u} \xrightarrow{v} = \begin{cases} \sigma_0 & \text{if } uv \in \{\bot, \top\}^* \\ \mathrm{id} & \text{otherwise} \end{cases} \\ (q_n')^{-1} \xrightarrow{u} \xrightarrow{v} =_\mathcal{T} \begin{cases} (\sigma_0)^{-1} & \text{if } u = \langle \mathcal{A} \rangle \text{ s.t. } \mathcal{A} \text{ satisfies } \varphi_n' \text{ and } v \in \{\bot, \top\}^* \\ \mathrm{id} & \text{otherwise} \end{cases} \end{cases}$$

$$\tag{6}$$

where $q_0' = q_0$ and we use the convention that the empty assignment satisfies a (closed)[7] formula if and only if the formula holds. Note that the (black) "otherwise" case includes the case that u or v is not from $\{\bot, \top\}^*$ and the case that u encodes an assignment not satisfying φ_n'.

As soon as we have established the invariant for some n, we immediately also get the gray additions for the above-mentioned trick to simulate a logical negation (by cross diagram (2) from the proof of Theorem 1). Note that the product of the state sequences on the right-hand side acts trivially if $u = \langle \mathcal{A} \rangle$ for some $\mathcal{A}$ which satisfies φ_n' (this is the case if and only if $\mathcal{A}$ does not satisfy $\varphi_n = \neg\varphi_n'$) and $v \in \{\bot, \top\}^*$. It also acts trivially if $uv \notin \{\bot, \top\}^*$. On the other hand, it acts like σ_0 (and, thus, non-trivially) if $u = \langle \mathcal{A} \rangle$ for some $\mathcal{A}$ which does satisfy $\varphi_n = \neg\varphi_n'$ and $v \in \{\bot, \top\}^*$. This shows, in particular, that q_N acts non-trivially if $\varphi = \varphi_N$ holds (i.e. if the empty assignment satisfies it) and trivially otherwise.

The induction invariant (i.e. the black part of cross diagram (6)) holds for $n = 0$ by the cross diagram (4) from the proof of Theorem 1. For the inductive step from $n - 1$ to n, consider a word $u \in \Sigma^*$ of length $N - n$, $a \in \Sigma$ and $v \in \Sigma^*$

---

[7] A formula is *closed* if it does not have any free variables, i.e. if all appearing variables are bound by a quantifier.

of length $n - 1$. We have the black part of the cross diagram

$$q'_n = \begin{cases} & \begin{array}{ccc} u & a & v \\ q_{n-1} + & + & + \; p_{n,0} \\ & u & a & v \\ t_{N-n} + & + \; \text{id} \; + \; \text{id} \\ & u & \tilde{a} & v \\ q_{n-1} + & + & + \; p_{n,1} \\ & u & \tilde{a} & v \\ t_{N-n}^{-1} + & + \; \text{id} \; + \; \text{id} \\ & u & a & v \end{array} \end{cases} \tag{7}$$

where we have

$$p_{n,0} =_\mathcal{T} \begin{cases} \sigma_0 & \text{if } ua = \langle \mathcal{A}' \rangle \text{ s.t. } \mathcal{A}' \text{ satisfies } \varphi_{n-1} \text{ and } v \in \{\bot, \top\}^* \\ \text{id} & \text{otherwise} \end{cases}$$

$$p_{n,1} =_\mathcal{T} \begin{cases} \sigma_0 & \text{if } u\tilde{a} = \langle \tilde{\mathcal{A}}' \rangle \text{ s.t. } \tilde{\mathcal{A}}' \text{ satisfies } \varphi_{n-1} \text{ and } v \in \{\bot, \top\}^* \\ \text{id} & \text{otherwise.} \end{cases}$$

The shaded parts are due to induction and lines involving t_{N-n} follow from cross diagram (5). By Fact 3 (and the cross diagram (1) from the proof of Theorem 1), we may add balanced iterated commutators obtaining the gray additions.

We conclude with a case distinction. If we have $uav \notin \{\bot, \top\}^*$, we get $p_{n,0} =_\mathcal{T} p_{n,1} =_\mathcal{T} \text{id}$ and, thus, $B_0[p_{n,1}, p_{n,0}] =_\mathcal{T} \text{id}$ on the right. Now, assume $uav \in \{\bot, \top\}^*$ and, in particular, $a \in \{\bot, \top\}$. In this case, we have $u = \langle \mathcal{A} \rangle$ for some $\mathcal{A} : \{x_{n+1}, \ldots, x_N\} \to \mathbb{B}$ and $\tilde{a} = \neg a$ (see cross diagram (5)). Let $ua = \langle \mathcal{A}' \rangle$ and $u\tilde{a} = \langle \tilde{\mathcal{A}}' \rangle$. Note that we have $\mathcal{A}'(x_n) = a = \neg \tilde{\mathcal{A}}'(x_n)$ (and $\mathcal{A}'(x_m) = \tilde{\mathcal{A}}'(x_m) = \mathcal{A}(x_m)$ for all $n < m \leq N$). If $\mathcal{A}$ satisfies $\varphi'_n = \forall x_n : \varphi_{n-1}$, we, therefore, have that $\mathcal{A}'$ and $\tilde{\mathcal{A}}'$ both satisfy φ_{n-1}. This yields $p_{n,0} =_\mathcal{T} p_{n,1} =_\mathcal{T} \sigma_0$ and, thus, $B_0[p_{n,1}, p_{n,0}] =_\mathcal{T} \sigma_0$ on the right by Fact 5. On the other hand, if $\mathcal{A}$ does not satisfy φ'_n, then $\mathcal{A}'$ or $\tilde{\mathcal{A}}'$ does not satisfy φ_{n-1} and we have $p_{n,0} =_\mathcal{T} \text{id}$ or $p_{n,1} =_\mathcal{T} \text{id}$. On the right, this yields $B_0[p_{n,1}, p_{n,0}] =_\mathcal{T} \text{id}$ by Fact 1, which shows the invariant.

Acknowledgements. The authors would like to thank Armin Weiß for many discussions around the presented topic. The results are part of the first author's Bachelor thesis, which was advised by the second author (while he was at FMI).

References

1. Mix Barrington, D.A.: Bounded-width polynomial-size branching programs recognize exactly those languages in NC^1. J. Comput. Syst. Sci. **38**(1), 150–164 (1989)

2. Bartholdi, L., Figelius, M., Lohrey, M., Weiß, A.: Groups with ALogTime-hard word problems and PSpace-complete circuit value problems. In: Saraf, S. (ed.) 35th Computational Complexity Conference (CCC 2020). Leibniz International Proceedings in Informatics (LIPIcs), vol. 169, pp. 29:1–29:29. Schloss Dagstuhl-Leibniz-Zentrum für Informatik, Dagstuhl, Germany (2020)
3. Bartholdi, L., Mitrofanov, I.: The word and order problems for self-similar and automata groups. Groups Geom. Dyn. **14**, 705–728 (2020)
4. Bartholdi, L., Silva, P.: Groups defined by automata. In: Pin, J.E. (ed.) Handbook of Automata Theory, vol. II, chap. 24, pp. 871–911. European Mathematical Society (2021)
5. Bassino, F., et al.:Complexity and Randomness in Group Theory. De Gruyter (2020)
6. Bishop, A., Elder, M.: Bounded automata groups are co-ET0L. In: Martín-Vide, C., Okhotin, A., Shapira, D. (eds.) Language and Automata Theory and Applications, pp. 82–94. Springer International Publishing (2019)
7. Bondarenko, I., Wächter, J.Ph.: On orbits and the finiteness of bounded automaton groups. Internat. J. Algebra Comput. **31**(06), 1177–1190 (2021)
8. Bondarenko, I.V., Bondarenko, N.V., Sidki, S.N., Zapata, F.R.: On the conjugacy problem for finite-state automorphisms of regular rooted trees. Groups Geom. Dyn. **7**, 232–355 (2013)
9. Cook, S.A., McKenzie, P.: Problems complete for deterministic logarithmic space. J. Algorithms **8**(3), 385–394 (1987)
10. D'Angeli, D., Rodaro, E., Wächter, J.Ph.: On the complexity of the word problem for automaton semigroups and automaton groups. Adv. in Appl. Math. **90**, 160–187 (2017)
11. Gillibert, P.: The finiteness problem for automaton semigroups is undecidable. Internat. J. Algebra Comput. **24**(01), 1–9 (2014)
12. Gillibert, P.: An automaton group with undecidable order and Engel problems. J. Algebra **497**, 363–392 (2018)
13. Grigorchuk, R.I., Pak, I.: Groups of intermediate growth: an introduction. Enseign. Math. **54**(3–4), 251–272 (2008)
14. Hopcroft, J.E., Ullman, J.D.: Introduction to Automata Theory, Languages and Computation. Addison-Wesley, Boston (1979)
15. Lipton, R.J., Zalcstein, Y.: Word problems solvable in LogSpace. J. ACM **24**(3), 522–526 (1977)
16. Lohrey, M.: The Compressed Word Problem for Groups. SpringerBriefs in Mathematics, Springer (2014)
17. Nekrashevych, V.V.: Self-similar groups, Mathematical Surveys and Monographs, vol. 117. American Mathematical Society, Providence, RI (2005)
18. Papadimitriou, C.M.: Computational Complexity. Addison-Wesley (1994)
19. Sidki, S.N.: Automorphisms of one-rooted trees: growth, circuit structure, and acyclicity. J. Math. Sci. (N.Y.) **100**(1), 1925–1943 (2000)
20. Silva, P.V.: Groups and automata: a perfect match. In: Kutrib, M., Moreira, N., Reis, R. (eds.) Descriptional Complexity of Formal Systems, pp. 50–63. Springer, Berlin Heidelberg (2012)
21. Steinberg, B.: On some algorithmic properties of finite state automorphisms of rooted trees. Contemp. Math. **633**, 115–123 (2015)
22. Šunić, Z., Ventura, E.: The conjugacy problem in automaton groups is not solvable. J. Algebra **364**, 148–154 (2012)
23. Wächter, J.Ph., Weiß, A.: An automaton group with PSpace-complete word problem. Theory Comput. Syst. **67**(1), 178–218 (2022)

Separating Words Problem over Groups

Neha Kuntewar, S. K. M. Anoop, and Jayalal Sarma$^{(\boxtimes)}$

Indian Institute of Technology Madras, Chennai, India
`jayalal@cse.iitm.ac.in`

Abstract. The separating words problem asks - given two words $w, x \in \{0, 1\}^n$, the size of the smallest automaton (in terms of number of states, expressed as a function of n) which accepts one of them and rejects the other. The best lower bound known for the problem is $\Omega(\log n)$, whereas the best upper bound known is $O(n^{1/3} \log^7 n)$, due to (Chase 2021). Motivated by the applications to this problem, we study separating in the context of groups - a finite group G is said to separate w and x, if there is a substitution function from $\phi : \Sigma \to G$ such that the expressions $\phi(w)$ and $\phi(x)$ yield different elements in the group G. We show the following results:

- By a result of Robson [6], there is a permuting automaton of size $O(\sqrt{n})$ states which separate any two words w and x of length n. Hence, there is a group of size $2^{O(\sqrt{n} \log n)}$ which separate w and x. Using basic properties of one dimensional representations of the groups, we improve this to $O(\sqrt{n} 2^{\sqrt{n}})$.
- A class of groups $\mathcal{G}$ is said to be *universal* if for any two words $w, x \in \Sigma^*$, there exists a group $G \in \mathcal{G}$ for which a separating substitution map exists such that the yields of the words under the map are distinct. We show that the class of permutation groups, solvable groups, nilpotent groups and, in particular, p-groups, are universal.
- Class of Abelian groups and Dihedral groups are not universal. En route to this result, we derive sufficiency conditions for a class of groups to be non-universal.
- We can also translate separation using groups to separation using automaton. Any two words $w, x \in \Sigma^n$ which are separated by a group G can be separated using an automaton of size $|G|$. We show better bounds for permutation groups. We also study the natural computational problem in the context and show it to be NP-complete.

1 Introduction

Given any computational model and the measure of a resource in the model, one of the simplest questions that can be asked about it is that of the amount of resource required to distinguish between two distinct inputs. A meaningful instantiation of this general question was first studied by Goralcik and Koubek [4] (see also Johnson [5]) called the SEPARATING WORDS PROBLEM : given two words $w, x \in \Sigma^*$ (where the shorter word is of length n) over an alphabet Σ, what is the minimum number of states of DFA, denoted by $sep(w, x)$,

© IFIP International Federation for Information Processing 2023
Published by Springer Nature Switzerland AG 2023
H. Bordihn et al. (Eds.): DCFS 2023, LNCS 13918, pp. 109–120, 2023.
https://doi.org/10.1007/978-3-031-34326-1_8

that distinguishes between the two (by accepting w and rejecting x or vice versa) where the size of DFA is the number of states in the automaton.

Indeed, the smallest automaton which accepts only w, and hence achieves separating, will be of size $O(|w|)$ - hence the trivial upper bound is $O(n)$ number of states. Goralcik and Koubek [4] provided non-trivial saving on the number of states - with an $o(n)$ upper bound. They attribute a conjecture to Choffrut - later known as *Choffrut Conjecture* - given distinct words of length n, for all $\epsilon > 0$, the value $sep(w, x) \in \mathcal{O}(n^\epsilon)$. The best known lower bound for the problem is $\Omega(\log n)$. When the two words are of different length it is known that they can be separated by an automaton of size $O(\log n)$. Three years later, Robson [7] improved the bound to $O\left(n^{2/5} \log^{3/5} n\right)$ number of states. More recently, Chase [2] proved that there exists a smaller automaton of size $O\left(n^{1/3} \log^7 n\right)$ for the separating words problem, thus indicating that this question is far from well-understood.

If we require the automaton to satisfy more properties, then it is possible that there are stronger lower bounds than $\Omega(\log n)$. For example, Robson [6] considered the restriction when the automaton should be a permuting one (that is, for each $a \in \Sigma$, the transition function is a permutation of the set of states). Surprisingly, it turns out [6] that there is a permuting automaton with $O(\sqrt{n})$ states for separating any two given words.

A different approach was proposed by Bulatov *et al* [1]. Let T be a semigroup. Consider $w, x \in \Sigma^*$. The expression $w = x$ is said to be an identity of T if for any substitution function $\phi : \Sigma \to T$, the element of T yielded by $\phi(w)$ and $\phi(x)$ are identical. If w and x is not an identity of T, then the trivial automaton with $|T|$ many states (see Sect. 2) can separate the two words w and x.

Notice that this connection goes in the reverse direction too. That is, suppose there exists an automaton which separates w and x using k states. The transformation monoid of the automaton (which is a submonoid of T_k the set of all functions from $[k] \to [k]$ with composition) has words of length n which gives different yields and hence gives a non-identity of length n. This approach gives a way for exploring lower bounds - that is, if we can prove that transformation monoid T_k cannot have any identity of length less than n, then it implies that $sep(w, x) > k$ for any two words of length n. Bulatov *et al* [1] computed the length of the shortest identity in T_5 and proved some properties about irreducible identities in T_k in general. It turns out that the any non-binary identity can be converted to a binary identity without increasing the length. In similar terms, Robson's result on permutation automaton [6] can be equivalently interpreted as showing that for any n, there are no identities in the symmetric group S_n which are shorter than $\frac{n^2}{4}$ elements.

Our Results: Motivated by the above approach, in this paper, we study the variant of the problem to separate words with groups. Let G be a group. Let Σ be a finite alphabet and let $\phi : \Sigma \to G$ be a function which can be extended to a monoid homomorphism between Σ^* and G. A word $w = w_1 w_2 \ldots w_n \in \Sigma^n$, is said to *yield* a $g \in G$ if $\prod_{i=1}^n \phi(w_i) = g$ where the product symbol is the operation of the group. Given $w, x \in \Sigma^*$, a group G is said to *separate* w and x if there exists a function ϕ such that $\phi(w) \neq \phi(x)$. The question we ask is - *given any w and x, does there always exist a group G that separates them?* Indeed, the fact that the separating automaton constructed by Robson is a permuting automaton implies an affirmative answer.

Size of the Separating Group: Given two words $w, x \in \Sigma^*$, what is the smallest size of the group which separates them in terms of the lengths $|w|$ and $|x|$? We show the following upper bound by carefully analyzing the transformation group of permuting automaton construction in [6].

Theorem 1. *For any $w, x \in \Sigma^*$, with $|w| = |x| = n$, there is a group of size $O\left(\sqrt{n}2^{\sqrt{n}}\right)$ that separates them. If $|w| \neq |x|$, then there is a group of size $\max\{|w|, |x|\}$ which separates them.*

Notice that the result of [6] constructs a permuting automaton of size $O(\sqrt{n})$ and the size of the transformation group is $2^{O(\sqrt{n}\log n)}$ and the above estimate is an improvement of the same. The best lower bound that we have is $\Omega(\log n)$ which follows from Proposition 1.

Structure of the Separating Group: We study the natural question whether we have groups with more structure separating words. A class of groups $\mathcal{G}$ is said to be *universal* if for any $w, x \in \Sigma^*$, there is a group $G \in \mathcal{G}$ in the class that separates the two words. As a first step, we establish the following results about universality of different classes of groups:

Theorem 2. *The class of groups $\mathcal{G}$ is universal where $\mathcal{G}$ is either permutation groups, solvable groups or p-groups.*

The first part in the above proposition is an easy consequence of Robson's automaton construction, which by construction, is a permutation group. The case of solvable groups is proved by analyzing the transformation group of Robson's permuting automaton that separates the two words and proving that it is indeed solvable. One the other hand, we also show classes of groups which are not universal.

Theorem 3. *The class of groups $\mathcal{G}$ is not universal where $\mathcal{G}$ is either Abelian groups or dihedral group.*

We also prove sufficient conditions for a class of groups to be not universal.

Separating Words : From Groups to Automaton. One of the uses of separating two words by groups is to apply it for separating words by automaton which can be derived from the groups. Towards this, we make the following definition - the separating group words problem asks to design an automaton to separate two words $w, x \in \Sigma^*$ (equipped with a mapping $\phi : \Sigma \to G$) with the additional guarantee that the yields of $\phi(w)$ and $\phi(x)$ as words in the group are different. This problem can potentially be done with smaller number of states than the general separating words problem since we may have more structural information about the words because their yields are different.

Define $d_G(n)$ to be the minimum $d(w, x)$ over words whose yields are different. $d_G(n) = \max\limits_{\substack{w, x \in G^n \\ yield(w) \neq yield(x)}} d(w, x)$. It is easy to see that $d_G(n) \leq$ $\min\{d(n), |G|\}$. A natural question to ask is whether there can be a better dependence on $|G|$ and n. Indeed, when G is a permutation group, there is a smaller automaton.

Theorem 4. *If w and x is separated by a group $G \leq S_m$, then, $d_G(n) \leq$ $\min\{d(n), m\}$*

Notice that the $|G|$ can be exponentially larger than m. Similarly, when G is an Abelian group, there is a better automaton.

Theorem 5. *If w and x and separated by an Abelian group G, then, $d_G(n) \leq$ $O(\log n)$.*

Complexity of Separating Groups: We consider the natural computational version of the problem in this context, denoted as SEPGROUPWORDS problem - given two words $w, x \in \Sigma^*$, a set of permutations S that generates a group $G \leq S_n$ and a function $\phi : \Sigma \to S$ and an integer k, check if there is an automaton of size k which separates w and x. Indeed, given a set of generators of a permutation group it is possible to estimate the $|G|$ in polynomial time, and if $k \geq |G|$, then the answer is trivially YES. However, we show that the problem is still NP-hard in general by reducing from the separating words problem in general. We show the following theorem:

Theorem 6. SEPGROUPWORDS *is* NP-*complete.*

2   Preliminaries

A group G is a set equipped with an operation $\circ$ that satisfies associativity, closure, existence of identity and inverse with respect to the operation. Furthermore, if the operation $\circ$ is commutative, we say that the group is *Abelian*. A group is said to be a p-group, if the order of the group is some power of a prime number p. Symmetric group S_n is the set of all bijections from the set $[n]$ to itself. Permutation group is any subgroup of the symmetric group.

The commutator of $g, h \in G$, denoted as $[g, h]$ is the element $ghg^{-1}h^{-1}$. The commutator subgroup is the group generated by the set of commutators $\forall g, h \in G\}, \{[g, h]|$. Subgroups H of G which are invariant under conjugation are called normal subgroups of G and are represented as $H \lhd G$. i.e., $\forall g \in G, h \in H$, $ghg^{-1} \in H$. A group G is said to be solvable if there exists an n, such that $G = G_{(0)} \rhd G_{(1)} \rhd \ldots \rhd G_{(n)} = \{e\}$, where $\forall i \in [n-1]$, $G_{(i+1)} = [G_{(i)}, G_{(i)}]$. A group G is said to be nilpotent if $G = G_0 \rhd G_1 \rhd \ldots \rhd G_n = \{e\}$, where $\forall i \in [n-1]$, $G_{(i+1)} = [G, G_{(i)}]$. All nilpotent groups are solvable.

The dihedral group is a group of symmetries of a regular n-gon, with n rotations and n reflections. The order of the group D_n is $2n$. We write $D_n = \{r_0, r_1, \ldots r_{n-1}, s_0, s_1 \ldots s_{n-1}\}$. Dihedral group has the group presentation $D_n = \langle r, s \mid r^n = s^2 = e \rangle$.

The following proposition follows by the standard constructions of an automaton from the syntactic monoid.

Proposition 1. *For any $w \neq x \in \Sigma^*$ which are separated by a group G, there is an automaton which separates w and x with at most $|G|$ states.*

By considering the transformation monoid, the following can also be proved.

Proposition 2. *For any $w \neq x \in \Sigma^*$ which are separated by a permuting automaton having k states, then there is a group of size $k!$ which separates the two words.*

We know the following result from Robson's [6] construction.

Proposition 3 ([6] **See** [8]). *For any $w \neq x$ of length n, there is a permuting automaton, with at most $O(\sqrt{n})$ states, that separates w and x.*

We outline some of the ideas involved in the proof of the above theorem, due to [6]. Firstly, they define the permuting automaton as follows : For integers i, m such that $0 \leq i < m$, let $M_{i,m}$ be an automaton that accepts words, for which the parity of the number of 1's at positions congruent to i $(mod\ m)$ is odd. More formally: $M_{i,m} = (Q, \{0,1\}, q_0, \delta, F)$, where $Q = \{(p,q) \mid p \in \{0,1\}$ and $q \in \{0, ..m-1\}\}$, $|Q| = 2m$, with $q_0 = (0,0)$. The transition function $\delta : Q \times \Sigma \longrightarrow Q$, defined as $\delta((p,q), 0) = (p, (q+1)\ \mod\ m$, and $\delta((p,q), 1) = (p, (q+1)\ \mod\ m)$ if $q \neq i$, and $(1-p, (q+1)\ \mod\ m)$ otherwise. Finally the set of final states $F = \{(1,q) | q \in (0, ..m-1)\}$.

Let $D(w, x) = \{i \mid w_i \neq x_i\}$. For any integers i, m the *residue class* R_S of given set S is defined as : $R_S(i, m) = \{a \mid a \in S \text{ and } a \equiv i \mod m\}$. There is a simple characterization in terms of differing index set about when the permuting automaton actually separates w and x.

Proposition 4 ([6]). *For any two distinct words w, x with length at most n, for any integers i, m such that $0 \leq i < m \leq n$, the following two statements are equivalent: (a) The set $R_{D(w,x)}(i, m)$ has odd cardinality. (b) The permuting automaton $M_{i,m}$ separates w, x.*

The remaining argument due to [6], is to prove that for any two words $w, x \in \Sigma^*$, there has to be a $m \leq \sqrt{n}$ such that $R_{D(w,x)}$ has odd cardinality.

3   Size of the Separating Groups

As mentioned in the previous section, Robson [6] proved that there is a permuting automaton having $O(\sqrt{n})$ states that separates w and x. However, if we apply

Proposition 1, the size of the group is trivially upper bounded by $O(\sqrt{n}!)$ which is $2^{O(\sqrt{n}\log n)}$. In this section we improve this bound. This proves Theorem 1.

Let the transformation monoid of the permuting automaton defined in the previous section be denoted by G_m with two generators g and h, with g corresponding to the transitions on 0, and the generator h corresponding to the transitions on 1. Our goal is to estimate the size of this group. .

Theorem 7. $|G_m| = m2^m$

Proof. We start with the following Lemma which is easy to prove (we defer the proof to the full version).

Lemma 1. $|G_m|$ *is independent of the offset* $0 \leq i < m$.

In light of the above lemma, without loss of generality, we can assume i to be 0. Now we estimate $|G_m|$. The proof idea is as follows. We consider the commutator subgroup H_m of Robson's group G_m. We will show that $|H_m| = 2^{m-1}$ and that $[H_m : G_m] = 2m$.

Step 1: Estimating the size of the commutator subgroup: Towards the first step, we will show that the commutator subgroup H_m can be generated by a set of $m-1$ transpositions and that it is Abelian. Then by the following lemma it follows that $|H_m| = 2^{m-1}$.

Proposition 5. *Let* $G = \langle S \rangle$ *be an Abelian group such that every generator* $g \in S$ *is a transposition. Then,* $|G| = 2^m$ *where* $m = |S|$.

Proof. The proof is by induction on m. Note that since every element $g \in S$ is a transposition the order of each generator is 2. Consider the base case where $m = 1$. Let $G = \langle g \rangle$. Since $g^2 = e$ where e is the identity element we have $G = \{g, e\}$. Hence, $|G| = 2$.

Choose $g \in S$ arbitrarily and let $S' = S \setminus \{g\}$. Now, consider $H = \langle S' \rangle$. By induction hypothesis, we have $|H| = 2^{m-1}$. Now we add the generator g to the set S', and observe the new elements that can be generated. Since G is Abelian and order of each generator is 2, the only possible elements that can be generated are $A = \{hg \mid h \in H\}$. Furthermore, each element in A is distinct since $hg = h'g$ for some $h, h' \in H$ implies $h = h'$. This gives $|A| = |H|$ and $|G| = 2|H| = 2^m$.

Lemma 2. *Consider a Robson's group* G_m. *Let* H_m *be the commutator subgroup of* G_m. *Consider* $S = \{(1, m+1)(m-i+1, 2m-i+1)|\forall i \in [m-1]\}$. *Then* $H_m = \langle S \rangle$.

Proof. Consider the Robson's group $G_m = \langle g, h \rangle$ where $g = (1, 2\ldots m)(m+1,\ldots 2m)$ and $h = (1, m+2, m+3\ldots 2m, m+1, 2\ldots m)$. Suffices to show that:(1) $S \subseteq H_m$ and (2) $H_m \subseteq \langle S \rangle$.

First we will show that $S \subseteq H_m$. Observe that $[g, h^i] = (1, m+1)(m-i+1, 2m-i+1) \; \forall i \in [m-1]$. Hence, for all $\gamma \in S$ there exist $\sigma, \rho \in G_m$ such that $[\sigma, \rho] = \gamma$. Hence $S \subseteq H_m$ which implies that $\langle S \rangle \subseteq H_m$.

Now, we want to show that $H_m \subseteq \langle S \rangle$. It suffices to show that $\forall \sigma, \rho \in G_m$ we have that $[\sigma, \rho] \in \langle S \rangle$. We will prove this by double induction on the lengths of generating sequences of σ, ρ.

Consider the base case when $\sigma, \rho \in \{g, h\}$. By inspection, $[g, h] = [h, g] = (1, m+1)(m, 2m) \in \langle S \rangle$. Now, consider $\sigma, \rho \in G_m$. We want to show that $[\sigma, \alpha] \in \langle S \rangle$ implies that $[\sigma\beta, \alpha] \in \langle S \rangle$ where $\alpha, \beta \in \{g, h\}$. Clearly, if $\alpha = \beta$ then, $[\sigma\beta, \alpha] = \sigma\beta\alpha\beta^{-1}\sigma^{-1}\alpha^{-1} = \sigma\alpha\sigma^{-1}\alpha^{-1} \in \langle S \rangle$ (by induction step).

Now, consider the case when $\alpha \neq \beta$. Wlog assume that $\alpha = g, \beta = h$. The other case is symmetric. Now, $[\sigma h, g] = \sigma h g h^{-1}\sigma^{-1}g^{-1} = \sigma(1, m+1)(m, 2m)g\sigma^{-1}g^{-1}$ where the last equality is because $ghg^{-1}h^{-1} = (1, m+1)(m, 2m)$. By applying induction hypothesis, for some $s \in \langle S \rangle$ it becomes $\sigma(1, m+1)(m, 2m)s\sigma^{-1} = \sigma s'\sigma^{-1}$ where $s' \in \langle S \rangle$).

We will show by induction on length of σ that $\sigma s = s'\sigma$ for some $s' \in \langle S \rangle$. The base case is when $\sigma \in \{g, h\}$. Again by inspection we have that $\sigma(i, i+m) = (i-1, i+m-1)\alpha$ for all $2 \leq i \leq m$ and $\sigma(1, 1+m) = (m, 2m)\sigma$. Since, these transpositions are commute with each other, we immediately get that $\forall s \in \langle S \rangle$ there exists $s' \in \langle S \rangle$ such that $\alpha s = s'\alpha$.

We would like to argue that $\sigma s = s'\sigma$ implies $\sigma\alpha s = s''\sigma\alpha$ where $\alpha \in \{g, h\}, s', s'' \in \langle S \rangle$. Now, $\sigma\alpha s = \sigma s'\alpha$ by the base case, and it can be written as $s''\sigma\alpha$ by applying induction hypothesis.

Substituting this above we get that $[\sigma h, g] = \sigma s'\sigma^{-1} = s''\sigma\sigma^{-1} = s'' \in \langle S \rangle$. Hence, we have that $[\sigma, \alpha] \in \langle S \rangle \implies [\sigma\beta, \alpha] \in \langle S \rangle$ for $\alpha, \beta \in \{g, h\}$.

Now, we induct on the length of ρ to show that $[\sigma, \rho] \in \langle S \rangle$ implies $[\sigma, \rho\alpha] \in \langle S \rangle$ for $\alpha \in \{g, h\}$.

Consider $[\sigma, \rho\alpha] = \sigma\rho\alpha\sigma^{-1}\alpha^{-1}\rho^{-1}$. By the base case, this can be written as, $\sigma\rho\sigma^{-1}s\rho^{-1}$, for some $s \in \langle S \rangle$. Now for some $s \in \langle S \rangle$ by induction hypothesis, it can further be written as $s'\rho s\rho^{-1}$. By the above discussion, it becomes $s' * s''\rho\rho^{-1} = \tilde{s} \in \langle S \rangle$.

Thus, $\forall \sigma, \rho \in G_m$ we have that $[\sigma, \rho] \in \langle S \rangle$. Hence, $H_m \subseteq \langle S \rangle$. Hence, the elements in S generate the commutator subgroup H_m. $\square$

Observe that the elements of S commute with each other. Hence, H_m is an Abelian subgroup with $m - 1$ generators which are transpositions. By Proposition 5, we have that $|H_m| = 2^{m-1}$.

Step 2: Bounds on the Index: Now we show that $[H_m : G_m] = 2m$. Then by Lagrange's theorem we have $|G_m| = 2m|H_m| = m2^m$. We use the following fact from group representation theory:

Lemma 3 ([3]). *The number of degree one representations of a finite group G, which is defined as the number of group homomorphisms $\phi : G \longrightarrow \mathbb{C}^\times$, is $[G : H]$ where H is a commutator subgroup of G.*

Thus, our task in hand is to find the number of degree one representations for the Robson's group G_m. We observe the following from the generators of the group itself.

Lemma 4. *The Robson's group G_m has a presentation $\langle g, h : g^m = h^{2m} = (gh^2)^{2m/3} = e \rangle$ when $m = 3k$ and $\langle g, h : g^m = h^{2m} = (gh^2)^m = e \rangle$ otherwise, where e is the identity element and $k \in \mathbb{N}$.*

Lemma 5. *The number of degree one representations of the Robson's group G_m is $2m$.*

Proof. To count the number of degree one representations of G_m we count the number of homomorphisms $\phi : G_m \longrightarrow \mathbb{C}^\times$. Since $g^m = e$, we have $(\phi(g))^m = 1$. Hence, $\phi(g)$ must be an mth root of unity. Similarly, it follows from $h^{2m} = e$ that $\phi(h)$ must be a $2m^{th}$ root of unity. For the third relation we get $(\phi(g)\phi(h)^2)^p = 1$ where $p = 2m/3$ when $m = 3k$ and $p = m$ otherwise. Thus we have the following equation $e^{\frac{2\pi i p}{m}} \left(e^{\frac{2\pi j p}{2m}} \right)^2 = 1$ where $0 \le i, p \le m - 1, 0 \le j \le 2m - 1$. Hence, $e^{\frac{2\pi i p}{m}} e^{\frac{2\pi j p}{m}} = e^{2\pi \ell}$ where $\ell \in \mathbb{N}$. This gives, $i + j = \left(\frac{\ell}{p} \right) m$. For a fixed value of j there is a unique $0 \le i \le m - 1$ satisfying the equation. Hence, the number of solutions to the equation is $2m$. This implies that there are $2m$ many one dimensional representations of G_m

4   Structure of the Separating Groups - Universality

In this section, we study the structure of the groups that can separate two words. Recall from the introduction that, a class of groups $\mathcal{G}$ is universal, if for any $w, x \in \Sigma^*$ with $|w| = |x| = n$, there is a group $G \in \mathcal{G}$ that separates w and x. We study this for different classes of groups.

Universal Groups: By inspecting the proof of Theorem 7, we notice that the commutator subgroup of Robson's group is Abelian and hence Robson's group is a solvable group. We have the following proposition:

Proposition 6. *The class of solvable groups is universal.*

We now concentrate on the case of nilpotent groups. In fact, we will show that p-groups are universal. We show that for any pair of words $w \ne x$, there is a 2-group separating w from x.

Lemma 6. *Given a pair of distinct words $w, x \in \{0, 1\}^n$ there exists $0 \le i < m \in [2n]$ and $m = 2^k$ for some $k \in \mathbb{N}$ such that $|R_S(i, m)|$ is odd.*

Proof. Consider two words $w \ne x \in \{0, 1\}^n$. Let j be the largest index such that $w_j \ne x_j$. Clearly, such a j must exist since $w \ne x$. Let $m = j, i = 0$. Observe that $R_S(i, m) = \{j\}$ since $w_i = x_i$ beyond position $j = m$. We have that $|R_S(i, m)|$ is odd but we also must ensure that m is a power of two.

If $m = 2^k$ for some $k \in [n]$ then we are already done. Consider the case when this does not hold. Let r be the smallest number such that $m + r = 2^k$ for some $k \in [n]$. Now set $i' = m, m' = m + r = 2^k$. Now $R_S(i', m') = \{j\} = \{m\}$. So, $|R_S(i', m')|$ is odd. Notice that $m' \le 2n$.

Hence, there exist $m \in [2n], 0 \le i < m$ such that m is a power of two and $|R_S(i, m)|$ is odd.

Continuing with the proof of universality of p-groups. Given $w, x \in \{0,1\}^n$, consider $w' = w0^n$ and $x' = x0^n$. Note that $w', x' \in \{0,1\}^{2n}$ and any deterministic finite automaton that separates w' and x' also separates w and x.

By Proposition 4, since $|R_S(i, m)|$ is odd (even for w' and x') there is a permutation automaton of size $2m$ separating w', x' and hence separating w and x. From Theorem 7 we have that there is a group of size $m.2^m$ separating w', x', and hence separating w and x. By the above claim $|G| = 2^k.2^m = 2^{2^k+k}$. Hence, G is a a 2-group.

Non-universal Groups: We identify group classes that are not universal. We first show that Abelian groups cannot be universal. This follows from the fact that in the case of Abelian groups the yield depends on the number of occurrences of the generators and not the positions at which they occur. We defer the details of the proof to full version.

Proposition 7. *The class of Abelian groups are not universal.*

We show non-universality for dihedral groups using the group structure.

Theorem 8. *The class of dihedral groups are not universal.*

Proof. Consider any dihedral group $G = \{r_0, r_1, \ldots r_{m-1}, s_0, s_1 \ldots s_{m-1}\}$. By properties of dihedral group, we know that $r_i r_j = r_{i+j}$ and $s_i s_j = r_{i-j}$. Now consider the following pair of words: $w = 0^{2k}1^{2k}$, $x = 1^{2k}0^{2k}$ where $k \in \mathbb{N}$. Consider a mapping from the elements in the alphabet to elements of the group. Consider the following cases:

Case 1: The elements in the group that get mapped are $\{r_i, r_j\}$. Then $yield(w) = (r_i)^{2k}(r_j)^{2k} = (r_j)^{2k}(r_i)^{2k} = yield(x)$.
Case 2: Suppose at least one of the elements gets mapped to some s_j. Then $(s_j)^{2k} = (s_j s_j)^k = (r_0)^k = r_0$. Then $yield(w) = h^{2k}r_0 = r_0 h^{2k} = yield(x)$ where $h \in G \setminus \{s_j\}$.

In either case, the yields of the two words are the same. Hence, G cannot separate w, x.

We generalize this idea to derive a sufficient condition for non-universality.

Proposition 8. *Let $\mathcal{G}$ be a family of groups such that $\forall G \in \mathcal{G}, \forall g \in G$ order of $g \leq k$ for some finite $k \in \mathbb{N}$. Then $\mathcal{G}$ is not universal.*

The above theorem implies non-universality of several other classes of groups as well. For example, it implies, if $\mathcal{G}$ is a finite family of groups, then $\mathcal{G}$ is not universal. Now, we use this idea to construct an explicit bad pair of words for separating over any group G.

Proposition 9. *Let G be a group of some finite order $k \in \mathbb{N}$, then there is a pair of words such that $yield(w) = yield(x)$ over G for any mapping.*

Proof. Let L be the *lcm* of order of all elements in G. Clearly, L is finite. Then as earlier, the pair of words $w = 0^L 1^L, x = 1^L 0^L$ have the same yield over any mapping. Hence, $yield(\phi(w)) = yield(\phi(x))$ irrespective of the mapping of $\phi : \Sigma \rightarrow G$.

Using the argument used above, we have the following proposition:

Proposition 10. *If $\exists c \ \forall m$ such that $H_m \leq G_m$ is a maximal Abelian subgroup of G_m and $\mathrm{lcm}(G_m \setminus H_m) \leq c$ then $\{G_m\}_{m \geq 0}$ is not universal.*

We remark that the converse of the above proposition does not hold and defer the details of this to the full version.

5   Separating Group-Separated Words

In this section, we consider the question of separating group-separated words. Let $w, x \in \Sigma^*$ and $\phi : \Sigma \rightarrow G$, such that $yield(\phi(w)) \neq yield(\phi(x))$. We start with the following proposition which shows an improvement to the trivial bound when G is a permutation group.

Proposition 11. *Given two words $w \neq x \in \Sigma^*$ which are separated by a group G that $G \leq S_m$ is a permutation group for $m \geq 0$, then there is an automaton which separates w and x with at most m states.*

Proof. We prove the second part of the proposition. The first part follows from it by noting that any group G is isomorphic to a subgroup of S_m where $m = |G|$. Given two distinct words $w, x \in \Sigma^n$ and a permutation group $G \leq S_m$ such that $yield(w) \neq yield(x)$, we construct an automaton A which separates w from x. Each element $g \in G$ is a bijection on the set $[m]$. Let $g(i)$ denote the image of $i \in [m]$ in g.

We now describe the construction of the automaton $M = (Q = [m], \Sigma, q_0, \delta, F)$ separating w from x. Define the transition function as $\forall a \in \Sigma, q \in Q, \delta(q, a) = g_a(q)$ where g_a denotes the element in G which is mapped to $a \in \Sigma$. Let the yields of w, x be $g, h \in G$. Since the yields are different, we have $g \neq h$. Hence, there must be an index $i \in [m]$ such that $g(i) \neq h(i)$. Taking $q_0 = i$ and $F = g(i)$ ensures that A separates w, x. The automaton separates w, x in m states.

Noticing that any abstract group G acts on itself faithfully, it follows that G is isomorphic to a subgroup of S_m where $m = |G|$. Hence by the above proposition, there is an automaton which separates w and x, with at most $|G|$ states. We note that the bound in Proposition 1 is still not asymptotically better than the trivial $|G|$ bound mentioned above since the cyclic group with $(2, 3 \ldots m, 1)$ as generator will still require $m = |G|$ states for separating by automaton M.

The case when G is Abelian: We also show an improved bound when G is an Abelian group. Tightness is also easy to argue.

Proposition 12. *Let G be an Abelian group of order k. Then any two words $w, x \in \Sigma^n$ and an injective mapping $\phi : \Sigma \to G$, such that $yield(w) \neq yield(x)$ can be separated by an automaton with $O(\log n)$ states.*

Hardness of the decision version: We now address the natural computational version of separating group separated words.

Theorem 9. SepGroupWords *is* NP-*complete.*

Proof. We recall the SepGroupWords problem - given two words $w, x \in \Sigma^*$, a set of permutations S that generates a group $G \leq S_n$ and a function $\phi : \Sigma \to S$ and an integer k, check if there is an automaton of size k which separates w and x. The problem is clearly in NP since given an automaton checking whether it separates w and x can be done efficiently.

Recall the separating words problem - given $w, x \in \Sigma^*$ and $k \in \mathbb{N}$, test whether there is a finite automaton with k states that accepts the string x and rejects w (or vice versa). The input to the problem is tuple (w, x, S, ϕ, k). We know the separating words problem in NP-Hard [1] even for binary alphabet. We show that this problem reduces to the SepGroupWords problem.

Consider an input instance (w, x, k) of the separating words problem, where $w, x \in \Sigma^*$ and $k \in \mathbb{N}$. We construct a group $G \leq S_n$ with a set of generators S that generates a group $G \leq S_n$ and a function $\phi : \Sigma \to S$, such that the yields of $\phi(w)$ and $\phi(x)$ as words over G are different. From Robson's construction [6], we know that there is an $m \in O(\sqrt{n})$ and a permuting automaton with $2m$ states that separates w, x. The generators of the transformation group (which is a subgroup of S_{2m} of this automaton are given by $g = (1, 2 \ldots m)(m+1, \ldots 2m), h = (1, m+2, \ldots 2m, m+1, 2, \ldots m)$. We can search through the range $\{1, 2 \ldots \sqrt{n}\}$ to find a value of m for which the group $\langle g, h \rangle$ separates w, x. Indeed, for a given value of m, consider the mapping $\phi : \Sigma \to S$ as $\phi(0) = g$ and $\phi(1) = h$. We check whether the yields of $\phi(x)$ and $\phi(y)$ are different. This takes $O(m)$ time. Hence the reduction takes time $O(m^2) = O(n)$. It is easy to observe that (w, x, k) is a yes instance for separating words problem if and only if (w, x, S, ϕ, k) is a yes instance of the group separating problem.

Acknowledgements. The authors would like to thank the anonymous reviewers of DCFS 2023 for the helpful comments.

References

1. Bulatov, A.A., Karpova, O., Shur, A.M., Startsev, K.: Lower bounds on words separation: Are there short identities in transformation semigroups? Electron. J. Comb. **24**(3), 3 (2017)
2. Chase, Z.: Separating words and trace reconstruction. In: STOC 2021, pp. 21–31. Association for Computing Machinery (2021)

3. Fulton, W., Harris, J.: Representation Theory. GTM, vol. 129. Springer, New York (2004). https://doi.org/10.1007/978-1-4612-0979-9
4. Goralčík, P., Koubek, V.: On discerning words by automata. In: Kott, L. (ed.) ICALP 1986. LNCS, vol. 226, pp. 116–122. Springer, Heidelberg (1986). https://doi.org/10.1007/3-540-16761-7_61
5. Johnson, J.H.: Rational Equivalence Relations. In Laurent Kott, editor, Automata, Languages and Programming, pp. 167–176, Berlin, Heidelberg, 1986. Springer, Berlin Heidelberg
6. Robson, J.M.: Separating words with machines and groups. RAIRO - Theoretical Informatics and Applications - Informatique Théorique et Appl. **30**(1), 81–86 (1996)
7. Robson, J.M.: Separating strings with small automata. Inf. Process. Lett. **30**(4), 209–214 (1989)
8. Wiedermann, J.: Discerning Two Words by a Minimum Size Automaton. Technical report, Institute of Computer Science, The Czech Academy of Sciences (2015)

Complexity of Exclusive Nondeterministic Finite Automata

Martin Kutrib[ID], Andreas Malcher[(✉)][ID], and Matthias Wendlandt

Institut für Informatik, Universität Giessen, Arndtstr. 2, 35392 Giessen, Germany
{kutrib,andreas.malcher,matthias.wendlandt}@informatik.uni-giessen.de

Abstract. Exclusive nondeterministic finite automata (XNFA) are non-deterministic finite automata with an exclusive-or-like acceptance condition. An input is accepted if there is exactly one accepting path in its computation tree. If there are none or more than one accepting paths, the input is rejected. It turns out that, from a descriptional complexity point of view, XNFAs differ significantly from the known types of finite automata. In particular the state costs for the simulation of an XNFA by a DFA are $3^n - 2^n + 1$ states, while the costs for simulating an XNFA by an NFA are $n \cdot 2^{n-1}$ states. Both bounds are also shown to be tight. On the other hand, NFAs may have advantages in comparison to XNFAs. A tight bound is given by $2^n - 1$ states for the simulation by XNFAs. Finally, we investigate the computational complexity of different decision problems for XNFAs and it turns out that emptiness, universality, inclusion, and equivalence are PSPACE-complete.

1 Introduction

Nondeterminism for finite state automata does not increase their computational power, albeit deterministic finite automata might need exponentially more states than an equivalent one-way nondeterministic finite automaton [14,15]. This explosion arises, since the deterministic finite automaton may be forced to store the given information of an input symbol that is read, while the nondeterministic variant is able to guess a certain situation.

Further structural extensions of finite automata have been examined in the literature. For example, two-way finite automata do also not increase the computational power of finite automata [16], but from a descriptional complexity point of view they enhance the classical model, namely, the costs for one-way deterministic finite automata for the simulation of two-way deterministic finite automata can be exponential in the number of states [15]. Similarly, two-way nondeterministic finite automata can be exponentially more succinct than equivalent one-way nondeterministic finite automata [17].

The question of whether nondeterminism is more powerful than determinism also triggers a closer look on the definition of nondeterminism. Out of a single state, it can be seen as the union of all possible ways on which the remaining input word leads the automaton to final states. Thus, it is natural to consider

© IFIP International Federation for Information Processing 2023
Published by Springer Nature Switzerland AG 2023
H. Bordihn et al. (Eds.): DCFS 2023, LNCS 13918, pp. 121–133, 2023.
https://doi.org/10.1007/978-3-031-34326-1_9

also the intersection of all possible ways or a combination of Boolean operations. This leads to the concept of alternating finite automata. Alternation has been introduced in [3] as a generalization of nondeterminism. For alternating finite automata, the transition function applied to the state set is then a Boolean function. It is well known that alternating finite automata are double-exponentially more succinct than deterministic finite automata [3,11].

The extensions of finite automata mentioned above are all structural. In this paper, we want to examine an extension that is based on the acceptance condition of the automaton and we call the model *exclusive* nondeterministic finite automaton (XNFA). In particular, we consider nondeterministic finite automata that accept an input word w if and only if there is *exactly one* accepting path for w. If there is no accepting path for w or more than one accepting path for w, then the input is rejected. Hence, acceptance can be seen as an exclusive decision of the automaton. A related model are unambiguous finite automata [18] (UFA), which are nondeterministic finite automata, where there must be at most one accepting path for each input word. In contrast, XNFAs may have more than one accepting path for an input word w with the consequence that w is not accepted then. It is clear that every unambiguous finite automaton can be considered as an XNFA, since every word accepted by an UFA has exactly one accepting path. On the other hand, an XNFA cannot be considered as an UFA in general, since words with more than one accepting path may exist. From a descriptional complexity perspective it is known that the trade-off from unambiguous finite automata to deterministic finite automata is exponential [12,13].

A computational model with exactly one accepting computation on every accepted input has already been studied in the context of complexity theory, where the class US (unique solution) is defined (see [2]) as the class of languages L for which there exists a nondeterministic polynomial time Turing machine M such that $w \in L$ if and only if M has on input w exactly one accepting computation path. A short overview on the class US may be found in [6]. Another related model are Xor-NFA [19] or $\oplus$-NFA [20] which are nondeterministic finite automata with a different interpretation of their transition function δ. While in traditional NFAs the set of states reachable from state q on input word w is the union of states $q' \in \delta(q, w)$, in Xor-NFAs or $\oplus$-NFAs the set of states reachable from state q on input word w is the symmetric difference of states $q' \in \delta(q, w)$. Hence, such automata accept only input words for which an odd number of accepting computation paths exist. This is in contrast to traditional NFAs where at least one accepting path is sufficient, and XNFAs where exactly one accepting path is necessary. This difference is also reflected in the descriptional complexity of the automata. n-state $\oplus$-NFAs can be determinized using the classical power set construction which results in an upper bound of at most 2^n [20]. In this paper, we will show that n-state XNFAs can be determinized as well, but the upper bound turns out to be $3^n - 2^n + 1$ and is shown to be tight.

The paper is structured as follows. In Sect. 2, we give the basic definitions that are used in the further sections. In Sect. 3, we show that exclusive nondeterministic finite automata are equally powerful to deterministic finite automata concerning their computational power. Moreover, we establish a trade-off between XNFAs and DFAs of $3^n - 2^n + 1$ states and show its tightness. The costs for the simulation of an XNFA by an NFA are then shown to be $n \cdot 2^{n-1}$ states. In addition, the tightness of the bound can be proven as well. Finally, the bound for the simulation costs of simulating NFAs by XNFAs is shown to be exactly $2^n - 1$ states. This bound is identical to the known bound for simulating NFAs by UFAs. In Sect. 4, we investigate the complexity of different decision problems. It turns out that the general membership problem for XNFAs is in NL, whereas the problems of deciding emptiness, universality, inclusion, and equivalence are PSPACE-complete.

2   Definitions and Preliminaries

Let Σ^* denote the set of all words over the finite alphabet Σ. The *empty word* is denoted by λ, and $\Sigma^+ = \Sigma^* \setminus \{\lambda\}$. The *reversal* of a word w is denoted by w^R. For the *length* of w we write $|w|$. We use $\subseteq$ for *inclusions* and $\subset$ for *strict inclusions*. We write 2^S for the power set and $|S|$ for the cardinality of a set S.

A *nondeterministic finite automaton* (NFA) is a system $M = \langle Q, \Sigma, \delta, q_0, F \rangle$, where Q is the finite set of *states*, Σ is the finite set of *input symbols*, $q_0 \in Q$ is the *initial state*, $F \subseteq Q$ is the set of *accepting states*, and $\delta \colon Q \times \Sigma \to 2^Q$ is the *transition function*.

With an eye towards further modes of acceptance, we define the *acceptance of an input* in terms of computation trees. For any input $w = a_1 a_2 \cdots a_n \in \Sigma^*$ read by some NFA M, a *(complete) path for* w is a sequence of states $q_0, q_1, \ldots, q_n$ such that $q_{i+1} \in \delta(q_i, a_{i+1})$, $0 \le i \le n-1$. All possible paths on w are combined into a *computation tree* of M on w. So, a computation tree of M is a finite rooted tree whose nodes are labeled with states of M. In particular, the root is labeled with the initial state, and the successor nodes of a node labeled q are the nodes $p_1, p_2, \ldots, p_m$ if and only if $\delta(q, a) = \{p_1, p_2, \ldots, p_m\}$, for the current input symbol a. A path in the computation tree is an *accepting path* if it ends in an accepting state.

Now, an input w is accepted by an NFA if at least one path in the computation tree of w is accepting.

The *language accepted* by M is $L(M) = \{\, w \in \Sigma^* \mid w \text{ is accepted by } M \,\}$.

An NFA, where for acceptance it is required that *exactly* one path is accepting, is called an *exclusive nondeterministic finite automaton* (XNFA).

Finally, an NFA is a *deterministic finite automaton* (DFA) if and only if $|\delta(q, a)| = 1$, for all $q \in Q$ and $a \in \Sigma$. In this case we simply write $\delta(q, a) = p$ for $\delta(q, a) = \{p\}$ assuming that the transition function is a mapping $\delta \colon Q \times \Sigma \to Q$. So, any DFA is complete, that is, the transition function is total, whereas for the other automata types it is possible that δ maps to the empty set.

3   Descriptional Complexity

In this section, we investigate the descriptional costs for converting exclusive nondeterministic finite automata to equivalent deterministic and nondeterministic finite automata. Finally, we study the costs for converting nondeterministic finite automata to equivalent exclusive nondeterministic finite automata.

3.1   Determinization

We start with a construction for the determinization of XNFAs which delivers an upper bound for the descriptional costs.

Theorem 1. *Let $n \geq 1$ and M be an n-state XNFA. Then $3^n - 2^n + 1$ states are sufficient for a DFA to accept $L(M)$.*

Proof. Given an n-state XNFA $M = \langle Q, \Sigma, \delta, q_0, F \rangle$, we are going to construct an equivalent DFA $M' = \langle Q', \Sigma, \delta', q_0', F' \rangle$. The basic idea of the construction is to use an extended version of the power set construction used for the determinization of NFAs. Basically, the idea of the power set construction is to consider the computation trees of the NFA, and to remember all states that appear on the same level of the tree, respectively. Finally, if at least one leaf is labeled with an accepting state, the input is accepted. This is due to the fact, that then there exists a path (a computation) from the root of the tree (the initial state) to some accepting leaf on which the input has been consumed entirely. The power set construction can also be applied to computation trees of XNFAs. However, it is not enough to remember all states that appear on the same level of the tree, respectively. For example, some state could appear on different branches of the tree on the same level, but is remembered only once. If this state would lead to acceptance, two branches in the tree would be accepting and, thus, the total input has to be rejected. So, the idea of the extension is to remember all states that appear on the same level of the computation tree together with an information whether they appeared on a single branch only or on at least two branches.

Let $Q = \{q_0, q_1, \ldots, q_{n-1}\}$. Then, for $i \in \{1, 2\}$, we consider the two disjoint copies $Q^{(i)} = \{q^{(i)} \mid q \in Q\}$ of Q. The state set of M' is set to be

$$Q' = \{\emptyset\} \cup \{N \in 2^{Q^{(1)} \cup Q^{(2)}} \setminus 2^{Q^{(2)}} \mid |N \cap \{q_i^{(1)}, q_i^{(2)}\}| \leq 1 \text{ for } 0 \leq i \leq n-1\},$$

where $q_0' = \{q_0^{(1)}\}$ is the initial state.

Next, we construct the transition function $\delta' \colon Q' \times \Sigma \to Q'$ of M'. For all $a \in \Sigma$, we define $\delta'(\emptyset, a) = \emptyset$, and for all $N \in Q' \setminus \{\emptyset\}$ we define $\delta'(N, a)$ as follows. For $0 \leq i \leq n-1$, first, we set $K_i = \{q_j^{(x_j)} \in N \mid q_i \in \delta(q_j, a)\}$. Next, we define a set K according to the following rules. If $K_i = \emptyset$, then neither $q_i^{(1)}$ nor $q_i^{(2)}$ is put into set K. Otherwise, we set $x_i = \min\{2, \sum_{q_j^{(x_j)} \in K_i} x_j\}$ and put $q_i^{(x_i)}$ into K. Finally, $\delta'(N, a)$ is defined to be K if $K \notin 2^{Q^{(2)}}$, and $\delta'(N, a) = \emptyset$ otherwise.

Let us take a closer look at this construction. We claim that the current state N of M' contains all states of M that appear on the current level of the computation tree of M (on the current input) as long as not all of these states appear with superscript (2). In this case, N is the empty set. Moreover, the superscript of each state indicates whether the state occurs at this level on exactly one branch (superscript (1)) or on at least two branches (superscript (2)).

The claim is certainly true for the initial state at the topmost level, that is, the root of the computation tree. Arguing inductively, for any $0 \leq i \leq n - 1$, the set K_i includes exactly the states belonging to N that together with the current input symbol are mapped to q_i by δ (where the mapping ignores the superscript). If K_i is empty, the state q_i has no predecessor under the current input symbol and, thus, does not belong to the next level of the computation tree. Correspondingly, state q_i is not put into K, for any superscript. If, however, K_i is not empty then q_i occurs on the next level and it is put into K. Its superscript is determined by the sum of the superscripts of its predecessors, that is, by the sum of the superscripts of states in K_i. This sum depends on the number of branches on which state q_i occurs on the next level. So, we set the superscript of q_i in K to (1) if the sum is 1. If the sum is larger than 1, the superscript is set to (2). Finally, the successor state of N is set to K if K includes at least one state with superscript (1) and set to $\emptyset$ otherwise. Therefore, the claim is true.

We conclude the construction by defining the set of accepting states of M'. We know that the XNFA M accepts if and only if exactly one branch of its computation tree is accepting. Whether or not this is true can be derived from the state of M'. If it contains accepting states (of M) the sum of whose superscripts is at least two, at least two branches are accepting and the current input has to be rejected by M' as well. It has to be accepted if the sum of these superscripts is exactly 1. So, we define $F^{(i)} = \{ q^{(i)} \mid q \in F \}$, for $i \in \{1, 2\}$, and

$$F' = \{ N \in Q' \mid |N \cap F^{(1)}| = 1 \text{ and } |N \cap F^{(2)}| = 0 \}.$$

Finally, by this construction it is evident that M and M' are equivalent as long as the transition function δ' does not map to the empty set since the set K does not include a state with superscript (1). However, if this happens then all states in K appear on at least two branches of the computation tree. Therefore, it is impossible to have exactly one accepting branch in the end. This means that the input cannot be accepted in this case, and the state reached is equivalent to the state $\emptyset$.

We conclude $L(M) = L(M')$ and, clearly, $|Q'| = 3^n - 2^n + 1$, which shows the theorem. □

The tightness of the upper bound presented in Theorem 1 is established in the following theorem.

Theorem 2. *Let $n \geq 3$. There exists an n-state XNFA M such that every DFA accepting $L(M)$ has at least $3^n - 2^n + 1$ states.*

Proof. Let $M = \langle Q, \Sigma, \delta, q_0, F \rangle$ be the XNFA, where $Q = \{0, 1, \ldots, n-1\}$, $\Sigma = \{a, b, c, d\}$, $F = \{n-1\}$, and δ is defined as

$\delta(i, a) = \{i+1\}$, if $1 \le i \le n-2$, $\delta(n-1, a) = \{0\}$, and $\delta(0, a) = \{0, 1\}$,

$\delta(i, b) = \{i\}$, if $i \in \{0, 2, 3, \ldots, n-1\}$, and $\delta(1, b) = \{0, 1\}$,

$\delta(i, c) = \{i-1\}$, if $1 \le i \le n-1$, and $\delta(0, c) = \{n-1\}$,

$\delta(i, d) = \{i\}$, if $1 \le i \le n-1$.

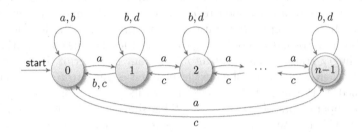

Fig. 1. An n-state XNFA where each equivalent DFA has at least $3^n - 2^n + 1$ states.

We use M (see Fig. 1) as witness automaton for the proof. To this end, let $M' = \langle Q', \Sigma, \delta', q_0', F' \rangle$ be the equivalent DFA constructed in the proof of Theorem 1. It is sufficient to show that M' is minimal.

Recall that the state set of M' is

$$Q' = \{\emptyset\} \cup \{ N \in 2^{Q^{(1)} \cup Q^{(2)}} \setminus 2^{Q^{(2)}} \mid |N \cap \{i^{(1)}, i^{(2)}\}| \le 1 \text{ for } 0 \le i \le n-1 \},$$

where $q_0' = \{0^{(1)}\}$ is the initial state. For all $N \in Q'$ and $z \in \Sigma$, the transition function $\delta'(N, z)$ is as follows. We have $K_i = \{ j^{(x_j)} \in N \mid i \in \delta(j, z) \}$, for $0 \le i \le n-1$. If $K_i = \emptyset$ then neither $i^{(1)}$ nor $i^{(2)}$ belongs to the set $\hat{K}$. Otherwise, $i^{(x_i)}$ belongs to $\hat{K}$, where $x_i = \min\{2, \sum_{j^{(x_j)} \in K_i} x_j\}$. Then we have $\delta'(N, z) = \hat{K}$ if $\hat{K} \cap Q^{(1)} \ne \emptyset$, and $\delta'(N, z) = \emptyset$ otherwise.

In order to show the minimality of M', we first show that all states in Q' are reachable. This is evident for $\emptyset \in Q'$, since $\delta'(\{0^{(1)}\}, d) = \emptyset$. Now, let $P \in Q'$ be an arbitrary state of M'.

The idea for the construction of an input word that drives M' from the initial state $\{0^{(1)}\}$ to state P is as follows. The first task is to reach the state P_1 of M' that includes all states of M, in particular, exactly the states in P with superscript (2) appear with superscript (2) in P_1. So, let $\{j_1^{(2)}, j_2^{(2)}, \ldots, j_\ell^{(2)}\} \subset P$ be the set of all states in P having superscript (2). Here and in the sequel we always assume that the states of M' are ordered sets. That is, for the state $\{j_1^{(2)}, j_2^{(2)}, \ldots, j_\ell^{(2)}\}$ we have $0 \le j_1 < j_2 < \cdots < j_\ell \le n-1$.

For the implementation of the first task, it is convenient to define the distances between consecutive states as $t_1 = j_1$, $t_i = j_i - j_{i-1}$ for $2 \le i \le \ell$, and $t_{\ell+1} = n - j_\ell$. Moreover, let $t_{r,s} = t_r + t_{r+1} + \cdots + t_s = j_s - j_{r-1}$, for $2 \le r \le s \le \ell$, and $t_{r,\ell+1} = t_r + t_{r+1} + \cdots + t_{\ell+1} = n - j_{r-1}$, for $2 \le r \le \ell+1$.

Now, input a^{n-1} drives M' from the initial state $\{0^{(1)}\}$ to state

$$\{0^{(1)}, 1^{(1)}, \ldots, (n-1)^{(1)}\}.$$

Next, the input symbol b yields state

$$\{0^{(2)}, 1^{(1)}, \ldots, (n-1)^{(1)}\}.$$

By processing the input c^{t_2}, automaton M' reaches state

$$\{0^{(1)}, 1^{(1)}, \ldots, (n-t_2)^{(2)}, \ldots, (n-1)^{(1)}\},$$

where all states $1, 2, \ldots, n-1$ appear with some superscript and all states represented by dots have superscript (1). Now, the input is extended by alternating the symbol b and c^{t_i}. So, reading b gives the state

$$\{0^{(2)}, 1^{(1)}, \ldots, (n-t_2)^{(2)}, \ldots, (n-1)^{(1)}\},$$

and subsequently processing c^{t_3} the state

$$\{0^{(1)}, 1^{(1)}, \ldots, (n-t_{2,3})^{(2)}, \ldots, (n-t_3)^{(2)}, \ldots, (n-1)^{(1)}\}.$$

Continuing the input by $bc^{t_4}bc^{t_5}\cdots bc^{t_\ell}$ yields the state

$$\{0^{(1)}, 1^{(1)}, \ldots, (n-t_{2,\ell})^{(2)}, \ldots, (n-t_{3,\ell})^{(2)}, \ldots, (n-t_\ell)^{(2)}, \ldots, (n-1)^{(1)}\}.$$

Finally, with input symbol b state

$$\{0^{(2)}, 1^{(1)}, \ldots, (n-t_{2,\ell})^{(2)}, \ldots, (n-t_{3,\ell})^{(2)}, \ldots, (n-t_\ell)^{(2)}, \ldots, (n-1)^{(1)}\}$$

is entered and the input $c^{t_{\ell+1}}$ drives M' into the state

$$\{0^{(1)}, \ldots, (n-t_{2,\ell+1})^{(2)}, \ldots, (n-t_{3,\ell+1})^{(2)}, \ldots, (n-t_{\ell+1})^{(2)}, \ldots, (n-1)^{(1)}\}.$$

Since $t_{r,\ell+1} = n - j_{r-1}$, we have reached the desired state P_1

$$\{0^{(1)}, \ldots, j_1^{(2)}, \ldots, j_2^{(2)}, \ldots, j_\ell^{(2)}, \ldots, (n-1)^{(1)}\},$$

and the first task is completed.

The second task is to reach the state P of M'. Since $P \subseteq P_1$, to this end, it is sufficient to remove all states with superscript (1) from P_1 that do not appear in P. So, let $D = \{i_1^{(1)}, i_2^{(1)}, \ldots, i_k^{(1)}\} \subset P_1$ be the set of all states in $P_1 \setminus P$ (having superscript (1)). Clearly, if D is empty then $P_1 = P$ and we are done. So, let us assume that D includes at least one state. Then P is reached from P_1 by the input

$$c^{i_1} dc^{i_2 - i_1} dc^{i_3 - i_2} \cdots dc^{i_k - i_{k-1}} dc^{n - i_k}.$$

By c^i, the components of P_1 are shifted circularly to the left. So, by c^{i_1} the i_1-th component is mapped to 0 together with its superscript. By a following d all components remain as they are but the leftmost one, the current state 0. It is deleted. By another $c^{i_2-i_1}$ the formerly i_2-th component is mapped to 0. It is deleted by the following d. We conclude that all of the components that were initially in D are deleted by processing the input sequence. Moreover, since the total number of circularly shifts is n, each undeleted component is mapped to itself. Finally, since all superscripts are shifted together with the components, we derive that the state reached after processing the input sequence is P.

So far, we have shown that all states of M' are reachable. It remains to be shown that they are pairwise inequivalent. To this end, let P and R be two different states of M'. We distinguish two cases.

Case 1: There is some component $i^{(1)}$ with superscript (1) in the symmetric difference of P and R, say $i^{(1)} \in P \setminus R$.

The input c^{i+1} maps the i-th components of P and R to $n-1$. So, from state P automaton M' accepts c^{i+1}. However, dependent on whether $i^{(2)} \in R$ or $i^{(2)} \notin R$, the state reached by M' from R after processing c^{i+1}, either includes $(n-1)^{(2)}$ or neither $(n-1)^{(1)}$ nor $(n-1)^{(2)}$. So, from state R automaton M' does not accept c^{i+1}. It follows that P and R are inequivalent in Case 1. In particular, since all states except the empty set include at least one component with superscript (1), Case 1 shows that the empty set is inequivalent with all other states from M'.

Case 2: All components with superscript (1) in P do belong to R and vice versa. Since P and R are different, there must exist some component $i^{(2)}$ with superscript (2) in the symmetric difference of P and R, say $i^{(2)} \in P \setminus R$. Since all states except the empty set include at least one component with superscript (1) and we are in Case 2, we conclude that there is some component $j^{(1)}$ with superscript (1) in P and R, say $j^{(1)} \in P \cap R$.

To design some input that is accepted by M' from P but is rejected from R, we first proceed as in the second task above by deleting all components from P and R that are different from $i^{(2)}$ and $j^{(1)}$. Let $i < j$. Then we reach the states $P' = \{i^{(2)}, j^{(1)}\}$ and $R' = \{j^{(1)}\}$. Now, by processing c^j, states P' and R' are mapped to $\{0^{(1)}, (n-j+i)^{(2)}\}$ and $\{0^{(1)}\}$. Further, the input a^{j-i} maps then to $\{0^{(2)}, 1^{(1)}, 2^{(1)}, \ldots, (j-i)^{(1)}\}$ and $\{0^{(1)}, 1^{(1)}, 2^{(1)}, \ldots, (j-i)^{(1)}\}$. Finally, extending the input by c yields the states $\{0^{(1)}, 1^{(1)}, \ldots, (j-i-1)^{(1)}, (n-1)^{(2)}\}$ and $\{0^{(1)}, 1^{(1)}, \ldots, (j-i-1)^{(1)}, (n-1)^{(1)}\}$. Therefore, M' accepts the designed input from R but rejects it from P. Similarly, we derive the same result when we assume $j < i$. It follows that P and R are inequivalent in Case 2 as well.

So, all states of M' are reachable and are pairwise inequivalent. Since we have $|Q'| = 1 + 3^n - 2^n$, the theorem follows. □

3.2   Nondeterminization

Next, we address the problem of "nondeterminizing" a given XNFA. We present a construction in the following theorem which leads to an upper bound of $n \cdot 2^{n-1}$ states. In Theorem 4 it will be shown that this upper bound is exactly reached.

Theorem 3. *Let $n \geq 1$ and M be an n-state XNFA. Then $n \cdot 2^{n-1}$ states are sufficient for an NFA to accept $L(M)$.*

Proof. Given an n-state XNFA $M = \langle Q, \Sigma, \delta, q_0, F \rangle$, we are going to construct an equivalent NFA $M' = \langle Q', \Sigma, \delta', q_0', F' \rangle$.

The construction follows the idea that, on the one hand, on a given input M' guesses an accepting path of M in one state component and, on the other hand, M' ensures that all 'non-guessed' states do not lead to acceptance. These non-guessed states are maintained in a second state component.

So, we set $Q' = \{ (q, P) \mid q \in Q, P \in 2^Q, \text{ and } q \notin P \}$ with initial state $q_0' = (q_0, \emptyset)$ and $F' = \{ (q, P) \mid q \in F \text{ and } P \cap F = \emptyset \}$.

Next, we construct the transition function $\delta' : Q' \times \Sigma \to 2^{Q'}$ of M'. To this end, for all $(q, P) \in Q'$ and $a \in \Sigma$, we first consider all $q' \in \delta(q, a)$. If and only if $q' \notin \delta(P, a)$ then $(q', \delta(P, a) \cup \delta(q, a) \setminus \{q'\})$ is put into $\delta'((q, P), a)$.

In order to verify that $L(M) = L(M')$, we consider the computation tree of M on some input w. We claim that the current state (q, P) of M' contains the component q reached by M on a path from the root such that q does not appear on any other branch of the tree (of M) at the same level, and that the component P contains all states different from q on the same level of the computation tree of M.

The claim is true for the initial state $(q_0, \emptyset)$ at the root of the tree.

Arguing inductively, all successor states $(q', P') \in \delta'((q, P), a)$ have a first component that extends the path to q since $q' \in \delta(q, a)$. Moreover, since $q' \notin \delta(P, a)$, state q' does not appear on any other branch of the tree (of M) at the same level. Finally, all states different from q' on the same level of the computation tree of M are collected in $P' = \delta(P, a) \cup \delta(q, a) \setminus \{q'\}$. Therefore, the claim is true.

By the construction of the set F', we conclude that M' reaches an accepting state (q'', P'') after processing input w if and only if q'' belongs to F and appears as leaf of the computation tree of M on w, and all other leaves of the computation tree are labeled with non-accepting states. Thus, if and only if M accepts w. This implies $L(M) = L(M')$.

Concerning the size of the state set of M', we note that every state of M appears in half of the elements of 2^Q. That is, it does not appear in 2^{n-1} elements. Since M has n states we obtain $|Q'| = n \cdot 2^{n-1}$. $\square$

Next, we obtain a matching lower bound for the XNFA to NFA conversion. To this end, we use the so-called (extended) *fooling set* technique (see, for example, [1,5,7]) that is widely used for proving lower bounds on the number of states necessary for an NFA to accept a given language. The proof is omitted here, but the witness automaton is depicted in Fig. 2.

Theorem 4. *Let $n \geq 3$. There exists an n-state XNFA M such that every NFA accepting $L(M)$ has at least $n \cdot 2^{n-1}$ states.*

3.3   NFA-to-XNFA Conversion

Finally, we turn to the descriptional complexity of converting an NFA into an XNFA. The upper bound for the number of states for this conversion can be

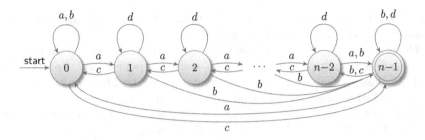

Fig. 2. An n-state XNFA where each equivalent NFA has at least $n \cdot 2^{n-1}$ states.

derived from the determinization of the NFA. Concerning the lower bound, we recall that XNFAs and UFAs somehow share the same restriction with respect to acceptance, but are different with respect to rejection. For example, the determinizations of UFAs and XNFAs show that this difference is significant. However, for every n, an n-state NFA was exhibited in [12] (see Fig. 3) whose smallest equivalent UFA cannot do better in the number of states than the smallest equivalent incomplete DFA. The proof of the lower bound is based on a method given in [18] which is based on a rank argument on certain matrices. This method has been generalized and extended in [12] to obtain the result mentioned. After a thorough analysis of the arguments of the method, it turns out that exclusively accepting computations of the UFAs are used. In other words, the arguments can be applied to XNFAs as well. Again, the detailed proof is omitted here.

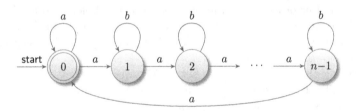

Fig. 3. An n-state NFA where each equivalent XNFA has at least $2^n - 1$ states.

Theorem 5. *Let $n \geq 1$ and M be an n-state NFA. Then $2^n - 1$ states are sufficient for an XNFA to accept $L(M)$. Moreover, there exists an n-state NFA M such that every XNFA accepting $L(M)$ has at least $2^n - 1$ states.*

4   Computational Complexity

In this section, we investigate the computational complexity of XNFAs where we obtain the complexity of several decidability questions for finite automata. It is known (see, for example, the survey given in [8]) that for DFAs the questions of testing emptiness, universality, inclusion, or equivalence are NL-complete. Moreover, the general membership problem is known to be L-complete. For NFAs the general membership problem as well as the emptiness problem are NL-complete, whereas the questions of testing universality, inclusion, or equivalence turn out to be PSPACE-complete.

For XNFAs we get here a different picture: First, the general membership problem is shown to belong to NL. Hence, this property is shared with NFAs. Second, the emptiness problem turns out to be PSPACE-complete and is therefore as difficult as for alternating finite automata. Finally, the questions of testing universality, inclusion, or equivalence are shown to be PSPACE-complete as well.

Theorem 6. *The general membership problem for XNFAs belongs to* NL.

It is not clear yet whether the general membership problem for XNFAs is also NL-hard. So, the NL-completeness of the problem is currently an open question. In contrast to NFAs we now show that the emptiness problem for XNFAs is PSPACE-complete.

Theorem 7. *The emptiness problem for XNFAs is* PSPACE-*complete.*

Proof. First, we show that the problem of non-emptiness belongs to PSPACE. Since PSPACE is closed under complementation, emptiness belongs to PSPACE as well. We describe a nondeterministic Turing machine M which receives a binary encoding $\mathrm{cod}(A)$ of an XNFA A on its read-only input tape and accepts the input if and only if A accepts a non-empty language while the space used on its working tape is bounded by a polynomial in $|\mathrm{cod}(A)|$.

It is shown in Theorem 1 that A can be converted into an equivalent DFA A' with at most 3^n states. This construction basically simulates the computation tree level by level and ensures that not more than one computation path is accepting. To this end, A' has to keep track of up to n states of A either with superscript (1) or with superscript (2). The basic idea for the Turing machine M is to guess a word and to check "on the fly" whether it is accepted by A. To simulate A on the guessed input we apply the construction described above and simulate A' on the guessed input. Thus, we have to keep track of at most n current states of A together with the corresponding superscript. Since each state can be encoded using $O(n)$ tape cells, it is clear that $O(n^2)$ tape cells are sufficient to encode a current state of A'.

Now, the Turing machine M guesses one input symbol a and updates all stored states of A according to the construction in Theorem 1. Additionally, we have to ensure that M stops in reasonable time if $L(A)$ is empty. Hence, we count the length of the guessed word by updating a binary counter and can definitively stop the simulation if the length exceeds 3^n. This behavior of M is now iterated until either an accepting state of A' is entered or the binary counter exceeds 3^n. In the first case, M halts accepting and M halts rejecting in the second case. The first case can be realized using at most $O(n^2)$ tape cells. For the second case we can implement on M's working tape a binary counter that counts up to 3^n. With the usual construction this needs at most $O(\lg(3^n)) = O(n)$ tape cells.

Altogether, we obtain that M decides the non-emptiness of A using an amount of tape cells which is at most polynomial in the length of the input.

To show the PSPACE-hardness of the emptiness problem we reduce the membership problem for linear bounded automata (LBA) which is known to be PSPACE-complete (see, e.g., [4]). Our reduction largely follows a similar reduction given in [9] which proves the PSPACE-hardness of the "Concatenation Equivalence problem" (see Theorem 4.1. in [9]). Let M be an LBA and w be an input to M. Furthermore, let $S = Q \cup \Gamma$, where Q denotes the state set of M and Γ its work-tape alphabet. It is shown in [9] that it is possible in polynomial time to construct two DFAs M_1 and M_2 such that $L(M_1) \cdot L(M_2) = S^*$ if and only if $w \notin L(M)$.

Now, we construct an NFA M' such that $L(M') = L(M_1) \cdot L(M_2)$ in the usual way. This means that we add transitions from all accepting states in M_1 to those states in M_2 which are reached in one step from the initial state of M_2, whereby the transitions are suitably labeled. Moreover, we construct a one-state DFA M'' that accepts S^*. Next, we construct an XNFA M''' as follows. M''' initially guesses whether it simulates for the complete input the NFA M' or the DFA M''. Since M''' is an XNFA we obtain that $L(M') = S^*$ if and only if $L(M''') = \emptyset$. Hence, we have $L(M''') = \emptyset$ if and only if $L(M_1) \cdot L(M_2) = S^*$ if and only if $w \notin L(M)$. Since the constructions of M', M'', and M''' can be realized in polynomial time, we obtain the PSPACE-hardness of the emptiness problem for XNFAs. $\square$

Next, it turns out that the remaining problems are PSPACE-complete as well.

Theorem 8. *The problems of testing universality, inclusion, and equivalence for XNFAs are PSPACE-complete.*

5   Future Work

At least three lines of future research result from our findings. First, the lower bounds shown in Theorem 2 for DFAs and in Theorem 4 for NFAs are making use of a four-letter alphabet. It is a natural question whether the tightness of the lower bounds can also be shown with a smaller alphabet size consisting of three or two letters. Another question is how and to which extent upper and lower bounds are changing in case of a unary alphabet. Second, the NL-hardness and, hence, the NL-completeness of the general membership problem for XNFAs is currently an open problem. Finally, it would be interesting to investigate the state complexity costs of converting XNFAs to alternating finite automata and vice versa.

References

1. Birget, J.C.: Intersection and union of regular languages and state complexity. Inform. Process. Lett. **43**, 185–190 (1992)
2. Blass, A., Gurevich, Y.: On the unique satisfiability problem. Inf. Control **55**, 80–88 (1982)
3. Chandra, A., Kozen, D., Stockmeyer, L.: Alternation. J. ACM **21**, 114–133 (1981)
4. Garey, M.R., Johnson, D.S.: Computers and Intractability: A Guide to the Theory of NP-Completeness. Freeman (1979)
5. Glaister, I., Shallit, J.: A lower bound technique for the size of nondeterministic finite automata. Inform. Process. Lett. **59**, 75–77 (1996)
6. Hemaspaandra, L.A., Ogihara, M.: The Complexity Theory Companion. Springer (2002)
7. Holzer, M., Kutrib, M.: Nondeterministic finite automata - Recent results on the descriptional and computational complexity. Int. J. Found. Comput. Sci. **20**, 563–580 (2009)
8. Holzer, M., Kutrib, M.: Descriptional and computational complexity of finite automata - A survey. Inform. Comput. **209**, 456–470 (2011)
9. Jiang, T., Ravikumar, B.: Minimal NFA problems are hard. SIAM J. Comput. **22**, 1117–1141 (1993)
10. Jones, N.D.: Space-bounded reducibility among combinatorial problems. J. Comput. Syst. Sci. **11**, 68–85 (1975)
11. Leiss, E.L.: Succinct representation of regular languages by Boolean automata. Theor. Comput. Sci. **13**, 323–330 (1981)
12. Leung, H.: Separating exponentially ambiguous finite automata from polynomially ambiguous finite automata. SIAM J. Comput. **27**, 1073–1082 (1998)
13. Leung, H.: Descriptional complexity of NFA of different ambiguity. Int. J. Found. Comput. Sci. **16**, 975–984 (2005)
14. Meyer, A.R., Fischer, M.J.: Economy of description by automata, grammars, and formal systems. In: Symposium on Switching and Automata Theory (SWAT 1971), pp. 188–191. IEEE (1971)
15. Moore, F.R.: On the bounds for state-set size in the proofs of equivalence between deterministic, nondeterministic, and two-way finite automata. IEEE Trans. Comput. **20**, 1211–1214 (1971)
16. Rabin, M.O., Scott, D.: Finite automata and their decision problems. IBM J. Res. Dev. **3**, 114–125 (1959)
17. Sakoda, W.J., Sipser, M.: Nondeterminism and the size of two way finite automata. In: Symposium on Theory of Computing (STOC 1978), pp. 275–286. ACM (1978)
18. Schmidt, E.M.: Succinctness of Dscriptions of Context-Free, Regular and Finite Languages. Ph.D. thesis, Cornell University, Ithaca, NY (1978)
19. Vuillemin, J., Gama, N.: Efficient equivalence and minimization for non deterministic Xor automata. Tech. Rep, Ecole Normale Supérieure, Paris (2010)
20. van Zijl, L.: On binary $\oplus$-NFAs and succinct descriptions of regular languages. Theor. Comput. Sci. **328**, 161–170 (2004)

Shortest Accepted Strings for Two-Way Finite Automata: Approaching the 2^n Lower Bound

Olga Martynova and Alexander Okhotin[(✉)]

Department of Mathematics and Computer Science, Saint Petersburg State University, 7/9 Universitetskaya nab., Saint Petersburg 199034, Russia
alexander.okhotin@spbu.ru

Abstract. The maximum length of the shortest string accepted by an n-state two-way finite automaton is known to be at least of the order $\Omega(1.626^n)$ and at most $\binom{2n}{n+1} = O(\frac{1}{\sqrt{n}}4^n)$. In this paper, a family of n-state automata with shortest accepted strings of length $\frac{3}{4} \cdot 2^n - 1$ is constructed, thus improving the lower bound. For the special case of direction-determinate automata (those that always remember in the current state whether the last move was to the left or to the right), the maximum length of the shortest accepted string is determined precisely as $\binom{n}{\lfloor \frac{n}{2} \rfloor} - 1 = \Theta(\frac{1}{\sqrt{n}}2^n)$.

1   Introduction

A natural question about automata and related models of computation is the length of the shortest string an automaton accepts. A function mapping the size of an automaton to the maximum length of the shortest accepted string, with the maximum taken over all automata of that size, is a certain complexity measure for a family of automata.

For one-way finite automata, this measure is trivial: the length of the shortest string accepted by a nondeterministic finite automaton (NFA) with n states is at most $n - 1$: this is the length of the shortest path to an accepting state. On the other hand, Ellul et al. [4] proved that the length of shortest strings *not* accepted by an n-state NFA is exponential in n. Similar questions were studied for other models and some variants of the problem. Chistikov et al. [2] investigated the length of shortest strings in counter automata. The length of shortest strings in formal grammars under intersections with regular languages was studied by Pierre [10], and recently by Shemetova et al. [11]. Alpoge et al. [1] investigated shortest strings in intersections of deterministic one-way finite automata (DFA).

The maximum length of shortest strings for deterministic two-way finite automata (2DFA) has been investigated in two recent papers. First of all, from the well-known proof of the PSPACE-completeness of the emptiness problem for 2DFA by Kozen [7] it is understood that the length of the shortest string

---

This work was supported by the Russian Science Foundation, project 23-11-00133.

H. Bordihn et al. (Eds.): DCFS 2023, LNCS 13918, pp. 134–145, 2023.
https://doi.org/10.1007/978-3-031-34326-1_10

accepted by an n-state 2DFA can be exponential in n. There is also an exponential upper bound on this length, given by transforming a 2DFA to an NFA: the construction by Kapoutsis [6] uses at most $\binom{2n}{n+1} = \Theta(\frac{1}{\sqrt{n}}4^n)$ states, and hence the length of the shortest string is slightly less than 4^n. Overall, the maximum length of the shortest string is exponential, with the base bounded by 4.

The first attempt to determine the exact base was made by Dobronravov et al. [3], who constructed a family of n-state 2DFA with shortest strings of length $\Omega((\sqrt[5]{10})^n) \geqslant \Omega(1.584^n)$. The automata they have actually constructed belong to a special class of 2DFA: the *direction-determinate automata*. These are 2DFA with the set of states split into states accessible only by transitions from the right and states accessible only by transitions from the left: in other words, direction-determinate automata always remember the direction of the last transition in their state.

Later, Krymski and Okhotin [8] extended the method of Dobronravov et al. [3] to produce automata of a more general form, with longer shortest accepted strings. They constructed a family of non-direction-determinate 2DFA with shortest strings of length $\Omega((\sqrt[4]{7})^n) \geqslant \Omega(1.626^n)$.

This paper improves these bounds. First, the maximum length of the shortest string accepted by n-state direction-determinate 2DFA is determined precisely as $\binom{n}{\lfloor \frac{n}{2} \rfloor} - 1 = \Theta(\frac{1}{\sqrt{n}}2^n)$. The upper bound on the length of the shortest string immediately follows from the complexity of transforming direction-determinate 2DFA to NFA, see Geffert and Okhotin [5]. A matching lower bound is proved by a direct construction of a family of n-state automata.

The second result of this paper is that not remembering the direction helps to accept longer shortest strings: a family of n-state non-direction-determinate automata with shortest strings of length $\frac{3}{4} \cdot 2^n - 1$ is constructed. This is more than what is possible in direction-determinate automata.

2 Definitions

Definition 1. *A two-way deterministic finite automaton (2DFA) is a quintuple* $\mathcal{A} = (\Sigma, Q, q_0, \delta, F)$, *in which:*

- Σ *is a finite alphabet, which does not contain two special symbols: the left end-marker (⊢) and the right end-marker (⊣);*
- Q *is a finite set of states;*
- $q_0 \in Q$ *is the initial state;*
- $\delta \colon Q \times (\Sigma \cup \{\vdash, \dashv\}) \to Q \times \{-1, +1\}$ *is a partial transition function;*
- $F \subseteq Q$ *is the set of accepting states, effective at the right end-marker (⊣).*

An input string $w = a_1 \ldots a_m \in \Sigma^*$ *is given to an automaton on a tape* $\vdash a_1 \ldots a_m \dashv$. *The automaton starts at the left end-marker* $\vdash$ *in the state* q_0. *At each moment, if the automaton is in a state* $q \in Q$ *and sees a symbol* $a \in \Sigma \cup \{\vdash, \dashv\}$, *then, according to the transition function* $\delta(q, a) = (r, d)$, *it enters a new state* r *and moves to the left or to the right depending on the direction* d. *If the requested value* $\delta(q, a)$ *is not defined, then the automaton rejects.*

The automaton accepts the string, if it ever comes to the right end-marker ⊣ in any state from F. The automaton can also loop.

    The language recognized by an automaton A, denoted by L(A), is the set of all strings it accepts.

This paper also uses a subclass of 2DFA, in which one can determine the direction of the previous transition from the current state.

Definition 2 ([9]). *A 2DFA is called direction-determinate, if there is a partition of the set of states $Q = Q^+ \cup Q^-$, with $Q^+ \cap Q^- = \varnothing$, such that for each transition $\delta(q, a) = (r, +1)$, the state r must belong to Q^+, and for each transition $\delta(q, a) = (r, -1)$, the state r is in Q^-.*

The known upper bounds on the length of the shortest accepted string are different for direction-determinate 2DFA and for 2DFA of the general form. These bounds are inferred from the complexity of transforming two-way automata with n states to one-way NFA: for 2DFA of the general form, as proved by Kapoutsis [6], it is sufficient and in the worst case necessary to use $\binom{2n}{n}$ states in a simulating NFA, whereas for direction-determinate 2DFA the simulating NFA requires $\binom{n}{\lfloor \frac{n}{2} \rfloor}$ states in the worst case, see Geffert and Okhotin [5]. Since the shortest string in a language cannot be longer than the shortest path to an accepting state in an NFA, the following bounds hold.

Proposition 1 (Dobronravov et al. [3]). *Let $n \geqslant 1$, and let A be a 2DFA with n states, which accepts at least one string. Then the length of the shortest string accepted by A is at most $\binom{2n}{n} - 1$. If the automaton A is direction-determinate, then the length of the shortest accepted string does not exceed $\binom{n}{\lfloor \frac{n}{2} \rfloor} - 1$.*

The first result of this paper is that this upper bound for direction-determinate automata is actually precise.

3 Shortest Accepted Strings for Direction-Determinate Automata

In this section, direction-determinate automata with the maximum possible length $\binom{n}{\lfloor \frac{n}{2} \rfloor} - 1$ of shortest accepted strings, where n is the number of states, will be constructed.

    Automata are constructed for every k and ℓ, where k is the number of states reachable by transitions to the right and ℓ is the number of states reachable in the left direction. The following theorem shall be proved.

Theorem 1. *For every $k \geqslant 2$ and $\ell \geqslant 0$ there exists a direction-determinate 2DFA with the set of states $Q = Q^+ \cup Q^-$, where $|Q^+| = k$ and $|Q^-| = \ell$, such that the length of the shortest string it accepts is $\binom{k+\ell}{\ell+1} - 1$.*

The automaton constructed in the theorem works as follows. While working on its shortest string, it processes every pair of consecutive symbols by moving back and forth between them, thus effectively comparing them to each other.

Table 1. All pairs (P, R) for sets of states $Q^+ = \{1, 2, 3\}$ and $Q^- = \{1', 2'\}$.

pairs (P, R)	sequences
$\varnothing, \{1\}$	(1)
$\{2'\}, \{1, 2\}$	$(1, -2', 2)$
$\{2'\}, \{1, 3\}$	$(1, -2', 3)$
$\{1'\}, \{1, 2\}$	$(1, -1', 2)$
$\{1', 2'\}, \{1, 2, 3\}$	$(1, -1', 2, -2', 3)$
$\{1'\}, \{1, 3\}$	$(1, -1', 3)$
$\varnothing, \{2\}$	(2)
$\{2'\}, \{2, 3\}$	$(2, -2', 3)$
$\{1'\}, \{2, 3\}$	$(2, -1', 3)$
$\varnothing, \{3\}$	(3)

Eventually it moves on to the next pair and processes it in the same way. It cannot come back to the previous pair anymore, because it has no transitions for that.

The automaton's motion between two neighbouring symbols begins when it first arrives from the first symbol to the second in some state from Q^+. Then it moves back and forth, alternating between states from Q^+ at the second symbol and states from Q^- at the first symbol, and finally leaves the second symbol to the right. Among the states visited by the automaton during this back-and-forth motion, the number of states from Q^+ is greater by one than the number of states from Q^-. Two such sets of states will be denoted by a pair (P, R), where $P \subseteq Q^-$, $R \subseteq Q^+$ and $|R| = |P| + 1$.

Proposition 2. There are $\binom{k+\ell}{\ell+1}$ different pairs (P, R), such that $P \subseteq Q^-$, $R \subseteq Q^+$ and $|R| = |P| + 1$.

The proof is standard and is therefore omitted.

Let the sets Q^+ and Q^- be linearly ordered. Then one can define an order on the set of pairs (P, R) as follows. In every such pair, let $P = \{p_1, \ldots, p_m\}$, where $p_1 < \ldots < p_m$, and $R = \{r_1, \ldots, r_{m+1}\}$, where $r_1 < \ldots < r_{m+1}$. There is a corresponding sequence to each pair, of the form $r_1, -p_1, r_2, -p_2, \ldots, r_m, -p_m, r_{m+1}$, and different pairs are compared by the lexicographic order on these sequences. In Table 1, all pairs (P, R), for $k = 3$ and $\ell = 2$, are given in increasing order, along with the corresponding sequences.

Let $N = \binom{k+\ell}{\ell+1}$ be the number of pairs. Then all pairs are enumerated in increasing order as $(P^{(1)}, R^{(1)}) < \ldots < (P^{(N)}, R^{(N)})$, where $P^{(i)} = \{p_1^{(i)}, \ldots, p_{m_i}^{(i)}\}$ and $R^{(i)} = \{r_1^{(i)}, \ldots, r_{m_i+1}^{(i)}\}$. In particular, the least pair is $(P^{(1)}, R^{(1)}) = (\varnothing, \{\min Q^+\})$, because the corresponding sequence $(\min Q^+)$ is lexicographically the least. The greatest pair is $(P^{(N)}, R^{(N)}) = (\varnothing, \{\max Q^+\})$.

The desired direction-determinate automaton A with the shortest accepted string of length $N - 1$ is defined over an alphabet $\Sigma = \{a_1, \ldots, a_{N-1}\}$, and the

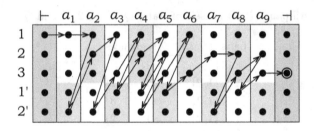

Fig. 1. The accepting computation of the automaton A on the string w, for $k = 3$ and $\ell = 2$.

shortest accepted string will be $w = a_1 \ldots a_{N-1}$. The set of states is defined as $Q = Q^+ \cup Q^-$, where $Q^+ = \{1, \ldots, k\}$ and $Q^- = \{1', \ldots, \ell'\}$. The initial state is $q_0 = 1$. The only transition by the left end-marker ($\vdash$) leads from the initial state to the least state in $R^{(1)}$.

$$\delta(q_0, \vdash) = (r_1^{(1)}, +1) \tag{1a}$$

For each symbol a_i, transitions are defined in the states $R^{(i)} \cup P^{(i+1)}$. If the automaton is at the symbol a_i in any state from $R^{(i)}$ (except for the greatest state), then it moves to the left in the corresponding state from $P^{(i)}$.

$$\delta(r_j^{(i)}, a_i) = (p_j^{(i)}, -1) \qquad (j \in \{1, \ldots, m_i\}) \tag{1b}$$

For the greatest state in $R^{(i)}$, there is no corresponding state in $P^{(i)}$, and so the automaton moves to the right (and this is the only way to move from Q^+ to Q^+, and hence the only way to advance from the symbol a_i to the next symbol for the first time).

$$\delta(r_{m_i+1}^{(i)}, a_i) = (r_1^{(i+1)}, +1) \tag{1c}$$

In each state from $P^{(i)}$, the automaton moves to the right in the next available state from $R^{(i)}$.

$$\delta(p_j^{(i+1)}, a_i) = (r_{j+1}^{(i+1)}, +1) \qquad (j \in \{1, \ldots, m_{i+1}\}) \tag{1d}$$

There are no transitions at the right end-marker, and there is one accepting state: $F = \{r_{m_N+1}^{(N)}\}$.

The computation of the automaton on the string $w = a_1 \ldots a_{N-1}$ is illustrated in Fig. 1. The automaton gradually advances, and moves between every two subsequent symbols, a_{i-1} and a_i, according to the sets P_i and R_i. Transitions at a_i expect that there is a_{i-1} to the left, whereas transitions at a_{i-1} expect a_i to the right. As long as every symbol is followed by the next symbol in order, these expectations will be fulfilled each time, and the automaton accepts in the end.

Lemma 1. *The automaton A accepts the string $w = a_1 \ldots a_{N-1}$.*

The proof proceeds by showing that the automaton, executed on the string w, eventually arrives at each symbol a_i in the corresponding state $r^{(i)}_{m_i+1}$, which is the only state in Q^+ with a transition by a_i going to the right. This is established inductively on i; the details are omitted due to space constraints.

Next, it is claimed that the automaton A cannot accept any shorter string. It cannot accept the empty string; if it did, then the first transition would lead to the right end-marker in the state 1, and the automaton would reject, because $k \neq 1$. Every accepted non-empty string must satisfy a number of conditions.

Lemma 2. *Every string accepted by the automaton A begins with the symbol a_1.*

Indeed, a_1 is the only symbol with a transition to the right in the state 1 (and any transition to the left leads to rejection at the left end-marker).

The next property is obtained by a symmetric argument.

Lemma 3. *Every string accepted by the automaton A ends with the symbol a_{N-1}.*

Here, since there are no transitions to the left at the right-end marker, in order to accept, the automaton should arrive there in the accepting state $\max Q^+$ at the first time. Among all the symbols, a_{N-1} is the only one with a transition to $\max Q^+$ from some state in Q^+.

Finally, it is proved that the automaton cannot skip any number, that is, the number of every next symbol, as compared to the number of the previous symbol, cannot increase by more than 1. If the number decreases or does not change, this would make the string only longer; but in order to reach a_{N-1} from a_1 without skipping any number, the automaton would have to move through all symbols of the alphabet, and therefore an accepted string cannot be shorter than $N - 1$ symbols.

Lemma 4. *No string accepted by the automaton A may contain any substring of the form $a_i a_j$, where $j > i + 1$.*

The general idea is that once the automaton first moves from a_i to a_j, it starts an exchange of transitions between these two symbols. If the symbols match each other, that is, if $i + 1 = j$, then all transitions by both symbols are used one by one, and eventually the automaton advances to the right from a_j. Let $i + 1 < j$. As always, the transitions at a_i expect to see a_{i+1} to the right, and transitions at a_j expect a_{j-1} to the left. For a while, the sequences of transitions assumed at a_i and at a_j may coincide, and the automaton moves between the symbols while it is so. But eventually a mismatch between the sequences is reached, and it follows from the lexicographic order that the next transition will be undefined.

Together, Lemmata 1–4 show that the shortest string accepted by the automaton is of length $N - 1 = \binom{k+\ell}{\ell+1} - 1$, which completes the proof of Theorem 1. Taking $k = \lceil \frac{n}{2} \rceil$ states in Q^+ and $\ell = \lfloor \frac{n}{2} \rfloor$ states in Q^- yields the following lower bound (which is precise in view of Proposition 1).

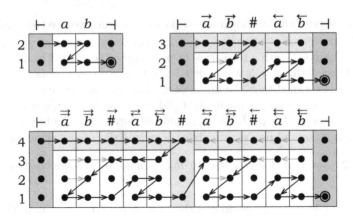

Fig. 2. Computations of automata A_2, A_3 and A_4 from the proof of Theorem 2 on their shortest strings w_2, w_3 and w_4.

Corollary 1 (from Theorem 1). *For every $n \geqslant 2$, there is a direction-determinate 2DFA with n states, such that the length of the shortest string it accepts is $\binom{n}{\lfloor \frac{n}{2} \rfloor} - 1$.*

4 Longer Shortest Strings for Automata of the General Form

The main result of this section is the construction of a family of 2DFA with shortest strings of length $3 \cdot 2^{n-2} - 1$, where n is the number of states in an automaton. This is more than the maximum possible length of shortest strings for direction-determinate automata; in other words, *forgetting the direction is useful*.

Theorem 2. *For each $n \geqslant 2$ there exists a 2DFA with n states, such that the shortest string it accepts is of length $3 \cdot 2^{n-2} - 1$.*

Proof. The automata and the shortest strings they accept are constructed inductively; for small values of n they are given in Fig. 2.

For the inductive proof to work, the following set of properties is ensured for every n.

Claim. For each $n \geqslant 2$ there exists a 2DFA $A_n = (\Sigma_n, Q_n, \delta_n)$ with no transitions by end-markers, no initial state and no accepting states, with the set of states $Q_n = \{1, \ldots, n\}$, and there exists a string $w_n \in \Sigma_n^*$ of length $3 \cdot 2^{n-2} - 1$, such that the following two properties hold.

1. If A_n starts at any symbol of w_n in the state n, then it eventually leaves this string by a transition from its rightmost symbol to the right in the state 1.

2. If for some non-empty string u there exists a position, in which the automaton A_n can start in the state n and eventually leave the string u by a transition from its rightmost symbol to the right in the state 1, then u is at least as long as w_n.

The first observation is that Theorem 2 follows from this claim. Let $n \geqslant 2$, and let A_n and w_n be an automaton and a string that satisfy the conditions in the claim. Then A_n is supplemented with an initial state n, a set of accepting states $\{1\}$ and a single transition by the left end-marker: from the state n to the state n; no transitions by the right end-marker are defined. The resulting automaton A'_n becomes a valid 2DFA, and it accepts the string w_n as follows: from the initial state at $\vdash$ it moves to the first symbol of w_n in the state n, then, by the first point of the claim, the automaton eventually leaves w_n to the right in the state 1, and thus arrives to the right end-marker $\dashv$ in an accepting state.

To see that every string accepted by A'_n is of length at least $|w_n|$, let u be any accepted string. It is not empty, because on the empty string the automaton steps on the right end-marker in the state n and rejects. Then, after the first step the automaton A'_n is at the first symbol of u in the state n. It cannot return to $\vdash$, because it has already used the only transition at this label, and if it ever comes back, it will reject or loop. Also the automaton cannot come to $\dashv$ in states other than 1. In order to accept, it must arrive to $\dashv$ in the state 1, and this is the first and the only time when it leaves the string u. Then, by the second point of the claim, the length of u cannot be less than the length of w_n.

It remains to prove the claim, which is done by induction on n.

Base case: $n = 2$. The automaton $A_2 = (\Sigma_2, Q_2, \delta_2)$ for $n = 2$ is constructed as follows. The alphabet is $\Sigma_2 = \{a, b\}$, the set of states is $Q_2 = \{1, 2\}$, and the string w_2 is ab. The transitions of A_2 are defined by its computation on w_2 presented in Fig. 2 (top left). The string w_2 meets the first condition of the claim, and none of the shorter strings (that is, a or b) violate the second condition.

Induction step: $n \to n + 1$. Let an n-state 2DFA $A_n = (\Sigma_n, Q_n, \delta_n)$ and a string $w_n \in \Sigma_n^*$ satisfy the claim. The $(n + 1)$-state automaton A_{n+1} satisfying the claim is constructed as follows. Let $A_{n+1} = (\Sigma_{n+1}, Q_{n+1}, \delta_{n+1})$.

- Its alphabet is $\Sigma_{n+1} = \overrightarrow{\Sigma_n} \cup \overleftarrow{\Sigma_n} \cup \{\#\}$, where $\overrightarrow{\Sigma_n} = \{\overrightarrow{a} \mid a \in \Sigma_n\}$ and $\overleftarrow{\Sigma_n} = \{\overleftarrow{a} \mid a \in \Sigma_n\}$.
- The set of states is $Q_{n+1} = Q_n \cup \{n + 1\} = \{1, \ldots, n + 1\}$.
- The transition function is defined as follows. In the new state $n + 1$, the automaton moves by all symbols with arrows in the directions pointed by the arrows.

$$\delta_{n+1}(n + 1, \overrightarrow{a}) = (n + 1, +1), \qquad \text{for } a \in \Sigma$$
$$\delta_{n+1}(n + 1, \overleftarrow{a}) = (n + 1, -1), \qquad \text{for } a \in \Sigma$$

In all old states $1, \ldots, n$, on symbols with arrows, the new automaton works in the same way as the automaton A_n on the corresponding symbols without arrows.

$$\delta_{n+1}(i, \overrightarrow{a}) = \delta_{n+1}(i, \overleftarrow{a}) = \delta_n(i, a), \qquad \text{for } a \in \Sigma \text{ and } i \in \{1, \ldots, n\}$$

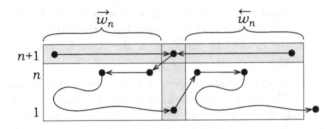

Fig. 3. Computation of the automaton A_{n+1} on the string w_{n+1}.

By the new separator symbol #, only two transitions are defined. In the state $n + 1$, the automaton moves to the left in the state n, thus starting the automaton A_n on the substring to the left.

$$\delta_{n+1}(n + 1, \#) = (n, -1)$$

And if the automaton gets to # in the state 1 (which happens after concluding the simulation of A_n on the substring to the left), then the automaton moves to the right in the state n to start the simulation of A_n also on the substring to the right of the separator #.

$$\delta_{n+1}(1, \#) = (n, +1)$$

The rest of transitions are undefined.

Note that once the automaton A_{n+1} leaves the state $n + 1$, it never returns to it, because there are no transitions to $n+1$ from any other state. Let $h \colon (\overrightarrow{\Sigma_n} \cup \overleftarrow{\Sigma_n})^* \to \Sigma_n^*$ be a string homomorphism which removes the arrow from the top of every symbol, that is, $h(\overrightarrow{a}) = h(\overleftarrow{a}) = a$ for all $a \in \Sigma_n$. The automaton A_{n+1} works in the states $1, \ldots, n$ on symbols from $\overrightarrow{\Sigma_n} \cup \overleftarrow{\Sigma_n}$ as A_n works on the corresponding symbols from Σ_n. Then, if $h(w) = w_n$ for some $w \in (\overrightarrow{\Sigma_n} \cup \overleftarrow{\Sigma_n})^*$, it follows that the automaton A_{n+1}, having started in the state n at any symbol of w, eventually leaves the string w by moving to the right in the state 1. Furthermore, if $|w| < |w_n|$ for some string $w \in (\overrightarrow{\Sigma_n} \cup \overleftarrow{\Sigma_n})^*$, then the automaton A_{n+1}, having started in the state n at any symbol of w, cannot leave the string by moving to the right in the state 1.

The string w_{n+1} is defined as $\overrightarrow{w_n} \# \overleftarrow{w_n}$, where $\overrightarrow{a_1 \ldots a_\ell} = \overrightarrow{a_1} \ldots \overrightarrow{a_\ell}$ and $\overleftarrow{a_1 \ldots a_\ell} = \overleftarrow{a_1} \ldots \overleftarrow{a_\ell}$ for every string $a_1 \ldots a_\ell \in \Sigma_n^*$. The length of w_{n+1} is $|w_{n+1}| = 2|w_n| + 1 = 2(3 \cdot 2^{n-2} - 1) + 1 = 3 \cdot 2^{n-1} - 1$, as desired.

First, it is proved that the automaton A_{n+1} works on the string w_{n+1} as stated in the first point of the claim. As shown in Fig. 3, it moves to the separator #, and then simulates the computation of A_n on the string w_n while working on the string $\overrightarrow{w_n}$ to the left of the separator. By the induction hypothesis, the automaton reaches the separator in the state 1. From there, it proceeds with simulating the computation of A_n an w_n again, this time while working on $\overleftarrow{w_n}$

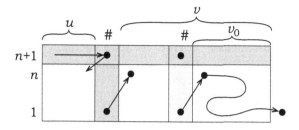

Fig. 4. The partition $w = u\#v$ and the suffix v_0 of v.

to the right of the separator. Finally, by the induction hypothesis, it leaves to the right in the state 1, as claimed.

Turning to the second point of the claim, it should be proved that computations of a certain form are impossible on any strings shorter than w_{n+1}. Let $w \in \Sigma_{n+1}^*$ be a string, and let there be a position in w, such that the automaton A_{n+1}, having started at this position in the state $n + 1$, eventually leaves the string w by a transition to the right in the state 1. It is claimed that $|w| \geqslant |w_{n+1}|$.

Consider the computation of A_{n+1} leading out of w to the right in the state 1. It begins in the state $n + 1$, and the automaton maintains the state $n + 1$ at all symbols except #. In order to reach the state 1, there should be a moment in the computation on w when the automaton arrives at some symbol # in the state $n+1$. Let u be the prefix of w to the left of this #, and let v be the suffix to the right of this #; note that the substrings u and v may contain more symbols #. It is sufficient to prove that $|u| \geqslant |w_n|$ and $|v| \geqslant |w_n|$.

Consider first the case of the suffix v. Let v_0 be the longest suffix of v that does not contain the symbol #; then the symbol preceding v_0 in w is the separator #, as shown in Fig. 4. Once the automaton A_{n+1} steps from the last # in w to the right, it arrives to the first symbol of v_0 in the state n (by the unique transition to the right at #). The string v_0 cannot be empty, because $n \neq 1$. Once the automaton is inside v_0, it cannot return to # anymore, since it has already used the only transition to the right from #, and cannot use it again without looping. Therefore, the automaton A_{n+1} starts on the string $v_0 \in (\Sigma_{n+1} \setminus \{\#\})^*$ in the state n, and, operating as A_n, eventually leaves this string to the right in the state 1. Then $|v_0| \geqslant |w_n|$ by the induction hypothesis, and hence $|v| \geqslant |w_n|$.

For the prefix u, the proof is generally analogous, but is divided into two cases: the case when the automaton does not encounter any separators # inside u, and the case when a separator inside u is reached. In either case, the induction hypothesis is ultimately invoked to prove that $|u| \geqslant |w_n|$. Here the details are omitted due to space constraints.

This confirms that $|w| = |u|+1+|v| \geqslant |w_n|+1+|w_n| = |w_{n+1}|$ and completes the proof. □

Table 2. The maximum length of shortest accepted strings for n-state 2DFA, for small n.

n	direction-determinate 2DFA $\binom{n}{\lfloor n/2 \rfloor} - 1$	2DFA of the general form		
		lower bound $3 \cdot 2^{n-2} - 1$	computed values	upper bound $\binom{2n}{n+1} - 1$
2	1	2	2	3
3	2	5	6	14
4	5	11	17	55
5	9	23	32	209
6	19	47		791

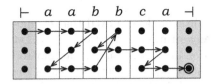

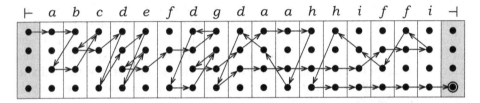

Fig. 5. Automata found by computer programs, and their shortest strings: (top) 3 states, string of length 6; (bottom) 4 states, string of length 17.

5 Conclusion

The maximum length of the shortest accepted string for direction-determinate 2DFA has been determined precisely, whereas for 2DFA of the general form, a lower bound of the order 2^n has been established. The known upper bound on this length is of the order ca. 4^n. Bounds on the maximum length of shortest strings for small values of the number of states n are given in Table 2.

In the table, besides the theoretical bounds, there are also some computed values of the length of shortest strings in some automata. The example for $n = 3$ was obtained by exhaustive search, while the examples for $n = 4$ and $n = 5$ were found by heuristic search. Therefore, the maximum length of the shortest string for 3-state automata is now known precisely, for 4-state automata it is at least 17 and possibly more, and the given length of strings for 5 states is most likely much less than possible. The computations of the automata found for $n = 3$ and $n = 4$ on their shortest strings are presented in Fig. 5.

It should be noted that these computed values exceed the theoretical lower bound $\frac{3}{4} \cdot 2^n - 1$ proved in this paper, and are much less than the known upper bound $\binom{2n}{n+1} - 1$. Thus, the bounds for 2DFA of the general form are still in need of improvement.

Another parameter to be refined is the size of the alphabet of the construction. Both constructions in this paper use an alphabet of exponential size. For a fixed alphabet, the maximum known length of shortest strings is $\Omega(1.275^n)$ [8]. Would it be possible to encode the construction in the present paper over a fixed alphabet to surpass this bound? What is the exact maximum length of shortest strings accepted by n-state 2DFAs over an m-symbol alphabet?

References

1. Alpoge, L., Ang, T., Schaeffer, L., Shallit, J.: Decidability and shortest strings in formal languages. In: Holzer, M., Kutrib, M., Pighizzini, G. (eds.) DCFS 2011. LNCS, vol. 6808, pp. 55–67. Springer, Heidelberg (2011). https://doi.org/10.1007/978-3-642-22600-7_5
2. Chistikov, D., Czerwiński, W., Hofman, P., Pilipczuk, M., Wehar, M.: Shortest paths in one-counter systems. In: Jacobs, B., Löding, C. (eds.) FoSSaCS 2016. LNCS, vol. 9634, pp. 462–478. Springer, Heidelberg (2016). https://doi.org/10.1007/978-3-662-49630-5_27
3. Dobronravov, E., Dobronravov, N., Okhotin, A.: On the length of shortest strings accepted by two-way finite automata. Fundam. Informaticae **180**(4), 315-331 (2021). https://doi.org/10.3233/FI-2021-2044
4. Ellul, K., Krawetz, B., Shallit, J., Wang, M.-W.: Regular expressions: new results and open problems. J. Automata Lang. Comb. **10**(4), 407-437 (2005). https://doi.org/10.25596/jalc-2005-407
5. Geffert, V., Okhotin, A.: One-way simulation of two-way finite automata over small alphabets. In: Proceedings of Non-Classical Models for Automata and Applications (NCMA 2013) Umeå, Sweden, 13–14 August 2013
6. Kapoutsis, C.: Removing bidirectionality from nondeterministic finite automata. In: Jedrzejowicz, J., Szepietowski, A. (eds.) MFCS 2005. LNCS, vol. 3618, pp. 544–555. Springer, Heidelberg (2005). https://doi.org/10.1007/11549345_47
7. Kozen, D.: Lower bounds for natural proof systems. In: Proceedings og 18th Annual Symposium on Foundations of Computer Science (FOCS 1977), pp. 254-266 (1977). https://doi.org/10.1109/SFCS.1977.16
8. Krymski, S., Okhotin, A.: Longer shortest strings in two-way finite automata. In: Jirásková, G., Pighizzini, G. (eds.) DCFS 2020. LNCS, vol. 12442, pp. 104–116. Springer, Cham (2020). https://doi.org/10.1007/978-3-030-62536-8_9
9. Kunc, M., Okhotin, A.: Reversibility of computations in graph-walking automata. Inf. Comput. **275**, 104631 (2020). https://doi.org/10.1016/j.ic.2020.104631
10. Pierre, L.: Rational indexes of generators of the cone of context-free languages. Theor. Comput. Sci. **95**(2), 279-305 (1992). https://doi.org/10.1016/0304-3975(92)90269-L
11. Shemetova, E.N., Okhotin, A., Grigorev, S.V.: Rational index of languages with bounded dimension of parse trees. In: Proceedings of Developments in Language Theory (DLT 2022), pp. 263-273 (2022). https://doi.org/10.1007/978-3-031-05578-2_21

Pushdown and One-Counter Automata: Constant and Non-constant Memory Usage

Giovanni Pighizzini[iD] and Luca Prigioniero[✉][iD]

Dipartimento di Informatica, Università degli Studi di Milano, Milan, Italy
`{pighizzini,prigioniero}@di.unimi.it`

Abstract. It cannot be decided whether a one-counter automaton accepts each string in its language using a counter whose value is bounded by a constant. Furthermore, when the counter is bounded by a constant, its value cannot be limited by any recursive function in the size of the machine. We consider three measures: the costs of all computations (**strong** measure), all accepting computations (**accept** measure), and the least expensive accepting computation (**weak** measure). By taking into account the **strong** and **accept** measures, the above-mentioned problem becomes decidable for both pushdown automata and one-counter automata. Moreover, the bounds for the pushdown height or the value of the counter, when non constant, are recursive in the size of the machine. We also prove that, under the **weak** measure, if a one-counter automaton accepts with a counter that, with respect to the input length is not bounded by any constant, then the counter grows at least as a logarithmic function. This bound can be reached. This is in contrast with the case of pushdown automata in which the optimal bound is double logarithmic. For the **strong** and **accept** measures these bounds are shown to be linear, for both pushdown and one-counter automata.

Keywords: Descriptional complexity · One-counter automata · Pushdown automata

1 Introduction

The relative succinctness of devices describing the same class of languages is a classical topic in formal languages and automata theory and, for sure, it is the central topic in the field of descriptional complexity. In this respect, many results have been obtained for devices describing the class of regular languages. Among them, besides several variants of finite automata (as one-way and two-way, deterministic and nondeterministic), *constant-height pushdown automata* have been considered (see, e.g., [5,9,11]). These devices are pushdown automata that can accept each word in their languages by making use of a constant (namely not depending on the input length) amount of pushdown store. This allows to simulate these devices by finite automata. However, for some languages, constant-height

© IFIP International Federation for Information Processing 2023
Published by Springer Nature Switzerland AG 2023
H. Bordihn et al. (Eds.): DCFS 2023, LNCS 13918, pp. 146–157, 2023.
https://doi.org/10.1007/978-3-031-34326-1_11

pushdown automata can be significantly smaller than nondeterministic finite automata [5].

In [11] we investigated the problem of deciding whether a pushdown automaton accepts in constant height. Namely, given a pushdown automaton $\mathcal{M}$, the question is to decide whether there exists a constant h such that any input string in the language accepted by $\mathcal{M}$ has an accepting computation in which the height of the pushdown store is at most h. We proved that this problem, in general, is undecidable. Furthermore, for pushdown automata accepting in constant height, it does not exists any recursive function bounding the height of the pushdown store with respect to the size of the description of the machine. We also proved that in the restricted case of pushdown automata over a one-letter input alphabet the above-mentioned problem is decidable. Furthermore, under the same restriction, in the case of acceptance in constant height, the height can be at most exponential in the size of the machine and, in the worst case, it cannot be reduced.

In this paper we investigate another restriction, by considering *one-counter automata*. These devices are pushdown automata in which the pushdown alphabet is restricted to one symbol, plus another symbol used only to indicate the bottom of the pushdown. Hence, the pushdown height can be seen as the value of a non-negative counter, which in one move can be incremented, decremented (if not negative), or left unchanged. It is also possible to test whether the counter contains zero. It easy to observe that the class of languages accepted by these devices properly contains the class of regular languages and it is properly included in that of context-free languages. We prove that the above-mentioned problem remains undecidable for these devices, namely, given a one-counter automaton it cannot be decided if there exists a constant h such that any accepted string has an accepting computation in which the value of the counter is bounded by h. Furthermore, in the case of a bounded counter, its value cannot be upper limited by any recursive function of the size of the machine.

We point out that all the above-mentioned results refer to the so-called weak measure, where the cost of the least expensive accepting computation is considered [3]. This is related to the idea of nondeterminism that, among all possible computations, allows to choose not only an accepting one, but also the *least expensive accepting computation*. However, it is quite natural to ask what happens if we consider the maximum cost among of *all* computations (strong measure) or among *all accepting* computations (accept measure). We prove that, for both these measures, in contrast with the weak one, the problem of deciding whether a pushdown automaton accepts in constant height is decidable. Hence also the corresponding problem for one-counter automata is computable. Furthermore, we are able to prove an upper bound for the height, with respect to the size of the machine, in the case of acceptance in constant height. These results are obtained by using a technique which is partially inspired by [12] and reduces the investigation for these measures to the case of deterministic pushdown automata, already considered in [9]. Essentially, we extend the input alphabet with symbols encoding the transitions used during a computation in such a way that the original machine, modified to work on this extended alphabet, becomes deterministic, but makes the same use of the pushdown store.

In the second part of the paper we study how much the height of the push-down grows, with respect to the length of the input, when it is not constant. For the weak measure we already proved a double-logarithmic optimal lower bound [11]. In the case of one-counter automata here we increase such a lower bound to a logarithmic function, also showing that it can be reached. For the strong and accept measures, we prove that the lower bound, in both cases of pushdown and one-counter automata, is linear. Even these results are obtained by the above-mentioned technique that reduces the investigation to the deterministic case, and by making use of some results on deterministic pushdown automata from [4].

For brevity reasons, many of the proofs are only outlined in this version of the paper.

2   Preliminaries

We assume the reader familiar with the standard notions from formal language and automata theory as presented in classical textbooks, e.g., [8]. As usual, the cardinality of a set S is denoted by $\#S$, the length of a string x is denoted by $|x|$, and the empty string is denoted by ε.

We first recall the notion of pushdown automata and present the form for these devices that will be used in the paper. A *pushdown automaton* (PDA, for short) is a tuple $\mathcal{M} = \langle Q, \Sigma, \Gamma, \delta, q_I, Z_0, q_F \rangle$ where Q is the finite *set of states*, Σ is the *input alphabet*, Γ is the *pushdown alphabet*, $q_I \in Q$ is the *initial state*, $Z_0 \in \Gamma$ is the *start symbol*, $q_F \in Q$ is the *final state*. Without loss of generality, we make the following assumptions about PDAs:

1. at the start of the computation the pushdown store contains only the start symbol Z_0, being at height 0, the input head scans the first input symbol, and the finite control contains the initial state q_I;
2. the input is accepted if and only if the automaton reaches the final state q_F, the pushdown store contains only Z_0, and all the input symbols have been scanned;
3. when the automaton reads an input symbol, it moves the head to the next symbol, and it does not make any change to the pushdown. Notice that this implies that the contents of the pushdown store can be changed only by ε-moves;
4. every push operation adds exactly one symbol on the pushdown.

The *transition function* δ of a PDA $\mathcal{M}$ in this form can be written as

$$\delta : Q \times (\Sigma \cup \{\varepsilon\}) \times \Gamma \to 2^{Q \times (\{-, \mathrm{pop}\} \cup \{\mathrm{push}(A) | A \in \Gamma\})}.$$

In particular, for $q, p \in Q$, $A, B \in \Gamma$, $\sigma \in \Sigma$, $(p, -) \in \delta(q, \sigma, A)$ means that the PDA $\mathcal{M}$, in the state q, with A at the top of the pushdown, by consuming the input σ, can reach the state p without changing the pushdown contents; $(p, \mathrm{pop}) \in \delta(q, \varepsilon, A)$ $((p, \mathrm{push}(B)) \in \delta(q, \varepsilon, A)$, $(p, -) \in \delta(q, \varepsilon, A)$, respectively) means that $\mathcal{M}$, in the state q, with A at the top of the pushdown, without reading any input symbol, can reach the state p by popping off the pushdown the symbol A from the top (by pushing the symbol B onto the top of the pushdown, without changing the pushdown, respectively).

Notice that in any accepting computation the occurrence of the start symbol Z_0 at the bottom of the pushdown is never removed, otherwise the next move would be undefined, so halting in a non-accepting configuration.

Now we present the main measure we consider in the paper, namely the *pushdown height*. The height of a PDA $\mathcal{M}$ in a given configuration is the number of symbols in the pushdown store in addition to the occurrence of the start symbol Z_0 at the bottom. Hence, in the initial and accepting configurations the height is 0. The *height of a computation* $\mathcal{C}$ is the maximum height reached in the configurations occurring in $\mathcal{C}$.

We say that $\mathcal{M}$ uses height $h(x)$ on an accepted input $x \in \Sigma^*$ if and only if $h(x)$ is the minimum pushdown height necessary to accept such a string, namely, there exists a computation accepting x of height $h(x)$, and no computation accepting x of height smaller than $h(x)$. Moreover, if x is rejected, then $h(x) = 0$. To study pushdown height with respect to the input length, we consider the worst case among all possible inputs of the same length. Hence, for each integer $n \geq 0$, we define $h(n) = \max \{h(x) \mid x \in \Sigma^*, |x| = n\}$. When there is a constant H such that, for each n, $h(n)$ is bounded by H, we say that $\mathcal{M}$ *accepts in constant height*. Each PDA accepting in constant height can be easily transformed into an equivalent finite automaton. So the language accepted by it is regular.

We point out that the above-given definition of acceptance in constant height considers the minimum height that is sufficient to accept inputs of length n. This measure is called weak. In contrast, by taking into account the costs of *all computations*, we obtain the strong measure. We can also give an intermediate measure, called accept, that considers the costs of *all accepting computations*. By summarizing, $\mathcal{M}$ works in strong (resp., accept) height $h(n)$ if each computation (resp., any accepting computation) on every input of length n uses at most height $h(n)$. For more details on these notions see, e.g., [3].

In the following, by the *size of a* PDA we mean the length of its description. Notice that for each PDA in the above-defined form, over a fixed input alphabet Σ, the size is $O((\#Q)^2(\#\Gamma)^2)$, namely a polynomial in the cardinalities of the set of states and of the pushdown alphabet. If we consider PDAs in different forms, as that given in [8] in which any push operation can replace the top of the pushdown by a string of symbols, to define the size we have to take into account also the number of symbols that can be pushed on the store in one single operation. However, PDAs in that form can be turned into the form we consider here with a polynomial increase in size and by preserving the property of being constant height.

A *one-counter automaton* (OCA, for short) is a PDA where the working alphabet Γ consists of the bottom symbol Z_0, which can occur only at the bottom of the pushdown store, plus another symbol Z, in such a way that the string on the pushdown store has always the form $Z_0 Z^h$, where $h \geq 0$ is the height. We also say that h is the *value of the counter*. All the notions and notation for pushdown automata can be used for one-counter automata. Languages accepted by OCAs are called *one-counter lanuguages*.

3   Undecidability and Non-recursive Bounds

In this section we show that the undecidability result proved in [11] for pushdown automata holds also if we restrict to one-counter automata. In particular, the problem of whether a given OCA $\mathcal{M}$ accepts with counter values bounded by a constant is not decidable. In addition, with respect to the size of $\mathcal{M}$ that does accept with a constant counter, neither the maximal value of the counter of $\mathcal{M}$ nor the number of states of the minimum finite automaton equivalent to $\mathcal{M}$ can be bounded by any recursive function.

These results are proven by refining a technique introduced by Hartmanis based on the fact that the complement of the language composed by suitable encodings of single-tape Turing machine computations is context free [7]. The language we define is a modification of the one used by Hartmanis. Roughly, configurations of a single-tape Turing machine $\mathcal{T}$ with state set Q and tape alphabet Γ are denoted in the standard way as strings in $\Gamma^* Q \Gamma^*$. A computation is encoded as a string $\alpha_1 \$ \alpha_2 \$ \ldots \$ \alpha_m \$$, where the blocks α_i, $i = 1, \ldots, m$, are encodings of configurations of $\mathcal{T}$ and $\$ \notin Q \cup \Gamma$ is a delimiter. Hence, the (encoding of a) *valid computation* of $\mathcal{T}$ on input w is a string $\alpha_1 \$ \alpha_2 \$ \cdots \$ \alpha_m \$$, for some integer $m \geq 1$ such that:

1. $\alpha_i \in \Gamma^* Q \Gamma^*$, i.e., α_i encodes a configuration of $\mathcal{T}$, $i = 1, \ldots, m$;
2. α_1 is the initial configuration on input w, encoded by the string $q_I w$, where q_I is the initial state of $\mathcal{T}$;
3. α_m is a halting configuration of $\mathcal{T}$, namely a configuration from which no move is possible;
4. α_{j+1} is reachable in one step from α_j, $j = 1, \ldots, m-1$.

Following Hartmanis' idea, to prove our undecidability result, we can show that the set of all the strings not representing valid computations of $\mathcal{T}$ on the input word w, denoted $(valid(\mathcal{T}, w))^c$, is a one-counter language. This allows us to prove the main result of this section.

Theorem 1. *It is undecidable whether a OCA accepts with bounded counter.*

Proof (sketch). We give a reduction from the blank-tape halting problem. Let $\mathcal{T}$ be a deterministic Turing machine. With an easy modification, we suppose that arbitrarily long computations use arbitrarily large amounts of tape (to this end, it is sufficient to modify $\mathcal{T}$ by adding to the tape a track where the machine, between every pair of consecutive moves of the original device, marks a tape cell not yet visited).

It is possible to define a OCA $\mathcal{M}_{\mathcal{T},\varepsilon}$ accepting the language $(valid(\mathcal{T}, \varepsilon))^c$, with the following property: Given $\mathcal{D} = \beta_1 \$ \beta_2 \$ \cdots \$ \beta_m \$$, with $\beta_j \in (Q \cup \Gamma)^*$,

$j = 1, \ldots, m$, if $\mathcal{D}$ does not satisfy Conditions 1, 2, or 3, then $\mathcal{M}_{\mathcal{T},\varepsilon}$ has an accepting computation that does not use the counter (so the value remains 0), otherwise $\mathcal{M}_{\mathcal{T},\varepsilon}$ has an accepting computation in which the counter is bounded by the length of the first block β_j for which Condition 4 is not satisfied, i.e., the block corresponding to the largest j such that $\beta_k = \alpha_k$ for $k = 1, \ldots, j$, where $\alpha_1, \alpha_2, \ldots$ is the (possibly infinite) sequence of configurations in the computation of $\mathcal{T}$ on ε. Hence a counter bounded by $|\alpha_k|$ is sufficient to accept such a string.

If $\mathcal{T}$ halts on ε in m steps, then the maximum value of the counter sufficient to accept strings in $(valid(\mathcal{T}, \varepsilon))^c$ is equal to $|\alpha_m|$. Otherwise, for each arbitrarily large integer h, we can find an index $j > 0$ such that $|\alpha_j| > h$. To accept a string $\alpha_1 \$ \alpha_2 \$ \cdots \$ \alpha_j \$ \beta \$\$$, with $\beta \in \Gamma^* Q \Gamma^*$ and β differs from α_{j+1} in the rightmost symbol (of α_{j+1}), it would require a counter equal to $|\alpha_j| > h$.

This allows to conclude that $\mathcal{T}$ halts on input ε if and only if $\mathcal{M}_{\mathcal{T},\varepsilon}$ accepts with constant counter. Hence, it cannot be decided whether a OCA accepts with the counter bounded by any constant.   □

In the general case of pushdown automata, each PDA $\mathcal{M}$ accepting in height h can be converted into an equivalent PDA $\mathcal{M}'$ in which the height of each computation is bounded by h. This can be done by attaching a counter either to the pushdown symbols or to the states to keep track, in every configuration, of the current height, in order to stop and reject when a computation tries to exceed the height limit. By encoding the pushdown store of $\mathcal{M}'$ in a finite control, equivalent NFAs and DFAs with a number of states exponential and double exponential in h, respectively, are easily obtained. In the worst case these bounds cannot be reduced [5]. As a corollary, in the restricted case of OCAs, these bounds are polynomial and exponential in h, respectively, because only a counter from 0 to h is attached to the states. Using an argument derived from [10, Prop. 7], we can show that, however, the value h cannot be bounded by any recursive function in the size of $\mathcal{M}$.

Theorem 2. *For any recursive function $f : \mathbb{N} \to \mathbb{N}$ and for infinitely many integers n there exists a OCA of size n accepting with counter bounded by a value $H(n)$, which is constant with respect to the length of the input, but exceeds $f(n)$.*

We point out that the question in Theorem 1 is decidable in the cases of *deterministic* and *unambiguous* PDAs, as well as in the case of PDAs with *unary input alphabet* [11]. Hence, in all these cases it is decidable for OCAs.

4   Counter Lower Bound for One-Counter Automata

From the results concerning the minimal space necessary for Turing machines to accept nonregular languages, it turns out that if a PDA does not work in constant height, then the height must grow, with respect to the input length, at least as a double-logarithmic function [1]. Furthermore, there exists a language accepted by a PDA using such a height [2]. Here, we prove that in the case of one-counter automata the optimal lower bound is higher. In fact, we show that if a OCA accepts a language L using an unbounded counter, then the value of the counter must grow, with respect to the input length, at least as a logarithmic function. Furthermore, this bound is optimal.

Given a OCA and a string $u \in \Sigma^*$ and an integer $h \geq 0$, let us denote by $Q_h(u)$ the set of *internal configurations*, i.e., pairs (q, t) where q is a state and t is the value of the counter, which are reachable after reading u, by a sequence of moves where the value of the counter is *at most* h.

Lemma 1. *Let* $x = a_1 a_2 \cdots a_n \in \Sigma^*$ *be a string of length* $n \geq 0$ *and* $h > 0$ *an integer. Suppose that* x *is accepted by a computation in which the counter is bounded by* h, *but it cannot be accepted by any computation in which the value of the counter never reaches* h. *If there are two indices* i, j *with* $0 \leq i < j \leq n$ *such that* $Q_h(a_1 \cdots a_i) = Q_h(a_1 \cdots a_j)$ *and* $Q_{h-1}(a_1 \cdots a_i) = Q_{h-1}(a_1 \cdots a_j)$, *then also the string* $x' = a_1 \cdots a_i a_{j+1} \cdots a_n$ *is accepted by a computation with the counter always bounded by* h, *but it cannot be accepted by any computation in which the value of the counter never reaches* h.

We are now able to prove the main result of this section:

Theorem 3. *Let* $\mathcal{M}$ *be a* OCA *using counter at most* $h(n)$. *Then either* $h(n) \in O(1)$, *or* $h(n) \notin o(\log n)$.

Proof. Let $L[k]$ be the set of strings that are accepted by computations of $\mathcal{M}$ with counter bounded by k, but are not accepted by any computation with counter smaller than k. Suppose $L[k] \neq \emptyset$ and consider a shortest string $x \in L[k]$. Let $n = |x|$ and $x = a_1 a_2 \cdots a_n$. By definition, $h(n) \geq k$.

If there are two integers i, j with $0 \leq i < j \leq n$ such that $Q_k(a_1 \cdots a_i) = Q_k(a_1 \cdots a_j)$ and $Q_{k-1}(a_1 \cdots a_i) = Q_{k-1}(a_1 \cdots a_j)$, then by Lemma 1, also the string $x' = a_1 \cdots a_i a_{j+1} \cdots a_n$ should belong to $L[k]$, which contradicts the minimality of x. Since for each integer h there are at most $2^{\#Q \cdot (h+1)}$ different sets $Q_h(u)$, $u \in \Sigma^*$, to avoid such a contradiction we need more than n pairwise-different pairs $(Q_k(u), Q_{k-1}(u))$, we obtain $2^{\#Q \cdot (2k+1)} > n$. Hence $h(n) \geq k \geq c \log n$, for a suitable constant c that only depends on $\#Q$.

We complete the proof by observing that if $h(n) \notin O(1)$ then there are infinitely many k such that $L[k] \neq \emptyset$. Hence, by applying the previous argument to any such k we can conclude that there are infinitely many n such that $h(n) \geq c \cdot \log n$, i.e., $h(n) \notin o(\log n)$. $\qquad\square$

In Gabarro [4, Thm. 4], a language accepted with an unbounded $O(\log n)$ counter is presented.

5   The Extended Language of a Pushdown Automaton

All the results presented in [11] for PDAs and in the previous sections for OCAs refer to the weak measure where, for each accepted word, the cost of least expensive accepting computation is considered. In the next sections of the paper we

will inspect the **strong** and **accept** measures, in which the costs of all computations and of all accepting computations, respectively, are taken into account.
We will prove that, with respect to these measures, the situation is completely
different: first, it becomes decidable whether or not a PDA uses constant height.
Furthermore, for PDAs not using constant height the lower bound for the height
increases to a linear function in the input length. Such a bound can be reached
even in the case of one-counter automata.

To obtain such results, we will make a reduction to the deterministic case.
Roughly, for any given PDA $\mathcal{M}$, we consider a *deterministic* PDA $\mathcal{M}_{ext}$, with
the same structure and the same internal configurations as $\mathcal{M}$, which recognizes
a language, called the *extended language* of $\mathcal{M}$, whose input strings describe
accepting computations of $\mathcal{M}$. Each string in such a language is obtained by
padding a string $w \in L(\mathcal{M})$ with some symbols encoding the transitions used in
a computation accepting w. In this way, we obtain a bijection between the set of
accepting computations of $\mathcal{M}$ and the set of strings in the extended language.
Furthermore, as we will show, the extended language is *deterministic* context
free and it is regular if and only if $\mathcal{M}$ accepts in constant height. Thus, we can
apply to $\mathcal{M}_{ext}$ the known results for the deterministic case, recovering from them
the properties of the original machine $\mathcal{M}$.[1]

Let us start by introducing some notation:

- Given a finite alphabet Γ, let us consider the set $\Gamma^{-1} = \{A^{-1} \mid A \in \Gamma\}$ and
  define the *Dyck language* over Γ, denoted as D_Γ, as the set of sequences of
  balanced brackets over $\Gamma \cup \Gamma^{-1}$, where each $A \in \Gamma$ represents an opening
  bracket and A^{-1} is the corresponding closing bracket.
  If A^{-1} is interpreted as the *right inverse* of A, then in any string from
  $(\Gamma \cup \Gamma^{-1})^*$ we can replace a factor AA^{-1}, $A \in \Gamma$, with the empty word,
  obtaining a shorter string. Hence, starting from a string $x \in (\Gamma \cup \Gamma^{-1})^*$, we
  can iteratively apply the previous process until obtaining a string that cannot
  be further reduced, namely that does not contain any factor AA^{-1}. Such a
  string, denoted as $\mu(x)$, is unique (see [6, Prop. 10.4.1]).
- Given two alphabets Σ, Δ, with $\Sigma \subseteq \Delta$, for each $x \in \Delta^*$, let us denote
  by $\pi_\Sigma(x)$ the *projection* of x on Σ, i.e., the string obtained by removing
  from x all the symbols not in Σ. This notion can be extended to languages
  by defining $\pi_\Sigma(L) = \{\pi_\Sigma(x) \mid x \in L\}$, for $L \subseteq \Delta^*$.

From now on let us fix a PDA $\mathcal{M} = \langle Q, \Sigma, \Gamma, \delta, q_I, Z_0, q_F \rangle$.

Let us consider the *global alphabet* $\Delta = \Sigma \cup \{\mathcal{E}\} \cup \Gamma \cup \Gamma^{-1}$, where $\mathcal{E} \notin \Sigma \cup \Gamma$
is a new symbol which will be used to encode transitions on the empty word
that do not change the pushdown contents.

We consider strings in $(\Delta \cdot Q)^+$. The rough idea is to use a string $x = a_0 p_0 a_1 p_1 \cdots a_m p_m$, $m > 0$, $a_i \in \Delta$, $p_i \in Q$, $i = 0, \ldots, m$, to represent a computation path which starts with $a_0 \in \Gamma$ on the top of the stack in the state p_0
and makes m moves, where the ith move is encoded by the factor $p_{i-1} a_i p_i$,

---

[1] The idea of padding the input of a PDA with some encoding of the transitions used
by the machine during the computations was firstly shown in [12].

$i = 1, \ldots, m$. For $a_i \in \Sigma \cup \{\mathcal{E}\}$, the move does not change the pushdown store and reads $a_i \in \Sigma$ from the tape, or does not read any input symbol, if $a_i = \mathcal{E}$; for $a_i \in \Gamma$, the move is a push of a_i on the stack; for $a_i \in \Gamma^{-1}$, the move pops off the stack A, where $a_i = A^{-1}$. In all the cases, the move changes the state from p_{i-1} to p_i.

The moves also depend on the symbol on the top of the stack. Such a symbol and the entire stack content can be recovered from the string x, provided that it effectively represents a computation path. To this end, we associate with x a string $\mathtt{stack}(x) \in (\Gamma \cup \Gamma^{-1})^*$, a symbol $\mathtt{top}(x) \in \Gamma \cup \Gamma^{-1}$, and a string $\mathtt{input}(x) \in \Sigma^*$, defined as follows:

- $\mathtt{stack}(x) = \mu(\pi_{\Gamma \cup \Gamma^{-1}}(x))$, intuitively it represents the stack content after the moves specified in x (with the topmost symbol to the right),
- $\mathtt{top}(x)$ is the rightmost symbol of $\mathtt{stack}(x)$, if $\mathtt{stack}(x)$ is not empty, otherwise it is undefined; it represents the top of the stack after the moves specified by x,
- $\mathtt{input}(x) = \pi_\Sigma(x)$.

Let $x = a_0 p_0 a_1 p_1 \cdots a_m p_m \in (\Delta \cdot Q)^+$, $m > 0$. For $i = 0, \ldots, m$, let us denote by x_i the prefix of length $2i + 2$ of x, namely $x_i = a_0 p_0 a_1 p_1 \cdots a_i p_i$. We say that x is *well formed* when:

- For $i = 0, \ldots, m$, $\mathtt{stack}(x_i) \in \Gamma^*$ and, if $i < m$, $\mathtt{stack}(x_i) \neq \varepsilon$;
- For $i = 1, \ldots, m$, let $A = \mathtt{top}(x_{i-1})$, then:
  - if $a_i \in \Sigma$ then $(p_i, -) \in \delta(p_{i-1}, a_i, A)$;
  - if $a_i = \mathcal{E}$ then $(p_i, -) \in \delta(p_{i-1}, \varepsilon, A)$;
  - if $a_i \in \Gamma$ then $(p_i, \mathtt{push}(a_i)) \in \delta(p_{i-1}, \varepsilon, A)$;
  - if $a_i \in \Gamma^{-1}$ then $(p_i, \mathtt{pop}) \in \delta(p_{i-1}, \varepsilon, A)$ and $a_i = A^{-1}$.

Notice that the first condition implies $a_0 \in \Gamma$. Intuitively, if x is well formed then it represents a computation path that starts with the pushdown store containing some string γ plus the symbol a_0 on the top, which is never removed except possibly in the last step, consumes the string $\mathtt{input}(x)$ from the input tape and ends with the pushdown store containing the original string γ in the bottom part plus the string $\mathtt{stack}(x)$. Such a computation path does not depend on γ.

At this point we are able to define the *extended language* of $\mathcal{M}$ as the set of well-formed strings encoding accepting computations of $\mathcal{M}$, namely:

$$EL(\mathcal{M}) = \{x = a_0 p_0 a_1 p_1 \cdots a_m p_m \mid x \text{ is well formed,}$$
$$a_0 = Z_0, \, p_0 = q_I, \, p_m = q_F, \text{ and } \mu(x) = Z_0\}$$

Lemma 2. *For each* PDA *$\mathcal{M}$ there exists a* DPDA *$\mathcal{M}_{\mathrm{ext}}$ accepting $EL(\mathcal{M})$ such that, for each integer $h \geq 0$, $\mathcal{M}_{\mathrm{ext}}$ accepts a string $x \in \Delta^*$ using height h if and only if $\mathcal{M}$ has an accepting computation on $\mathtt{input}(x)$ using height h.*

Lemma 3. *The language $EL(\mathcal{M})$ is a deterministic context-free language. Furthermore, it is regular if and only if there exists a constant h such that each accepting computation of $\mathcal{M}$ uses at most height h.*

6   Decidability and Lower Bounds

In [11] it has been proved that it is not decidable whether a PDA accepts in constant height. That result is proved for the weak measure, namely by considering the cost, on each accepted input, of the least expensive computation. As a consequence of Lemma 2, here we prove that the problem becomes decidable if we take into account the amount of pushdown store used in *all* accepting computations.

Theorem 4. *It is decidable whether a* PDA *works in constant height under the* accept *measure.*

Proof. With each PDA $\mathcal{M}$, we associate the *deterministic* PDA $\mathcal{M}_{\text{ext}}$ of Lemma 2. Hence, for any fixed constant h, *each* accepting computation of $\mathcal{M}$ uses at most height h if and only if on each accepted input $\mathcal{M}_{\text{ext}}$ uses height at most h. The result follows from the decidability of acceptance in constant height for deterministic PDAs [9].   □

We can also prove the following:

Theorem 5. *Let $\mathcal{M}$ be a* PDA *such that any accepting computation of $\mathcal{M}$ uses at most height h, for some constant h. Then h can be bounded by $n^2 m$, where n and m are the cardinalities of state set and pushdown alphabet of $\mathcal{M}$, respectively.*

We point out that, in contrast to Theorem 5, in the case of the weak measure there is no recursive function which gives an upper limit to the height of a PDA accepting in constant height with respect to the size of the PDA [11].

We continue the analysis of the accept case, by proving that if under this measure the height is not constant with respect to the length of the input, then it must grow at least linearly.

Theorem 6. *Let $\mathcal{M}$ be a* PDA. *Let us denote by $h_{\mathcal{M},acc}(n)$ the maximum height used in accepting computations on inputs of length n. Then either $h_{\mathcal{M},acc}(n) \in O(1)$, or $h_{\mathcal{M},acc}(n) \notin o(n)$.*

Proof. If $h_{\mathcal{M},acc}(n) \notin O(1)$, then by Lemma 3 the language $EL(\mathcal{M})$ is not regular. However, by Lemma 3, $EL(\mathcal{M})$ is a deterministic context-free language. By Theorem 1 in [4], it turns out that to accept it a linear height is necessary. Hence the PDA $\mathcal{M}_{\text{ext}}$ accepting $EL(\mathcal{M})$ uses height $h'(n') \notin o(n')$, where h' is the height used by the DPDA $\mathcal{M}_{\text{ext}}$, where n' is the length of the input of $\mathcal{M}_{\text{ext}}$; i.e., there exists $c > 0$, such that for infinitely many x, $h'(x) > c \cdot |x|$. We notice that $h'(x) \leq h_{\mathcal{M},acc}(\text{input}(x))$. This implies $h_{\mathcal{M},acc}(\text{input}(x)) > c \cdot |x| \geq c \cdot |\text{input}(x)|$. Hence $h_{\mathcal{M},acc}(n) > c \cdot n$ for infinitely many n, thus implying $h_{\mathcal{M},acc}(n) \notin o(n)$.   □

We now consider the strong measure, which is defined by taking into account the cost of *each* computation. To extend the results in Theorems 4, 5, and 6 to this case, we could try to make each computation accepting. However, a PDA can have computations that stop before reading all the input and computations that enter infinite loops, which will not be considered using this approach.

To overcome this problem, from any given PDA $\mathcal{M}$ we build another PDA $\widetilde{\mathcal{M}}$ that in any configuration can nondeterministically enter a special state q_e, where it consumes input and pushdown symbols, finally reaching the accepting configuration. In this way, each configuration reachable in $\mathcal{M}$ on input w belongs to some accepting computation of $\widetilde{\mathcal{M}}$ on w, that does not use any extra amount of pushdown store. So $h_{\mathcal{M},strong}(n) = h_{\widetilde{\mathcal{M}},acc}(n)$, where $h_{\mathcal{M},strong}(n)$ denotes the maximal height used by $\mathcal{M}$ on inputs of length n. As a consequence, using Theorems 4, 5, and 6, we obtain the following results:

Theorem 7. *Let $\mathcal{M}$ be a PDA. Thus:*

- *It is decidable whether $\mathcal{M}$ works in constant height under the strong measure.*
- *If every accepting computation of $\mathcal{M}$ uses at most height h, for some constant h, then h is upper bounded by $n^2 m$, where n and m are the cardinalities of state set and pushdown alphabet of $\mathcal{M}$, respectively.*
- *Either $h_{\mathcal{M},strong}(n) \in O(1)$, or $h_{\mathcal{M},strong}(n) \notin o(n)$.*

7   Conclusion

Table 1 summarizes the lower bounds for the height of the pushdown store and the value of the counter, with respect to the length of the input, when they are non constant. For any of these bounds it is possible to show a language witnessing that it can be reached.

We could ask if it is also possible to give some upper bound for the height of the pushdown store with respect to the length of the input. It is known that each context-free language can be recognized by a pushdown automaton accepting with a height which is at most linear in the length of the input. However, we could ask if we are able to state such an upper bound *after having given* a PDA. In general the answer is negative, because due to ε-transitions some PDAs can have even accepting computations using arbitrarily large height. However, we have been able to prove that for each computation C there always exists a "reduced" computation C_r using at most linear height, where in this context "reduced" means that C_r can be obtained from C by removing some "redundant" sequences of the ε-transitions, while it performs exactly the same transitions as C on "real" input symbols. (Due to space limitation, this result is not included in this version of the paper.)

We finally mention that all the results we presented for one-counter automata also hold for one-counter automata *without zero test*; namely those that, when the counter is 0, can perform exactly the same transitions as when the counter is greater than zero, except those decreasing the counter.

Table 1. Bounds for the height, if non constant

	strong	accept	weak
Pushdown Automata	n (Th. 7)	n (Th. 6)	$\log\log n$ ([11])
One-Counter Automata	n (Th. 7)	n (Th. 6)	$\log n$ (Th. 3)

References

1. Alberts, M.: Space complexity of alternating Turing machines. In: Budach, L. (ed.) FCT 1985. LNCS, vol. 199, pp. 1–7. Springer, Heidelberg (1985). https://doi.org/10.1007/BFb0028785

2. Bednárová, Z., Geffert, V., Reinhardt, K., Yakaryilmaz, A.: New results on the minimum amount of useful space. Int. J. Found. Comput. Sci. **27**(2), 259–282 (2016). https://doi.org/10.1142/S0129054116400098

3. Bertoni, A., Mereghetti, C., Pighizzini, G.: Strong optimal lower bounds for Turing machines that accept nonregular languages. In: Wiedermann, J., Hájek, P. (eds.) MFCS 1995. LNCS, vol. 969, pp. 309–318. Springer, Heidelberg (1995). https://doi.org/10.1007/3-540-60246-1_137

4. Gabarro, J.: Pusdown space complexity and related full-A.F.L.s. In: Fontet, M., Mehlhorn, K. (eds.) STACS 1984. LNCS, vol. 166, pp. 250–259. Springer, Heidelberg (1984). https://doi.org/10.1007/3-540-12920-0_23

5. Geffert, V., Mereghetti, C., Palano, B.: More concise representation of regular languages by automata and regular expressions. Inf. Comput. **208**(4), 385–394 (2010). https://doi.org/10.1016/j.ic.2010.01.002

6. Harrison, M.A.: Introduction to Formal Language Theory. Addison-Wesley Longman Publishing Co., Inc, Boston, MA, USA (1978)

7. Hartmanis, J.: Context-free languages and Turing machine computations. In: Mathematical Aspects of Computer Science. Proceedings of Symposia in Applied Mathematics, vol. 19, pp. 42–51. American Mathematical Society (1967)

8. Hopcroft, J.E., Ullman, J.D.: Introduction to Automata Theory. Addison-Wesley, Languages and Computation (1979)

9. Malcher, A., Meckel, K., Mereghetti, C., Palano, B.: Descriptional complexity of pushdown store languages. J. Automata Lang. Comb. **17**(2–4), 225–244 (2012). https://doi.org/10.25596/jalc-2012-225

10. Meyer, A.R., Fischer, M.J.: Economy of description by automata, grammars, and formal systems. In: 12th Annual Symposium on Switching and Automata Theory, pp. 188–191. IEEE Computer Society (1971). https://doi.org/10.1109/SWAT.1971.11

11. Pighizzini, G., Prigioniero, L.: Pushdown automata and constant height: decidability and bounds. Acta Informatica **60**, 123–144 (2023). https://doi.org/10.1007/s00236-022-00434-0

12. Salomaa, K., Wood, D., Yu, S.: Pumping and pushdown machines. RAIRO Theor. Inform. Appl. **28**(3–4), 221–232 (1994). https://doi.org/10.1051/ita/1994283-402211

Construction of a Bi-infinite Power Free Word with a Given Factor and a Non-recurrent Letter

Josef Rukavicka[✉] [ID]

Department of Mathematics, Faculty of Nuclear Sciences and Physical Engineering,
Czech Technical University in Prague, Prague, Czech Republic
josef.rukavicka@seznam.cz

Abstract. Let $L_{k,\alpha}^{\mathbb{Z}}$ denote the set of all bi-infinite α-power free words over an alphabet with k letters, where α is a positive rational number and k is a positive integer. We prove that if $\alpha \geq 5$, $k \geq 3$, $v \in L_{k,\alpha}^{\mathbb{Z}}$, and w is a finite nonempty factor of v, then there are $\widetilde{v} \in L_{k,\alpha}^{\mathbb{Z}}$ and a letter x such that w is a factor of $\widetilde{v}$, x occurs in w, and x has only finitely many occurrences in $\widetilde{v}$.

Keywords: Power Free Words · Extension property · Recurrent factor

1 Introduction

An α-*power* of a nonempty word r is the word $r^\alpha = rr \cdots rt$ such that $|r^\alpha| = \alpha|r|$ and t is a prefix of r, where α is a positive rational number. For example $(1234)^3 = 123412341234$ and $(1234)^{\frac{7}{4}} = 1234123$.

Let $\mathbb{N}$ denote the set of positive integers and let $\mathbb{Q}$ denote the set of positive rational numbers. Let w be a (finite or infinite) word. Let

$$\Theta(w) = \{(r, \alpha) \mid r \text{ is a nonempty word and } \alpha \in \mathbb{Q}$$
$$\text{such that } r^\alpha \text{ is a factor of } w\}.$$

We say that w is α-*power free* if

$$\{(r, \beta) \in \Theta(w) \mid \beta \geq \alpha\} = \emptyset$$

and we say that w is α^+-*power free* if

$$\{(r, \beta) \in \Theta(w) \mid \beta > \alpha\} = \emptyset.$$

The power free words include well known square free (2-power free), overlap free (2+-power free), and cube free (3-power free) words. In [2] and [7], the reader can find some surveys on the topic of power free words.

In 1985, Restivo and Salemi presented a list of five problems concerning the extendability of power free words [3]. For the current article, Problem 4 and Problem 5 are of interest:

- Problem 4: Given finite α-power-free words u and v, decide whether there is a transition word w such that uwv is α-power free.

© IFIP International Federation for Information Processing 2023
Published by Springer Nature Switzerland AG 2023
H. Bordihn et al. (Eds.): DCFS 2023, LNCS 13918, pp. 158–168, 2023.
https://doi.org/10.1007/978-3-031-34326-1_12

– Problem 5: Given finite α-power-free words u and v, find a transition word w, if it exists.

In 2009, a conjecture related to Problem 4 and Problem 5 of Restivo and Salemi appeared in [6]:

Conjecture 1. Let L be a power-free language and let $e(L) \subseteq L$ be the set of words of L that can be extended to a bi-infinite word respecting the given power-freeness. If $u, v \in e(L)$ then $uwv \in e(L)$ for some (transition) word w.

In 2018, Conjecture 1 was presented also in [5] in a slightly different form using the so-called "Restivo Salemi property"; it was defined that a language L has the *Restivo Salemi property* if Conjecture 1 holds for the language L.

In [1], a recent survey on the solution of all the five problems of Restivo and Salemi can be found. In particular, Problem 4 and Problem 5 are solved for some overlap free binary words. In addition, in [1] the authors prove that: For every pair (u, v) of cube free words over an alphabet with k letters, if u can be infinitely extended to the right and v can be infinitely extended to the left respecting the cube-freeness property, then there exists a transition word w over the same alphabet such that uwv is cube free.

Definition 1. *(see [4, Definition 1])*

$$\Upsilon = \{(k, \alpha) \mid k \in \mathbb{N} \text{ and } \alpha \in \mathbb{Q} \text{ and } k = 3 \text{ and } \alpha > 2\}$$
$$\cup \{(k, \alpha) \mid k \in \mathbb{N} \text{ and } \alpha \in \mathbb{Q} \text{ and } k > 3 \text{ and } \alpha \geq 2\}$$
$$\cup \{(k, \alpha^+) \mid k \in \mathbb{N} \text{ and } \alpha \in \mathbb{Q} \text{ and } k \geq 3 \text{ and } \alpha \geq 2\}.$$

Remark 1. (see [4, Remark 1]) The definition of Υ says that: If $(k, \alpha) \in \Upsilon$ and α is a "number with +" then $k \geq 3$ and $\alpha \geq 2$. If $(k, \alpha) \in \Upsilon$ and α is "just" a number then $k = 3$ and $\alpha > 2$ or $k > 3$ and $\alpha \geq 2$.

In [4], it was shown that if $(k, \alpha) \in \Upsilon$ then we have that: For every pair (u, v) of α-power free words over an alphabet Σ_k with k letters, if u can be infinitely extended to the right and v can be infinitely extended to the left respecting the α-power freeness property, then there exists a transition word w over the alphabet Σ_k such that uwv is α-power free. Also it was shown how to construct the word w. Less formally said, the results from [4] solve Problem 4 and Problem 5 for a wide variety of power free languages.

To prove the results in [4], the author showed that: If v is a right (left) infinite α-power free word with a factor w and x is a letter, then there is a right (left) infinite α-power free word $\tilde{v}$ such that $\tilde{v}$ contains w as a factor and x is not recurrent in $\tilde{v}$. In other words, $\tilde{v}$ has only a finite number of occurrences of the letter x. Also the construction of $\tilde{v}$ has been presented. The infinite α-power free words with the non-recurrent letter x have then been used to construct the transition words.

Let

$$\tilde{\Upsilon} = \{(k, \alpha) \mid k \in \mathbb{N} \text{ and } \alpha \in \mathbb{Q} \text{ and } k \geq 3 \text{ and } \alpha \geq 5\}.$$

In the current article, we generalize the construction of right and left infinite power free words with a non-recurrent letter to bi-infinite power free words. We prove our result for α-power free words over an alphabet with k letters, where $(k, \alpha) \in \widetilde{\Upsilon}$. Note that $\widetilde{\Upsilon} \subset \Upsilon$. Let $L_{k,\alpha}^{\mathbb{Z}}$ denote the set of all bi-infinite α-power free words over an alphabet with k letters, where α is a positive rational number and k is a positive integer. Formally, our main theorem (Theorem 2) states that if $(k, \alpha) \in \widetilde{\Upsilon}$, $v \in L_{k,\alpha}^{\mathbb{Z}}$, and w is a finite nonempty factor of v, then there are $\widetilde{v} \in L_{k,\alpha}^{\mathbb{Z}}$ and a letter x such that w is a factor of $\widetilde{v}$, x is a factor of w, and x has only finitely many occurrences in $\widetilde{v}$.

To prove the current result, we apply some ideas and results from [4]. The proof is rather technical using several elaborated observations of recurrent factors in infinite words.

Following the construction of the transition word based on left and right α-power free infinite words with the non-recurrent letter x in [4], we suppose that the bi-infinite α-power free words with the non-recurrent letter x could be used in order to prove Conjecture 1. The result of the current article shows how to construct the bi-infinite words with a given factor and a non-recurrent letter for $(k, \alpha) \in \widetilde{\Upsilon}$; as such, the current article offers the first step in the construction of transition words from Conjecture 1. Although the current result works "only" for $\alpha \geq 5$ and $k \geq 3$, it is still a valuable result, since Conjecture 1 is currently, to our best knowledge, open for all $\alpha > 1$ and $k \geq 2$.

2   Preliminaries

Let Σ_k denote an alphabet with k letters, where k is a positive integer. Let Σ_k^+ denote the set of all nonempty finite words over Σ_k, let ϵ denote the empty word, and let $\Sigma_k^* = \Sigma_k^+ \cup \{\epsilon\}$. Let $\Sigma_k^{\mathrm{N},R}$ denote the set of all right infinite words over Σ_k, let $\Sigma_k^{\mathrm{N},L}$ denote the set of all left infinite words over Σ_k, and let $\Sigma_k^{\mathbb{Z}}$ denote the set of all bi-infinite words over Σ_k.

Let $\Sigma_k^\infty = \Sigma_k^{\mathrm{N},L} \cup \Sigma_k^{\mathrm{N},R} \cup \Sigma_k^{\mathbb{Z}}$. We call $w \in \Sigma_k^\infty$ an *infinite* word.

Let $\mathrm{occur}(w, t)$ denote the number of all occurrences of the nonempty factor $t \in \Sigma_k^+$ in the word $w \in \Sigma_k^* \cup \Sigma_k^\infty$. If $w \in \Sigma_k^\infty$ and $\mathrm{occur}(w, t) = \infty$, then we say that t is a *recurrent* factor of w; otherwise we say that a factor t is *non-recurrent* in w.

Let $F(w)$ denote the set of all finite factors of a finite or infinite word $w \in \Sigma_k^* \cup \Sigma_k^\infty$. The set $F(w)$ contains the empty word ϵ and if w is finite then also $w \in F(w)$. Let $F_{\mathrm{rec}}(w) \subseteq F(w)$ denote the set of all recurrent nonempty factors of $w \in \Sigma_k^\infty$.

Let $\mathrm{Prf}(w) \subseteq F(w)$ denote the set of all prefixes of $w \in \Sigma_k^* \cup \Sigma_k^{\mathrm{N},R}$ and let $\mathrm{Suf}(w) \subseteq F(w)$ denote the set of all suffixes of $w \in \Sigma_k^* \cup \Sigma_k^{\mathrm{N},L}$. We define that $\epsilon \in \mathrm{Prf}(w) \cap \mathrm{Suf}(w)$ and if w is finite then also $w \in \mathrm{Prf}(w) \cap \mathrm{Suf}(w)$.

Let $L_{k,\alpha}$ denote a language of all α-power free words over Σ_k, where α is a positive rational number. We have that $L_{k,\alpha} = \{w \in \Sigma_k^* \mid w \text{ is } \alpha\text{-power free}\}$. Let

$$L_{k,\alpha}^\infty = \{w \in \Sigma_k^\infty \mid F(w) \subseteq L_{k,\alpha}\}.$$

Thus $L_{k,\alpha}^{\infty}$ denotes the language of all infinite α-power free words over Σ_k. In addition we define $L_{k,\alpha}^{N,R} = L_{k,\alpha}^{\infty} \cap \Sigma_k^{N,R}$, $L_{k,\alpha}^{N,L} = L_{k,\alpha}^{\infty} \cap \Sigma_k^{N,L}$, and $L_{k,\alpha}^{\mathbb{Z}} = L_{k,\alpha}^{\infty} \cap \Sigma_k^{\mathbb{Z}}$; it means the languages of right infinite, left infinite, and bi-infinite α-power free words over Σ_k, respectively.

Let $\mathbb{Z}$ denote the set of integers. We define the *reverse* w^R of a finite or infinite word $w = \Sigma_k^* \cup \Sigma_k^{\infty}$ as follows:

- $\epsilon^R = \epsilon$.
- If $w \in \Sigma_k^+$ and $w = w_1 w_2 \cdots w_m$, where $w_i \in \Sigma_k$ and $1 \le i \le m$, then $w^R = w_m \cdots w_2 w_1$.
- If $w \in \Sigma_k^{N,L}$ and $w = \cdots w_2 w_1$, where $w_i \in \Sigma_k$ and $i \in \mathbb{N}$, then $w^R = w_1 w_2 \cdots \in \Sigma_k^{N,R}$.
- If $w \in \Sigma_k^{N,R}$ and $w = w_1 w_2 \cdots$, where $w_i \in \Sigma_k$ and $i \in \mathbb{N}$, then $w^R = \cdots w_2 w_1 \in \Sigma_k^{N,L}$.
- If $w \in \Sigma_k^{\mathbb{Z}}$ and $w = \cdots w_{-2} w_{-1} w_0 w_1 w_2 \cdots$, where $w_i \in \Sigma_k$ and $i \in \mathbb{Z}$, then $w^R = \cdots w_2 w_1 w_0 w_{-1} w_{-2} \cdots$.

Remark 2. It is obvious that the reverse function preserves the power-freeness and that every factor of an α-power free word is also α-power free.

The next proposition is a "reformulation" of Corollary 1 from [4] using only the notation of the current article.

Proposition 1. *(reformulation of [4, Corollary 1])* If $(k,\alpha) \in \Upsilon$, $v \in L_{k,\alpha}^{N,L}$, $z \in \mathrm{Suf}(v)$, $x \in F_{\mathrm{rec}}(v) \cap \Sigma_k$, $s \in L_{k,\alpha}^{N,L}$, and $x \notin F(s)$, then there is a finite word $u \in \Sigma_k^*$ such that $z \in \mathrm{Suf}(su)$ and $su \in L_{k,\alpha}^{N,L}$.

Remark 3. Proposition 1 says that if z is a finite power free word that can be extended to a left infinite power free word having a letter x as a recurrent factor and s is a left infinite power free word not containing the letter x as a factor, then there is a left infinite power free word containing z as a suffix and having only a finite number of occurrences of x.

The following elementary lemma was shown in [4]. For the reader's convenience we present the lemma with the proof.

Lemma 1. *(reformulation [4, Lemma 2])* If $k \ge 3$ and $\alpha > 2$ then $L_{k-1,\alpha}^{N,R} \ne \emptyset$.

Proof. Thue Morse words are well known overlap-free (2^+-power free) right infinite words on two letters [5]. Let $x \in \Sigma_k$ and let $t \in L_{k,\alpha}^{N,R}$ be a Thue Morse word on two letters such that $x \notin F(t)$. Since $k \ge 3$, we have that such t exists. This ends the proof.

3   Bi-infinite α-power Words

For the rest of the article suppose that $(k,\alpha) \in \widetilde{\Upsilon}$; it means $k \ge 3$ and $\alpha \ge 5$.

We define two technical sets Γ and Δ.

Definition 2. *Let Γ be a set of triples such that $(w, \eta, u) \in \Gamma$ if and only if*

- $w \in \Sigma_k^+$, $\eta, u \in \Sigma_k^*$, *and*
- *if $|u| \leq |w|$ then $|\eta| \geq (\alpha + 1)\alpha^{|w|-|u|}|w|$.*

Remark 4. The set Γ contains triples of finite words w, η, u such that w is nonempty, and if u is shorter than w, then the word η is "sufficiently" longer than w.

Definition 3. *Let Δ be a set of 6-tuples such that $(s, \sigma, w, \eta, x, u) \in \Delta$ if and only if*

1. $s \in \Sigma_k^{\mathbb{N},L}$, $\sigma, \eta, u \in \Sigma_k^*$, $w \in \Sigma_k^+$, $x \in \Sigma_k$,
2. $s\sigma w \eta x u \in L_{k,\alpha}^{\mathbb{N},L}$,
3. $(w, \eta, u) \in \Gamma$,
4. $\mathrm{occur}(s\sigma w, w) = 1$, *and*
5. $x \notin F(s) \cup F(u)$.

Remark 5. The set Δ contains 6-tuples of strings s, σ, w, η, x, u, where the triple (w, η, u) is from the set Γ, σ is a finite word, x is a letter, s is an α-power free left infinite word, and the letter x is not contained as a factor in s and u. Moreover the concatenation $s\sigma w\eta xu$ is an α-power free left infinite word and the left infinite word $s\sigma w$ contains exactly one occurrence of w.

Given $(s, \sigma, w, \eta, x, u) \in \Delta$, we will identify in this section a prefix $\bar\eta$ of η and a letter y such that $(s, \sigma, w, \bar\eta, x, uy) \in \Delta$; it means that the word $s\sigma w\bar\eta xuy$ is α-power free and $y \neq x$. By iterative application of this procedure we will be able to construct a bi-infinite α-power free word with w as a factor and with a finite number of occurrences of the letter x.

Given $(s, \sigma, w, \eta, x, u) \in \Delta$ and $y \in \Sigma_k$ with $uy \in L_{k,\alpha}$, let

$$\Pi(s, \sigma, w, \eta, x, u, y) = \{(r, \beta) \mid r \in \Sigma_k^+ \text{ and } \beta \in \mathbb{Q} \text{ and } \beta \geq \alpha \text{ and}$$
$$r^\beta \in \mathrm{Suf}(s\sigma w\eta xuy)\}.$$

Remark 6. Realize that the set $\Pi(s, \sigma, w, \eta, x, u, y)$ is empty if and only if the left infinite word $s\sigma w\eta xuy$ is α-power free; just consider that $s\sigma w\eta xu$ is α-power free, since $(s, \sigma, w, \eta, x, u) \in \Delta$.

The following lemma is obvious from the definitions of Π and Δ. We omit the proof. Just note that $(w, \eta, u) \in \Gamma$ and $y \in \Sigma_k$ imply that $(w, \eta, uy) \in \Gamma$.

Lemma 2. *If $(s, \sigma, w, \eta, x, u) \in \Delta$, $y \in \Sigma_k$, $uy \in L_{k,\alpha}$, $\Pi(s, \sigma, w, \eta, x, u, y) = \emptyset$, and $y \neq x$ then $(s, \sigma, w, \eta, x, uy) \in \Delta$.*

For the rest of this section, suppose that $(s, \sigma, w, \eta, x, u) \in \Delta$, $y \in \Sigma_k$, $r \in \Sigma_k^+$, and $\beta \in \mathbb{Q}$ are such that $y \neq x$, $uy \in L_{k,\alpha}$, $\Pi(s, \sigma, w, \eta, x, u, y) \neq \emptyset$, and $(r, \beta) \in \Pi(s, \sigma, w, \eta, x, u, y)$.

Remark 7. Note that $s\sigma w\eta xuy$ is not α-power free, whereas $s\sigma w\eta xu$ is α-power free.

We show that xuy is a suffix of r.

Lemma 3. *We have that* $xuy \in \mathrm{Suf}(r)$.

Proof. Realize that if $r \in \mathrm{Suf}(uy)$ then $x \notin F(r)$ and consequently $r^\beta \in \mathrm{Suf}(uy)$. This is a contradiction since $uy \in L_{k,\alpha}$. Hence we have that $r \notin \mathrm{Suf}(uy)$. It follows that $|r| > |uy|$ and hence $xuy \in \mathrm{Suf}(r)$. This completes the proof.

Let $\bar{r} \in \Sigma_k^*$ be such that $r = \bar{r}xuy$; Lemma 3 asserts that $\bar{r}$ exists and is uniquely determined.

We show that if r^β is shorter than ηxuy then there is a prefix $\bar{\eta}$ of η such that $s\sigma w\bar{\eta}xuy$ is α-power free.

Proposition 2. *If* $r^\beta \in \mathrm{Suf}(\eta xuy)$ *then there is* $\bar{\eta} \in \mathrm{Prf}(\eta)$ *such that*

$$(s, \sigma, w, \bar{\eta}, x, uy) \in \Delta.$$

Table 1. Case $r^\beta \in \mathrm{Suf}(\eta xuy)$

s	σ	w	η		x	uy
			$\bar{\eta}$	$xuy\bar{r}$		
			$zr^{\beta-2}\bar{r}$		$xuyr$	
			zr^β			

Proof. Let z be such that $\eta xuy = zr^\beta$. Let $\bar{\eta} = zr^{\beta-2}\bar{r}$. Hence we have that $\eta xuy = zr^{\beta-2}rr = zr^{\beta-2}\bar{r}xuyr = \bar{\eta}xuyr$. Then $\sigma w\bar{\eta}xuy \in \mathrm{Prf}(\sigma w\eta xu)$ and consequently Property 2 of Definition 3 implies that

$$s\sigma w\bar{\eta}xuy \in L_{k,\alpha}^{\mathrm{N},L}. \tag{1}$$

We have that

$$\beta|r||z| \geq (\beta - 2)|r||z|$$
$$\implies \beta|r||z| + (\beta - 2)\beta|r||r| \geq (\beta - 2)|r||z| + (\beta - 2)\beta|r||r|$$
$$\implies (|z| + (\beta - 2)|r|)\,\beta|r| \geq (|z| + \beta|r|)(\beta - 2)|r|$$
$$\implies \frac{|z| + (\beta - 2)|r|}{|z| + \beta|r|} \geq \frac{(\beta - 2)|r|}{\beta|r|}. \tag{2}$$

It follows from (2) and $\beta \geq \alpha \geq 5$ that

$$\frac{|\bar{\eta}|}{|\eta|} = \frac{|zr^{\beta-2}\bar{r}|}{|zr^\beta| - |xuy|} \geq \frac{|zr^{\beta-2}|}{|zr^\beta|} = \frac{|z| + (\beta - 2)|r|}{|z| + \beta|r|} \geq$$
$$\frac{(\beta - 2)|r|}{\beta|r|} = \frac{\beta - 2}{\beta} = 1 - \frac{2}{\beta} \geq \frac{3}{5}. \tag{3}$$

From Property 3 of Definition 3, (3) and $\frac{3}{5} > \frac{1}{5} \geq \frac{1}{\alpha}$ we have that if $|u| \leq |w|$ then

$$|\overline{\eta}| \geq \frac{3}{5}|\eta| \geq \frac{1}{\alpha}|\eta| \geq \frac{1}{\alpha}(\alpha+1)\alpha^{|w|-|u|}|w| > (\alpha+1)\alpha^{|w|-(|u|+1)}|w|. \quad (4)$$

From (1) and (4) we have that $(w, \overline{\eta}, uy) \in \Gamma$ and $(s, \sigma, w, \overline{\eta}, x, uy) \in \Delta$. Realize that Property 2 of Definition 3 is asserted by (1) and Property 3 of Definition 3 is asserted by (4). Other properties of Definition 3 are obvious. Table 1 illuminates the structure of the words.

This completes the proof.

The next lemma shows that if r^β is longer than $\eta x u y$ then r is longer than w.

Lemma 4. If $r^\beta \notin \mathrm{Suf}(\eta x u y)$ then $|r| > |w|$.

Proof. Property 2 of Definition (3) implies that

$$\beta \leq \alpha + 1. \quad (5)$$

From $r^\beta \notin \mathrm{Suf}(\eta x u y)$ it follows that $|r^\beta| > |\eta|$. Hence from Property 3 of Definition 3 it follows that

$$|r^\beta| = \beta|r| > |\eta| \geq (\alpha+1)|w|. \quad (6)$$

From (5) and (6) we have that $|r| > |w|$. This ends the proof.

The next lemma shows that if r^β is longer than $\eta x u y$ then $\eta x u y$ contains $r^{\beta-2}$ as a factor.

Lemma 5. If $r^\beta \notin \mathrm{Suf}(\eta x u y)$ then $r^{\beta-2} \in \mathrm{Suf}(\eta x u y)$.

Proof. We distinguish two cases:

- $r^\beta \in \mathrm{Suf}(w\eta x u y)$. Then from Lemma 4 it follows that $r^{\beta-1} \in \mathrm{Suf}(\eta x u y)$ and consequently also $r^{\beta-2} \in \mathrm{Suf}(\eta x u y)$.
- $r^\beta \notin \mathrm{Suf}(w\eta x u y)$. Then Lemma 4 implies that $w \in F(rr)$ and in consequence Property 4 of Definition 3 implies that $r^{\beta-1} \in \mathrm{Suf}(w\eta x u y)$. Then from Lemma 4 we have that $r^{\beta-2} \in \mathrm{Suf}(\eta x u y)$.

This completes the proof.

We show that if r^β is longer than $\eta x u y$ then there is a prefix $\overline{\eta}$ of η such that $s\sigma w\overline{\eta} x u y$ is α-power free.

Proposition 3. If $r^\beta \notin \mathrm{Suf}(\eta x u y)$ then there is $\overline{\eta} \in \mathrm{Prf}(\eta)$ such that

$$(s, \sigma, w, \overline{\eta}, x, uy) \in \Delta.$$

Proof. Lemma 5 implies that $r^{\beta-2} \in \mathrm{Suf}(\eta x u y)$. From Lemma 3 we have that $r = \bar{r} x u y$. It follows that

$$|\eta| \geq |r^{\beta-3}| \tag{7}$$

and it follows also that there is unique $\bar{\eta} \in \mathrm{Prf}(\eta)$ such that

$$\eta x u y = \bar{\eta} x u y \bar{r} x u y. \tag{8}$$

From $r^{\beta} \notin \mathrm{Suf}(\eta x u y)$ it follows that

$$|\eta| \leq |r^{\beta}|. \tag{9}$$

From (8) we have that

$$|\bar{\eta}| = |\eta| - |r|. \tag{10}$$

Since $\beta \geq \alpha \geq 5$, it follows from (7), (9), and (10) that

$$\frac{|\bar{\eta}|}{|\eta|} \geq \frac{|\bar{\eta}|}{|r^{\beta}|} = \frac{|\eta| - |r|}{|r^{\beta}|} \geq \frac{|r^{\beta-3}| - |r|}{|r^{\beta}|} = \frac{|r^{\beta-4}|}{|r^{\beta}|} = \frac{\beta - 4}{\beta} \geq \frac{1}{5}. \tag{11}$$

From Property 3 of Definition 3, 11, and $\frac{1}{5} \geq \frac{1}{\alpha}$ we have that if $|u| \leq |w|$ then

$$|\bar{\eta}| \geq \frac{1}{5}|\eta| \geq \frac{1}{\alpha}(\alpha + 1)\alpha^{|w|-|u|}|w| > (\alpha + 1)\alpha^{|w|-(|u|+1)}|w|. \tag{12}$$

It is clear that $w\bar{\eta} x u y \in \mathrm{Prf}(w\eta x u)$, hence $s\sigma w\bar{\eta} x u y \in L^{N,L}_{k,\alpha}$. Then it is easy to verify that $(s, \sigma, w, \bar{\eta}, x, uy) \in \Delta$. Note that Property 3 of Definition 3 follows from (12).

Table 2 illuminates the structure of the words for this case.

Table 2. Case $r^{\beta} \notin \mathrm{Suf}(\eta x u y)$

s	σ	w	η		x	uy
			$\bar{\eta} x u y$	$\bar{r}$		
			$\ldots r^{\beta}$			

This completes the proof.

A consequence of the previous two propositions is that in every case there is a prefix $\bar{\eta}$ of η such that $s\sigma w\bar{\eta} x u y$ is α-power free.

Lemma 6. *There is $\bar{\eta} \in \mathrm{Prf}(\eta)$ such that $(s, \sigma, w, \bar{\eta}, x, uy) \in \Delta$.*

Proof. We distinguish two cases:

- $r^{\beta} \in \mathrm{Suf}(\eta x u y)$. In this case the lemma follows from Proposition 2.
- $r^{\beta} \notin \mathrm{Suf}(\eta x u y)$. In this case the lemma follows from Proposition 3.

This completes the proof.

4   Transition Words

The first theorem of this section shows that if $(s, \sigma, w, \eta, x, \epsilon) \in \Delta$ and t is a right infinite α-power free word with no occurrence of the letter x then there is a bi-infinite α-power free word containing the factor w and having only a finite number of occurrences of x.

Theorem 1. *If* $(s, \sigma, w, \eta, x, \epsilon) \in \Delta$, $t \in L_{k,\alpha}^{N,R}$, *and* $x \notin F(t)$ *then there is* $\widehat{\eta} \in \mathrm{Prf}(\eta)$ *such that* $s\sigma w\widehat{\eta}xt \in L_{k,\alpha}^{\mathbb{Z}}$.

Proof. Given $i \in \mathbb{N} \cup \{0\}$, let $\phi(i) \in \mathrm{Prf}(t) \cap \Sigma_k^i$ be the prefix of t of length i. We have that $\phi(0) = \epsilon$. Let $y_j \in \Sigma_k$ be such that $\phi(j-1)y_j = \phi(j)$, where $j \in \mathbb{N}$; it means that y_j is the last letter of the prefix $\phi(j)$.

Let $\omega(0) = \eta$. We have that $(s, \sigma, w, \omega(0), x, \phi(0)) \in \Delta$. Given $j \in \mathbb{N}$, we define $\omega(j) \in \mathrm{Prf}(\omega(j-1))$ as follows:

- If $\Pi(s, \sigma, w, \omega(j-1), x, \phi(j-1), y_j) = \emptyset$ then we define that $\omega(j) = \omega(j-1)$. Lemma 2 implies that $(s, \sigma, w, \omega(j), x, \phi(j)) \in \Delta$.
- If $\Pi(s, \sigma, w, \omega(j-1), x, \phi(j-1), y_j) \neq \emptyset$ then Lemma 6 implies that there is $\overline{\eta}_j \in \mathrm{Prf}(\omega(j-1))$ such that $(s, \sigma, w, \overline{\eta}_j, x, \phi(j)) \in \Delta$. We define that $\omega(j) = \overline{\eta}_j$.

It follows that $\omega(j)$ is well defined for all $j \in \mathbb{N} \cup \{0\}$ and also it follows that $(s, \sigma, w, \omega(j), x, \phi(j)) \in \Delta$ for all $j \in \mathbb{N} \cup \{0\}$.

Since $\omega(0) = \eta$ is a finite word and since $\omega(j) \in \mathrm{Prf}(\omega(j-1))$ for all $j \in \mathbb{N}$, obviously there is $m \in \mathbb{N}$ such that $\omega(i) = \omega(m)$ for all $i \geq m$. Consequently we have that $(s, \sigma, w, \omega(m), x, \phi(i)) \in \Delta$ for all $i \geq m$. Let $\widehat{\eta} = \omega(m)$. We conclude that $s\sigma w\widehat{\eta}xt \in L_{k,\alpha}^{\mathbb{Z}}$.

This completes the proof.

If a factor w is recurrent in a bi-infinite word v, then it is possible that w is recurrent only on the "left or the right side" of v. For the next proposition we will need that the letter x is recurrent "on the right side". We define formally this notion.

Definition 4. *Suppose* $v \in L_{k,\alpha}^{\mathbb{Z}}$ *and* $w \in F(v) \setminus \{\epsilon\}$. *If there are* $v_1 \in L_{k,\alpha}^{N,L}$ *and* $v_2 \in L_{k,\alpha}^{N,R}$ *such that* $v = v_1 v_2$ *and* $w \in F_{\mathrm{rec}}(v_2)$ *then we say that* w *is on-right-side recurrent in* v.

Remark 8. Note in Definition 4 that no restriction is imposed on the recurrence of w in v_1. It means that w may be recurrent also in v_1.

If v is a bi-infinite α-power free word and the letter x is on-right-side recurrent in v, then we prove that the main result of the current article holds for v; it means that there is a bi-infinite α-power free word containing the factor w and having a non-recurrent letter x.

Proposition 4. *If* $v \in L_{k,\alpha}^{\mathbb{Z}}$, $w \in F(v) \setminus \{\epsilon\}$, $x \in F(w) \cap \Sigma_k$, *and* x *is on-right-side recurrent in* v *then there is* $\widehat{v} \in L_{k,\alpha}^{\mathbb{Z}}$ *such that* $w \in F(\widehat{v})$ *and* $x \notin F_{\mathrm{rec}}(\widehat{v})$.

Proof. It is clear that there are $\widetilde{v} \in L_{k,\alpha}^{N,L}$, $\ddot{v} \in L_{k,\alpha}^{N,R}$ and $\widetilde{\eta} \in \Sigma_k^*$ such that $v = \widetilde{v} w \widetilde{\eta} x \ddot{v}$ and $(w, \widetilde{\eta}, \epsilon) \in \Gamma$. Just note that x is on-right-side recurrent in v; hence $\widetilde{\eta}$ can be chosen to be longer than any arbitrarily chosen positive number.

Let t be a right infinite α-power free word on the alphabet $\Sigma_k \setminus \{x\}$. Since $\alpha \geq 5$ and $k \geq 3$, Lemma 1 asserts that t exists. We define a left infinite α-power free word $\overline{s} \in L_{k,\alpha}^{N,L}$ with $x \notin F(\overline{s})$ and a finite word $p \in \Sigma_k^+$ as follows:

- If $x \notin F_{\text{rec}}(\widetilde{v})$, then let $\overline{s} = \widetilde{v}$ and let $p = w \widetilde{\eta} x$.
- If $x \in F_{\text{rec}}(\widetilde{v})$, then let $\overline{s} = t^R$. Clearly $\overline{s}$ is a left infinite α-power free and $x \notin F(s)$. Let p be such that $\overline{s}p \in L_{k,\alpha}^{N,L}$, and $w \widetilde{\eta} x \in \text{Suf}(\overline{s}p)$; Proposition 1 asserts that such p exists.

Then, obviously, there are $s \in L_{k,\alpha}^{N,L}$ and $\sigma, \eta \in \Sigma_k^*$ such that

$$(s, \sigma, w, \eta, x) \in \Delta \quad \text{and} \quad s\sigma w \eta x = \overline{s}p.$$

Note that since $x \in F(w)$ and $x \notin F_{\text{rec}}(\overline{s})$, we have that s, σ, η are uniquely determined by Property 4 of Definition 3.

Theorem 1 implies that there is $\widehat{\eta}$ such that $s\sigma w \widehat{\eta} x t \in L_{k,\alpha}^{\mathbb{Z}}$. Let $\widehat{v} = s\sigma w \widehat{\eta} x t$. Clearly $w \in F(\widehat{v})$ and $x \notin F_{\text{rec}}(\widehat{v})$. This completes the proof.

Now, we can step to the main theorem of the current article.

Theorem 2. *If $v \in L_{k,\alpha}^{\mathbb{Z}}$, $w \in F(v) \setminus \{\epsilon\}$, then there are $\overline{v} \in L_{k,\alpha}^{\mathbb{Z}}$ and $x \in \Sigma_k$ such that $w \in F(\overline{v})$, $x \in F(w)$, and $x \notin F_{\text{rec}}(\overline{v})$.*

Proof. Let $\Omega = (F(w) \setminus F_{\text{rec}}(v)) \cap \Sigma_k$ be the set of letters of w that are non-recurrent in v. We define a bi-infinite α-power free word $\overline{v} \in L_{k,\alpha}^{\mathbb{Z}}$ and a letter $x \in \Sigma_k$ as follows:

- If $\Omega \neq \emptyset$ then let $x \in \Omega$ and let $\overline{v} = v$.
- If $\Omega = \emptyset$ then let $x \in F(w) \cap \Sigma_k$. We have that $x \in F_{\text{rec}}(v)$. It follows that either x is on-right-side recurrent in v or x is on-right-side recurrent in v^R.
  - If x is on-right-side recurrent in v then Proposition 4 implies that there is $\widehat{v} \in L_{k,\alpha}^{\mathbb{Z}}$ such that $w \in F(\widehat{v})$ and $x \notin F_{\text{rec}}(\widehat{v})$. Let $\overline{v} = \widehat{v}$.
  - If x is on-right-side recurrent in v^R. Proposition 4 implies that there is $\widehat{v}$ such that $w^R \in F(\widehat{v})$ and $x \notin F_{\text{rec}}(\widehat{v})$. Let $\overline{v} = \widehat{v}^R$. Then obviously $w \in F(\overline{v})$ and $x \notin F_{\text{rec}}(\overline{v})$.

For every case we showed that $\overline{v} \in L_{k,\alpha}^{\mathbb{Z}}$, $w \in F(\overline{v})$, and $x \notin F_{\text{rec}}(\overline{v})$. This ends the proof.

Acknowledgment. This work was supported by the Grant Agency of the Czech Technical University in Prague, grant No. SGS20/183/OHK4/3T/14.

References

1. Petrova, E.A., Shur, A.M.: Transition property for cube-free words. Theory of Computing Systems **65**(3), 479–496 (2020). https://doi.org/10.1007/s00224-020-09979-4
2. Rampersad, N.: Overlap-free words and generalizations. A thesis, University of Waterloo (2007). http://hdl.handle.net/10012/3421
3. Restivo, A., Salemi, S.: Some decision results on nonrepetitive words. In: Apostolico, A., Galil, Z. (eds.) Combinatorial Algorithms on Words, pp. 289–295. Springer, Berlin Heidelberg, Berlin, Heidelberg (1985). https://doi.org/10.1007/978-3-642-82456-2_20
4. Rukavicka, J.: Transition Property for α-Power Free Languages with $\alpha \geq 2$ and $k \geq 3$ Letters. In: Jonoska, N., Savchuk, D. (eds.) DLT 2020. LNCS, vol. 12086, pp. 294–303. Springer, Cham (2020). https://doi.org/10.1007/978-3-030-48516-0_22
5. Shallit, J., Shur, A.: Subword complexity and power avoidance. Theor. Comput. Sci. **792**, 96–116 (2019)
6. Shur, A.M.: Two-sided bounds for the growth rates of power-free languages. In: Diekert, V., Nowotka, D. (eds.) DLT 2009. LNCS, vol. 5583, pp. 466–477. Springer, Heidelberg (2009). https://doi.org/10.1007/978-3-642-02737-6_38
7. Shur, A.M.: Growth properties of power-free languages. In: Mauri, G., Leporati, A. (eds.) DLT 2011. LNCS, vol. 6795, pp. 28–43. Springer, Heidelberg (2011). https://doi.org/10.1007/978-3-642-22321-1_3

Merging Two Hierarchies of External Contextual Grammars with Subregular Selection

Bianca Truthe[(✉)] [iD]

Institut für Informatik, Justus-Liebig-Universität Giessen, Arndtstr. 2,
35392 Giessen, Germany
bianca.truthe@informatik.uni-giessen.de

Abstract. In this paper, we continue the research on the power of contextual grammars with selection languages from subfamilies of the family of regular languages. In the past, two independent hierarchies have been obtained for external and internal contextual grammars, one based on selection languages defined by structural properties (finite, monoidal, nilpotent, combinational, definite, ordered, non-counting, power-separating, suffix-closed, commutative, circular, or union-free languages), the other one based on selection languages defined by resources (number of non-terminal symbols, production rules, or states needed for generating or accepting them). In the present paper, we compare the language families of these hierarchies for external contextual grammars and merge the hierarchies.

Keywords: Contextual grammars · subregular selection languages · computational capacity

1 Introduction

Contextual grammars were introduced by S. Marcus in [15] as a formal model that might be used in the generation of natural languages. The derivation steps consist in adding contexts to given well formed sentences, starting from an initial finite basis. Formally, a context is given by a pair (u, v) of words and the external adding to a word x gives the word uxv whereas the internal adding gives all words $x_1 u x_2 v x_3$ when $x = x_1 x_2 x_3$. In order to control the derivation process, contextual grammars with selection in a certain family of languages where defined. In such contextual grammars, a context (u, v) may be added only if the surrounded word x or x_2 belongs to a language which is associated with the context. Language families were defined where the all selection languages in a contextual grammar belong to some language family $\mathcal{F}$. Contextual grammars have been studied where the family $\mathcal{F}$ is taken from the Chomsky hierarchy (see [13,18,19] and references therein).

In [4], the study of external contextual grammars with selection in special regular sets was started. Finite, combinational, definite, nilpotent, regular suffix-closed, regular commutative languages and languages of the form V^* for some

H. Bordihn et al. (Eds.): DCFS 2023, LNCS 13918, pp. 169–180, 2023.
https://doi.org/10.1007/978-3-031-34326-1_13

alphabet V were considered. The research was continued in [6–8,14] where further subregular families of selection languages were considered and the effect of subregular selection languages on the generative power of external and internal contextual grammars was investigated. A recent survey can be found in [25] which presents for each type of contextual grammars (external and internal ones) two hierarchies, one based on selection languages defined by structural properties (finite, monoidal, nilpotent, combinational, definite, ordered, non-counting, power-separating, suffix-closed, commutative, circular, or union-free languages), the other one based on selection languages defined by resources (number of non-terminal symbols, production rules, or states needed for generating or accepting them). In the present paper, we compare the language families of these hierarchies for external contextual grammars and merge the hierarchies.

2   Preliminaries

Throughout the paper, we assume that the reader is familiar with the basic concepts of the theory of automata and formal languages. For details, we refer to [19]. Here we only recall some notation and the definition of contextual grammars with selection which form the central notion of the paper.

2.1   Languages, Grammars, Automata

Given an alphabet V, we denote by V^* and V^+ the set of all words and the set of all non-empty words over V, respectively. The empty word is denoted by λ. By V^k, we denote the set of all words of the alphabet V with exactly k letters. For a word w and a letter a, we denote the length of w by $|w|$ and the number of occurrences of the letter a in the word w by $|w|_a$. For a set A, we denote its cardinality by $|A|$.

A right-linear grammar is a quadruple $G = (N, T, P, S)$ where N is a finite set of non-terminal symbols, T is a finite set of terminal symbols, P is a finite set of production rules of the form $A \to wB$ or $A \to w$ with $A, B \in N$ and $w \in T^*$, and $S \in N$ is the start symbol. Such a grammar is called regular, if all the rules are of the form $A \to xB$ or $A \to x$ with $A, B \in N$ and $x \in T$ or $S \to \lambda$. The language generated by a right-linear or regular grammar is the set of all words over the terminal alphabet which are obtained from the start symbol S by a successive replacement of the non-terminal symbols according to the rules in the set P. Every language generated by a right-linear grammar can also be generated by a regular grammar.

A deterministic finite automaton is a quintuple $A = (V, Z, z_0, F, \delta)$ where V is a finite set of input symbols, Z is a finite set of states, $z_0 \in Z$ is the initial state, $F \subseteq Z$ is a set of accepting states, and δ is a transition function $\delta : Z \times V \to Z$. The language accepted by such an automaton is the set of all input words over the alphabet V which lead letterwise by the transition function from the initial state to an accepting state.

The set of all languages generated by some right-linear grammar coincides with the set of all languages accepted by a deterministic finite automaton. All these languages are called regular and form a family denoted by REG. Any subfamily of this set is called a subregular language family.

2.2 Complexity Measures and Resources Restricted Languages

Let $G = (N, T, P, S)$ be a right-linear grammar, $A = (V, Z, z_0, F, \delta)$ be a deterministic finite automaton, and L be a regular language. Then we define

$$State(A) = |Z|,\ Var(G) = |N|,\ Prod(G) = |P|,$$
$$State(L) = \min\{\ State(A) \mid A \text{ is a det. finite automaton accepting } L\ \},$$
$$Var_{RL}(L) = \min\{\ Var(G) \mid G \text{ is a right-linear grammar generating } L\ \},$$
$$Prod_{RL}(L) = \min\{\ Prod(G) \mid G \text{ is a right-linear grammar generating } L\ \}.$$

We now define subregular families by restricting the resources needed for generating or accepting their elements:

$$RL_n^V = \{\ L \mid L \in REG \text{ with } Var_{RL}(L) \le n\ \},$$
$$RL_n^P = \{\ L \mid L \in REG \text{ with } Prod_{RL}(L) \le n\ \},$$
$$REG_n^Z = \{\ L \mid L \in REG \text{ with } State(L) \le n\ \}.$$

2.3 Subregular Language Families Based on the Structure

We consider the following restrictions for regular languages. Let L be a language over an alphabet V. We say that the language L – with respect to the alphabet V – is

- *monoidal* if and only if $L = V^*$,
- *nilpotent* if and only if it is finite or its complement $V^* \setminus L$ is finite,
- *combinational* if and only if it has the form $L = V^*X$ for some subset $X \subseteq V$,
- *definite* if and only if it can be represented in the form $L = A \cup V^*B$ where A and B are finite subsets of V^*,
- *suffix-closed* (or *fully initial* or *multiple-entry* language) if and only if, for any two words $x \in V^*$ and $y \in V^*$, the relation $xy \in L$ implies the relation $y \in L$,
- *ordered* if and only if the language is accepted by some deterministic finite automaton $\mathcal{A} = (V, Z, z_0, F, \delta)$ with an input alphabet V, a finite set Z of states, a start state $z_0 \in Z$, a set $F \subseteq Z$ of accepting states and a transition mapping δ where $(Z, \preceq)$ is a totally ordered set and, for any input symbol $a \in V$, the relation $z \preceq z'$ implies $\delta(z, a) \preceq \delta(z', a)$,
- *commutative* if and only if it contains with each word also all permutations of this word,

- *circular* if and only if it contains with each word also all circular shifts of this word,
- *non-counting* (or *star-free*) if and only if there is a natural number $k \geq 1$ such that, for any three words $x \in V^*$, $y \in V^*$, and $z \in V^*$, it holds $xy^k z \in L$ if and only if $xy^{k+1}z \in L$,
- *power-separating* if and only if, there is a natural number $m \geq 1$ such that for any word $x \in V^*$, either $J_x^m \cap L = \emptyset$ or $J_x^m \subseteq L$ where $J_x^m = \{ x^n \mid n \geq m \}$,
- *union-free* if and only if L can be described by a regular expression which is only built by product and star.

We remark that monoidal, nilpotent, combinational, definite, ordered, and union-free languages are regular, whereas non-regular languages of the other types mentioned above exist. Here, we consider among the commutative, circular, suffix-closed, non-counting, and power-separating languages only those which are also regular.

Some properties of the languages of the classes mentioned above can be found in [20] (monoids), [10] (nilpotent languages), [12] (combinational and commutative languages), [17] (definite languages), [2,11] (suffix-closed languages), [21] (ordered languages), [3] (circular languages), [16] (non-counting languages), [22] (power-separating languages), [1] (union-free languages).

By *FIN, MON, NIL, COMB, DEF, SUF, ORD, COMM, CIRC, NC, PS, UF*, and *REG*, we denote the families of all finite, monoidal, nilpotent, combinational, definite, regular suffix-closed, ordered, regular commutative, regular circular, regular non-counting, regular power-separating, union-free, and regular, languages, respectively.

As the set of all families under consideration, we set

$$\mathfrak{F} = \{ FIN, MON, NIL, COMB, DEF, SUF, ORD, COMM, CIRC, NC, PS, UF \}$$
$$\cup \{ RL_n^V \mid n \geq 1 \} \cup \{ RL_n^P \mid n \geq 1 \} \cup \{ REG_n^Z \mid n \geq 1 \}.$$

2.4   Hierarchy of Subregular Families of Languages

We present here a hierarchy of the families of the aforementioned set $\mathfrak{F}$ with respect to the set theoretic inclusion relation.

Theorem 1. *The inclusion relations presented in Fig. 1 hold. An arrow from an entry X to an entry Y depicts the proper inclusion $X \subset Y$; if two families are not connected by a directed path, then they are incomparable.*

For proofs and references to proofs of the relations, we refer to [24].

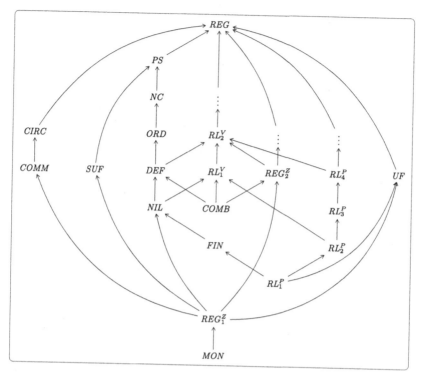

Fig. 1. Hierarchy of subregular language families

2.5 Contextual Grammars

Let $\mathcal{F}$ be a family of languages. A contextual grammar with selection in $\mathcal{F}$ is a triple $G = (V, \mathcal{S}, A)$ where

- V is an alphabet,
- $\mathcal{S}$ is a finite set of selection pairs (S, C) with a selection language S over some subset U of the alphabet V which belongs to the family $\mathcal{F}$ with respect to the alphabet U and a finite set $C \subset V^* \times V^*$ of contexts where, for each context $(u, v) \in C$, at least one side is not empty: $uv \neq \lambda$,
- A is a finite subset of V^* (its elements are called axioms).

Let $G = (V, \mathcal{S}, A)$ be a contextual grammar with selection. A direct external derivation step in G is defined as follows: a word x derives a word y (written as $x \Longrightarrow y$) if and only if there is a pair $(S, C) \in \mathcal{S}$ such that $x \in S$ and $y = uxv$ for some pair $(u, v) \in C$. Intuitively, one can only wrap a context $(u, v) \in C$ around a word x if x belongs to the corresponding selection language S.

By $\Longrightarrow^*$ we denote the reflexive and transitive closure of the relation $\Longrightarrow$. The language generated by G is $L = \{\, z \mid x \Longrightarrow^* z \text{ for some } x \in A \,\}$. By $\mathcal{EC}(\mathcal{F})$, we denote the family of all languages generated externally by contextual grammars with selection in $\mathcal{F}$. When a contextual grammar works in the external mode, we call it an external contextual grammar.

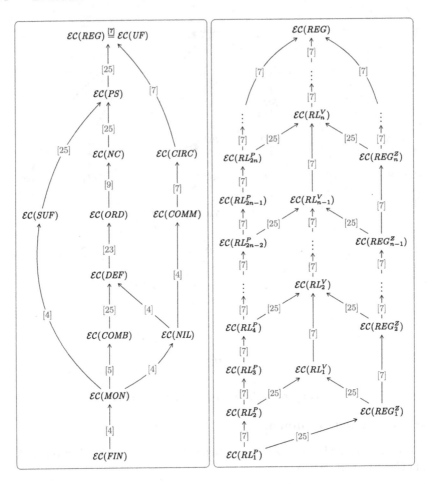

Fig. 2. Hierarchies of the language families by external contextual grammars with selection languages defined by structural properties (left) or restricted resources (right). An edge label refers to the paper where the respective inclusion is proved.

From previous research, we have the two hierarchies depicted in Fig. 2. An arrow from an entry X to an entry Y depicts the proper inclusion $X \subset Y$. If two families X and Y are not connected by a directed path, then X and Y are incomparable. The label at an edge shows in which paper the relation was proved. In the following section, we relate the families of these two hierarchies.

From the definition follows that the subset relation is preserved under the use of contextual grammars: if we allow more, we do not obtain less.

Lemma 2. *For any two language classes X and Y with $X \subseteq Y$, we have the inclusion*

$$\mathcal{EC}(X) \subseteq \mathcal{EC}(Y).$$

3   Results

When we speak about contextual grammars in this section, we mean external contextual grammars (whose languages are generated in the external mode).

First, we present languages which will serve later as witness languages for proper inclusions or incomparabilities.

Lemma 3. *Let $L = \{\, a^n \mid n \geq 1 \,\} \cup \{\, ba^{2n}b \mid n \geq 1 \,\}$. Then the relation*

$$L \in (\mathcal{EC}(RL_2^P) \cap \mathcal{EC}(REG_2^Z) \cap \mathcal{EC}(RL_1^V)) \setminus \mathcal{EC}(PS)$$

holds.

Proof. The language L is generated by the contextual grammar

$$G = (\{a, b\}, \{(S_1, C_1), (S_2, C_2)\}, \{a\})$$

with $S_1 = \{a\}^*$, $C_1 = \{(\lambda, a)\}$, $S_2 = \{aa\}^*$, and $C_2 = \{(b, b)\}$. Thus, we obtain $L \in \mathcal{EC}(RL_2^P) \cap \mathcal{EC}(REG_2^Z) \cap \mathcal{EC}(RL_1^V)$. The relation $L \notin \mathcal{EC}(PS)$ was proved already in [25].

Lemma 4. *Let $L = \{ab\}^+ \cup \{ba\}^+ \cup \{\, c(ba)^n c \mid n \geq 1 \,\}$. Then the relation*

$$L \in (\mathcal{EC}(RL_2^P) \cap \mathcal{EC}(REG_2^Z) \cap \mathcal{EC}(RL_1^V)) \setminus \mathcal{EC}(CIRC)$$

holds.

Proof. The language L is generated by the contextual grammar

$$G = (\{a, b, c\}, \{(S_1, C_1), (S_2, C_2)\}, \{ab, ba\})$$

with $S_1 = \{ab\}^+$ or $S_1 = \{a, b\}^*\{b\}$ and $C_1 = \{(\lambda, ab)\}$ as well as $S_2 = \{ba\}^+$ or $S_2 = \{a, b\}^*\{a\}$ and $C_2 = \{(\lambda, ba), (c, c)\}$. Hence, we obtain the first relation $L \in \mathcal{EC}(RL_2^P) \cap \mathcal{EC}(REG_2^Z) \cap \mathcal{EC}(RL_1^V)$. Since the letters c are wrapped around a word for which also a circular shift belongs to the language L, the usage of a circular selection language would yield a wrong word. Hence, the language L cannot be generated by a contextual grammar where every selection language is circular.

Lemma 5. *Let $L = \{a\}^+ \cup \{a\}^*\{b\}\{a, b\}^* \cup \{c\}\{a\}^*\{b\}\{a, b\}^*\{c\}$. Then the relation $L \in \mathcal{EC}(REG_2^Z) \setminus \mathcal{EC}(COMB)$ holds.*

Proof. The language L is generated by the contextual grammar

$$G = (\{a, b, c\}, \{(S_1, C_1), (S_2, C_2)\}, \{a, b\})$$

with

$$
\begin{aligned}
S_1 &= \{a\}^*, & C_1 &= \{(\lambda, a)\}, \\
S_2 &= \{a\}^*\{b\}\{a, b\}^*, & C_2 &= \{(a, \lambda), (\lambda, a), (\lambda, b), (c, c)\}.
\end{aligned}
$$

It is easy to see that S_1 and S_2 belong to the family REG_2^Z. Thus, we obtain that $L \in \mathcal{EC}(REG_2^Z)$.

The letters c are wrapped around a word of L with at least a letter b (but with an arbitrary last letter a or b). Since the language L also contains words without a b but with last letter a, the usage of a combinational selection language would yield a word which does not belong to the language L. This contradiction shows that the language L cannot be generated by a contextual grammar where every selection language is combinational.

Lemma 6. *Let $n \geq 1$ be a natural number, $V_n = \{a_1, a_2, \ldots, a_n\}$ be an alphabet with n letters, and $L_n = V_n^*$. Then the relation $L_n \in \mathcal{EC}(MON) \backslash \mathcal{EC}(RL_n^P)$ holds.*

Proof. The language L_n is generated by the contextual grammar

$$G_n = (V_n, \{(V_n^*, \{ (\lambda, a_i) \mid 1 \leq i \leq n \})\}, \{\lambda\})$$

with a monoidal selection language only. Thus, $L_n \in \mathcal{EC}(MON)$.

In any contextual grammar generating the language L, there is a selection language S where the number of each letter of the alphabet is unbounded (if, for every selection language, there would be a letter with a bounded number of occurrences in the words of that language, then the union of the selection languages would not contain a word with an arbitrary number of occurrences of each letter). For generating the selection language S, a non-terminating rule is necessary for each letter of the alphabet V_n and a terminating rule is also needed. Hence, at least $n + 1$ rules are necessary. Thus, $L \notin \mathcal{EC}(RL_n^P)$.

Lemma 7. *Let $n \geq 1$ be a natural number and $L_n = I_n \cup T_n$ for two languages $I_n = \{ a^i \mid 1 \leq i \leq n \}$ and $T_n = \{ a^{k(n+1)} \mid k \in \mathbb{N}, k \geq 2 \}$. Then the relation $L_n \in \mathcal{EC}(NIL) \setminus \mathcal{EC}(REG_n^Z)$ holds.*

Proof. Let $V = \{a\}$ and $n \geq 1$ be a natural number. The language L_n is generated by the contextual grammar

$$G_n = (V, \{(V^*V^{n+1}, \{(\lambda, a^{n+1})\})\}, I_n \cup \{a^{2(n+1)}\})$$

with a nilpotent selection language only. Thus, $L_n \in \mathcal{EC}(NIL)$.

For generating the language L_n by a contextual grammar, no selection language has words of I_n and T_n at the same time (otherwise wrong words would be generated) and one needs a selection language with infinitely many words of T_n (where every word has at least $n + 1$ letters a). This 'counting' cannot be done by a deterministic finite automaton with at most n states. Therefore, we obtain that $L_n \notin \mathcal{EC}(REG_n^Z)$.

In a similar way, the following result is proved.

Lemma 8. *Let $n \geq 1$ be a natural number and $L_n = I_n \cup T_n$ for two languages $I_n = \{ ba^i \mid 1 \leq i \leq n \}$ and $T_n = \{ ba^{k(n+1)} \mid k \in \mathbb{N}, k \geq 2 \}$. Then the relation $L_n \in \mathcal{EC}(SUF) \setminus \mathcal{EC}(REG_n^Z)$ holds.*

Proof. Let $V = \{a, b\}$. The language L_n is generated by the contextual grammar

$$G_n = (V, \{(Suf(T_n), \{(\lambda, a^{n+1})\})\}, I_n \cup \{ba^{2(n+1)}\})$$

with a suffix-closed selection language only ($Suf(X)$ is the set of all suffixes of words of X). Thus, $L_n \in \mathcal{EC}(SUF)$.

As in the previous proof, some selection language must 'count' $n+1$ letters a which cannot be done by a deterministic finite automaton with at most n states. Therefore, we obtain that $L_n \notin \mathcal{EC}(REG_n^Z)$.

Lemma 9. *Let* $n \geq 1$ *be a natural number,* $M_n = \{ w \mid w \in \{a, b\}^*, |w|_a \leq n \}$, *and* $L_n = \{a, b\}^+ \cup \{c\} M_n \{c\}$. *Then the relation*

$$L_n \in (\mathcal{EC}(SUF) \cap \mathcal{EC}(COMM) \cap \mathcal{EC}(ORD)) \setminus \mathcal{EC}(RL_n^V)$$

holds.

Proof. The language L_n is generated by the contextual grammar

$$G_n = (\{a, b, c\}, \{(\{a, b\}^*, \{(\lambda, a), (\lambda, b)\}), (M_n, \{(c, c)\})\}, \{a, b, cc\}).$$

Both the selection languages $\{a, b\}^*$ and M_n are suffix-closed and commutative. The selection language $\{a, b\}^*$ is accepted by a deterministic finite automaton with exactly one state, hence, an ordered automaton. The selection language M_n can also be accepted by an ordered deterministic finite automaton (according to [24]). Thus, we have $L_n \in \mathcal{EC}(SUF) \cap \mathcal{EC}(COMM) \cap \mathcal{EC}(ORD)$.

For generating the language L_n by a contextual grammar, one needs a selection language with infinitely many words of M_n where the number of the letter b in every 'block' is unbounded (otherwise, not every word of the subset $\{c\} M_n \{c\}$ is generated). On the other hand, this selection language has no words with more than n letters a (or more than $n + 1$ unbounded b-blocks). For this 'counting' while generating the selection language, one needs at least $n + 1$ non-terminal symbols (one for each b-block). Therefore, we obtain that $L_n \notin \mathcal{EC}(RL_n^V)$.

We now state the relations between the language families.

Lemma 10. *The language families* $\mathcal{EC}(FIN)$ *and* $\mathcal{EC}(RL_1^P)$ *coincide.*

Proof. From [4], we know $\mathcal{EC}(FIN) = FIN$; from [7], $\mathcal{EC}(RL_1^P) = FIN$.

Lemma 11. *Every language family* $\mathcal{EC}(RL_n^P)$ *for* $n \geq 2$ *is incomparable to each of the families* $\mathcal{EC}(MON)$, $\mathcal{EC}(NIL)$, $\mathcal{EC}(COMM)$, $\mathcal{EC}(CIRC)$, $\mathcal{EC}(SUF)$, $\mathcal{EC}(COMB)$, $\mathcal{EC}(DEF)$, $\mathcal{EC}(ORD)$, $\mathcal{EC}(NC)$, *and* $\mathcal{EC}(PS)$.

Proof. Due to the inclusion relations stated in Theorem 1, depicted in Fig. 1, proofs of the following relations are sufficient (which have been presented above):

1. $\mathcal{EC}(RL_2^P) \setminus \mathcal{EC}(PS) \neq \emptyset$ (Lemma 3),
2. $\mathcal{EC}(RL_2^P) \setminus \mathcal{EC}(CIRC) \neq \emptyset$ (Lemma 4),
3. $\mathcal{EC}(MON) \setminus \mathcal{EC}(RL_n^P) \neq \emptyset$ for every natural number n with $n \geq 2$ (Lemma 6).

Regarding the families which are defined by the number of states necessary for accepting the selection languages, we obtain the following results.

Lemma 12. *The language families $\mathcal{EC}(MON)$ and $\mathcal{EC}(REG_1^Z)$ coincide.*

Proof. This follows from the fact that $REG_1^Z = MON \cup \{\emptyset\}$ and that the empty set has no influence as a selection language.

Lemma 13. *The relation $\mathcal{EC}(COMB) \subset \mathcal{EC}(REG_2^Z)$ holds.*

Proof. From [24], we know that $COMB \subset REG_2^Z$. By Lemma 2, we obtain that $\mathcal{EC}(COMB) \subseteq \mathcal{EC}(REG_2^Z)$ holds. By Lemma 5, this inclusion is proper.

Lemma 14. *Every language family $\mathcal{EC}(REG_n^Z)$ for $n \geq 2$ is incomparable to each of the families $\mathcal{EC}(NIL)$, $\mathcal{EC}(COMM)$, $\mathcal{EC}(CIRC)$, $\mathcal{EC}(SUF)$, $\mathcal{EC}(DEF)$, $\mathcal{EC}(ORD)$, $\mathcal{EC}(NC)$, and $\mathcal{EC}(PS)$.*

Proof. Due to the inclusion relations stated in Theorem 1, depicted in Fig. 1, proofs of the following relations are sufficient (which have been presented above):

1. $\mathcal{EC}(REG_2^Z) \setminus \mathcal{EC}(PS) \neq \emptyset$ (Lemma 3),
2. $\mathcal{EC}(REG_2^Z) \setminus \mathcal{EC}(CIRC) \neq \emptyset$ (Lemma 4),
3. $\mathcal{EC}(NIL) \setminus \mathcal{EC}(REG_n^Z) \neq \emptyset$ for every $n \geq 2$ (Lemma 7),
4. $\mathcal{EC}(SUF) \setminus \mathcal{EC}(REG_n^Z) \neq \emptyset$ for every $n \geq 2$ (Lemma 8).

Regarding the families which are defined by the number of non-terminal symbols necessary for generating the selection languages, we obtain the following results.

Lemma 15. *The relation $\mathcal{EC}(DEF) \subset \mathcal{EC}(RL_1^V)$ holds.*

Proof. We first prove the inclusion $\mathcal{EC}(DEF) \subseteq \mathcal{EC}(RL_1^V)$.
   Let $G = (V, \{ (S_i, C_i) \mid 1 \leq i \leq n \}, A)$ be a contextual grammar where every selection language can be represented in the form $S_i = A_i \cup V^* B_i$ $(1 \leq i \leq n)$ for finite subsets A_i and B_i of V^*. The same language $L(G)$ is also generated by the contextual grammar

$$G' = (V, \{ (A_i, C_i) \mid 1 \leq i \leq n \} \cup \{ (V^* B_i, C_i) \mid 1 \leq i \leq n \}, A).$$

Every such selection language can be generated by a right-linear grammar with one non-terminal only. Hence, $\mathcal{EC}(DEF) \subseteq \mathcal{EC}(RL_1^V)$.
   The properness follows from Lemma 3.

Lemma 16. *Every language family $\mathcal{EC}(RL_n^V)$ for $n \geq 1$ is incomparable to each of the families $\mathcal{EC}(COMM)$, $\mathcal{EC}(CIRC)$, $\mathcal{EC}(SUF)$, $\mathcal{EC}(ORD)$, $\mathcal{EC}(NC)$, and $\mathcal{EC}(PS)$.*

Proof. Due to the inclusion relations stated in Theorem 1, depicted in Fig. 1, proofs of the following relations are sufficient (which have been presented above):

1. $\mathcal{EC}(RL_1^V) \setminus \mathcal{EC}(PS) \neq \emptyset$ (Lemma 3),
2. $\mathcal{EC}(RL_1^V) \setminus \mathcal{EC}(CIRC) \neq \emptyset$ (Lemma 4),
3. $\mathcal{EC}(COMM) \setminus \mathcal{EC}(RL_n^V) \neq \emptyset$ for every $n \geq 1$ (Lemma 9),
4. $\mathcal{EC}(SUF) \setminus \mathcal{EC}(RL_n^V) \neq \emptyset$ for every $n \geq 1$ (Lemma 9),
5. $\mathcal{EC}(ORD) \setminus \mathcal{EC}(RL_n^V) \neq \emptyset$ for every $n \geq 1$ (Lemma 9).

The following theorem summarizes the results.

Theorem 17. *The relations depicted in Fig. 3 hold. An arrow from an entry X to an entry Y denotes the proper inclusion $X \subset Y$. If two families are not connected by a directed path then they are incomparable.*

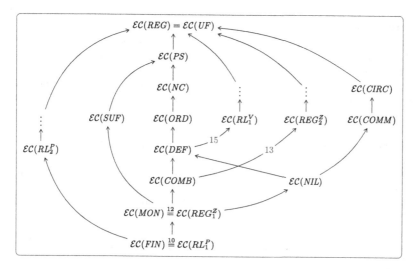

Fig. 3. Hierarchy of language families by contextual grammars; an edge label refers to the corresponding lemma (where the relation was not already shown in Fig. 2). The incomparabilities were proved in the Lemmas 11, 14, and 16.

References

1. Brzozowski, J.A.: Regular Expression Techniques for Sequential Circuits. Ph.D. thesis, Princeton University, Princeton, NJ, USA (1962)
2. Brzozowski, J.A., Jirásková, G., Zou, C.: Quotient complexity of closed languages. Theor. Comput. Syst. **54**, 277–292 (2014)
3. Dassow, J.: On the circular closure of languages. Elektronische Informationsverarbeitung und Kybernetik/J. Inform. Process. Cybern. **15**(1–2), 87–94 (1979)
4. Dassow, J.: Contextual grammars with subregular choice. Fundamenta Informaticae **64**(1–4), 109–118 (2005)

5. Dassow, J.: Contextual languages with strictly locally testable and star free selection languages. Analele Universității București **62**, 25–36 (2015)
6. Dassow, J., Manea, F., Truthe, B.: On contextual grammars with subregular selection languages. In: Holzer, M., Kutrib, M., Pighizzini, G. (eds.) DCFS 2011. LNCS, vol. 6808, pp. 135–146. Springer, Heidelberg (2011). https://doi.org/10.1007/978-3-642-22600-7_11
7. Dassow, J., Manea, F., Truthe, B.: On external contextual grammars with subregular selection languages. Theor. Comput. Sci. **449**(1), 64–73 (2012)
8. Dassow, J., Manea, F., Truthe, B.: On subregular selection languages in internal contextual grammars. J. Automata, Lang. Combinatorics **17**(2–4), 145–164 (2012)
9. Dassow, J., Truthe, B.: Relations of contextual grammars with strictly locally testable selection languages. RAIRO Informatique théorique et Applications/Theoretical Informatics and Applications (2023), submitted
10. Gécseg, F., Peak, I.: Algebraic Theory of Automata. Academiai Kiado, Budapest (1972)
11. Gill, A., Kou, L.T.: Multiple-entry finite automata. J. Comput. Syst. Scie. **9**(1), 1–19 (1974)
12. Havel, I.M.: The theory of regular events II. Kybernetika **5**(6), 520–544 (1969)
13. Istrail, S.: Gramatici contextuale cu selectiva regulata. Stud. Cerc. Mat. **30**, 287–294 (1978)
14. Manea, F., Truthe, B.: On internal contextual grammars with subregular selection languages. In: Kutrib, M., Moreira, N., Reis, R. (eds.) DCFS 2012. LNCS, vol. 7386, pp. 222–235. Springer, Heidelberg (2012). https://doi.org/10.1007/978-3-642-31623-4_17
15. Marcus, S.: Contextual grammars. Revue Roum. Math. Pures Appl. **14**, 1525–1534 (1969)
16. McNaughton, R., Papert, S.: Counter-free Automata. MIT Press, Cambridge, USA (1971)
17. Perles, M., Rabin, M.M., Shamir, E.: The theory of definite automata. IEEE Trans. Electron. Comput. **12**, 233–243 (1963)
18. Păun, Gh.: Marcus Contextual Grammars. Kluwer Publ. House, Doordrecht (1998)
19. Rozenberg, G., Salomaa, A. (eds.): Handbook of Formal Languages. Springer-Verlag, Berlin (1997)
20. Shyr, H.J.: Free Monoids and Languages. Hon Min Book Co., Taichung, Taiwan (1991)
21. Shyr, H.J., Thierrin, G.: Ordered Automata and Associated Languages. Tankang J. Math. **5**(1), 9–20 (1974)
22. Shyr, H.J., Thierrin, G.: Power-Separating Regular Languages. Math. Syst. Theor. **8**(1), 90–95 (1974)
23. Truthe, B.: A Relation Between Definite and Ordered Finite Automata. In: Bensch, S., Freund, R., Otto, F. (eds.) Sixth Workshop on Non-Classical Models of Automata and Applications (NCMA), Kassel, Germany, July 28–29, 2014, Proceedings. books@ocg.at, vol. 304, pp. 235–247. Österreichische Computer Gesellschaft (2014)
24. Truthe, B.: Hierarchy of subregular language families. Tech. rep., Justus-Liebig-Universität Giessen, Institut für Informatik, IFIG Research Report 1801 (2018)
25. Truthe, B.: Generative capacity of contextual grammars with subregular selection languages. Fundamenta Informaticae **180**, 1–28 (2021)

A Tight Upper Bound on the Length of Maximal Bordered Box Repetition-Free Words

Jean Weight, Trienko Grobler, Lynette van Zijl[✉], and Carlyle Stewart

Department of Computer Science, Stellenbosch University, Stellenbosch, South Africa
{25493515,tlgrobler,lvzijl,24915793}@sun.ac.za

Abstract. A bordered box repetition-free word is a finite word w where any given factor of the form axa, with $a \in \Sigma$ and $x \in \Sigma^*$, occurs at most once. It is known that the length of a bordered box repetition-free word is at most $B(n) = n(2 + B(n-1))$, with $B(1) = 2$, where n denotes the size of the alphabet. An alternative approach is given to prove that $B(n)$ is an upper bound, which enables a proof that this upper bound is tight.

1 Introduction

Combinatorics of words is the study of symbol sequences [3,4,13]. Early studies on the topic [17,18] included the investigation of square-free words, which is a word with no two adjacent identical factors. A square can in fact be seen as a pattern that has to be avoided. This in turn resulted in a large body of work which investigates the avoidance of certain patterns in words, and the realization that there are some patterns in words that are unavoidable [1,2,20]. Other work on such patterns consider words that do not contain repeating factors – that is, the situation where a specified factor occurs, but does so only once.

One of the early studies that investigated this notion, is that of Martin [14]. Martin investigated words that contain only one occurrence of a specified pattern. In particular, he considered the lexicographically largest De Bruijn word of length k, over an alphabet with n symbols, that do not repeat in a word. He showed a greedy algorithm that can generate a finite word w where no permutation of length k repeats. Later work considered a generalisation of this idea, namely, universal cycles of different combinatorial objects such as permutations [7], which do not repeat. The concern in this field is to consider cyclic words where patterns of length k do not repeat, for some k.

In this work, we focus on a related but somewhat different issue. Similar to De Luca [5], we consider finite words rather than cycles. Furthermore, instead of looking at patterns of a given length k that do not repeat, we consider the combinatorial generation of a single word w where no patterns of any length k repeats. Initially, we focus on the case where the patterns are factors that are bordered by the same symbol [9,10]. That is, we consider factors of the form axa, with x any string from the alphabet. In other words, we look for words that contain **no** repetitions of the form axa, with the length of x any value between

© IFIP International Federation for Information Processing 2023
Published by Springer Nature Switzerland AG 2023
H. Bordihn et al. (Eds.): DCFS 2023, LNCS 13918, pp. 181–196, 2023.
https://doi.org/10.1007/978-3-031-34326-1_14

zero and (one less than) the alphabet size. We call these factors *bordered boxes*, or bboxes for short.

In a previous work, we presented different search algorithms which attempt to find ever larger bbox repetition-free words [9,10]. There, we showed that the maximal length of a bbox repetition-free word over an alphabet with n symbols, is at most $B(n) = n(2 + B(n-1))$, with $B(1) = 2$. In particular, we proved that $B(n)$ is an upper bound and conjectured that this upper bound was tight [9,10].

In this paper we give an alternative proof to show that $B(n)$ is an upper bound, and then continue to show that this upper bound is tight. The proof rests on extending an existing bbox repetition-free word by the maximum number of alphabet symbols before another bbox can occur, leading quite naturally to an upper bound.

To show that $B(n)$ is a tight upper bound, a directed graph G_n will be constructed, having as its vertices permutations of the n alphabet symbols, with its edges labelled by specific bboxes (so-called inner bboxes; see below). A subgraph $G*$ of G_n will then be identified, so that this subgraph will contain no repeating inner bbox labels. Moreover, traversing this graph results in a bbox repetition-free word, with the additional property that the left and right boundary of any two successive inner bboxes are n symbols apart. We will then prove that $G*$ has a directed Eulerian path, and as such contains a path which utilizes all inner bboxes over an alphabet of size n, which in turn ensures that at least one bbox repetition-free word of the maximal length $B(n)$ can be found.

Some basic definitions are presented in Sect. 2. The (alternative) proof that $B(n)$ is an upper bound is presented in Sect. 3. The proof that this is a tight upper bound is given in Sect. 4. The paper ends with some concluding remarks.

2 Background and Definitions

We assume that the reader has a general background in combinatorics on words, such as in [6,15,16] and others. Let Σ_n indicate a finite alphabet with n symbols. A word w over Σ_n is an element of Σ_n^*, where Σ_n^* is the Kleene closure of Σ_n. For notational convenience, we write $w = w_0 w_1 w_2 \cdots w_k$, where each $w_i \in \Sigma_n$. The length of w is indicated as $|w|$. A factor is any consecutive string of symbols in w; that is, x is a factor of w if $w = uxv$ for some words $u, v \in \Sigma_n^*$. A bbox x is a factor of a word w such that $x = aya$, with $a \in \Sigma_n$, and $y \in \Sigma_n^*$. A bbox is called an inner bbox if it does not contain a bbox as a proper factor. In other words, an inner bbox is a bbox that does not contain another bbox. Note that any bbox $x = aya$ has $|x| \geq 2$. That is, the empty string, and also a single symbol, are not considered to be bboxes. A bbox that is not an inner bbox is called an outer bbox. Note that, in a given word, bboxes can overlap (similar to the factors in a De Bruijn word [8]).

Algorithmically, bbox repetition-free (BRF) words can be generated in many different ways [10], usually by attempting to append a symbol from the alphabet to the end of the word, and making sure that the appended symbol does not cause a repetition. If it is not possible to append any alphabet symbol to a word w without causing a repetition, then w is called a maximal bbox repetition-free word. Over an alphabet Σ_n, the longest possible BRF word is called the longest maximal bbox repetition-free word.[1] That is, for any longest BRF word w over Σ_n, it must hold that $|v| \leq |w|$ for any other BRF word v. Note that, since there is a finite number of inner bboxes over a given alphabet, and at most a finite distance between bboxes (see the next section), such a longest word must exist.

Example 1. Let $\Sigma_3 = \{a, b, c\}$. Consider the word $w = aababcbacba$ over Σ_3. By inspection, there are no repeating bboxes and hence w is a BRF word. The first two inner bboxes in w are aa and aba, and these two bboxes overlap. For the inner bbox $bacb$, note that it contains no proper factors that are bboxes. Moreover, ac is a permutation of the symbols in $\Sigma_3 \setminus \{b\}$.   □

Some self-evident properties of bboxes and inner bboxes include that, for Σ_n, any inner bbox x has length $2 \leq |x| \leq n + 1$ (property P1); and, for a word w over Σ_n^* with factors s and x, if s is an (outer) bbox containing the inner bbox x, then if s repeats in w, it must hold that x also repeats. Hence, by contrapositive, if each inner bbox appears at most once, then each bbox appears at most once (property P2). This means that only inner bboxes need to be considered when deciding whether a word w is a bbox repetition-free word.

3   An Upper Bound on the Length of a BRF Word

In this section, it is shown that an upper bound on the length of a BRF word over Σ_n is given by $B(n) = n + \sum_{k=1}^{n} \frac{kn!}{(k-1)!}$ which, as proven in [10], is equivalent to the recursive form given before.

Let w be a BRF word over alphabet Σ_n. For each symbol a, consider the longest factor that ends on symbol a and that does not contain an inner bbox. When advancing from one symbol to the next, one of two situations can occur.

1. The new symbol is the last symbol of an inner bbox: The new factor cannot extend back to the first symbol of this inner bbox, as else it would include an inner bbox. Hence, the factor can extend back to at most the symbol after the start of this inner bbox. As an inner bbox cannot contain an inner bbox, this factor satisfies the conditions and is the longest such factor. Note that the new factor length will be one less than the length of the inner bbox – this is termed a length reset.
2. The new symbol is not the last symbol of an inner bbox: The old factor with the new symbol cannot contain a bbox – if the new symbol formed an inner bbox it would be the end of the inner bbox. This is a contradiction to the case, so the new factor is the old factor with the new symbol added. Note the new factor length will be one more than that of the factor ending on the previous symbol.

---

[1] In [9], the terminology LMRF is used.

As any factor that contains duplicate symbols will contain an inner bbox, the length of the factor is at most n. This means that when advancing to the next symbol after a factor of length n, a new inner bbox must be formed that ends on that symbol. If this were not the case, the length would need to increase to $n + 1$, which is impossible.

Consider now the length of the factor as one advances over the symbols from the beginning of w. The length either increases by one or gets reset to a lower value on each inner bbox formed with the length depending on the length of the inner bbox. After every inner bbox formed of length $x + 1$ with $1 \leq x \leq n$, the factor length will be reset to x on the last symbol of the bbox. After that there can be at most $n - x$ symbols before a new inner bbox is formed.

For notational convenience, a label string $l(w)$ is assigned to any BRF word w. In $l(w)$, each symbol is assigned a 1 if it is the last symbol of an inner bbox and a 0 otherwise. Furthermore, let the longest factor not containing an inner bbox ending at index i be $f(i)$.

Example 2. Let $\Sigma_3 = \{a, b, c\}$. Consider the BRF word $w = aababcbacbac$ over Σ_3. Looking at the fourth symbol, the longest factor not containing an inner bbox is ba. It is the last symbol of the inner bbox aba. It is hence given a 1 as label and $f(4) = ba$. On the other hand, consider the sixth symbol. Here, $f(6) = abc$ and the symbol is not the last symbol of an inner bbox and is given 0 as label. The reader can verify that the label string $l(w)$ for this example is given by $l(w) = 010110101111$.   □

It is interesting to consider the sequences of 0s and 1s that can occur in a label string $l(w)$. When a 1 occurs in the label string at an index i where the factor is reset to length x, that is, $|f(i)| = x$, there can be at most $n - x$ consecutive 0s before another label value 1 must occur. Hence, each inner bbox of length $x + 1$ can be responsible for at most $1 + n - x$ symbols. Also note there can be at most n leading 0s before an inner bbox forms.

Lemma 1. *Let w be a BRF word and $l(w)$ its associated label string. Then there are at most $\frac{n!}{(n-x)!}$ different i where $l(w)[i] = 1$ and $|f(i)| = x$.*

Proof. To reset the length of the factor to x, an inner bbox of length $k = x + 1$ must have been formed. Each inner bbox can occur only once in a BRF word, and from [9] there are $\frac{n!}{(n-k+1)!}$ inner bboxes of length k. By substituting $k = x + 1$, the lemma holds.   □

By adding all the inequalities above together, accounting for the number of inner bboxes per length and simplifying, one gets an upper bound on the length of w.

Theorem 1. *Let w be an BRF word over an alphabet Σ_n. Then $|w| \leq B(n)$.*

Proof.

$$\underbrace{00\cdots 0}_{\leq n}\overset{\text{length set to }x_1}{\underbrace{1\,00\cdots 0}_{\leq 1+n-x_1}}\overset{\text{length set to }x_2}{\underbrace{1\,00\cdots 0}_{\leq 1+n-x_2}}\overset{\text{length set to }x_3}{\underbrace{1\,00\cdots 0}_{\leq 1+n-x_3}}\overset{\text{length set to }x_4}{\underbrace{1\,00\cdots 0}_{\leq 1+n-x_4}}\cdots$$

Let w be a BRF word, and $l(w)$ its associated label string. From Lemma 1, there are at most $\frac{n!}{(n-x)!}$ occurrences of symbol 1, that indicates the resetting of the suffix to size x. Before the symbol 1 appears in $l(w)$ for the first time, there can be at most n occurrences of the symbol 0. Every symbol 1 that represents the resetting of the suffix length to x can be followed by at most $n - x$ occurrences of 0's. Hence there can be at most $n + \sum_{x=1}^{n}((n - x) + 1)(\frac{n!}{(n-x)!})$ symbols in $l(w)$ which is equal to $n + \sum_{k=1}^{n}\frac{kn!}{(k-1)!}$ by the flipping of summation.

As each symbol in $l(w)$ is mapped from a symbol in w, and w is BRF, it follows that the maximal length of a BRF word is indeed $B(n) = n + \sum_{k=1}^{n}\frac{kn!}{(k-1)!}$.
□

Furthermore, suppose that every inner bbox is used exactly once. At every step the factor is pushed to length n (a permutation) before a new inner bbox is formed. Hence all the inequalities in the upper bound proof are equalities, since they were set up knowing that at every step the length of the factor is at most n. Therefore, such a sequence results in a BRF of length $B(n)$. This forms the premise for the proof that words of length $B(n)$ exist.

Assume that there exists a z which is a BRF with the maximal allowable length as per Theorem 1. From the above arguments, it can be seen that $l(z)$ contains at most $J(n) = \sum_{x=1}^{n}\frac{n!}{(n-x)!}$ occurrences of the symbol 1 (which represents the number of inner bboxes in z). On the other hand, there are $n + \sum_{x=1}^{n}\frac{n!}{(n-x)!}(n - x)$ occurrences of the symbol 0 in $l(z)$. From the results in [10], it follows that the number of occurrences of the 1 and 0 symbols in $l(z)$ are in fact equal. This implies that the length of z will be equal to twice the number of inner bboxes that it contains; in other words, $B(n) = 2J(n)$. Moreover, it is straightforward to prove by induction that $B(n) = n(2 + B(n - 1))$ [10]. Interestingly, the sequence obtained by evaluating $J(n)$ for successive values of n appears in the Online Encyclopedia of Integer Sequences (OEIS) with designation A007526[2]. This gives rise to another expression equivalent to $B(n)$, namely, $B(n) = 2\sum_{x=0}^{n-1}\frac{n!}{x!}$.

---

[2] https://oeis.org/A007526.

4 The Upper Bound on the Maximal Length of BRF Words Is Tight

To show that the upper bound of Theorem 1 is tight, a digraph G_n is constructed so that a path in G_n satisfying certain conditions can be turned into a BRF. We then find a subgraph $G*$ of G_n that has an Eularian path satisfying the conditions. Traversal of this Eulerian path will lead to a BRF word of the required length.

Henceforth, for notational convenience, *permutation* is taken to mean any permutation of all the symbols of the alphabet Σ_n. Also, an s-string is a string of length s consisting of symbols from the alphabet Σ_n such that each symbol is used at most once, and $1 \leq s \leq n$. For example, *abd* is a 3-string over Σ_4.

Consider a digraph G_n where every vertex is labelled by a different permutation of the alphabet symbols in Σ_n. Vertices are connected by edges labelled by inner bboxes. Let $I = i_0 i_1 \cdots i_k$ be an inner bbox over Σ_n, with $1 \leq k \leq n$. Consider two vertices $A = a_0 a_1 \cdots a_{n-1}$ and $B = b_0 b_1 \cdots b_{n-1}$. Then A has an edge to B, labelled by the inner bbox I, if $i_0 i_1 \cdots i_{k-1}$ is a suffix of A and $i_1 i_2 \cdots i_k$ is a prefix of B. Informally, for an inner bbox of length $s + 1$, vertex A is connected to vertex B if the last $s - 1$ symbols of A is the same as the first $s - 1$ symbols of B, and the s-th last symbol of A is the same as the s-th symbol of B. For example, suppose A is the vertex *abcdef* and B is the vertex *defcab* over alphabet Σ_6. Then *cdefc* is an inner bbox with *cdef* a suffix of A, and *defc* a prefix of B. Therefore, vertices A and B are connected in graph G_n with an edge labelled *cdefc*.

Note that a word over Σ_n corresponds to a path in G_n. For example, the word *abcdefcba* corresponds to the path from vertex *abcdef* to vertex *defcba*, via edge *cdefc*.

More formally, let $G_n = (V, E)$ be the graph of alphabet Σ_n. To turn a path in the graph into a BRF the following process is performed: Start a word w with the starting permutation of the path. The path is then traversed and at each permutation some symbols are appended to w, depending on the inner bbox that connected to the permutation. At permutation $v_i = a_0 a_1 \cdots a_{n-1}$, when traversed through an inner bbox of length $s + 1$, append $a_{s-1} a_s \cdots a_{n-1}$ to w. Informally, the last $n - s + 1$ symbols of v_i are appended.

For clarity, we refer to the graph G_n as a bbox graph. Note that in a bbox graph G_n, the outgoing edges of a given vertex are determined by the value s together with the last s symbols of the vertex label. For example, if $s = 1$, then vertex *abc* has an edge labelled *cc* to a vertex with c as the first symbol.

Theorem 2. *For an alphabet Σ_n and bbox graph G_n, if a path p in G_n contains no edges with the same edge label, then the word w associated with the path is a BRF. Furthermore, if each edge label occurs exactly once, then w is of length $B(n)$.*

Proof. Let G_n be the bbox graph over Σ_n, and consider a path in G_n and the process to turn it into a word.

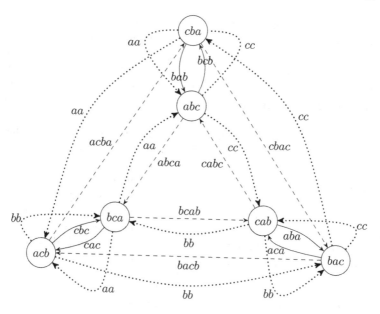

Fig. 1. The graph G_3. The dotted, solid and dashed edges are respectively associated with the inner bboxes of length two, three and four.

Notice that by the construction of the graph the last $s - 1$ symbols of a vertex is the same as the first $s - 1$ symbols of any permutations it connects to through an inner bbox of length $s + 1$. Hence at ever step the word w ends on the permutation just considered as the last $n - s + 1$ symbols are appended and w already ended on the first $s - 1$ symbols of the considered permutation. Furthermore since w ended on a permutation the first appended symbol at each step forms a new inner bbox and by construction this inner bbox is the label of the traversed edge. Using the terminology from the proof of the upper bound this symbol will reset the factor to length s and then the rest of the $n - s$ appended symbols will each increase the factor length by one till the length is n. Since each inner bbox occurs at most once in the path the final word w has no inner bboxes repeated and is hence a BRF.

Furthermore, if every inner bbox is used exactly once, and since at every point the factor is pushed to length n before a new inner bbox is formed, all the inequalites in the upper bound proof are equalities. Hence such a path results in a BRF of length $B(n)$.

$\square$

The reader may note the similarity between the construction in Theorem 2 above, and the two cases that occur when a word w is extended by a new symbol, in Sect. 3, when a new suffix length is determined. A path in G_n connects permutations using inner bboxes, which means that extending a path in the graph forces the first case (without resetting the suffix length), until a new permutation forms (the next vertex in the path), when the second case occurs.

By Theorem 2, if there is a path through a bbox graph G_n which contains all the possible inner bbox labels over an alphabet Σ_n, and none of these inner bbox labels repeat in the path, then the BRF associated with the path must be a BRF of maximal length. In the rest of this section, we therefore show that there exists a subgraph $G*$ of G_n with all edge labels unique, so that $G*$ has an Eulerian path. Recall that an Eularian path exists in a digraph if the digraph is strongly connected, and the indegree of every vertex is equal to its outdegree.

To construct the desired subgraph $G*$, the first step is to define different subgraphs G_n^s of G_n, based on the length of the inner bbox labels. That is, in subgraph G_n^s of G_n, with $1 \leq s \leq n$, the edge labels of graph G_n^s have length $s + 1$. We refer to these subgraphs as s-layers. Importantly, the subgraph G_n^s may not contain duplicate edge labels. We will then show how to connect these s-layers to form the subgraph G^* of G_n, so that G^* has an Eulerian path, and all its edge labels are unique. As an example, in Fig. 1, the subgraph G_3^3 is the graph with all six the vertices, but only the dashed edges.

Definition 1. *A subgraph G_n^s of G_n is a valid s-layer if*

- *each edge of G_n^s corresponds to a different inner bbox of length $s + 1$;*
- *for every inner bbox of length $s + 1$ over Σ_n there is a corresponding edge in G_n^s; and*
- *every vertex of G_n^s has an indegree of one and an outdegree of one.*

For example, G_3^3 forms a valid 3-layer, with all the dashed edges labelled with length four inner bboxes, and all the vertices having indegree and outdegree one. All the edge labels are unique, and every possible inner bbox of length four over Σ_3 occurs in G_3^3. Note that duplicate edge labels are possible; in that case, a valid s-layer would exclude some of the duplicate edges – we expand on this later.

The aim is now to show how to construct valid s-layers, which could ultimately be combined into a subgraph G^* of G_n. Consider a grouping S of the vertices in G_n.

The reader is reminded that each of the vertices in G_n has a label which is a permutation over Σ_n. Also, an s-string is a string of length s consisting of symbols from the alphabet Σ_n such that each symbol is used at most once, and $1 \leq s \leq n$.

Definition 2. *For a certain s, define a set of permutations S as s-graphable if and only if for every s-string, there is exactly one permutation in S that has the s-string as a suffix and there is exactly one permutation that has the s-string as a prefix.*

For example, in G_3 in Fig. 1, for Σ_3, choose $s = 2$. Then G_3^3 is the subggraph of G_3 that contains only the dashed edges. Then the set of permutations $\{abc, acb, bac, bca, cab, cba\}$ is s-graphable. A possible 2-string is bc, and only the permutation

bca starts with bc, and only permutation abc ends with bc. The reader can easily verify the case for any other 2-strings in Fig. 1. However, for $s = 1$, the set of permutations above are not s-graphable. In this case, $\{abc, bca, cab\}$ would be a valid s-graphable set. As a larger example, for Σ_4 and $s = 2$, the set of permutations $\{abcd, acbd, adbc, badc, bcad, bdac, cadb, cbda, cdab, dacb, dbca, dcba\}$ is s-graphable.

Lemma 2. *Let s be a value with $1 \leq s \leq n$, and let S be an s-graphable set of permutations over Σ_n for the value s. Let G_n^s be the subgraph of G_n that has as vertices all the vertices of G_n with labels in S, and has as edges the edges of G_n that are labelled by an inner bbox of length $s + 1$ and are between vertices with labels in S. Then G_n^s is a valid s-layer.*

Proof. The proof rests on the definition of a s-graphable set, namely, that there is only one pair of permutations, for every s-string, which has the required prefix and suffix property. Hence, by construction, every edge in G_n^s corresponds to a different inner bbox of length $s + 1$. Since S is s-graphable, every s-string has a corresponding permutation pair, and it therefore follows that for every inner bbox of length $s + 1$, there is a corresponding edge in G_n^s. Finally, it remains to show that each vertex in G_n^s has an indegree and outdegree of exactly one. By contradiction. Suppose there is a vertex v with an outdegree greater than one. That would imply that there are two different inner bboxes of length $s + 1$, starting with the same s symbols. This is a contradiction. The same argument holds for the indegree of the vertices.

It follows that G_n^s is a valid s-layer. $\square$

The strategy now is, for each value of s, to find a s-graphable set. The resulting subgraphs G_n^s can then be constructed and combined to form G^*.

Assign a linear ordering to the alphabet Σ_n. Let u, v be strings in Σ_n^* with $|u| = |v|$. Then u and v is said to have the same ordering if the i-th smallest symbol in u and the i-th smallest symbol in v both occur at the same index k in (respectively) u and v. For example, if $n = 6$, then acb and dfe have the same ordering.

For a large enough value of s, it is straightforward to find a s-graphable set for s. We therefore consider two cases, namely, the case where $\frac{n}{2} \leq s \leq n$, and the case where $s < \frac{n}{2}$. In each case, we show a s-graphable set S_s.

Definition 3. *Define S_s for $\frac{n}{2} \leq s \leq n$ to be the set of permutations that have the first $n - s$ symbols in the same ordering as the last $n - s$ symbols.*

For example, for $n = 4$, consider $s = 2$. Then $abcd, bdac, cadb$ and $dacb$ are some of the permutations in S_2, but $abdc, bdca, cabd$ and $dabc$ are not in S_2.

Note that, because s is at least half the length of a given permutation in S_s, it implies that the first s symbols of a permutation in S_s determines the permutation – this follows from the ordering requirement for S_s. Hence, for any s-string, there is at most one permutation in S_s having s as a prefix, and at most one having s as a suffix in S_s. Given any s-string there is at least one permutation in S_s that has it as a prefix, as the constraint only forces the last $n - s$ symbols to be in the same ordering of the first $n - s$ symbols, and the first s symbols have no overlap with the last $n - s$ symbols. The same is true for the suffix. Hence, for every s-string, there is exactly one permutation in S_s that has it as a prefix and exactly one permutation that has it as a suffix. Hence S_s is s-graphable.

To find a s-graphable set for small s is somewhat more involved. It requires the construction of an invertable function g.

Assume a cyclic ordering of Σ_n. Let $next(a, k)$ for some symbol a and natural number k be the value found by applying the successor function of the cyclic ordering k times to a. Define $prev(a, k)$ similarly in terms of the predecessor function.

Assume now that $s < \frac{n}{2}$ (that is, s is small). For a given value of such a small s, let the set of all s-strings over Σ_n be K. To find a s-graphable set, an invertible function from K to itself is constructed, with the restriction that the function input may not share any symbols with the output.

Define the function $g : K \to K$ as follows. For any s-string $u \in K$, let $g(u) = v$ where v is constructed by the following process. Form a set X, and assign all the symbols in u to X. Let $u = u_0 u_1 \cdots u_{s-1}$ and $v = v_0 v_1 \cdots v_{s-1}$. Start at step $k = 1$, and apply $next(u_i, k)$ for $0 \le i \le s - 1$. At every i, if $next(u_i, k) \notin X$, add $next(u_i, k)$ to X and let $v_i = next(u_i, k)$. Repeat for increasing values of k, until all the v_i had been assigned values. This gives the value of v. Given that all the symbols in u are unique, it follows that all the symbols in v are also unique, and the intersection of the symbols in u and the symbols in v is empty. The assignment of symbols to v must terminate for some finite value of k, as there are initially $n - s > s$ available symbols for assignment to v. We say that u_i maps forward to v_i.

Example 3. Let $n = 7$, with $\Sigma_7 = \{a, b, c, d, e, f, g\}$ and $s = 3 < n/2$ (see Fig. 2 in appendix). Let $u = u_0 u_1 u_2 = abd$, and attempt to construct v. Set $X = \{a, b, d\}$. For $k = 1$, $next(a, 1) = b$. But $b \in X$, and no value is assigned to v_0. Now $next(u_1, 1) = next(b, 1) = c \notin X$, and so $v_1 = c$ and $X := X \cup \{c\}$. Similarly, $next(u_2, 1) = next(d, 1) = e$, and so $v_2 = e$. Note that at this stage $X = \{a, b, c, d, e\}$, so that only symbols f and g are available for assignment. Increase k to $k = 2$, and consider $u_0 = a$. $next(u_0, 2) = c \in X$ and c cannot be assigned. This situation also occurs for $k = 3$, when $next(u_0, 3) = d$, and $k = 4$, when $next(u_0, 4) = e$. When $k = 5$, $next(u_0, 5) = f$, and $v_0 = f$ is assigned. The process now terminates, as $v = fce$ had been fully assigned. Note that $\{a, b, d\} \cap \{f, c, e\}$ is empty. □

Let $g' : K \to K$ be the function defined as for g above, except that all occurrences of $next(u_i, k)$ are replaced by $prev(u_i, k)$.

Let (i, j), with $i, j \in \Sigma_n$, denote an interval along the cyclic ordering of Σ_n, excluding i and j. As an example, for $n = 5$, it holds that $(a, d) = \{b, c\}$ and that $(d, a) = \{e\}$.

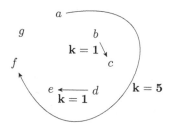

Fig. 2. Forward mapping in Example 3.

Note that the function g restricts all forward mapping of symbols to be non-overlapping.

Lemma 3. *Let u be an s-string over Σ_n, and $g(u) = v$. Let $p = u_i$ be a symbol in u that forward maps to a symbol q in v. Then all symbols in u that are elements of (p, q) must forward map to symbols that are in (p, q).*

Proof. By contradiction. Suppose that there is a symbol x in (p, q) which forward maps to a symbol not in (p, q). But, by the definition of function g, the smallest k such that $next(x, k) = q$ is smaller than the smallest k such that $next(p, k) = q$. This means that function g will attempt to assign x before p is assigned. But, by assumption, p forward maps to q, and hence p is not assigned at the time when x is assigned, and therefore x must forward map to q. This is a contradiction. Analogously, no symbol outside (p, q) can forward map into (p, q) when p mapped to q. □

The above lemma implies that if $x = u_i$ for some i, and $x \in (p, q)$, then x maps to (x, q). Also notice that there is no symbol x in (p, q) that is in neither u nor v, since then p would forward map to x instead of q. Clearly, the same properties hold for backward maps, with the appropriate changes to the ranges.

Lemma 4. *g' is the inverse of g.*

Proof. It must be shown that for every s-string $u \in K$, it holds that $g'(g(u)) = u$. In other words, if $g(u) = v$ and $g'(v) = w$, then it should hold that $u = w$. This will hold true if, for any symbol a in u that forward maps to a symbol b in v, it is the case that b maps backwards to a. The argument is based on strong mathematical induction. Let $u \in K$ be any s-string, and let k be the step number of the forward mapping. Also, for notational convenience, let a be a symbol in u and b a symbol in v.
Base case $k = 0$: No steps have occurred yet, and the result holds by default.
Induction step: Consider k, with $1 \leq k \leq m$, for some m with $0 \leq m < n$. For all such k, assume that for any symbol a that forward mapped to symbol b in step $k = m$, it holds that b maps backward to a. Furthermore, no symbol b has backward mapped in step k if it was not the result of a forward map in step k. That is, up until step $k = m$, any forward map of a symbol a to b will have b

mapping backwards to a.

Let $k = m + 1$. Consider every symbol b in v where b is the symbol to be mapped backwards. Three possibilities arise.

Case 1: Suppose there is a symbol x that forward mapped to b in step $k < m + 1$. Then, by the induction hypothesis, b maps backward to x.

Case 2: Suppose there is a symbol x that forward mapped to b in step $k = m+1$. Then, by the induction hypothesis, x will be unassigned as of yet. Applying $prev(b, k)$ then maps b back to x.

Case 3: Suppose there is a symbol x that forward mapped to b in step $k > m + 1$. We show by contradiction that b cannot be mapped backward at step $m + 1$. Assume that b does map backward at step $m + 1$ to symbol z. Note that $z \in (x, b)$ and that $(z, b) \subset (x, b)$. Since x maps to b, z must map to $c \in (z, b)$ at some $\hat{k} < m + 1$. By the induction hypothesis c must have already been mapped back to z at step $\hat{k}$, making it impossible for b to do so at step k, which results in a contradiction.

Hence, if a symbol a forward maps to b in step $k = m + 1$, then the symbol b will backward map to a in step $k = m + 1$. And, if a symbol was not mapped to in step $k = m + 1$, it cannot be backward mapped to that symbol in step $k = m + 1$ and the strong induction is complete.

Since all symbols must map back on or before step $k = n - 1$ (since that is the size of the alphabet), it holds that g' is the inverse of g.   □

Since g' is the inverse of g, we will denote it as g^{-1} from here onwards.

Now consider the first part of a permutation, and the last part – in particular, the first s symbols and the last s symbols. Then g can be used to find a s-graphable set S_s, when $s < \frac{n}{2}$.

Definition 4. *Define S_s for $s < \frac{n}{2}$ to be the set of permutations satisfying the following conditions:*

- *Let the first s symbols of the permutation be u and the last s symbols of the permutation be v. Then $g(u) = v$.*
- *The middle $n - 2s$ symbols are linearly ordered over the alphabet.*

For example, consider $n = 3$ and $s = 1$. That is, $s < \frac{n}{2}$. Take the permutation acb. Here, $g(u) = v$ and $g^{-1}(v) = u$ as is required by the above definition. Moreover, since c is the only remaining alphabet symbol, $acb \in S_1$. The remaining permutations of S_1 can be found in a similar way, and $S_1 = \{acb, cba, bac\}$. In contrast, the permutations bca, abc and cab do not belong to S_1.

Notice that the last s symbols of a permutation in S_s determines what the permutation is, as the first s symbols can be found from the last s symbols by applying g^{-1}. The remaining symbols that are not in the first or last s symbols of the string, must be in between, in sorted order. Also notice that this permutation does exist, given the last s symbols. Hence there is exactly one permutation in S_s having a specific s-string as a suffix. Similarly, the permutation can be uniquely determined from the first s symbols of the permutation, using g to find the end; and again it does exist. Therefore, for every s-string there is exactly one permutation in S_s that has it as a prefix and exactly one permutation that has it as a suffix. It follows that S_s is s-graphable.

From the previous argument, it follows that there is a s-graphable set for every such s. Therefore, it is possible to construct valid s-layers from the subgraphs G_n^s, for $s \in \{1, \cdots, n\}$, as defined in Definition 1. The graph $G*$ can be constructed by joining these valid s-layers together; that is, all the vertices of G_n are vertices in $G*$, and the edges in $G*$ are all the edges in each of the individual s-layers. The next step is to show that the graph $G*$ is strongly connected.

Lemma 5. *The graph $G*$ found by joining the valid s-layers from Lemma 2, is strongly connected.*

Proof. We will show that $G*$ is strongly connect by the edges from the layers corresponding to the two largest values of s.

Consider any inner bbox I of length $n + 1$ (an inner bbox from layer n). As all inner bboxes must occur as en edge in $G*$, one has that I must also be an edge. Notice that it can only join a permutation A to a permutation B if the first n symbols of I is equal to the last n symbols of A, and the last n symbols of I is equal to the first n symbols of B. Notice that there is only one pair A and B that satisfy these conditions and hence the edge must be between them. Since the first and last symbols of I are equal, it follows that B is A cycled one symbol left. For example, $abcde$ maps to $bcdea$ through $abcdea$ in an alphabet of size 5.

Since for every permutation there is an inner bbox of length $n + 1$ with that permutation as prefix, it follows that every permutation has an out-edge corresponding to an inner bbox of size $n + 1$. Hence for every permutation there is an out-edge in $G*$ that can be followed to get the same permutation back but cycled one left. By repeating this process, any permutation can reach any other cycle of itself.

Consider now any inner bbox I of length n (that is, an inner bbox from layer $n - 1$). Again, one has that I must correspond to an edge in $G*$. Notice that the edge can only join a permutation A to a permutation B if the first $n - 1$ symbols of I is equal to the last $n - 1$ symbols of A. The first symbol in A is then forced to be the only symbol that does not appear in I, as there is only one unused symbol and one unused position in the permutation. Similarly, the last $n - 1$ symbol of I is equal to the first $n - 1$ symbols of B and the last symbol of B is forced to be the same unused symbol in I. Notice that there is again only one pair A and B that satisfy these conditions and hence the edge must be between them. Following this edge corresponds to taking the first two symbols of A, swapping them and putting them at the back; equivalently, swapping the first two symbols and then cycling left twice. For example, $abcde$ maps to $cdeba$ through $bcdeb$ in an alphabet of size 5.

Hence, for any permutationan, an edge in $G*$ can be followed to a new permutation which is the old one cycled left twice and then swapping the last two symbols.

By chaining these operations together, one can advance from any permutation to any other permutation that only differs in the two adjacent symbols to be swapped – one can follow edges to cycle the permutation such that the above two symbols are at the front, then follow an edge that results in the first two being swapped, followed by two left cycles. One can then cycle further until the permutation is in the correct position; that is, until the original and current permutations are equal apart from the two above symbols being swapped. Hence, there are edges that can be followed that allows the swapping of any two adjacent symbols in a permutation. It is known that any permutation can be reached from any other using only a sequence of moves corresponding to swapping pairs of adjacent symbols (using the Johnson-Trotter generation algorithm [12, 19]).

Therefore, all the vertices in $G*$ is reachable from any other vertex, and the result follows.   □

Consider again Fig. 1 on page 7. Here, G_3^1 is the subgraph with vertices acb, bac and cba, and the dotted edges that connect these vertices. Note that G_3^1 contains no duplicate dotted edges. G_3^2 is the subgraph with all the vertices of G_3, and the solid edges. G_3^3 is the subgraph with all the vertices of G_3, and the dashed edges. As an example, the subgraph formed by joining G_3^2 and G_3^3 is strongly connected.

The following result can now be established formally.

Lemma 6. *The graph $G*$, found by joining the valid s-layers from Lemma 2, has an Eulerian path, contains all the inner bbox edge labels over Σ_n, and has no duplicate edge labels.*

Proof. $G*$ is composed of valid s-layers (see Lemma 2). As such, $G*$ contains all the inner bbox edge labels over Σ_n, and has no duplicate edge labels. Moreover, since the indegree and outdegree of each vertex in G_n^s is one, the indegree and outdegree of every vertex in G^* must be equal. Recall that $G*$ is strongly connected (see Lemma 5). $G*$ must, therefore, contain an Eulerian path.   □

As an example, $G*$ constructed by joining G_3^3, G_3^2 and G_3^1, adheres to Lemma 6. Therefore, for $n = 3$, there does indeed exist a BRF of the conjectured length $B(n)$, which is the maximal length of a BRF over an alphabet of size n. Therefore,

Theorem 3. *For every Σ_n, there exists a longest BRF $w \in \Sigma_n^*$ such that $|w| = B(n)$.*

Proof. This follows from Theorem 2 and Lemma 6.   □

For the interested reader, we note that $B(3) = 30$, and an example of a longest BRF for Σ_3 is

$$w = abcacaccbcbcababaacabbaabcbcbacbacbacbababcccabc \ .$$

5   Conclusion

We proved that the length of the longest BRF over an alphabet Σ_n is at most $B(n) = n(2 + B(n - 1))$, with $B(1) = 2$, and that this bound is in fact tight. We gave a new graph representation with inner bboxes as edges, where Eulerian paths in $G*$ must be found to generate example instances of longest BRFs, as opposed to the existing approach in [9], where Hamiltonian paths are required instead. Eulerian paths in $G*$ can be found by employing Hierholzer's algorithm [11].

We are currently looking at further properties of the set of all longest BRFs for a given n. This includes, for example, the number of longest BRFs that exists for a given n. Another avenue to explore is the idea of cyclic BRFs.

References

1. Baena-Garcia, M., Morales-Bueno, R., Carmona-Cejudo, J., Castillo, G.: Counting word avoiding factors. Electronic J. Math. Technol. **4**(3), 251–267 (2010)
2. Avoidable patterns in strings of symbols: Bean, D., Ehrenfeucht, A., G., M. Pac. J. Math. **85**, 261–294 (1979)
3. Berstel, J., Karhumäki, J.: Combinatorics on words: a tutorial. Bull. EATCS **79**, 178–228 (2003)
4. Berstel, J., Perrin, D.: The origins of combinatorics on words. Eur. J. Comb. **28**, 996–1022 (2007)
5. Carpi, A., De Luca, A.: Words and special factors. Theoret. Comput. Sci. **259**, 145–182 (2001)
6. Charalambides, C.A.: Enumerative Combinatorics. CRC Press, Boca Raton, USA (2002)
7. Chung, F., Diaconis, P., Graham, R.: Universal cycles for combinatorial structures. Discret. Math. **110**(1), 43–59 (1992)
8. Fredricksen, H.: A survey of full length nonlinear shift register cycle algorithms. SIAM Rev. **24**(2), 195–221 (1982)
9. Grobler, T., Habeck, M., Van Zijl, L., Geldenhuys, J.: Search algorithms for the combinatorial generation of bordered box repetition-free words. J. Univ. Comput. Sci. **29**(2), 100–117 (2023)
10. Habeck, M.: The generation of maximum length box repetition-free words. Master's thesis, Stellenbosch University, South Africa (2021)
11. Hierholzer, C.: Über die Möglichkeit, einen Linenzug ohne Wiederholung und ohne Unterbrechung zu umfahren. Math. Ann. **6**(1), 30–32 (1873)
12. Johnson, S.: Generation of permutations by adjacent transposition. Math. Comput. **17**(83), 282–285 (1963)
13. Lothaire, M.: Combinatorics on Words. Cambridge University Press, Cambridge Mathematical Library (1997)
14. Martin, M.: A problem in arrangements. Bull. Am. Math. Soc. **40**(12), 859–864 (1934)
15. Ruskey, F.: Combinatorial generation. Preliminary working draft. University of Victoria, Victoria, BC, Canada 11, 20 (2003)
16. Stanley, R.: What is enumerative combinatorics? Springer (1986)

17. Thue, A.: Über unendliche Zeichenreihen. Norske Vid Selsk. Skr. I Mat-Nat Kl. (Christiana) 7, 1–22 (1906)
18. Thue, A.: Über die gegenseitige Lage gleicher Teile gewisser Zeichenreihen. Jacob Dybwad (1912)
19. Trotter, H.: Algorithm 115: Perm. Commun. ACM 5(8), 434–435 (1962)
20. Zimin, A.: Blocking sets of terms. Sbornik: Math. 47(2), 353–364 (1984)

Author Index

© IFIP International Federation for Information Processing 2023
Published by Springer Nature Switzerland AG 2023
H. Bordihn et al. (Eds.): DCFS 2023, LNCS 13918, p. 197, 2023.
https://doi.org/10.1007/978-3-031-34326-1

Printed in the United States
by Baker & Taylor Publisher Services